WILLIAM CULLEN BRYANT

WILLIAM
CULLEN
BRYANT

Author of America

❧

Gilbert H. Muller

STATE UNIVERSITY OF NEW YORK PRESS

Bryant

Jacket image of William Cullen Bryant courtesy of the Library of Congress
Prints and Photographs Division, Washington, DC

Published by
State University of New York Press, Albany

© 2008 Gilbert H. Muller

For information, contact State University of New York Press, Albany, NY
www.sunypress.edu

Production by Kelli W. LeRoux
Marketing by Susan Petrie

Library of Congress Cataloging in Publication Data

Muller, Gilbert H., 1941-
  William Cullen Bryant : author of America / Gilbert H. Muller.
    p. cm.
  Includes bibliographical references (p.   ) and index.
  ISBN 978-0-7914-7467-9 (alk. paper)
  1. Bryant, William Cullen, 1794–1878. 2. Authors, American—19th
century—Biography. I. Title.

PS1181.M85 2008
811'.3--dc22
[B]
                                                          2007033406

10 9 8 7 6 5 4 3 2 1

CONTENTS

To
Laleh
Parisa, Darius, Sara
and
Sadie Rain

PREFACE

When William Cullen Bryant died in 1878 at the age of eighty-three, his fame was universal. Newspapers across the country and Europe ran extensive obituaries on America's great poet and principled editor. Flags flew at half-mast throughout Manhattan, which for half a century had embraced this transplanted Yankee from the Berkshires as its own unique celebrity.

Bryant's funeral at All Souls Church reflected his stature and fame. He had not wanted a public funeral but got one nevertheless, with friends, dignitaries, and citizens filling the pews and overflowing into the street. One mourner, Walt Whitman, vividly recalled the crowd's final salute to the great man. "The bard of river and wood," Whitman said of his old friend, was a poet who stood "among the first in the world."

My effort to capture the life, times, and career of Bryant has been guided by the iconic status that he enjoyed during most of the nineteenth century. Bryant was the first major American poet to experience celebrity—a public exposure and adulation so sustained that only Robert Frost rivals him in this regard. (Celebrity aside, Bryant was also, as Harold Bloom asserts, "a superb poet, always and still undervalued.") Moreover, Bryant compounded his literary fame by serving for fifty years as editor of the *New-York Evening Post*. As the respected owner and editor of the *Evening Post*, which was not the largest newspaper in New York City but arguably the most authoritative and influential, Bryant grappled with the conflicts and controversies of his day. No wonder that Bryant's contemporaries hailed him as Manhattan's first citizen and America's first poet.

With his dual celebrity, Bryant was a key participant in the nation's literary, cultural, and political life. He promoted a national literature and art, advanced Jacksonian democracy, attacked slavery and defended the Union, helped found the Republican Party, supported revolutions in Europe and South America, spearheaded municipal reform. One of New York City's leading boosters, he was instrumental in creating the National Academy of Design, the Century Association, Central Park, and the Metropolitan Museum of Art. A walker in the city, he could also be Gotham's most persistent critic, decrying its dirty streets, atrocious health conditions, haphazard development, rampant crime and corruption. In the end, Bryant helped make Manhattan the cultural and commercial heart of America.

Bryant offered a progressive—at times radical—vision for America. (One exception was his endorsement of Indian removal by the Jackson administration.) He took enlightened stands on workers and women; abolitionism and slavery; immigration and religion; the dangers of American expansionism and the inevitability of global revolutions. A force in American social and political life, he was unique among poets in harnessing his literary talent to the demands of daily editorial duties. In a sense, this poet of nature submerged his deepest impulses in order to serve his city and country. When Bryant in the *Evening Post* opposed capital punishment, reviled nativists, excoriated secessionists, or supported the rights of workers to unionize, the city and nation listened.

Bryant is a largely forgotten figure today, but his earlier fame is still with us in surprising ways. To stroll through Bryant Park behind the New York Public Library; walk down streets named after him in Roslyn, New York, or Palo Alto, California; visit Bryant libraries and schools in numerous states—above all to sample some of his finest poems like the superb "To a Waterfowl" or delicious "Summer Wind"—is to sense the hold that Bryant once had on American popular culture.

Bryant, as I present him in this book, was not only a celebrity but a flesh-and-blood character driven by complex and often combative emotions and opinions fueled by an American epic stretching from the age of Jefferson to the Gilded Age. By offering an account of his passions and preoccupations, triumphs and failures—all enacted on the stage of a great city linked to a turbulent nation—I try to restore Bryant to his rightful place as a compelling and exemplary figure in American life and letters.

☙

Anyone writing today on William Cullen Bryant must begin by acknowledging the collected *Letters*, astutely edited by William Cullen

Bryant II and Thomas G. Voss; these six volumes were unavailable to previous biographers. Here students, scholars, and critics will find a trove of information on Bryant's literary, philosophical, and political development. Moreover, in these letters, Bryant emerges as a thoughtful and modest soul, devoted family man, loyal friend, and consummate clubman. He was not the cold, "saturnine" figure depicted by his son-in-law Parke Godwin (whom Bryant excluded from his will) that influenced later accounts of his life.

In my research, I have been guided in my search for additional primary materials by unfailingly helpful staffs at the New York Public Library, New-York Historical Society, New York Society Library, Library of Congress, Roslyn Library, and Cedarmere. To all of these people I am indebted.

I want to especially thank James Peltz, the interim director at SUNY Press, for his support of and faith in this book. For a superb job in copyediting the manuscript, I thank Dana Foote and Sybil Sosin. To Kelli Williams-LeRoux, the senior production editor at the Press, I owe a special debt for keeping the project on track. The Press's readers guided my revisions and made the book better. Among the specialists who read the manuscript, I am most grateful to Bruce Michelson, who read the biography twice and improved it significantly each time.

1

AMERICA'S FIRST POET

In my ninth year I began to make verses, some of which were
utter nonsense.
—"An Autobiography of Mr. Bryant's Early Life"

I

William Cullen Bryant was a celebrity for almost seventy-five years.
For virtually the entire nineteenth century, he had been at the center of the nation's ferment—first as America's foremost poet and then,
for fifty years, as its most distinguished newspaper editor. No one had
greater cultural authority than this self-made man from rural New England. Already a famous poet when he left western Massachusetts for
Manhattan in 1825, he had reinvented himself as a metropolitan man and
in the process had helped to define the trajectory of American culture
and democracy.

Bryant was a unique celebrity in his intertwined influence as America's premier poet and crusading editor. Famous since childhood, celebrated for decades as "America's first poet" and New York City's "first
citizen," he had been instrumental in creating the lineaments of a distinctively American poetry and criticism. Moreover, as the nation's most
respected newspaper editor, he wielded political influence. As arguably
the country's foremost cultural authority, Bryant had championed a
national literature and art, freedom of speech and the press, Jacksonian
democracy, urban improvement, the Republican party of Frémont and
Lincoln, an end to slavery, and the preservation of the Union. He had
helped to create coherence for American culture.

1

Although not as flamboyant as his rival, Horace Greeley of the *Tribune*, over the years Bryant was the steadier and more reliable champion of liberal social and political causes. Bryant's old adversary Greeley, never consistent in his opinions or predictable in his behavior, had gone crazy following his quixotic presidential bid in 1872 and died a broken man. Bryant was still moving well on the public stage. With his gnomish head and white, flowing beard, he seemed to many Americans the mythic embodiment of the nation's literature and the rise of American democracy. He was Emerson's representative man, Carlyle's poetic and literary—even prophetic—hero.

No wonder his brusque, boisterous friend, James Fenimore Cooper, who was so unlike the modest, self-conscious Bryant, had declared, "We others get a little praise now and then, but Bryant is the author of America." Cooper, Greeley, and so many of the other luminaries he had known were gone. But Bryant had survived—the result, he believed, of a diet rich in grains, fruits, and vegetables, of walking and strenuous exercise (he could still vault a split rail fence), and of the wonders of homoeopathy.

What turned out to be Bryant's last working day, a hot Wednesday in late May 1878, had not started smoothly. Three years earlier, his company had moved into the *Evening Post*'s new building at the corner of Broadway and Fulton Street in lower Manhattan. The Bryant Building, a ten-story complex that cost $750,000, was a monument both to the city's rapidly rising skyline and the owner's worldly success, for among other attributes Bryant was an enlightened capitalist. Despite the heat and humidity, Bryant did not take the building's elevator. Proud of his health, he climbed the stairs to the top floor and, after settling into his office, tackled his correspondence.

Bryant received hoards of unsolicited manuscripts from aspiring poets during the five decades he served as editor of the *Evening Post*. Two poems submitted by an acquaintance were in the day's mail. After perusing the lyrics, he strode into the office of the paper's literary editor, George Cary Eggleston, a man in his thirties whose keen knowledge of Cowper and other English poets impressed Bryant. Rarely given to raw emotion in public or private, Bryant complained that the woman's verse was "extremely poor stuff." Now he would have to write her about why her poetry was unsuitable for publication. "People expect too much of me—altogether too much!" To Eggleston, his employer's voice sounded like a "wail," a cry from the heart of a man unable to hold fame at arm's length.

That Wednesday morning, May 29, Bryant checked proofs and talked for more than an hour with Eggleston about American literature and criticism. He reviewed "the whole field," Eggleston recalled, "classifying and arranging the different branches of the subject as skillfully as he would have done it in an essay, and expressing some unconventional opinions which startled me by their vigorous originality, and by the apparent care with which they had been wrought out in his mind." Bryant had written some the nation's earliest literary criticism, including essays on early American poetry and the use of trisyllabic feet that appeared in the *North American Review* in 1818 and 1819 respectively. In 1825, when he was thirty-one years old and newly settled in Manhattan, he had delivered four seminal lectures on poetry before the New York Athenaeum. Bryant could still recite every line of verse he had written (especially when ladies like his charming neighbor, Leonice Moulton, were the auditors) and quote copious stanzas from other poets.

Today, however, the writer of "Thanatopsis," "To a Waterfowl," and other poems recited by schoolchildren and memorized by generations of Americans was fighting a spring cold. He preferred to stay at Cedarmere, his Roslyn estate twenty miles from Manhattan on the shores of Long Island Sound, but duty—yet another public speech—had called him to Manhattan that morning. Democracy, he believed, demanded sacrifice and accountability. For more than fifty years, Bryant had been one authority willing to raise fundamental questions about the character of American democracy.

Truth be told, he enjoyed metropolitan society. Bryant treasured a circle of close friends; he had a reputation for genteel clubiness; and he had delivered more than a hundred major speeches in his lifetime, most of them in Manhattan. Bryant's worldly celebrity—the outer man—had served to ameliorate the more self-conscious, shy, and solitary impulses of his inner self. Over a long lifetime, he had struggled and largely succeeded in creating an equilibrium in his private and public lives.

Bryant had accepted an invitation from the city's Italian American community to speak at the unveiling of a bust commemorating the Italian patriot and revolutionary, Giuseppe Mazzini, whom he had met in London in 1845. The previous Sunday, he had confessed to Dr. John Ordronaux, a close friend who occupied a cottage on Bryant's estate, that he did not look forward to delivering the Mazzini speech. "If you knew how I am followed up by people of every class asking for this and that kind of service, you would appreciate how I am tormented. I have no rest from this kind of importunity, and, having obliged one set of people,

4   WILLIAM CULLEN BRYANT

I can't well refuse another. Besides, Mazzini was a patriot, and Italy owes to him a large share of her independence." Once more he would harness his inner turmoil—his present melancholy and vexation—to the demands of democracy and the role of the public man. Once again he would use his celebrity status to instruct the democratic mass.

Today's unveiling was to take place at Central Park—the park for the citizens of Manhattan that Bryant had been instrumental in founding. (As early as 1833 he had lamented "a deficiency of public squares in the lower part of the city for the purposes of health and refinement.") Following a light lunch, Bryant was driven to the park in his carriage. Arriving thirty minutes before the ceremony, he entered Central Park at the West Drive opposite Sixty-Seventh Street, near where the bust of Mazzini stood veiled on a granite base. The heat had increased, and Bryant sought shelter from the sun under several elm trees, where he chatted with an old acquaintance, General James Grant Wilson.

At the start of the ceremony, Bryant mounted the platform and, hatless, sat with other dignitaries in the intense sunlight. A friend noticed that he seemed uncomfortable and insisted on holding an umbrella over Bryant's head. When Bryant finally rose to speak, he seemed weak. Gradually, however, his voice gained resonance and fire. He ended with an apostrophe to the bust of Mazzini: "Image of the illustrious champion of civil and religious liberty, cast in enduring bronze to typify the imperishable renown of thy original! Remain for ages yet to come, where we place thee in this resort of millions; remain till the day shall dawn—far distant though it may be—when the rights and duties of human brotherhood shall be acknowledged by all the races of mankind." Speaker and subject seemed perfectly matched. Here on a sultry spring day in the most populous and diverse city in the United States, a polyglot crowd of Americans could ponder in the bust of Mazzini and the presence of Bryant the very course of nineteenth-century democracy.

It was close to four o'clock when the ceremony ended. Wilson insisted that Bryant return with him and his daughter to the Wilsons' house at 15 East Seventy-Fourth Street for refreshments. Strolling through the Sheep Meadow and entering the Mall, they viewed the statues to Bryant's deceased friends, Fitz-Greene Halleck and Samuel F. B. Morse, and discussed national affairs. An astute student of botany and horticulture, Bryant identified birds, trees, and flowers as they passed Bethesda Fountain and walked out of Central Park onto Seventy-Second Street.

Reaching their destination, Wilson mounted the steps ahead of the poet to open the door, when suddenly, according to Wilson, Bryant pitched backward, striking his head on the paved steps. A passerby noticed the accident and offered his services while servants rushed from the Wilson residence to assist the semiconscious Bryant inside. Mrs. Wilson immediately brought him ice water and bathed his head until Bryant told her to stop. He was offered a glass of iced sherry, which he drank slowly, gradually regaining a degree of lucidity, but then groaned, "My head! My poor head! I don't feel well." Resisting entreaties from Wilson and his wife to rest in an upstairs bedroom, Bryant insisted on being taken home.

Wilson accompanied Bryant in a Madison Avenue car to Seventeenth Street and then by cab to the poet's brownstone at 24 West Sixteenth Street. From time to time, Bryant was able to string a few words and sentences together before lapsing into silence. Approaching his residence, he became disoriented, asking, "Whose house is this? What street is this?" But then he reached into his pocket, pulled out his key, and opened the door. A niece, Anna Fairchild, who was staying with him while Julia, his daughter and companion, was in Atlantic City, rushed to Bryant's assistance. Miss Fairchild called for the famous homoeopathist Dr. John F. Gray. Over the next few days, in consultation with other attending physicians, Dr. Gray concluded that Bryant was suffering from "haemorhage of the brain" and in all likelihood would not survive.

II

William Cullen Bryant's life began far from Manhattan and the "wilderness" that had been so artfully contrived for Central Park by his friend Frederick Law Olmsted. Cullen (as everyone called him) was born on November 3, 1794, in a roughhewn log cabin two miles from Cummington, a frontier enclave in the Berkshire range of western Massachusetts. The town was sparsely settled, remote, and lonely. Nevertheless, the backcountry residents of Hampshire County were famous for their resistance to the British Intolerable Acts of 1774 and, after the Revolutionary War, for their fierce adherence to democratic politics. The Whiskey Rebellion had broken out in the region in the year of Bryant's birth, rekindling the specter of Daniel Shays.

Wilderness—vast forests of beech, birch, ash, maple, and hemlock—surrounded and impinged on the hardscrabble settlement. The first family had come to Cummington in 1770. Three years later, Bryant's grandfather, Ebenezer Snell, moved his family from North Bridgewater to Cummington. Known as Deacon and Squire, Ebenezer, a stern, energetic Calvinist, cleared land in the highlands above the town and built a commodious house that became known as the Homestead. He planted fields of Indian corn and wheat, set aside grassland for cows and sheep, and started an apple orchard.

Both sides of Bryant's family had roots in New England. The ancestors of his father, Dr. Peter Bryant, had arrived in Massachusetts Bay Colony in 1632. His mother, Sarah Snell Bryant, could trace her ancestry to the *Mayflower* voyagers. Among Sarah's ancestors were Captain John Alden and Priscilla Mullins, the romantic figures depicted in *The Courtship of Miles Standish* by Bryant's younger friend, Henry Wadsworth Longfellow. Peter Bryant had set up his practice in Cummington in 1792. He boarded with Squire Snell, courted the Deacon's daughter, whom he might have known when he and the Snells lived in North Bridgewater, and married her that year.

When Cullen was four years old, he would move with his family into the Homestead, remaining there until he was twenty-two and ready to briefly embark on a career in law. The second son in a closely knit family that would number five boys and two girls, Cullen was formed by wilderness—the forests, verdant valleys, and high, rolling hills of western Massachusetts. Bryant recalled that his family "then lived in a house, which stands no longer, near the center of the township, amid fields which have a steep slope to the north fork of the Westfield River, a shallow stream, brawling over a bed of loose stones in a very narrow valley." Cummington itself consisted of a few dwellings and stores. Bryant described the surrounding area in "Lines on Revisiting the Country":

> Broad, round, and green, that in the summer sky
> With garniture of waving grass and grain,
> Orchards, and beechen forests, basking lie,
> While deep the sunless glens are scooped between,
> Where brawls o'er shallow beds the streams unseen.

The wild, pristine highlands of the Berkshire range, its hills rising to two thousand feet, would mold the boy and become summer and autumn retreat for Bryant in later age.

Many of Bryant's finest lyrics derive from the landscape surrounding the Homestead. He apostrophized a stream that ran through the

Snell property in "The Rivulet," a lyric that counterbalances Nature's joys against the loss of youth. It was by "childhood's favorite brook" that the fledgling poet tried his "first rude numbers," composing lines of Romantic verse that he would declaim to the delight of the family.

Across the road from the rivulet, a dense forest, described by Bryant in his early blank verse masterpiece, "Inscription for the Entrance to a Wood," challenged the most intrepid wanderer—as it does today:

> Stranger, if thou hast learned a truth which need
> No school of long experience, that the world
> Is full of guilt and misery, and hast seen
> Enough of all its sorrows, crimes, and cares,
> To tire thee of it, enter this wild wood
> And view the haunts of Nature. . . .

To enter the wood, Bryant declares, is to open oneself to self-discovery, setting aside any theologizing over mordant "guilt" and "Her pale tormentor, misery." Here, freed of dogma, the wanderer can apprehend nature and find the words to inscribe it:

> Throngs of insects in the shade
> Try their thin wings and dance in the warm beam
> That waked them into life. Even the green trees
> Partake the deep contentment; as they bend
> To the soft winds, the sun from the blue sky
> Looks in and sheds a blessing on the scene.

In recording this world literally and figuratively, Bryant developed a style—words, images, and cadences—designed to capture the discrete particulars of Nature. Typically, he merges the outer world with his inner emotions. As he writes at the start of the final version of "Thanatopsis":

> To him who in the love of Nature holds
> Communion with her visible forms, she speaks
> A various language. . .

Guided by Bryant's poetry, cultural enthusiasts would discover his part of the Berkshires in the late nineteenth century. Western Massachusetts would become the nation's own Lake Country—tonic for Americans and as inspiring to native writers and artists as any English landscape conjured by William Wordsworth.

Young Bryant immersed himself in this rural world. "I was always from my earliest years a delighted observer of external nature—the splendors of a winter daybreak over the wide wastes of snow seen from our window, the glories of the autumnal woods, the gloomy approaches of the thunderstorm, and its departure amid sunshine and rainbows, the return of spring, with its flowers, and the first snowfall of winter." A life-long student of botany and a horticulturalist of note, Bryant was the most specific and comprehensive recorder of nature in nineteenth-century American poetry. "He was a passionate botanist," his friend, Colonel Ralph Taylor, remembered, claiming that Bryant "knew the name of every tree, flower, and spire of grass." Even Bryant's lesser-known lyrics display remarkable detail, as in "The Old Man's Counsel":

> Within the woods,
> Whose young and half transparent leaves scarce cast
> A shade, gay circles of anemones
> Danced on their stalks; the shad-bush, white with flowers
> Brightened the glens; the new-leaved butternut
> And quivering poplar to the roving breeze
> Gave a balsamic fragrance.

Set against the exquisite detail in these lines is the elegiac tone of the lyric, for Bryant measures his ability to transcribe nature against his failing vision.

Ralph Waldo Emerson observed that Bryant was shrewd in tying his mind to "the northern landscape—its summer splendor, its autumn russets, its winter lights and glooms." To read Bryant's strongest poems—among them his lovely meditative lyric "To the Fringed Gentian," the wondrous "Summer Wind," or the cold, metaphysical "A Winter Piece"—is to discover the ways in which he seized truth from the Berkshire landscape and the seasons of his youth.

If Nature fostered vision, Bryant mastered the craft of transcribing this world in his father's well-appointed library. Dr. Bryant had accumulated an extensive collection of books, and Cullen poured over the classics and English poetry as well as books on botany, chemistry, and the natural sciences. Combining book knowledge with his constant rural rambles, Bryant became the first authoritative American poet to compose strong lyrics about the elemental forces and philosophical depths of the native landscape.

One elemental force—death—was an unavoidable aspect of Bryant's boyhood. Death was part of the "various language" of Nature, endemic in Berkshire society, a motif in the boy's reading, and a peril in his personal life. Bryant was a sickly infant; in later years he recalled that his "case was thought a doubtful one." A family acquaintance confirmed that "the poet was puny and very delicate in body, and of a painfully nervous temperament. There seemed little promise that he would survive the casualties of early childhood." Existence was tenuous in New England wilderness society, and Bryant almost succumbed at an early age.

Fortunately, Peter Bryant was an experienced and innovative physician. Worried about the enlarged size of his newborn son's head in proportion to the fragile body, Dr. Bryant devised an innovative cure. According to Senator Henry Dawes, himself a Cummington native: "In after years, when he had become famous, those who had been medical students with his father when he was struggling for existence with the odds very much against him, delighted to tell of the cold baths they were ordered to give the infant poet in a spring near the house each early morning of the summer months, continuing the treatment, in spite of the outcries and protestations of their patient, so late into the autumn as sometimes to break the ice which skimmed the surface."

Bryant survived infancy and a series of potentially fatal childhood illnesses. "My health was rather delicate from infancy," he said, "and easily disturbed." He was frequently sick and prone to fevers; on one occasion, his temperature was so high that his parents doubted "they could raise him." Bryant also suffered from "frequent and severe attacks of colic." Once, he was kicked by a horse and severely injured; copious bloodletting by Dr. Bryant complicated his recovery. Unlike his older brother Austin, he wilted under rural labors. He admits in "A Lifetime," a retrospective lyric, that he was a "delicate child and slender." In his autobiographical fragment he adds: "Sometimes the tasks of the farm were too great for my strength, and brought on a sick headache, which was relieved under my father's directions by taking a little soda dissolved in water." Bryant's infirmities would persist through his teenage years and early adulthood. From "Thanatopsis" to his final poem of consequence, "The Stream of Life," he would be preoccupied with the beauty and fragility of life.

Although Bryant would leave western Massachusetts to craft a version of himself as a new type of American—self-reliant, adventurous, multitalented, pragmatic, and democratic—he never fully escaped the region's culture and habits of being. The Puritan legacy bequeathed to him by his mother's side of the family would remain strong. Even as he moved away from the doctrinal rigidity of Calvinism as a young man to embrace the more expansive, egalitarian tenets of Unitarianism, Bryant retained a Calvinist conviction that life requires moral justification in personal, public, and even artistic endeavors. Bryant's character and art were formed in part by the Puritan myth of an elected people engaged in a divine drama, an unending primal errand in the wilderness.

Tutored by his mother, whose fifty-year diary reveals Sarah Bryant as a robust and pious soul committed to the Puritan virtues of economy and usefulness in life, Cullen mastered the alphabet at sixteen months. He also followed his older brother Austin's progress through the Scriptures, which he read at the age of four. What he learned from his "stately," devoutly religious mother was the libertarian side of biblical lore, which he acknowledged in "A Lifetime":

> Of the cruel King of Egypt
>   Who made God's people slaves,
> And perished, with all his army,
>   Drowned in the Red Sea waves;

"I ought to be fond of church-going," he observed, "for I began early, making my first appearance at church about the middle of my third year, though there is no note of how I behaved myself there." To Bryant, the preachers presiding over their Sunday congregations were "often poets in their extemporaneous prayers." From the ministers' mellifluous prayers and supplications, their dignified and plain style, he absorbed those rhetorical elements that would characterize his verse. At home, Bryant practiced his own sermonizing. Transfixed by the stately cadences and rhymed meter of the religious verse, he would stand on a chair and passionately recite the hymns of Isaac Watts.

Bryant's grandfather, Ebenezer Snell, also supervised the boy's spiritual instruction. Squire Snell was a justice of the peace, a deacon in the Congregational church, and a stern Calvinist immune to the more liberal winds of Unitarianism that were creeping into the Berkshires from Boston and that had already converted Bryant's father. Some of Bryant's earliest verse was a response to Grandfather Snell's instructions to turn the first chapter of the book of Job into heroic couplets. Typical of the young poet's efforts is this couplet:

His name was Job, evil he did eschew,
To him were born seven sons; three daughters too.

Peter Bryant, remembered by Cullen as possessing "a mild and indulgent temper" similar to the one the poet would cultivate, gently dismissed his son's efforts at biblical verse as mere doggerel.

Peter Bryant was the countervailing influence in his son's life. He fostered in Cullen a love of literature as well as a skeptical attitude about religious and intellectual orthodoxy. Dr. Bryant was a large, barrel-chested man who had experienced the world beyond the Calvinist confines of western Massachusetts. A respected physician and surgeon, he had trained under a French doctor and attended medical lectures at Harvard and had sailed as a ship's surgeon in late 1795. A disastrous business transaction involving investment in a merchant ship might have landed him in debtor's prison had he remained in Cummington. Captured by the French, Dr. Bryant spent a year on the island of Mauritius working in a hospital. After returning to Cummington in May 1798, Peter Bryant maintained a lively correspondence with physicians in Boston, where ideas were more progressive than in the stony predestinarian hills of the Berkshires. Bryant remembered that his father dressed like "a Boston gentleman" and projected a certain "metropolitan air"—an image the son would cultivate in adulthood. Dr. Bryant also was a lover of music and literature, a writer of verse in the Augustan tradition of Pope, a freethinker on matters of religion, and a staunch Federalist who, starting in 1806, served in the Massachusetts legislature for twelve years. He detected literary talent in his son and encouraged Cullen to write poetry.

Bryant recalled his early schooling as unsatisfactory. He entered the district school when he was four years old—so young and delicate that he would often awaken to find himself enfolded in the lap of the teacher, leading (according to family members) to furious outbursts of shame and indignation from the sleepy little fellow. "Reading, spelling, writing and arithmetic, with a little grammar and a little geography, were all that was taught, and these by persons much less qualified, for the most part, than those who now give instruction."

What distinguished the young student was his aptitude for language. Through long winter evenings, he and his brother Austin read voraciously in his father's "well chosen" library, part of the two-room office that the doctor added to the Homestead. Here he first encountered

Shakespeare, Spenser, Milton, Dryden, Pope, Goldsmith, Burns, Cowper, Scott, Byron, Wordsworth, and "American versifiers in abundance." He also listened to Dr. Bryant and his medical students as they discussed scientific matters or debated state, national, and global affairs. Young Bryant was curious about all forms of knowledge. He came readily to the notion that ideas exist in the world and drive history and nations.

III

"I was thought to be a precocious child," Bryant admitted; his literary talent impressed the citizens of Hampshire County. His first published verse appeared in the Northampton *Hampshire Gazette* on March 18, 1807; it was a poem in heroic couplets on the theme of progress that he had delivered three years earlier to local acclaim at a school commencement. The next year, he composed a long poem, *The Embargo, or Sketches of the Times: A Satire, by a Youth of Thirteen*, that his father arranged to have published in pamphlet form. The *Monthly Anthology* praised the poem as an "extraordinary performance," and Dr. Bryant's Federalist friends in the state legislature were delighted by its attack on the Jefferson administration. In 1809, a "Corrected and Enlarged" edition of *The Embargo* appeared, this time with the name of its author, William Cullen Bryant, on the title page. Young Bryant was learning the power of celebrity.

The Embargo adumbrates Bryant's admittedly facile understanding of the controversial political issues destined to mold his life and career. In the 420 lines of this juvenile satire, Cullen vilifies Jefferson and condemns the president's imposition of the Embargo Act of 1807. His best lines are vitriolic:

> Go, wretch, resign the presidential chair,
> Disclose thy secret measures foul or fair,
> Go, search, with curious eye, for horned frogs,
> 'Mongst the wild wastes of Louisianian bogs;
> Or where Ohio rolls his turbid stream,
> Dig for huge bones, thy glory and thy theme;
> Go scan, Philosophist, thy **** charms,
> And sink supinely in her sable arms;
> But quit to abler hands, the helm of state,
> No image ruin on thy country's fate!

This shrewd, bellicose boy uses the heroic couplet and the conventions of classical rhetoric to skewer Jefferson for a policy that had kept ships in New England ports, inflamed the entire region, and brought New England to the brink of secession. The little rascal even alludes to the president's alleged black mistress!

Much of *The Embargo* is little more than a muddled outpouring of Federalist cant. Cullen had uncritically absorbed his ideas about Jefferson from Peter Bryant and his father's Federalist friends, who, like much of New England, found the Republican president to be anathema. Jefferson was obsessed with the enforcement of the embargo, vilifying entire communities and accusing violators of treason. In the end, even some members of Jefferson's party broke ranks and joined the Federalist opposition in repealing the act on the day of the president's retirement in 1809. Bryant would regret his attack on Jeffersonian ideals. In time, he would become the champion of precisely those democratic masses ("each blockhead's vote") that in his youthful folly he accused the president of pandering to. One striking feature of Bryant's cultural authority was his ability to redefine himself and his opinions as the very idea of America also evolved.

More relevant to an impetuous boy's evolution into a mature poet and political thinker is the theme of American progress that appears, admittedly in a minor key, in *The Embargo*. To young Bryant's mind, the uniqueness of the American experiment resides in the happy marriage of Commerce and Agriculture, "a bright pair" bestowing its blessing on the nation:

> 'Tis done, behold the cheerful prospects rise!
> And splendid scenes the startled eye surprise;
> Lo! busy commerce courts the prosperous main;
> And peace and plenty glad our shores again!
> Th' industrious swain sees nature smile around
> His fields with fruit, with flocks, his pastures crown'd.

Raised on New England soil but destined to be a metropolitan man, Bryant would always subscribe to a doctrine of progress that was central to American democracy.

With the publication of *The Embargo*, Dr. Bryant concluded that his talented son deserved a broader prospect than the one Cummington provided. "It was decided," Bryant wrote, "that I should receive a college education, and I was accordingly taken by my father to the house of my mother's brother, the Rev. Dr. Thomas Snell, in North Brookfield, to begin the study of Latin." Bryant arrived in Brookfield, fifty miles east of Cummington, on November 8, 1808, five days after he celebrated his fourteenth birthday. Reverend Snell, who had been pastor of the Second Congregational Church in North Brookfield since 1798, was, according to Bryant, "a rigid moralist, who never held parley with wrong in any form." A graduate of Dartmouth and a former tutor at Haverhill Academy, Reverend Snell quickly recognized Bryant's talent for languages, rapidly advancing the boy from daily assignments in Horace and Cicero to reading Virgil's *Aeneid*. Bryant wrote a letter to his father detailing his progress in Latin and enclosing two translations from the *Aeneid* in heroic couplets. "Respected Father," he began, "You will doubtless find in the preceding lines much that needs emendation and much that characterizes the crude efforts of puerility." Peter Bryant demanded lucidity and exactness from his son, and much of Bryant's facility with metrical and verse forms can be ascribed to his influence.

Reverend Snell was another of the family's ardent Calvinists. He kept a skeptical eye on his young ward, who was prone to wandering the fields and meadows and reading unwholesome books, including the Gothic tales of Mrs. Radcliffe. Still, when Peter Bryant visited his son at Dr. Snell's home the following July, he was pleased with his son's progress in Latin and the boy's new aptitude for art.

In August, following a return to Cummington and a summer working on the Snell farm, where he was occasionally goaded by Squire Snell for "making varses again," Bryant left to study Greek and mathematics with Reverend Moses Hallock in nearby Plainfield. His aptitude for Greek was so keen that by the end of October he had mastered the Greek New Testament "from end to end almost as if it had been English." In October 1810, after more study at home, Bryant was accepted by Williams College as a sophomore.

He was now sixteen and already something of a celebrity among the students at Williams (although some of the boys doubted that he actually had written *The Embargo*). A classmate, Charles Sedgwick, described Bryant as "tall and slender in his physical structure, and having a prolific growth of dark brown hair." Bryant quickly concluded that the college, a bastion of Calvinism and Federalism, offered a curriculum that was "meager and slight." Williams consisted of a president, one professor, and two tutors; and the college had endured several years of turmoil as students rebelled against their rude surroundings. Williams was not intellectual or urbane; it was no Concord or Boston.

To the delight of members of the Philotechnian Society, a literary club he had joined, Bryant composed a verse satire, *Descriptio Guliel-mopolis*, in which he lampooned the faculty, the dreary lives of the students, and the physical conditions at Williams:

Why should I sing those reverend domes
    Where science rests in grave repose?
Ah me! Their terrors and their glooms
    Only the wretched inmate knows.
Where through the horror-breathing hall
The pale-faced, moping students crawl
    Like spectral monuments of woe;
Or, drooping, seek the unwholesome cell
Where shade, and dust, and cobwebs dwell,
    Dark, dirty, dank, and low.

After seven months at Williams, Bryant received permission from his father to leave the college. Williams College, like Cummington, was a small backwater place, so demoralized that its president and students would soon escape to Amherst to start a new college. Bryant journeyed home at the end of May 1811, planning to transfer to Yale College with his roommate, John Avery, and another friend.

Cullen's family was delighted, as it always was on his return, to have its prodigal son at home. Within the family circle, Cullen was buoyant and even boisterous, the charming center of the Bryant household. The youngest brother, John, who would become a minor poet, recalled, "He was lively and playful, tossed me about, and frolicked with me in a way that made me look upon him as my best friend." With another brother, Arthur, the two boys would roam the Berkshire range, reciting strophe and antistrophe choral lines from *Oedipus Tyrannus*, in a translation by Cullen himself.

Bryant was sixteen, dreaming of Yale and a scholar's—perhaps a famous poet's—life. At Sunday evening prayer services, he had often prayed to the Lord that he might "receive the gift of poetic genius, and verses that might endure. I presented this petition in those early years with great fervor, but after a time I discontinued the practice; I can hardly say why." Nevertheless, in the evolving construction of democratic American society, anything seemed possible for a boy seeking fame and a new life.

2

PEDLAR OF
LAW AND POETRY

O'er Coke's black-letter page,
Trimming the lamp at eve, 'tis mine to pore,
Well pleased to see the venerable sage
Unlock his treasur'd wealth of legal lore.
—Verse letter to Jacob Porter, 1813

I

Bryant might never have achieved his remarkable position of cultural authority had he attended Yale and settled back into life in western Massachusetts. However, shortly after his return to Cummington in 1811, Bryant informed John Avery that the prospect of attending Yale was "very problematical." In fact, Dr. Bryant lacked the money to further Bryant's dream of a college education. Bryant, masking the hurt with humor, vowed to "quit study and go to farming or turn mechanic" or perhaps "go to cleaning cowstables." He would always lament the lost opportunity to attend Yale; it was a profound disappointment, for it had frustrated his deepest yearnings for a scholarly experience.

Dr. Bryant decided that Cullen would have to prepare for a profession. His own father and grandfather had been physicians, but Peter Bryant had not prospered, and he did not want to risk a similar fate for his son. The bent of the boy's genius might be for literature, but Dr. Bryant decided that Cullen needed a more lucrative prospect. Perhaps a law career would guarantee an income for his son and even political advancement.

In December 1811, Cullen Bryant began legal studies with his father's friend, Samuel Howe, at nearby Worthington. Initially, Bryant was not enamored of the town; he described it as "consisting of a black-smith-shop and cow-stable." Yet in another letter he waxed nostalgically about "Ward's Store and Mills's tavern and Taylor's grog-shop" and other "cool comfortable lounging places." In fact, Worthington was on the Boston–Albany stage line; it boasted three distilleries and five taverns and was the liveliest town in the western part of Hampshire County. It is hard to believe that Bryant, who enjoyed dances, hayrides, sleighing, and other rural pleasures, found that "the only entertainment it afforded was bound up in the pages of *Knickerbocker*." Bryant apparently had time to lounge in the grog shops, court local women, and read poetry. When the estimable Judge Howe caught his pupil reading Wordsworth's *Lyrical Ballads*, he admonished Bryant not to waste his time.

Bryant's relationship with Judge Howe's wife, Sarah Lydia Robbins Howe, the daughter of the lieutenant governor of Massachusetts, suggests a sexual awakening in the ardent young man. Judge Howe was a widower when Bryant had first arrived; he took Sarah Robbins as his new bride in October 1813. Sarah was educated, cultivated, and socially adept; she loved poetry and read it aloud beautifully and passionately. She found Bryant to be "quiet, reserved, and diffident," later recalling that he was a talented practical botanist who frequently went "to the woods and fields for his specimens." Their relationship was guarded and assuredly proper, but they were drawn to each other by a passion for literature. Bryant's letters to his favorite sister, Sally, and to friends after he left Worthington indicate that he was alternately intimidated and enchanted by Sarah.

Bryant was reconciled to Worthington but happy to leave for a more exciting destination on June 1, 1814. He moved to West Bridgewater, twenty-five miles from Plymouth on the eastern seaboard, to continue his legal studies with Congressman William Baylies. The change was to his liking. In a letter to his friend Elisha Hubbard, who had been a fellow student at Williams College and under Samuel Howe, he declared that "not the wealth of the Indies could tempt me back to my former situation" in Worthington. Confessing to "restlessness and desire of change," he wanted to move to Boston. He had a taste for urban life. However, Dr. Bryant, who was battling consumption, did not approve: "You have cost me already four hundred dollars at Mr. Howe's, and I have other children entitled to my care. Besides, my health is imperfect; I have suffered much from the fatigues of the last season, and, as I may not long be with you, I must do what I can for you all while I am still here."

Bryant was not unhappy to remain in Bridgewater. The town's women, "a whole army of them who were under my almost sole protection," were especially diverting. In a letter to his friend George Downes, Bryant described a picnic involving six couples. "We had a charming sail on the lake, and our ladies were wonderfully sociable and awake, considering that they were up till three o'clock the night before." Bryant bragged about the superiority of Bridgewater girls to those at Worthington, promising Downes "a liberal assignment of some half-dozen to your share" if his friend decided to study law with Congressman Baylies. His letter conjures for Downes an erotic feast.

At this juncture, Bryant had doubts about a law career, but he grew close to Congressman Baylies nevertheless. To Hubbard he wrote: "My situation here is perfectly agreeable—books enough—a convenient office and for their owner a good lawyer and an amiable man. The testimony which all classes of men and I might perhaps say every individual bear to the uprightness of Mr. Baylies' character is truly wonderful. Every body—even those who entertain the greatest dislike to lawyers in general concur in ascribing to him the merit of an honest lawyer." Baylies made Bryant his clerk and, during the time he spent in Washington, entrusted the affairs of his office to his pupil.

Bryant's correspondence at this time reveals a mind in turmoil over political issues confronting the state and nation and his incipient doubts about Federalist policies. In an October 1814 letter to Baylies, Bryant frets over the course of the war with England: "What are the views of the administration and the prospects of the nation? Is all probability of peace cut off? Is the war to be interminable?" He criticizes the obstinate political loyalties of Berkshires' citizens to his father, lamenting their uncritical acceptance of information from the staunchly Federalist *Hampshire Gazette*. "It is like the polypus taking its colour from every thing it devours, and imparting the same tinge to its young." Confessing that there was less party loyalty on the more liberal eastern seaboard of Massachusetts than in the Berkshires, Bryant questions his conservative political values. He embraces the republican rhetoric of independence.

With the British fleet blockading American ports throughout New England, Bryant hailed the militia defending the "goodly and important town of Plymouth." He had reservations about Federalist policies on the conduct of the war and about the war itself, referring to President James

Madison, who was thwarted by Congress in an attempt to raise money for the military, as "His Imbecility." Still, he was "almost ashamed to stay at home when almost every body else is gone," and he applied for a commission in the militia. He railed against plans to raise taxes, predicting that they would "cause violent and unstifled discontent" and even precipitate "dissolution of the Union." When Congress proposed a conscription law in late 1814, Bryant vowed that if "the people of New England acquiesce to this law I will foreswear federalism forever."

Bryant was unaware that a peace treaty had been signed at Ghent on Christmas Eve 1814; the news would not reach the United States until mid-February. When it did, he was not impressed by the terms. The Treaty of Ghent made no mention of American demands that England cease the practice of impressing American seamen. "I have been very curious to know what the democrats say about it—and the following seems to be a favorite method with them of getting rid of the unlucky stumbling block that we have obtained none of those objects for which the war was declared—It is true, say they, that there is no express stipulation in the treaty about sailors and impressments and the principle of search, but the British have received such a drubbing that they never will dare again to impress seamen nor search and American ship." While acknowledging the "extravagant joy" of the local population now that the war was over, Bryant thought the treaty to be a blunder.

Despite Bryant's reservations, the Treaty of Ghent produced joy in Atlantic ports from Boston to Baltimore—but even greater celebration in Manhattan. For a full week in February, jubilant New Yorkers marched in the streets, lurched from grog shops in tipsy revelry, and restocked stores with fine wares. The *New-York Evening Post*, where Bryant was destined to spend more than half a century, reported the festivities in detail, capturing the mood of the citizenry after three years of interrupted commerce.

II

In his spare time while preparing for life as a "pedlar of law," as he wrote sardonically to Elisha Hubbard, Bryant read Byron, Southey, and Cowper and composed poetry patterned after these Romantic poets. Preaching that nature was beautiful and a teacher of virtue, Cowper was his favorite. The influence of the British poet can be seen in a delicate lyric, "The Yellow Violet," which Bryant wrote in 1814 when he was twenty years old. Over the eight quatrains of "The Yellow Violet," Bryant creates a quietly dramatic encounter with the natural world. From the delight he feels in seeing the yellow violet's "modest bell" that reveals the advent of spring, Bryant enters into a dialogue with the flower, finding in its slight form and "humble stalk" the measure of his own interior life. The last two stanzas convey a statement about people's complex relationship to nature and society:

> So they, who climb to wealth, forget
> The friends in darker fortunes tried.
> I copied them—but I regret
> That I should ape the ways of pride.

> And when again the genial hour
> Awakes the painted tribes of light,
> I'll not o'erlook the modest flower
> That made the woods of April bright.

Wandering the woods, hills, and valleys of the Berkshires, young Bryant was composing some of his best work—and creating a new poetry indigenous to American soil.

In July 1815, Bryant wrote "To a Waterfowl," apparently after seeing the bird during one of his solitary walks in the country. Arguably the finest of Bryant's early poems, "To a Waterfowl" reveals a careful reading of *Lyrical Ballads* and an understanding of Wordsworth's concept of the association of ideas. The poem also reflects Bryant's knowledge of the Scottish Common Sense philosophers, whom he had read while preparing for admission to Williams College. Common Sense philosophy claims that nature stimulates moral feelings in men and women. Bryant popularized this influential idea in early nineteenth-century American literature, criticism, and art. In "To a Waterfowl," he transplanted the analogies and correspondences between nature and the human condition into native soil.

Bryant composed "To a Waterfowl" as a meditative lyric suggesting the greatness of a Supreme Being who created the natural world, including all its creatures. From the innovative form of the opening quatrain with its alternating tetrameter and pentameter lines,

Whither, midst falling dew,
While glow the heavens with the last steps of day,
Far, through their rosy depths dost thou pursue
Thy solitary way?

Bryant invokes the waterfowl as an emblem of our own passage through life. Like the waterfowl, we exist among the discrete particulars of this planet—the "falling dew," "weedy lake," and "rocking billows . . . on the chafed ocean side." The bird's "lone wandering," which is "painted on the crimson sky," serves as a trope for the human condition. In its migration, flying deliriously near the "abyss of heaven," the solitary bird becomes a symbol confirming the truth of a divine benevolence embracing all of creation in the concluding quatrain:

He who, from zone to zone,
Guides through the boundless sky thy certain flight,
In the long way that I must tread alone,
Will lead my steps aright.

Matthew Arnold and Hartley Coleridge claimed that "To a Waterfowl" was the best short poem in English. A contemporary poet and critic, Richard Wilbur, concurs: "I suppose, if there must be rankings and priorities, that 'To a Waterfowl' may be America's first flawless poem." The poem is exquisite, as impressive as "Thanatopsis."

Later that fall, Bryant probably wrote the first version of "Thanatopsis," which the critic Ivor Winters called the only truly great American poem written in the first half of the nineteenth century. Years afterward, Bryant recalled somewhat uncertainly that he had composed the poem "when I was seventeen or eighteen years old—I have not now at hand the memorandum which would enable me to be precise—and I believe it was composed in my solitary rambles in the woods." While the date of composition remains in doubt, it is clear that nature offered solace to a young man who was then preoccupied with the deaths in 1813 of his grandfather, Ebenezer Snell, and the young wife of Jacob Porter, a friend who had trained in medicine with Dr. Bryant. These deaths confirmed what Bryant had been reading in the English graveyard poets about the inevitable end of human existence. He found Robert Blair's "The Grave" and Bishop Porteus's "Death," with their Gothic horrors ameliorated by a redemptive God, especially compelling. Moreover, his concern about a typhus epidemic sweeping western Massachusetts and about his father's poor health help to explain Bryant's state of mind as he composed "Thanatopsis."

Bryant conceived "Thanatopsis" as both an acceptance of death and an affirmation of life. Eschewing conventional religious pieties, he departed from the rigid Calvinistic codes of his mother's family in composing a meditation on mortality and the cosmos. In place of a harsh, unforgiving God presiding over fallen and largely unredeemable humankind, the short first version of the poem conjures a raw, cosmic landscape:

> Yet a few days, and thee
> The all-beholding sun shall see no more
> In all his course; nor yet in the cold ground,
> Where thy pale form was laid, with many tears,
> Nor in the embrace of ocean, shall exist
> Thy image . . .

The expanded 1821 version of "Thanatopsis"—where at the end we serenely take our place in "The innumerable caravan, that moves / To that mysterious realm" that is our final destination—is more deistic than Christian in its contours.

The balance of tonalities that Bryant added to the original draft of "Thanatopsis" offers a clue to his maturing view of a moral universe:

> To him who in the love of Nature holds
> Communion with her visible forms, she speaks
> A various language; for his gayer hours
> She has a voice of gladness, and a smile
> And eloquence of beauty, and she glides
> Into his darker musings, with a mild
> And healing sympathy, that steals away
> Their sharpness, ere he is aware . . .

This sinuous first sentence, with its sprightly cadences and metrical variations suggesting a bright rather than gloomy vision of death, prepares readers for the poet's affirmation of the totality of existence and our unity with the natural world. In the body of "Thanatopsis"—the original forty-nine lines—readers join a caravan of millions who have moved through the ages and into the great unknown. By the end of the revised and greatly expanded 1821 version, Bryant weaves a filament over the chasm separating life and death, presenting a profound and strikingly premodern depiction of consciousness confronting the possibility of annihilation.

Dr. Bryant discovered "Thanatopsis" in a pigeonhole of his desk and submitted it to the *North American Review*, which published the poem and four others, including a blank verse fragment that later became "Inscription for the Entrance to a Wood," in its September 1817 issue. The editors of the *North American Review* were amazed by Bryant's work. Richard Henry Dana, who would become one of Bryant's closest friends and his most prolific correspondent, thought "Thanatopsis" so magnificent that it could not have been written "on this side of the Atlantic." Dana's cousin, Edward Tyrell Channing, told Bryant that the author of "To a Waterfowl," which was published in the March 1818 issue of the *North American Review*, was "under higher obligation than any other American bard to do more." With these poems, Bryant first gave expression to a truly national literature. His poetry had become a form of cultural negotiation.

III

Bryant dreaded his impending law career. Praising Downes for his agreeable manners and placid temper, he predicted that the practice of law would suit his friend well. By contrast, "I lay claim to nothing of all these, and the day when I shall set up my gingerbread-board is to me a day of fearful expectation. The nearer I approach to it the more I dread." Bryant was especially anxious about the need to argue in public.

Despite his forebodings, Bryant joined the fraternity, becoming, as he informed Judge Howe, "a limb of the law." He was admitted as an attorney of the Court of Common Pleas on August 15, 1815. Following a brief stay in Cummington and eight unhappy months in a solitary practice in Plainfield, he entered into a law partnership with George Ives in Great Barrington in August 1816. In a letter written from Great Barrington to his mentor Baylies in late May 1817, Bryant confessed to a conflict: "You ask whether I am pleased with my profession—Alas, Sir, the Muse was my first love and remains of that passion which not rooted out yet chilled into extinction will always I fear cause me to look coldly on the severe beauties of Themis. Yet I tame myself to its labors as well as I can." Earlier, in a verse letter to Jacob Porter written while studying under Congressman Baylies, Bryant had hinted at the sacrifice he had made in abandoning poetry for the law:

> O'er Coke's black-letter page,
> Trimming the lamp at eve, 'tis mine to pore,
> Well pleased to see the venerable sage
> Unlock his treasur'd wealth of legal lore;
> And I, that loved to trace the woods before
> And climb the hills, a playmate of the breeze,
> Have vowed to tune the rural lay no more,
> Have bid my useless classics sleep at ease,
> And left the race of bards to scribble, starve, and freeze.

Bryant was seemingly destined for a career that he didn't like. Soon he was complaining in letters to Baylies about the bigoted ideas of some of his local clients. Baylies admonished him: "Experience will teach you that it is from that class of society sometimes denominated—previously denominated—the lower—as *much*—probably *more* than any other, you are to expect zealous support, & disinterested friendship." Bryant listened to his mentor's advice about the classes of society but still was skeptical about his profession.

Bryant sought consolation from mundane legal work in the landscape around Great Barrington. "I had never before seen the southern part of Berkshire," he wrote in a reminiscence of Catharine Sedgwick, "and congratulated myself on being a resident of so picturesque a region." Talking about Great Barrington in a letter to Baylies, he admitted, "This is a pretty little village in a very pleasant part of the world."

Bryant found another compelling aspect to life in Great Barrington. We can only speculate about the young man's earlier interest in the attractive Mrs. Howe or about a disappointing love affair he might have had with a woman he addressed in several forlorn verses:

> I knew thee fair—I deemed thee free
>   From fraud and guile and faithless art,
> Yet had I seen as now I see,
>   Thine image ne'er had stained my heart.

Bryant's flirtatious escapades had brought him to the attention of the local women and had resulted in remonstrance from his father. But now he met

Frances Fairchild, an orphan of nineteen. Frances was living with her married sister at the time of their first encounter at a local dance in 1816.

In an unpublished memoir written after her death, Bryant remembered Frances as "a very pretty blonde, small in person, with light-brown hair, gray eyes, a graceful shape, a dainty foot, transparent and delicate hands, and a wonderfully frank and sweet expression of face." Over the decades, he wrote several poems to her, among them the frequently anthologized lyric beginning

> Oh fairest of the rural maids!
> Thy birth was in the forest shades;
> Green boughs, and glimpses of the sky,
> Were all that met thine infant eye.

The tenderness and sincerity of feeling evoked by the interplay of plain language and delicate metrical rhythms in this poem remind us of the best Renaissance love lyrics:

> The forest depths, by foot unpressed,
> Are not more sinless than thy breast;
> The holy peace, that fills the air
> Of those calm solitudes, is there.

The allusion to female anatomy and the sharp rhymes of this last quatrain serve notice that Bryant was using traditional verse forms to express boldly modern sentiments.

Bryant is familiar, amusing, and at times avuncular in his correspondence with Frances. In his first surviving letter to her, which he wrote in March 1817 when Frances was visiting her brother near Canandaigua Lake in New York State, Bryant strikes a waggish note: "It is so long since we have heard from you that some of us begin seriously to doubt whether there ever was such a young lady as Frances Fairchild. Others pretend to say that the reason why we hear nothing of Frances Fairchild is that she has changed her name to Frances Wells—but I am pretty certain that if you were either dead or married or run away you would let us know it." He imagines that Frances might have become an Indian bride before cautioning her about her "delicate constitution" and urging her swift return "as soon as the roads become settled." The letter's tone is intimate and anticipatory.

Meanwhile, Bryant's new association with the editors of the *North American Review*, a "club" consisting of Harvard luminaries Edward Tyrell Channing, Richard Henry Dana, Willard Phillips, and Jared Sparks, offered him a venue for his poetry and also for essays and reviews that would make him a pioneer in American literary criticism. In October 1817, Bryant had written to Phillips praising the quality of the *North American Review*. Phillips in turn conveyed through Dr. Bryant his interest in having Cullen write "a short history of and criticism on our poetry." Cullen responded to Phillips, agreeing to undertake the article. In a letter to his father, Bryant had demonstrated a knowledge of "most of the American poets of any note—Dwight—Trumbull—Barlow—Humphreys—Paine—Cliffton—Honeywood," as well as Freneau and Hopkinson. He continued, "I imagine that we could hardly be said to have any poetry of our own—and indeed it seems to me that American poetry may justly enough be said to have had its rise with that knot of Connecticut poets Trumbull and others, most of whose works appeared about the time of the revolution or soon after."

The result of Bryant's thoughts on American poetry, which he shared with his father while visiting Cummington in late April, is the first of five essays he would write for the *North American Review* prior to his departure for New York City in 1825. Reviewing *An Essay on American Poetry* (1818), a verse production by Solyman Brown, which he had mentioned in a letter to his father as "poor stuff" that, having located the volume locally, he luckily didn't have to pay any money for, Bryant found American poetry to be in a dismal state: "We make but a contemptible figure in the eyes of the world, and set ourselves up as objects of pity to our posterity, when we affect to rank the poets of our own country with those mighty masters of song who have flourished in Greece, Italy, and Britain." He excoriated Philip Freneau as "a writer of inferior verse," while the so-called Hartford Wits rarely aspired to more than "a certain glow and interest in their manner" with their patriotic sentiments.

In a lucid, logical, and balanced style deriving from eighteenth-century classical models best represented by the critics of the *Edinburgh Review*, Bryant called for a higher standard of national taste: "The poetical adventurer should be taught that it is only the production of genius, taste, and diligence that can find favour at the bar of criticism—that his writings are not to be applauded merely because they are written by an American, and are not decidedly bad; and that he must produce some satisfactory evidence of his claim to celebrity than an extract from a in courts of justice and the Court of Common Pleas. Legal affairs took him as far as New York City in June 1818. On this, his first trip to Manhattan, he had written to his father of his illness aboard a Hudson River boat, but "running about continually" in the city had restored his health. That September, Bryant was admitted to full practice in the Judicial Court of Massachusetts. He was elected town clerk in February 1819, and the next month he became tithing-man, even though he was not a member of the Great Barrington Congregational Church. The unpaid position of tithing-man, a holdover from Puritan times, required Bryant to serve as a sort of spiritual sheriff, enforcing attendance at Sunday services and keeping an eye out for "nightwalkers, tipplers, Sabbath breakers . . . or whatever else tending toward debauchery, irreligion, profaneness and atheism." Bryant's civic duties expanded in May when he was appointed justice of the peace.

For the July 4, 1820, celebration at nearby Stockbridge, Bryant gave an oration in which he discussed the Missouri Compromise and for the first time publicly attacked the institution of slavery. Congress had passed the Missouri Compromise in March in an attempt to placate the Union's warring northern and southern factions. Under the compromise, Maine was admitted to the Union as a free state and Missouri as a slave state, with slavery excluded from all territory acquired in the Louisiana Purchase north of the line 36°30'. Bryant criticized the compromise as "extending the dangerous and detestable practice of enslaving men into territory yet unpolluted with the curse." According to Bryant, the law was a compromise with evil. Denouncing slavery on moral grounds, he urged the good people of Missouri to have the common sense to ignore it. Bryant's life was defined in part by the Puritan ethic of hard work and good deeds. But in his condemnation of slavery, Bryant rejected the Calvinistic notion that our lives are predestined. All Americans had to be defenders of liberty and champions of freedom.

Bryant had become a very busy public man. In a letter to the Unitarian preacher Henry D. Sewall, he described his frantic schedule: "a term of the Supreme Court which lasted a fortnight—one of the Court of Sessions and another of the Court of Common Pleas," along with other legal engagements. He argued cases in Great Barrington, in New Haven, and before the State Supreme Court in Boston, demonstrating a talent for the intricacies of legal debate. That December, Bryant was appointed to a seven-year term as justice of the peace. He had become an exemplary public figure.

intrigued Wallace Stevens, himself a descendant of the American Romantic tradition that Bryant pioneered, the poet presents himself as an observer and participant in a frozen landscape. The white world with its "pure clean air" offers Bryant a perception of life persistent and "Patient, and waiting the soft breath of Spring." He provides evidence of life within this winter landscape:

> The snow-bird twittered on the beechen bough,
> And 'neath the hemlock, whose thick branches bent
> Beneath its bright cold burden, and kept dry
> A circle, on the earth, of withered leaves,
> The partridge found a shelter. . . .

Bryant then proceeds to a vivid evocation of trees cased in crystal, a shimmering world that alternately can be viewed as "a glittery floor" or "spacious cavern" or "palace vault." "A Winter Piece" sparkles with sheer sensory audacity, but near the end, Bryant offers a simple, pristine picture of "blue sky and the white drifting cloud." Bryant typically comes back to earth—the world he knows—a practical trait central to his growing national recognition.

Another strong poem that Bryant wrote for the short-lived *Idle Man* (which ran to only two volumes despite Dana's and Bryant's strenuous efforts to promote it) is the lovely, wistful "Green River." The poem's opening and closing stanzas capture Bryant's abiding search for solace in nature amid the cares of the professional world.

> When breezes are soft and skies are fair,
> I steal an hour from study and care,
> And hie me away to the woodland scene,
> Where wanders the stream with waters of green,
> As if the bright fringe of herbs on its brink
> Had given their stain to the waves they drink;
> Have named the stream its own fair hue.
> . . . . .
> Though forced to drudge for the dregs of men,
> And scrawl strange words with the barbarous pen,
> And mingle among the jostling crowd,
> Where the sons of strife are subtle and loud—
> I often come to this quiet place,
> To breathe the airs that ruffle thy face,

And gaze upon thee in silent dream
For in thy lonely and lovely stream
An image of that calm life appears
That won my heart in my greener years.

Like Dana, who was also a lawyer and poet, Bryant lamented the legal
life he seemed destined to pursue. Even his prominence in political affairs
(he had been elected Secretary of the Federal Republican National Convention at Lenox in March 1823) was little consolation, for he had started
to question his Federalist loyalties. He also was starting to ponder the
rise of global democratic movements; in December 1823, he gave a
speech at Great Barrington in support of Greek independence.

The publication of *Poems* encouraged Bryant to consider a broader
arena for his literary activities. Perhaps it would be Boston, where
Phillips had hailed Bryant in the *North American Review* as a native
writer "of great genius." But this son of New England had come to the
attention of a wider audience. From New York, the writer and politician
Gulian C. Verplanck, initiating a friendship that would survive intermit-
tently for fifty years, had written in the *American* that Bryant's poems
were extraordinary in "their exquisite taste, their keen relish for the
beauties of nature, their magnificent imagery, and their pure and majestic
morality." And in England, a reviewer in *Blackwood's Edinburgh Magazine* predicted that Bryant would take his rank among the greatest English poets. Bryant reflected on his growing celebrity. An impulse—a
dissatisfaction with circumstances that often would dictate future decisions—seemed to be propelling him from the Berkshires toward New
York City. Both Bryant and Manhattan—a raw, dynamic, democratic
city—were in flux and in the process of becoming. As much as his poetry
and life were rooted in the Berkshires' hills, he would take the plunge
and become a metropolitan man.

3

THE DELECTABLE CITY
OF GOTHAM

It cost me more pains and perplexity than it was worth to live on friendly terms with my neighbours—and not having as I flatter myself any great taste for contention I made up my mind to get out of it as soon as I could and come to this great city where if it was my lot to starve I might starve peaceably and quietly.
—Letter to Richard Henry Dana, New York, May 25, 1825

I

In rebelling against life's limits, Bryant embarked, not without a certain amount of trepidation, on what would be a unique American odyssey. His dislike of contentious courtrooms and capricious clients led him to believe that his life had become paltry and inauthentic in the Berkshires and that he needed a radical change. Just as he had once dreamed of Boston as a stage on which he could create a new version of himself, Bryant began to imagine that New York City held similar promise.

With a population over 160,000 in 1825, Manhattan was the emblem of what John Lambert, an English tourist, called "pure republican equality." Bankers and merchants mixed with artisans and manual laborers. Old Knickerbockers strolling fashionable Broadway shared space with cartmen and prostitutes. The mercantile elite clustered in enclaves at the southern end of the island while sailors in Corlears Hook and poor blacks in Bancker Street in the Fifth Ward endured filthy, overcrowded quarters. Four percent of the population owned half of the city's wealth: what did pure republicanism mean?

When Henry and Robert Sedgwick invited Bryant to visit them in Manhattan in April 1824 to explore professional prospects, Bryant jumped at the opportunity. He had known the Sedgwicks, a distinguished family living near Great Barrington in Stockbridge, since 1820. He was on close terms with three Sedgwick brothers—Charles (who had been his classmate at Williams), Henry, and Robert. And he was a great admirer of their father, Theodore Sedgwick, who, though still nominally a Federalist, had become interested in European political economy and was revising his notions of what constituted a just society and polity. The Sedgwicks were both cosmopolitan and rural republican elite.

In a memoir written for *Griswald's Biographic Annual* (1839), Bryant extolled the liberal opinions held by Theodore Sedgwick, which clearly influenced his own evolving political thought. He approved of Sedgwick's book *Public and Private Economy*: "Its principal design was to promote the object that lay nearest the heart of the author, that of narrowing more and more the limits of poverty, ignorance, and vice among his countrymen, of inspiring them with the love of personal independence, giving them habits of reflection, teaching them reverence for one another's rights, and thus bringing about that equality of condition which is most favorable to the morals and happiness of society, and to the harmonious working of our institutions."

Bryant enjoyed a special relationship with the youngest of Theodore Sedgwick's three daughters, Catharine, who was thirty when she first met the poet. A smart, vivacious woman, Catharine liked Bryant immediately. Soon to join the ranks of American novelists with the anonymous publication in 1822 of her anti-Calvinist narrative, *A New England Tale*, Catharine was intelligent and well read. She found Bryant to be a convivial, unpretentious gentleman and invited him to contribute hymns to a songbook being prepared by the Unitarian Society of Massachusetts. He composed six hymns for the volume.

Catharine Sedgwick would later be famous on both sides of the Atlantic as a novelist and reformer. She dedicated her second novel, *Redwood* (1824), to Bryant. In return, Bryant wrote appreciatively of *Redwood* in the *North American Review* a year later, arguing for the creation of a native literature. American novelists, he asserted in his praise of Catharine's novel, "have a rich and varied field before them in the United States"; they can set their narratives in an exceptional landscape "of grandeur and beauty." For years, Cullen and Catharine would travel in the same social circles and spheres of mutual influence. Unlike Bryant (or perhaps because of him), Catharine Sedgwick would never marry.

Catharine apparently saw Bryant during the poet's first trip to New York City. "We have a great deal of pleasure from a glimpse of Bryant. I never saw him so happy, nor half so agreeable. I think he is very much animated with his prospects." One evening, at a soiree hosted by Catharine's brother, Robert, a lavishly dressed woman recited "To a Waterfowl" and "Thanatopsis" in the poet's presence. "Bryant's face 'brightened all over,'" wrote Catharine, "was one gleam of light, and, I am certain, at the moment he felt the ecstasy of a poet." Bryant was enjoying the power of celebrity.

Robert Sedgwick's Manhattan home was a popular salon, a patrician site of power, and Bryant met merchants, professionals, educators, and writers there. Chief among the writers were the poets Fitz-Greene Halleck and Robert C. Sands (who that May would start the *Atlantic Magazine*), and James Fenimore Cooper. Cooper stood out in Bryant's mind. Following a dinner hosted by Robert, he described America's acclaimed novelist to his wife. "Mr. Cooper engaged the whole conversation to himself—he seems a little giddy with [the] great success his works have met with." Years later, in a memorial speech in 1852, Bryant tempered his early assessment of the novelist, recalling that he had been "somewhat startled, coming from the seclusion of a country life, with a certain emphatic frankness in his manner, which, however, I came at last to like and to admire." Perhaps Bryant was self-conscious about his rural origins and intimidated in his initial encounter with Cooper; soon he would feel at home in metropolitan culture and learn to appreciate the garrulous novelist.

Bryant, now thirty, enjoyed Manhattan's energy and civic life. New York—"the delectable city of Gotham" as Washington Irving, his brother William, and James Kirke Paulding had drolly labeled the metropolis in their *Salmagundi* papers—might draw to its environs legions of fools and rascals, but Bryant sensed that the city also rewarded men and women of talent and ambition. Despite the bad spring weather, he notified Frances that he would extend his stay and see more of the metropolis.

Charles Sedgwick, seeing Bryant back in Great Barrington, noticed the poet's high spirits. "Every muscle of his face teemed with happiness. He kissed the children, talked much and smiled at every thing. He said more about your kindness to him than I have ever heard him express before in regard to any body."

That winter, following several months of vexing legal work, Bryant became "fixed" in his "determination to leave this beggarly profession." Dana encouraged his metropolitan prospects. "Cooper holds you in great admiration. G. C. Verplanck talked about you, too. So far as I could discover in a two days' visit in the city, you are mighty popular." Bryant later confessed to Dana, "[M]y residence in Great Barrington in consequence of innumerable local quarrels and factions which were springing up every day among an extremely excitable, and not very enlightened population had become quite disagreeable to me." His law practice threw him into nasty confrontations with the contentious citizenry of western Massachusetts, and when judges in *Bloss v. Tobey* reversed a decision favorable to his client on a technicality, Bryant was angered and disillusioned. His overt anger disturbed him: he prided himself on controlling tempestuous emotions. But Bryant already had threatened to thrash an opposing lawyer; and shortly after he assumed editorship of the *New-York Evening Post*, he would engage in a legendary Broadway battle with a rival newspaper publisher.

Bryant's state of mind darkened further when his sister Sally died of tuberculosis in December 1824. Bryant had been close to Sally, initiating a correspondence with her in 1817 when she was fifteen and soon to enter Miss Bancroft's school for girls in Great Barrington. "Next to her parents," he had written her, "a young lady ought to consider her brother as her best friend," and Bryant's letters were filled with moral advice for his younger sister. Sally had taught school for a brief period before marrying Dr. Samuel Shaw, one of Peter Bryant's former students, in 1821. At the time Bryant had been worried about the state of Sally's health, inviting her to visit him in Great Barrington, where she could seek restorative health by roaming the countryside and studying the unusual plant life with Bryant and Frances, who also had become an apt student of botany.

Shortly before Sally's death, Bryant wrote "Consumption," expressing his sorrow over his sister's impending fate:

> Ay, thou art for the grave; thy glances shine
>   Too brightly to shine for long; another Spring
> Shall deck her for men's eyes, but not for thine—
>   Sealed in a sleep which knows no wakening.
> The fields for thee have no medicinal leaf,
>   And the vexed ore no mineral of power;
> And they who love thee wait in anxious grief

Till the slow plague shall bring the fatal hour.
Glide softly to thy rest then; Death should come
   Gently, to one of gentle mould like thee,
As light winds wandering through groves of bloom
   Detach the delicate blossom from the tree.
Close thy sweet eyes, calmly, and without pain;
And we will trust in God to see thee yet again.

Edgar Allan Poe, who loathed most American poetry (and poets) but admired Bryant and his verse, regretted the last line of this sonnet; otherwise, he found it the perfect expression of what he claimed was one of poetry's great subjects, the death of a beautiful woman. Poe was astute; the commonplace sentiment about a heavenly reunion in the last line taints the gentle, heartfelt, and melancholy tribute to Bryant's dying sister.

In his sonnet to Sally, Bryant framed human experience in naturalistic terms, revealing that rural scenes and landscapes still animated his poetry and pulled at his heart. The sonnet, one of twenty-three poems he wrote for a new publication, the *United States Literary Gazette*, belongs to a prolific period of poetic production for Bryant. On the eve of his departure for New York, he entered into an agreement with Theophilus Parsons, the editor of the *Gazette*, who was "very anxious" to have Bryant's contributions. "If you can confer on me this great favour, will you have the goodness to inform me, how much money I may have the pleasure of sending you." The two men agreed that Bryant would supply poems at two dollars apiece, subsequently adjusted to two hundred dollars a year for one hundred lines monthly. The money was a welcome addition to Bryant's earnings, for his legal practice rarely brought in more than five hundred dollars annually.

As a result of the agreement with the *Gazette*, Bryant produced several impressive poems, including the superb lyric "Summer Wind," which opens:

It is a sultry day; the sun has drunk
The dew that lay upon the morning grass;
There is no rustling in the lofty elm
That canopies my dwelling, and its shade
Scarce cools me. All is silent, save the faint
And interrupted murmur of the bee,
Settling on the sick flowers, and then again
Instantly on the wing. The plants around

Feel the too potent fervors: the tall maize
Rolls up its long green leaves; the clover droops
Its tender foliage, and declines its blooms.

"Summer Wind" is pioneering poetry of the American landscape drawn from the Berkshires rather than from English hedgerows, fields of daffodils, or even the woods through which the sylvan Wye flows (in Wordsworth's "Tintern Abbey"). Bryant might have learned the language of common men and women from Wordsworth, but in "Summer Wind" he uses it to recreate a native scene. The images and rhythms shift from static, languid, oppressive heat to refreshing, almost homoerotic breezes willed or wooed into existence by the poet. Bryant's American wind sweeps from Berkshire's mountains into its fields and valleys. With the technical assurance of a poet at the height of his powers, Bryant animates his landscape; with an American voice presaging Robert Frost's nature poetry, he makes music out of the sound of sense—or in this case, sense out of sights and sounds captured in supple, innovative blank verse rhythms.

Bryant was writing accomplished poetry even as he was exasperated by constant courtroom skirmishes and overwhelmed by growing civic responsibilities. His New England upbringing had taught him to confront life's challenges and difficulties head-on. He finally decided that only new prospects would cure his nagging dissatisfaction with the law. Bryant had the foresight and daring to sense that Manhattan soon would eclipse all other American cities including Boston, which earlier had seemed a logical destination for the bard of the Berkshires. Imbibing the American entrepreneurial spirit, Bryant turned to Manhattan in search of his destiny.

Bryant made a second trip to New York in February 1825, referring to himself as a "literary adventurer" seeking a new life. As he traveled winter's frozen roads from Great Barrington to Manhattan, he recalled perhaps a verse letter he had written eleven years earlier to his friend, Elisha Hubbard. The letter, entitled "To a Discontented Friend" and composed as an ode in imitation of Horace, begins with the lines

The hills are white with new fall'n snow,
Beneath its weight the forests bow,
The ice-clad streams can scarcely flow,
    Constrained by hoary winter;

Haste, to the cheerful parlour fly,
And heap the generous fuel high,—
And then—whenever thou art dry,
    Why, broach the bright decanter.

To Providence resign the reign,
Nor vex with idle care thy brain,
To know if thou shalt go to Maine,
    Ohio, or Kentucky.
Nor give to moping dread thy mind;—
The man to gloomy dreams inclin'd
The ill he fears will always find,
    And always be unlucky.

Bryant had no intention of remaining in a small western Massachusetts town, aggravated by court cases, resigned to his fate.

Bryant's gloom lifted as soon as he reached Manhattan; he was energized by the prospect of starting anew. "I have got here at last after being three days and one night on the road," he wrote Frances. "The first day brought me to Hartford—the next carried me to New Haven, and finding no packet nor steam-boat there which would set for New York till Friday, I kept on in the stage, and the next morning at sunrise found that I had traveled the immense distance of twenty-six miles during the night. Yesterday at 7 o'clock I came into New York in the midst of a sharp shower of rain—and this morning after a good long night's sleep at the City Hotel, am as well as when I set out last Monday." The City Hotel, on the west side of Broadway in the block north of Trinity Church, had opened in 1794, the year of Bryant's birth. With 137 rooms, a bar, coffee room, concert hall, and the City Assembly room, it was the most celebrated hotel in the city. The hotel had hosted the Marquis de Lafayette at a lavish state dinner in 1824. From the hotel, Bryant could walk easily to commercial Wall Street or upscale Bowling Green, City Hall or the Battery. He wrote Frances: "My friends here are making some interest to obtain the approbation & patronage of the Athenaeum for a literary paper to be established here under my direction, and I think there is a pretty good prospect that they will succeed."

Bryant returned briefly to Great Barrington, then ventured to New York once again in March, this time traveling westward by coach to the hardscrabble town of Hudson, notorious for the taverns and brothels patronized by workers on the Erie Canal and other adventurers, and then down the Hudson River. This trip, like the one in February, proved difficult. He told Frances of blinding rain, a heavy cold that he contracted, a long delay, and the rough, nauseating eighteen-hour journey down the Hudson River by steamboat. (During a lifetime of travel that took him by boat to Mexico, the Caribbean, Europe, and the Middle East, Bryant stoically put up with seasickness.) On arriving in New York, he told Frances with self-deprecating humor, "Here I am trying to starve myself well, going hungry amid a profusion of good cheer, and refusing to drink good wine amid an ocean of it. But all will not do; I am continually in the steamboat. Sitting or standing, I feel the roll and swell of the water under me; the streets and floors of houses swing from side to side as if they were floating in a sea."

Bryant by now had resolved to tie his destiny to Manhattan. After three exploratory trips, he was ready to act. He informed Frances, who apparently had few reservations about the impending disruption of their lives, "At all events, I shall make the experiment." As a metropolitan man, he would be at the locus of the political and cultural transformations sweeping Manhattan and the nation in the next half-century.

With the support of the Sedgwick brothers and their friends, Bryant had been asked to launch a new literary publication, the *New-York Review and Athenaeum Magazine*. He would serve as coeditor with Henry James Anderson, the son of a wealthy New York family and a professor of mathematics and astronomy at Columbia College. The New York Athenaeum, a society created the previous year by a small group of New York's affluent patricians as a vehicle to improve the city's intellectual climate, would underwrite the *Review*. Gotham's learned leaders, drawn from the ranks of wealthy bankers, merchants, educators, and lawyers, believed in elevating the city's culture by supporting the arts and legislating standards of taste—a laudable Republican enterprise that seemed a bit anomalous in the democratic climate of the 1820s. Bryant, they imagined, was the ideal man to raise the city's cultural image.

Bryant closed his Great Barrington law office in May 1825 and settled for good in New York City. At the age of thirty-one, he was older than seventeen-year-old Benjamin Franklin had been when he strolled into Philadelphia from Boston a century earlier. But like Franklin, Bryant was a self-confessed "literary adventurer"—a person of several talents and numerous interests, a type of new American man. New York, which had surpassed both Philadelphia and Boston as the largest and most important commercial city in the United States, would offer Bryant a platform for his literary interests as well as a forum for his evolving cultural authority.

II

Bryant arrived in New York at a decisive moment in the city's history. Manhattan was on the cusp of greatness; with the completion of the Erie Canal in late 1825, it was soon to become the country's center of finance, commerce, and culture. The city, once it was linked to the American interior, would be the center of the emerging idea of the United States as a cauldron of commerce and democracy for a transcontinental nation. Bryant, who delighted in thinking of himself as an intrepid literary adventurer, an independent and self-made republican, would promote the city and nation's development.

Bryant had gradually renounced his Federalist principles. In fact, Federalism as a national movement was moribund. By 1825, Bryant had reconsidered the spacious political imagination of Jefferson, whom he had satirized so heartily as a youth. With the Louisiana Purchase in 1803, Jefferson had expanded the United States from the Mississippi to the Rockies, adding eight hundred thousand square miles to the nation. To strengthen this new American empire, President James Monroe's message to Congress on December 2, 1823, outlined the principles that would dictate the U.S. role in the Western hemisphere. Sprinkling ideas that became known as the Monroe Doctrine throughout his speech, the president, whose policies created what Boston's *Columbia Sentinel* termed approvingly an "Era of Good Feelings," asserted "that the American continents, by the free and independent condition which they have assumed and maintain, are henceforth not to be considered as subjects for future colonization by any European powers."

Bryant now embraced the liberal political principles that had emerged in the United States in the 1820s: liberty and self-determination (at least for white men), freedom from foreign entanglements, free trade, pan-Americanism, and—with slow but growing conviction—suppression of the slave trade. His political intelligence was not original, but it was malleable. He had moved far from the western Massachusetts soil that had nurtured his mother's orthodox Calvinism and his father's Federalist principles. Determined "to leave this beggarly profession," as he had informed Charles Sedgwick, he was ready to promote democratic cultural and political values in a new arena.

Moving to delectable Gotham, Bryant was caught up in a roiling population of 167,000 souls—40,000 more inhabitants than in 1820. Fenimore Cooper delighted in annoying residents by telling them that Manhattan was "a hobbledehoy metropolis, a rag fair sort of place," but Bryant liked the city's cultural vitality. One evening he attended a "soiree," as he called it, hosted by Dr. David Hosack, a professor at Columbia College and the College of Physicians and Surgeons and president of the New-York Historical Society. "There was a crowd of literary men—citizens & strangers—in fine apartments splendidly furnished—hung with pictures." Sir John Franklin, the British explorer whose 1823 *Narrative of a Journey to the Shores of the Polar Sea* Bryant had read, was there, along with two of his expedition's companions. On other occasions, Bryant joined Catharine Sedgwick and her brothers and friends for dinner.

Bryant could even enjoy rural rambles in the city, for Manhattan above Fourteenth Street still consisted largely of fields and farms. Greenwich was a rural retreat but changing rapidly; in 1825, the editor of the *Commercial Advertiser* remarked: "Greenwich is no longer a country village." Westward, in "Chelsea," an extensive farm owned by Clement Moore, hunters shot waterfowl. (Moore, a conservative Knickerbocker who objected to the city's northerly growth, in 1823 had anonymously published what became known as "The Night Before Christmas.") Even the city's downtown area was still somewhat wild: foxes roamed in the churchyard of St. Patrick's Church on Mulberry Street, which had been dedicated in 1815 to accommodate the city's growing population of Catholic immigrants.

Bryant had to embark on a search for lodgings because of a housing crisis that New York City arguably has never solved. In 1824 alone, approximately three thousand new houses had been built in a futile effort to accommodate Manhattan's exploding population. And in 1825, more than five hundred new businesses opened. Wealthy residents, like the conservative merchant Philip Hone, could purchase one sumptuous residence after another in an attempt to keep ahead of a population surge that brought less desirable elements to even the most stately streets. Most of the city's artisan and middle class residents did not own homes, renting instead modest two- to four-room dwellings or boarding in portions of them. For years Bryant would be part of these roaming masses.

All leases in Manhattan expired on May 1 of each year. The event, described in articles and captured vividly in magazine illustrations as "Moving Day," produced an urban eruption, with residents spewing forth from former domiciles in search of new lodgings. In fragmentary autobiographical notes that Frances Bryant kept, we have a chronicle of the nomadic lives that ordinary New Yorkers led: "We took lodgings [in 1825] at Monsieur Evrard, in Chambers Street. Then . . . we took lodgings with Mrs. Meigs in Canal Street. The next May 1826 we moved to Laight St. with Mrs. Meigs. . . . The next May 1827 I moved with Mrs. Meigs into Thomson St. . . . In the autumn we . . . took lodgings with Mrs. Tripler, corner of Market St. and Broadway. . . ." New Yorkers were in perpetual motion; the city never seemed to offer ordinary citizens sufficient rest. Witnessing the pandemonium on Moving Day, the acerbic English visitor Frances Trollope thought that the entire population looked as if it were "flying from the plague." Bryant, struggling to make ends meet, would not be able to settle down and rent a house of his own until December 1830.

On Moving Day in 1825, Bryant joined the urban cavalcade heading to new lodgings. He had found room and board on Chambers Street at the home of the Evrards, a French Catholic family that had owned a plantation in Haiti and had escaped the revolution there. Recalling the epidemic of 1822, Bryant appreciated the fact that the Evrard house was "at some distance from that part of the city in which the yellow fever made so many victims a few years since." Still the country boy, he liked his new dwelling's proximity to the river. "I see it whenever I put my head out the window." Like Ben Franklin, Bryant slept with the window open in all seasons. "I like my boarding house better and better," he confessed to Frances, who was in Great Barrington with Fanny. "It is almost impossible to conceive of a man of more goodness of heart and rectitude of principle than Mons. Evrard. He is very religious—very charitable—and very honest—a proof of the utter folly and presumption of all those who arrogate to their own sect the exclusive title Christians."

Bryant attended Roman Catholic services with the Evrards, who spoke only French at home, prompting him to polish a language that he had studied as a teenager. He sampled denominational services at other churches as well—sometimes three in one day. He was more inquisitive and intrigued by all aspects of the city's diverse culture than rigorously devout. Churchgoing was popular in New York City, and a new breed of minister, skilled in oratory and acting, had turned the pulpit into a source of both edification and entertainment. Bryant was amused by M. Evrard's attempts to convert him to Catholicism. He informed Frances on May 24: "I went yesterday to vespers in St. Peter's Church; but my convictions were not sufficiently strong to induce me to kneel at the elevation of the host." In June, an oppressively hot month in the city, he again humorously revealed his ecumenical bent: "On the whole, I think that a *good* Catholic is quite as good, and much more amiable, than a good Calvinist."

Bryant, his religious views tolerant, had gravitated to Unitarianism. He began attending the Congregational Church, which had been founded in the city in 1821 by the Unitarian minister William Ware. Bryant and Ware would be intimate friends until the minister's death in 1852.

Bryant's adjustment to his new urban surroundings was not always placid. He complained to Frances of "the heat, the noise, and the unpleasant odours of the city." New York was notoriously filthy. Herds of swine raised by butchers, grocers, and residents roamed freely, devouring garbage while leaving their own waste behind. Dead cats and dogs mingled with dust and ashes thrown into the streets. Bryant's future son-in-law, Parke Godwin, recalled: "Within the city the streets were narrow . . . they were then frequented by loose pigs, were badly lighted by rusty oil lamps, and poorly watched by constables in huge capes and leather caps."

William Coleman, the editor of the *Evening Post*, commented sardonically on the city's filth in an 1823 editorial: "To the Curious:—The collection of filth and manure now lying in heaps, or which had been heaped in Wall, Water, and Front Streets, near the Coffee-House, and left there, will astonish those who are fond of the wonderful, and pay them for the trouble of a walk there." Two years later, Coleman, whom Bryant had encountered in a courtroom during his very first trip to New York in 1818, renewed his diatribe against Gotham: "You can scarcely pass through any one street in the city without running against a greasy table, with plates of sickly oysters displayed, well peppered with dust, and swarms of fleas feeding upon them."

Still adjusting to urban realities, Bryant lamented the loss of his Berkshire summers, especially in June's oppressive heat: "I envy you very much the pure air, the breezes, the shade and the coolness which you must enjoy in the country," he wrote to Frances, "while I am sweltering under a degree of heat which I never experienced in my whole life time for so long a period. . . . Yesterday in the afternoon I rode out a few miles into the country—I found it worse if possible than the city. The roads were full of carts, barouches, chaises, hacks and people on horseback, passing each other; and a thick cloud of dust lay above the road as far as the eye could follow it; it was almost impossible to breathe the stifling element."

No longer able to wander Berkshire's gentle hills and expansive valleys, Bryant began to trudge around Manhattan. The city's streets clustered at the southern tip of the island, with the most elegant houses situated near the Battery. Here the Knickerbocker gentry resided, those pedigreed Dutch and English families that, despite the arrival of John Jacob Astor and other parvenus, still constituted the bedrock of New York society. This area was "downtown," a word popularized by the compulsive diarist Philip Hone. New Yorkers possessing or aspiring to any level of gentility lived south of Reade and Chatham streets. Mansions, many decorated with pillars and porticos, fronted State Street, which was known to New Yorkers as Quality Row. Maiden Lane, overrun occasionally by pigs, was the center of fashion.

A vigorous walker, insatiably curious about his new metropolitan universe, Bryant discovered that commerce radiated northward, typically mixing with the city's housing. The offices of the *New-York Evening Post*, founded in 1801 by Alexander Hamilton to advance a Federalist agenda and soon to be Bryant's base of operations, were located at 49 William Street. In *Reminiscences of the Evening Post*, which he wrote for the fiftieth anniversary of his newspaper in 1851, Bryant provided an account of the city when he had first arrived. "The space covered with houses had extended a little beyond Canal Street, and on each side of Broadway a line of dwellings, with occasional vacant spaces, had crept as far as Fourth Street. Preparations were making to take up the monuments in Potter's field, now the site of Washington Square, and fill it up to the level of Fourth Street. Workmen were employed in opening the street now called St. Mark's Place, and a dusty avenue had just been made through the beautiful farm of the old Governor Stuyvesant, then possessed by his descendants." Beyond Twelfth Street there were farms and orchards, fields stretching northward, undulating hills, swamps, and streams. The city's rough topography had not been leveled or drained yet; the grid imposed on Manhattan during the survey and subsequent adoption of the Commissioners' Plan in 1821 was not apparent.

After he became editor of the *New-York Evening Post*, Bryant would have much to say about the consequences of the Commissioners' Plan, which imposed a rigid blueprint of horizontal and vertical streets on all of Manhattan and accelerated the city's erratic expansion. Gone were the zigzag contours—the hobbledehoy features mentioned by Cooper—that had characterized the city's life during the Dutch and colonial eras and that can be seen today in the irregular design of certain streets in lower Manhattan. Hills had to be leveled, the Collect Pond and swamps drained, watercourses and ravines filled, and the shoreline extended—all in service to the flat, geometric design of the plan. Once settled into New York and comfortable with his bearings, Bryant often would stroll the streets with one or two close friends, searching for signs of the old New York that was rapidly vanishing.

To Bryant, the city seemed at times like Bedlam. Unbridled construction and development produced a monstrous urban mess. "New York never saw such days since it was a city," Coleman complained in the *New-York Evening Post* in 1825. "The streets are so obstructed by the great number of buildings going up and pulling down, that they have become almost impassable, and a scene of bustle, noise, and confusion prevails that no pen can describe, nor any but an eye witness imagine." A few years after he had become the *Evening Post*'s editor, Bryant would also complain about the metropolitan sprawl. In a typical editorial on February 12, 1833, Bryant used a pungent, pictorial style to criticize plans "for opening new streets, widening others, ploughing through church yards, demolishing block after block of buildings, for miles in length, filling up streets so that you can step out of your second story bed room window upon the side walk, and turning your first story parlors and dining rooms into cellars and kitchens, with various other magnificent projects for changing the appearance of the city, and for preventing any part of it from ever getting the look of antiquity." Learning from Coleman, he rapidly became a caustic and increasingly authoritative commentator on the social and political upheavals of the nineteenth century.

As Manhattan was changing, so were relationships among the populace. Bryant detected a newer, more egalitarian community in the making. Gone were the earlier Republican and patrician notions of personal bonds governing behavior between merchants, artisans, and urban dwellers and of civic institutions assembled coherently around public spaces—an essentially static concept of human behavior that had appealed to the Federalist mind. In place of this traditional civic culture, Bryant witnessed the rise of a grid-inspired commodity system based on the impersonal exchange of goods in an urban world increasingly fragmented by class and caste divisions. Bryant had learned something about political economy from the Sedgwick brothers, who encouraged him to study the laissez-faire writings of Adam Smith, David Ricardo, and others; he understood that the rough-and-tumble commercial spirit of Manhattan was creating fissures in the social order.

Bryant only had to stroll from Chambers Street to fashionable Broadway to experience the clashing democratic impulses of Manhattan. One of his destinations was Bliss and White, the firm commissioned to print the *New York Review and Athenaeum Magazine*, at 128 Broadway. The printing house was located along what one contemporary chronicler called the "great artery of life" and "the most cosmopolitan of streets." On Broadway, Bryant marveled over the panorama of changing America: millionaires and beggars; merchants and vendors; financiers and western land speculators; elegant women and suspiciously "undomesticated ladies." Races intermingled, leading an English visitor, Mrs. Felton, to declare that Broadway was "the fashionable lounge for all the black and white belles and beaux of the city." Just as he had studied nature, Bryant now turned his attention to an evolving urban society. As he studied the diverse population of enterprising New Yorkers who were adept at self-creation, he absorbed their entrepreneurial energy and democratic spirit.

Bryant sensed the dangers inherent in his metropolitan world—so unlike anything he had encountered in the bucolic Berkshires. He recounted disquieting events for Frances: "This week has been a chapter of terrible accidents in N.Y. Last Friday a Swiss who had just arrived in this country was murdered by two of his fellow passengers. Yesterday morning at 6 o'clock the boiler of one of the steam boats plying between this city and Brunswick, exploded at the wharf, as she was just setting out with about 100 passengers on board,—and four of [her] hands were scalded to death, and others badly injured—and this morning about 2 o'clock a Mr. Lambert returning from a party a little out of the city with some of his friends was assaulted by a party of drunken apprentices, and a fray ensued in which he was killed."

There were sections of the city, notably Five Points, where not even the peripatetic Bryant wanted to venture. (Located northeast of the present New York County Courthouse, Five Points took its name from the intersection of five streets.) This "Valley of Poverty" was a haphazard warren of dismal back alleys, dank passages, shacks, and outhouses that had been precariously erected over the drained and filled Collect Pond. By the time of Bryant's arrival in the city, the buildings in Five Points were sinking into the moist, unsettled soil and tilting precariously, like Hogarth's portrayal of Gin Lane.

But even Five Points with its beer gardens, oyster saloons, theaters, brothels, and teeming streets pulsed with urban life. It was a roiling mixed-race and working-class neighborhood—home to African Americans, immigrants, Irish gangs, the destitute, and the working poor. Five Points was a dangerous but alluring habitat. When Charles Dickens visited Manhattan in 1842, he expressed two wishes: he wanted to visit Five Points, and he insisted on meeting Bryant.

III

By the end of May 1825, Bryant had prepared the first issue of the short-lived *New-York Review and Athenaeum Magazine*. Neither the *Review* nor its successor, *The United States Review and Literary Gazette*, which together lasted thirty months, attracted sufficient writing of quality. New York and the nation were not yet supportive of literary journals. In Philadelphia, the venerable *Port Folio*, which once boasted of a phenemonal circulation of two thousand copies at five dollars annually, was on the verge of collapse. In Boston, the *North American Review* had barely five hundred subscribers and was constantly in need of contributors. Bryant contributed poetry to the *Review* and churned out dozens of reviews and notices to fill space in each issue. He confessed to Dana, "The business of sitting in judgment upon books as they come out is not the literary employment the most to my taste nor that for which I am best fitted." Still, he admitted, "It affords me for the present a certain compensation—which is a matter of consequence to a poor devil like myself."

Bryant managed to write a lengthy critical essay on the Troubadour poets that revealed his growing facility with French and Provençal. Possessing a talent for translation, he would introduce French, Spanish, Italian, and German writers to American readers and in later years would produce best-selling translations of the *Iliad* and *Odyssey*. Bryant also took notice of the talents of "H. W. L.," an unknown Boston poet who was an undergraduate at Bowdoin College, introducing Henry Wadsworth Longfellow to the American public. Moreover, he printed some of the earliest art criticism written in the United States, which was composed by yet another new acquaintance, Samuel F. B. Morse.

In a rare moment of cultural serendipity, Bryant had arrived in New York at the same time as Morse and another artist, Thomas Cole. First introduced to each other at the homes of the Sedgwicks, the three friends soon were moving in the same cultural circles. Morse had come from England to set up as a portrait painter and was soon commissioned to paint a portrait of the celebrated Lafayette for City Hall, thus launching an avalanche of commissions. Morse painted Bryant's portrait at this time—one of some fifty likenesses of the poet produced by artists and photographers throughout the nineteenth century. Morse's portrait depicts a slender, rather handsome man with curls swept forward in the fashion of the day. Bryant has a long face, a prominent forehead, deeply set and piercing gray eyes, a sharp nose, and lips suggesting a certain bemusement over life's uncertainties and contradictions. Morse highlights the large, cerebral head and one of the poet's hands against a chiaroscuro backdrop. Overall, the impression is of intelligence and strength.

Bryant struck up an equally close friendship with Thomas Cole, who had moved to New York from Philadelphia to join his parents. Working in the garret of their house on Greenwich Street, he painted Hudson River scenes. Exhibiting three of his landscapes in the window of William Colman's bookstore, Cole was hailed as a special talent by the domineering artist and entrepreneur John Trumbull and also by Hone. Each man purchased one of Cole's paintings from Colman's shop, and the artist Asher B. Durand, yet another artist who would become Bryant's friend, bought the third. Encouraged by the praise of his work, Cole then headed back to the Catskills to find more landscapes to paint, including three of his best compositions—*Falls of Kaaterskill* (1826), *The Clove, Catskills* (1827), and *Scene from "The Last of the Mohicans"* (1827).

Bryant would have a profound influence on Cole, Morse, Durand, and the other artists who constituted a new coterie of creative souls living and working in Gotham. The monumental paintings by Cole entitled *The Course of Empire* are pictorial representations of ideas in Bryant's "The Ages." Bryant in turn would use Catterskill Falls as the setting of a sentimental narrative poem on life's passages. Bryant's verse and criticism would inspire other artists, notably Durand, who produced several paintings based on themes from Bryant's poetry, among them *Landscape: Scene from 'Thanatopsis'* and *The Fountain*.

Bryant moved easily among the writers, artists, lawyers, merchants, and educators who were forming clubs, cultural organizations, and civic societies in New York City. He would always be part of genteel clubs and literary drawing rooms, not of the bawdy houses, oyster cellars, grog shops, and gambling halls that sustained Manhattan's workingmen. Bryant was reserved with strangers but gregarious and amiable among friends. Berkshires neighbors remembered that Bryant had always enjoyed parties, games, and "frolics." He displayed a "cheerful, entertaining, joyous way among his friends," and his penchant for walking revealed a "strange fondness for talking with queer and common people—farmers, woodsmen, and stage-drivers." Bryant delighted in the new kindred souls he found among the artists and writers in Gotham. And he gladly accepted the overtures of the city's patricians and merchant princes—Philip Hone, Luman Reed, Jonathan Sturges, and others—who viewed the poet as a welcome addition to the ideals of high culture they sought to propagate.

IV

Bryant found time to visit Cummington in July. Away from the city, luxuriating in the Berkshire landscape, and reunited with his family, he composed the lovely "Lines on Revisiting the Country." The lyric is an evocation of pastoral life, a loving tribute to his daughter Fanny in "her fourth bright year," and a confession that he was not yet completely reconciled to metropolitan life:

> Here, have I 'scaped the city's stifling heat,
>   Its horrid sounds, and its polluted air,
> And, where the season's milder fervors beat,
>   And gales, that sweep the forest borders, bear
> The song of bird and sound of running stream,
> Am come awhile to wander and to dream.

For the July 1825 issue of the *Review*, Bryant published a translation of Goethe's "The Indian God and the Bayadeer" by George Bancroft, then codirector of the experimental Round Hill School in Northampton. In accepting the piece, he had written Bancroft: "I yesterday received your beautiful translation of Goethe's ballad. We shall venture to print it—there is nothing in it with which true delicacy can be offended. I have however ventured to take the liberty you grant me, of slightly varying the phraseology in one or two instances,—not with a view of improving, but of softening the expression." Bryant and Bancroft, soon to distinguish himself as historian and diplomat, would become close friends.

Bryant corresponded frequently with Dana, whose poetry he revised before publishing it in the *Review*. With Dana he could offer candid comments on the literary and artistic skirmishes that he now surveyed from his editorial perch. In a September 1, 1825, letter to Dana he wrote, "I saw

Cooper yesterday. He is printing a novel entitled *The Last of the Mohicans*: the first volume is nearly finished.—You tell me that I must review him, next time, myself. Ah, sir, he is too sensitive a creature for me to touch. He seems to think his own works his own property instead of the property of the public, to whom he has given them." Bryant then touched obliquely on a rivalry between Cooper and Catharine Sedgwick, and certain "misunderstandings" that had led to a rupture in their friendship. Robert Sedgwick apparently had loaned Cooper money and was now suing for repayment.

Bryant's editorship of the *Review* provided the poet with an annual salary of one thousand dollars, giving him the means to settle in the city and bring Frances and Fanny there in September 1825. He had missed his wife and daughter during the summer, writing to his little girl in French so that she, like her father, would grow up with a love of languages. He informed Frances on June 20, "Notwithstanding the heat, the noise, and the unpleasant odours of the city, I think that if you and Frances were with me, I should pass my time here much more pleasantly than at Great Barrington." In September, he rejoiced in the break in summer's heat: "The weather is become quite cool—and you will find things quite convenient here—and I am impatient to have you and Frances with me."

Later in the fall, Bryant, Cole, and Morse were accepted as members of the Bread and Cheese Club. Also known as the Lunch, the club was an informal gathering of writers, artists, merchants, bankers, educators, and lawyers that had been launched by Fenimore Cooper in 1822. Bread and Cheese had evolved from gatherings that Cooper initially had hosted in the back room of Wiley's New Street bookstore—the publisher that had made Cooper a national celebrity with the 1821 publication of *The Spy*, his novel about the Revolutionary War. Cooper's club took its name from the way members voted for aspiring applicants—by casting a bit of bread for acceptance or cheese for rejection. The club met weekly at the Washington Hotel on the corner of Broadway and Chambers Street.

Bryant often saw Cooper who, with Washington Irving residing abroad, had assumed the role of the city's reigning novelist and literary celebrity. Raised on his family's baronial twenty-thousand-acre estate in upstate New York, kicked out of Yale, and subsequently sailing before the mast, Cooper had a blunt, forceful personality. On one occasion in the fall of 1825, Bryant ran into Cooper, who invited the poet to his house at 345 Greenwich Street. When Bryant asked Cooper to write down the address, Cooper replied brusquely, "Can't you remember *three-four-five*?" Bryant and Cooper shared an affinity for North America's untrammeled

natural landscape and the virtues it inspired. Bryant's "A Forest Hymn,"
with its memorable first line—"The groves were God's first temples"—
which he had written that year, was like a coda for Cooper's own ideas
about nature. Moreover, like Bryant, whose poetry reveals a keen interest
in North American tribes, Cooper was obsessed with Native Americans.
The novelist deplored eviction of the tribes from their lands east of the
Mississippi—unlike Bryant, who stoutly defended President Andrew
Jackson's policy of Indian removal.

Bryant shared with Cooper a broad interest in democratic culture.
Bryant, however, would become a reformer, while Cooper was a conservative at heart, an increasingly surly aristocrat at odds with the course of
American civilization. Natty Bumppo was his alter ego—at a deep psy-
chic level his ideal of the American Adam trying (like his later literary
cousin, Huck Finn) to stay one step ahead of an encroaching society. For
a brief time an admirer of Andrew Jackson, Cooper excoriated Jacksonian democracy in *The American Democrat* (1838). In his three novels of
the 1840s known as the Littlepage trilogy (*Satanstoe*, 1845; *The Chain-
bearer*, 1845; *The Redskins*, 1846), he presented a panorama of decline as
America's agrarian world, once held together by large landholdings like
the one created by Cooper's father, started to disappear.

Bryant's Lunch companions held decidedly disparate political and
social views but enjoyed one another's company. Cooper, in his typically
brash way, encouraged the clashing, roiling, competing ideas of his Bread
and Cheese friends. Prominent among the members was old, dictatorial
John Trumbull, who had painted portraits of Revolutionary War scenes
and heroes. Soon the irascible Trumbull would precipitate a rebellion
among the younger artists Cole and Morse, who, along with Durand,
Henry Inman, Robert Weir, and playwright-painter William Dunlap,
also were Lunch members.

Bryant formed strong friendships with the artists he encountered at
Lunch's weekly meetings and also made lasting literary friendships. His
new friend, Gulian C. Verplanck, was well known for his writings on law,
theology, and Shakespeare. Verplanck was a member of Congress who
provided Bryant, once he became associated with the *New-York Evening
Post*, with inside news on Washington machinations. Another of Bryant's
Lunch companions was Fitz-Greene Halleck, whom he had first met the
previous April at Robert Sedgwick's house. Halleck, who like Bryant had
a rural New England background—in his case, western Connecticut—
had arrived in New York in 1811, had served for a time as John Jacob
Astor's private secretary, and was a well-regarded poet. (Bryant published

Halleck's *Marco Bozzaris*, the poem taking its title from a Greek hero in the war for independence against the Turks, in the first issue of the *New-York Review*, praising it in a letter to Dana as "a very beautiful thing.") At Lunch gatherings he also saw Robert Sands, whose narrative poem *Yamoyden: A Tale of the Wars of King Philip* captured the popular interest in the Indian experience. And he found a companion in the decidedly uneven writer James Kirke Paulding of *Salmagundi* fame, who invented the tongue-twisting rhyme "Peter Piper picked a peck of pickled peppers." Paulding, a staunch nationalist who would later serve as secretary of the navy under another New Yorker, President Martin Van Buren, never hesitated to criticize John Bull in speech and print; and he could also turn a sharp eye on American society, offering depictions of the savagery of American slavery in *Letters from the South*.

With friendships cemented from his hours at Lunch meetings and other gatherings, Bryant joined a coterie of young artists and writers applying for admission to Trumbull's Academy of Fine Arts—the symbol of the city's patrician culture. Led by Morse and Cole, the group sought access to academy facilities in order to work on their drawings. They were prevented from entering by Trumbull, who told them, "Remember that beggars are not to be choosers." In retaliation, the younger artists and some of their literary companions, probably including Bryant, met in the rooms of the Historical and Philosophical Societies, located in the old Almshouse building behind City Hall, on November 8, 1825, and founded the rival New York Drawing Association, to be renamed the following year the National Academy of Design. (The next year, Bryant was appointed the academy's "Professor of Mythology and Antiquities," charged with offering talks on mythology and history and their relationship to the visual arts.) The new association presented itself to the public as an institution by and for artists rather than for the elitists, who previously had exercised their ancestral right to dictate taste and mold cultural values. Morse, the association's president, declared, "[E]very profession in a society knows what measures are necessary for its own improvement." His statement was a call to arms, a signal that artists and writers would be their own critics and would no longer be responsible to patrons or even to the public.

As he fashioned himself anew as man of the city, Bryant was caught up in the transformation of New York, which would rival London and Paris by the end of his career. Crucial to this transformation was the completion and opening of the Erie Canal, which cut through New York State and into Ohio, in October 1825. Building the canal took more than eight years of dangerous labor by thousands of workers, most of them Irish immigrants. The singular zeal of former New York mayor and state governor DeWitt Clinton had brought the "Big Ditch" to fruition at a cost of about eight million dollars. Many people thought that the "Governor's Gully" was a political boondoggle, the invention of an unscrupulous mind. (A popular jingle was "Clinton, the federal son of a bitch / taxes our dollars to build him a ditch.") Like Bryant, Clinton was also a visionary American. As mayor of New York City earlier in his career, he had predicted that in a hundred years the metropolis would stretch from the Battery to the northernmost reaches of Manhattan. Bryant lived to see the fulfillment of Clinton's prophecy.

When the 363-mile Erie Canal was completed, it was forty feet wide and four feet deep, and it linked Manhattan and other New York cities— Albany, Utica, Syracuse, Rochester, Buffalo—to the economy of the entire Middle West. It guaranteed that Manhattan, whose port already handled half the nation's imports and a third of its exports, would be the major market for the nation as well as the gateway to America for immigrants—the unrivaled Empire City.

Bryant, Frances, and their daughter were settled somewhat precariously in New York when the canal boat *Seneca Chief* carrying Governor Clinton and other notables, accompanied by a flotilla of forty-one boats, arrived in Manhattan on the splendid autumn day of November 4, 1825. Governor Clinton extolled the "wedding of the waters" by pouring a keg of water from Lake Erie into the Atlantic. The Grand Procession afterward through the streets of Manhattan, involving seven thousand marchers and witnessed by more than one hundred thousand bystanders—two-thirds of the city's population—was one of the largest gatherings in the nation's history. At ten o'clock that night, ten thousand people gathered in City Park to view a glorious fireworks display.

Bryant left no record of that day, but we can safely assume that he witnessed the spectacular events. After less than a year in Manhattan, he was already a public figure, part of a cluster of literary and artistic celebrities and enlightened leaders intent on producing a more democratic-minded culture. Despite ambivalent feelings about city life, Bryant was in the process of constructing a powerful cultural identity that required a metropolitan setting for its fullest and most authoritative expression.

4

APPRENTICE EDITOR

I drudge for the *Evening Post* and labor for the *Review*.
—Bryant to Richard Henry Dana, 1827

I

At the start of 1826, Bryant and his family were living in Mrs. Meigs's cluttered boarding house close to Canal Street. The street defined the northernmost reach of the city; it was a broad thoroughfare distinguished by rows of trees and houses fronting the canal. The Bryants shared space with seven members of the extended Meigs family and four other boarders. Bryant's modest lifestyle enhanced his expanding cultural cachet.

Bryant spent long hours working on the *Review and Athenaeum*, barely earning enough to cover expenses. He wrote to Dana: "If I keep to it I may possibly find it a source of some profit in time, but these things you know are built up slowly, and no man must expect in this country to grow rich by literature." The *Review* was headed for a merger with the *United States Literary Gazette* of Boston and eventual failure, hastened by the bankruptcy of the scandal-plagued Fulton Bank and a general financial downturn in the city's economy. Sensing the journal's precarious condition, Bryant applied reluctantly for a license to practice law in New York.

Even as he brooded over a possible return to his former profession, Bryant enjoyed new public successes. The previous December, he had been selected unanimously by members of the New York Athenaeum to lecture on poetry. In a series of four well-received discourses (which were paired with lectures on art by Samuel F. B. Morse) in March and

April 1826, Bryant staked out principles of poetic practice that would influence Longfellow, Lowell, and future generations of poets and critics. In his first lecture, Bryant offered a definition of poetry that derived from his passion for Wordsworth's preface to *Lyrical Ballads* and his reading, while preparing for admission to Williams College, of Edmund Burke's *A Philosophical Inquiry into the Origin of Our Ideas of the Sublime and Beautiful*. Bryant defines poetry "as that art which selects and arranges the symbols of thought in such a manner as to excite it the most powerfully and delightfully." Poetry should meld the emotional and intellectual faculties in order to produce "direct lessons of wisdom." Only poetry, with its powerful metrical harmonies—the major feature distinguishing it from prose—could move the mind from the emotional contemplation of experience to a higher state of knowledge. Bryant urged his listeners to turn away from neoclassicists like Dryden and Pope to more contemporary romanticists like Wordsworth, Coleridge, Shelley, and Byron.

In subsequent lectures, which drew overflow crowds, Bryant explained the doctrine of correspondences in which the poet "beholds between the things of the moral and natural world." He dismissed the idea that the United States, lacking a literary tradition, could not produce great poetry. If tradition was all that was required, then in due course "a multitude of interesting traditions will spring up in our land to ally themselves with every mountain, every hill, every forest, every river, and every tributary brook." Bryant's espousal of analogies, symbols, and correspondences to capture the sublimity of the natural world would influence Cole and the Hudson River School. The lectures on poetry, combined with the numerous reviews he wrote to fill the pages of the *Review*, constitute the "beginning of a more discriminating criticism in America."

The last issue of the *Review* appeared in May 1826, leaving Bryant with a one-fourth interest in its merged successor, the *United States Review and Literary Gazette*—scarcely enough work or income to sustain his family. Then, in an unexpected turn that confirmed Bryant's belief in a beneficent God, he was offered a new editorial position.

II

In June 1826, William Coleman, the editor of the *New-York Evening Post*, was thrown from his gig by a runaway horse, suffering injuries from which he would never recover fully. Coleman hailed from the same part of Massachusetts as Bryant; he was aware of the poet and admired his lyrics. He had reprinted "Thanatopsis" with warm words of praise when Bryant visited Manhattan in 1824. Subsequently, he published "The Death of the Flowers" and "To a Cloud," the latter containing lines on the struggle of Greece, "long fettered and oppressed," against the Ottoman power.

Bedridden for ten weeks, Coleman needed help running his paper. From a mutual friend, Gulian Verplanck, he learned of Bryant's financial difficulties and offered the poet employment as an assistant editor. Bryant promptly accepted. He wrote to Frances, who was attending to affairs in Great Barrington, "The establishment is an extremely lucrative one. It is owned by two individuals—Mr. Coleman and Mr. Burnham. The profits are estimated at about thirty thousand dollars a year—fifteen to each proprietor. This is better than poetry and magazines."

Coleman had edited the *Evening Post* since its founding on November 16, 1801, by Alexander Hamilton and a coterie of Federalist friends. The author of the *Federalist Papers* with James Madison and John Jay, Hamilton was a prominent Wall Street lawyer. He had seen the Federalists routed from national, state, and local offices by Jefferson and his Democratic Republicans. With the *Evening Post*, the sixth newspaper to be started in Manhattan, Hamilton and his Federalist associates would have an organ promoting strong central government and strict adherence to the Constitution. His friend William Coleman, also a lawyer, would edit the newspaper, with Hamilton—up to his death in 1804 from the duel with Aaron Burr—frequently dictating editorials to his companion.

Coleman was a crusading editor whose democratic principles and pet urban peeves would mold Bryant into an equally fierce civic gadfly and defender of the rights of common Americans: farmers and artisans, small merchants and shopkeepers, laborers and mechanics, immigrants and Catholics. Under Coleman, the *Evening Post* exposed municipal horrors: unsanitary food, fire hazards, yellow fever and other infectious diseases, patent medicines, filthy streets, noise, lotteries, and pigs. With his editorials set under the paper's masthead and framed by leaded lines on the second of the *Evening Post*'s four pages, Coleman wielded an acerbic pen in detailing the calamities besetting Gotham.

Like other journalists, Coleman attacked rivals in person and print. He had killed one opponent in a duel. In 1819, Henry B. Hagerman, a prominent Democrat who had molested a shopkeeper and incurred Coleman's editorial wrath, had beaten him severely. Left in a bloody heap at the corner of Murray and Church streets, Coleman survived but suffered periods of paralysis for the rest of his life.

When Bryant began work as assistant editor for the *Evening Post*, probably in July 1826 at a weekly salary of fifteen dollars, he became heir to the paper's tradition of personal invective and contentious political journalism. Politics was very much on the minds of Americans during the turbulent 1820s. By the time Bryant stepped into the editorial office of the *Evening Post*, a political maelstrom was realigning parties and creating strange political bedfellows. The Era of Good Feelings had never quite been that, and the Panic of 1819 had produced lingering animosities among social and economic classes. Moreover, with the Adams presidency under attack and John Quincy Adams himself unable to impose his Federalist sympathies even on members of his cabinet, a new party opposing the Adams camp was forming.

Bryant joined the *Evening Post* shortly after Coleman had cut the paper from its original doctrinal moorings and started to sail his newspaper, somewhat provisionally, in new political waters. By the election of 1824, Coleman's personal biases and dislikes had moved the paper from the staunchly Federalist agenda that Hamilton had laid out at the *Evening Post*'s founding to a Jeffersonian tone. That election had been decided in the House of Representatives and had denied Andrew Jackson the presidency despite the fact that he won the popular vote and had the most electoral votes, but not a majority of them.

Coleman had endorsed the Republican William H. Crawford, secretary of the treasury, heir to the Virginia dynasty, and a strict Jeffersonian, rather than one of the other contenders—Henry Clay, John Quincy Adams, or Old Hickory. Clay, a magnificent orator and consummate manipulator, had delivered the presidential election to Adams in exchange for the post of secretary of state. "So you see," wrote Jackson famously, "the Judas of the West has closed the contract and will receive the thirty pieces of silver." Coleman was appalled by the outcome of the election; he had a long-standing hatred of the new president because of Adams's support of the Embargo Act. The Federalist party might be moribund, but Coleman held grudges.

The supporters of Crawford, the followers of Martin Van Buren in New York, and the friends of John Calhoun (who wisely had dropped out of the 1824 presidential race) cast their lot with Andrew Jackson. The result was the formation of the Democratic National Party, or simply the Democratic Party, dedicated to upholding the Jeffersonian principles of limited government and a sound economy. Followers of Adams and

Clay, who propounded the ideals of a strong federal government, a national bank, and major internal improvements—Clay's so-called American Plan—suddenly had a serious rival.

Under Coleman, the *Evening Post* had moved away from its Federalist moorings and was now bobbing, rather haphazardly, on the rising tide of Jacksonian democracy. Writing years later in *Reminiscences of the Evening Post*, Bryant recalled that when he first joined the paper, it was "much occupied with matters of local interest, the sanitary conditions of the city, the state of its streets, its police, its regulation of various kinds." Settling into his new office at 49 William Street, Bryant learned from his ailing mentor how to be a crusading journalist and craft an authoritative editorial persona.

While learning how to run a newspaper, Bryant continued to turn out poetry in order to fill the pages of the *Review*. One poem in particular, "The Conjunction of Jupiter and Venus," published in the September 1826 issue of the *Review*, reflects Bryant's emerging political consciousness. Bryant opens with an invocation to the unifying power of reason and emotion as the guide for human conduct and artistic practice. He next offers a catalogue of dualities—country and city; reason and emotion; war and peace. Just as Jupiter and Venus meet fortuitously in the radiance of evening, the movements of Earth and its inhabitants—specifically in Bryant's adoptive city—are subject to forces of convergence. Bryant meditates on the organic unity of city and nation in succeeding lines:

> Meekly the mighty river, that infolds
> This mighty city, smooths his front, and far
> Glitters and burns even the rocky base
> Of the dark heights that bound him to the west;
> And a deep murmur, from the many streets,
> Rises like a thanksgiving. . . .

After expanding his poetic conceit by invoking a union of opposites—melancholy and happy days, feast and famine, summer and winter—he returns to the national subject:

> Emblems of power and beauty! well may they
> Shine brightest on our borders, and withdraw
> Toward the great Pacific, making out
> The path of empire . . .

Bryant ends the lyric with an apostrophe to young Americans destined to wed in this glorious age where, he hopes, "Men shall wear softer hearts, / And shudder at the butcheries of war, / As now at other murders."

In "The Conjunction of Jupiter and Venus," Bryant presents a providential view of American history. The striking feature of the poem (and of Bryant's personality) is the poet's tempered optimism as he interrogates the conflicts and problems of the world. Bryant seeks a convergence or reconciliation of conflicting elements—some principle of order in the affairs of men and women as well as in the affairs of the nation. Written as Bryant began to assume responsibility for the daily operations of the *Evening Post*, the poem hints at his editorial philosophy. Bryant would also have to reconcile clashing, oppositional, and potentially explosive issues of the day—local issues like the woeful condition of Manhattan streets and the most vexing national controversies, including the growing controversy over slavery.

But at the start of 1827, still the apprentice editor, Bryant had to handle varied assignments at the *Evening Post*. He covered the unusually cold winter—one of the coldest in the history of the Republic. Snow swept into New York State and continued for more than a week from New England to Georgia, with Gotham recording a total of twenty-seven inches. The temperature was numbing: ten degrees below zero in New York City and only eight degrees above in St. Augustine, Florida. Rivers, from the Hudson to the Ohio to the mouth of the Savannah, froze completely. "We now have a good bridge across the Hudson toll free," Bryant reported in the *Evening Post* in its Thursday, January 4, issue. Just as his poetry paints a comprehensive panorama of the seasons—"March," "Spring in Town," "Summer Wind," the impressive "Autumn Woods," the magnificent "A Winter Piece," and the three sonnets "Midsummer," "October," and "November"—at the *Evening Post* Bryant paid careful attention to the particulars of his world.

Supervised by Coleman but rapidly becoming the newspaper's de facto editor as the older man's condition deteriorated, Bryant inserted himself into the management of the editorial page during his first year at the *Evening Post*. Entries reveal his emerging political interests as well as the pithy, robust style that would characterize his editorials. Bryant's journalistic style—whether dealing with the weather or the complex issues and colorful personalities of the day—is plain but elegant. Assuming responsibility for filling the *Evening Post*'s police blotter, he filed the following account: "The watch were called in last evening to quell a row in the cellar of the house No. 65 Catherine street. On going in they found 30 or 40 men, women and children, bawling and quarreling, among themselves—smashing the chairs, glasses, decanters and bottles &etc—in plain English, kicking up a dust."

Bryant's penchant for "plain English" would become the *Evening Post's* trademark. He created a style manual, which he called his *Index Expurgatorius*, prescribing plain usage instead of the euphemistic words and phrases common to the journalism of the period. After he had become editor-in-chief and part owner, Bryant cautioned staffers to avoid dozens of "barbaric" constructions, among them:

Artiste (for artist)	Gents (for gentlemen)
Bagging (for capturing)	Juvenile (for boy)
Casket (for coffin)	Lengthy (for long)
Commence (for begin)	Repudiate (for reject)
Devouring element (for fire)	Sensation (for noteworthy event)

Bryant's insistence on plain style would turn the *Evening Post* into the best-written newspaper in the United States for most of the nineteenth century.

Even as he devoted more and more time to the *Evening Post*, Bryant struggled to save the *United States Review and Literary Gazette*, for he relied on the income from both positions to support his family in Manhattan. The previous May, the Bryants had moved with Mrs. Meigs from the house on Canal Street to a residence on Laight Street. Room and board with Mrs. Meigs now amounted to $540 annually. Bryant was desperate to cover expenses and provide comforts for Frances, including extended vacations for her to Orange Springs, Cummington, and Great Barrington during the sweltering summer months.

Unable to lure contributors to the *Review and Literary Gazette*, Bryant was forced to grind out his own writing for the fall and winter issues. He wrote reviews, two mediocre stories, and several poems, notably the fine sonnet "October." He also translated "Niagara" from the Spanish of Cuban poet José María Hérédia. Holding down two editorships, Bryant was fatalistic about his harried condition. "I drudge for the *Evening Post* and labor for the *Review*," he informed Dana, "and thus have a pretty busy life of it. I would give up one of these if I could earn my bread by the other, but that I cannot do." In late 1827, after thirteen months, the *Review and Literary Gazette* passed quietly from the literary scene.

III

In his first full year as Coleman's assistant editor, Bryant brought a new vigor to the *Evening Post*'s editorial page, projecting a more consistently forward-looking editorial stance than had Coleman. Even as Coleman looked backward to ancient insults and political battles, Bryant's editorials were based on current realities. He attacked Congress for "neglect of the public welfare and . . . instances of mischievous legislation" and pilloried the legislators for rejecting a bankruptcy bill, postponing payments to veterans, and passing the tariff. "Let us talk no more of our wisdom, or of our justice—let us boast no more of our enlightened legislator, until these errors have been atoned or forgotten."

Especially alarming to the *Evening Post*'s new assistant editor was the controversy between the state of Georgia and the federal government over the governance of the Creek tribe. In a February 8 editorial, Bryant warned about the potential consequences of violation by a state of a national treaty: "Instead of that harmony and initial cooperation between the general and state governments on which we have so much prided ourselves, we shall then present to the world the disgraceful and ill-omened spectacle of a nation torn with internal dissensions." To Bryant, the Union must not be endangered by states usurping federal powers.

As Coleman's condition deteriorated, Bryant slowly took charge of the *Evening Post*. He respected Coleman, remembering him in his "full make, with a broad chest, muscular arms, which he wielded lightly and easily, and a deep-toned voice; but his legs dangled like strings. He expressed himself in conversation with fluency, energy, and decision, particularly when any subject was started in which he had taken an interest in former years." Coleman still composed some editorials, remaining the irascible urban reformer to the end. In January 1827, he renewed his perennial assault on the lotteries lining Broadway: "The stranger that walks through this street might almost imagine that the city was one great lottery shop, and that one half of the citizens, at least, got their living by affording the opportunity of gambling to the rest." Throughout the winter months, Coleman railed against coal ashes in the streets, gangs, the flying of kites, and the growing prevalence of laws permitting divorce in editorials on a hodgepodge of local issues that Bryant probably helped to edit as he assumed greater responsibilities at the *Evening Post*. Urban democracy required constant improvement, and Bryant was learning how to serve as its advocate.

In April, Coleman's health declined precipitously. He was confined to his house for long weeks and months, leaving Bryant in complete control of the *Evening Post*'s daily editorials. Even before Coleman's confinement, Bryant had started to address new issues and controversies in the pages of the *Evening Post*. On Monday, January 8, the paper covered the cause of Greek independence. Reporting on the previous Saturday's Greek Meeting at the City Hotel, a writer described the group's "sympathy for the sufferings of the inhabitants of Greece." The list of participants constituted a pantheon of the city's elite, among them John Jacob Astor, Arthur Tappan, James Roosevelt, Jr., Philip Hone, and William Paulding. Their lofty resolution—that Greece, a democratic and Christian nation, should be free from war and suffering—resulted in six thousand dollars in contributions by the end of the month. Bryant saw to it that the *Evening Post* covered the Greek crisis throughout the winter and spring months.

Bryant was particularly interested in Greek literature and civilization. One of his favorite books in childhood had been Pope's translation of the *Iliad*, which Bryant himself would translate in his old age. Bryant recalled that he and his brother Austin, "in emulation of the ancient heroes, made for ourselves wooden shields, swords, and spears, and fashioned old hats in the shape of helmets, with plumes in tow, and in the barn, when nobody observed us, we fought the battles of the Greeks and Trojans over again." Bryant had even dreamed in Greek.

Bryant's first foray into Greece's struggle for independence came in an address to the Greek Meeting in Great Barrington on December 18, 1823. After outlining conventional notions about Greece as the source of civilization, the "cradle of liberty," and a bulwark of Christianity, Bryant described the massacre at Scio: "The Greeks are a nation of martyrs—and when Scio—the fertile and populous island of Scio, saw its old men and children butchered, and thirty thousand women sold into captivity to supply the seraglios of the Turks and seven hundred of its prisoners shot down in a day—and, when the Jews of Smyrna were employed to drag away the corpses that blocked up its streets and throw them into the sea, it was then that the world witnessed a spectacle of suffering for the cause of our holy religion such as has not had a parallel since the reign of Domitian." Not a naturally gifted speaker in an age of great orators, Bryant nevertheless was more than adequate owing to the elegance of his composition. He was adept at delivering effective speeches (which he wrote and memorized before presentation). Over time, his public would look forward to Bryant's appearances as a speaker at some of the most momentous events—including Lincoln's first appearance in Manhattan—of his era.

The poetry that Bryant produced about the Greek question is fairly conventional in subject matter and sentiment. It is remarkable, nevertheless, in the quality of execution. The variation in meter and line in "The Greek Partisan," a paean in three stanzas to sacrifice for one's country, is typical of Bryant's innovative method:

> They go to the slaughter,
>   To strike the sudden blow,
> And pour on earth, like water,
>   The best blood of the foe;
> To rush on them from rock and height,
>   And clear the narrow valley,
> Or fire their camp at dead of night,
>   And fly before they rally.
> —Chains are round our country pressed,
>   And cowards have betrayed her,
> And we must make her bleeding breast
>   The grave of the invader.

With metrical lines of three and four iambic feet, he invites readers to march rapidly and vigorously into battle, matching mood, thought, and movement to metrical line. In "The Greek Partisan" and the companion poems "The Greek Boy," "The Massacre at Scio," and "Song of the Greek Amazon" (the last lyric containing strikingly bold sexual overtones), Bryant conveys his hatred of oppression, his commitment to freedom, and his support of democracy on a global scale.

Another of Bryant's new editorial preoccupations was free trade. He had become an advocate under the influence of Theodore Sedgwick, and for more than half a century he would devote thousands of densely reasoned editorial lines to a defense of laissez-faire economics. Free trade, Bryant believed, created the necessary condition for economic and national progress.

With the Jackson-controlled Congress anticipating victory in the 1828 presidential election, Bryant moved the tariff issue to new prominence in the pages of the *Evening Post*, using the controversy as a weapon against the Adams administration. In Bryant's view, a protective tariff was inimical to the laws of economics and an unwarranted intrusion by government into the conduct of commerce. Only free trade, a cornerstone of Adam Smith's economic theories in *The Wealth of Nations*, could produce an equitable distribution of resources to worker and businessman alike. Influenced by Smith, who attacked the union of government and business as damaging to the working classes, Bryant promoted decidedly Jeffersonian ideas. He had come to believe that individual liberties guaranteed a healthy society. Not only was a tariff bad economic policy, but it was an even greater threat to the preservation of liberty.

Bryant realized that the tariff issue confronting the nation in the 1820s was complex. The decision to lower existing tariffs would benefit businesses and factories in one part of the nation but could harm economic interests in others. Nevertheless, Bryant asserted that free trade should be the bedrock of a nation's economic policies, and as editor he made the *Evening Post* a leading organ of free trade opinion. As early as February 1827, he criticized a bill before Congress that would make the importation of woolen goods prohibitive for American merchants:

> The members of Congress wear fine broadcloths, and those among them who support the new tariff have friends among the noisy and hungry manufacturers besieging the doors of Congress whose activity may have some influence on their own popularity at home.—What do these members care for the consumers of cheap woolens? Nothing at all. Their own interests are safe, and they will be able to buy fine clothes about as cheap as ever, and their manufacturing friends will get rich and send them again to Congress. They feel nothing for the distresses of the poor, but they hear the clamors of the woolen manufacturers, and to pacify them, they will set themselves to work without remorse of conscience to double the burdens of the poor.

Although dignified in his public bearing and conduct, Bryant could be waspish and combative in his editorials. It was as if dark impulses submerged in his inner self could find a healthy outlet in vitriolic editorial assaults on his opposition.

Free trade was the issue upon which Bryant typically distinguished political allies from opponents. He commiserated with Gulian Verplanck over the Tariff of Abominations, a bill that placed higher duties on raw materials than on manufactures, which had been passed that May by Jackson supporters. Verplanck, who had been elected to Congress in

1825 and was serving as a member of the House Ways and Means Committee, incurred the hostility of the city's mechanics over the tariff. Bryant reminded New York's workers of his friend's commitment to "the principles of free trade and unrestricted industry" so essential to the economic well-being of the city. Verplanck was reelected easily in the congressional elections two weeks later. (In his *Autobiography*, Martin Van Buren named Bryant's editorial "assaults" on the protective tariff as the "single influence" producing its "final overthrow.")

During his apprentice years at the *Evening Post*, Bryant found himself in the thick of other political controversies. In February 1828, he wrote to Dana about his new career as a crusading editor: "I am a small proprietor in the establishment, and am a gainer by the arrangement. It will afford me a comfortable living after I have paid for the *eighth part*, which is the amount of my share. I do not like politics any better than you do; but they get only my mornings, and you know politics and a belly-full are better than poetry and starvation." Coleman had offered Bryant a share in the *Evening Post* for two thousand dollars. (In his biography of Bryant, John Bigelow claimed that Henry Sedgwick loaned Bryant the money to purchase this share.) Bryant had not seen himself as a newspaper editor and owner. For years, he believed that his tenure at the *Evening Post* was temporary, that someday he would return to his rural origins and the full-time consolations of a literary life. If he had realized that he would remain with the *Evening Post* for the rest of his life, he might have paused before purchasing his share.

Bryant's immersion in the affairs of the *Evening Post* didn't prevent him from enjoying his expanding circle of friends, exploring the city and its environs, and embarking on new literary ventures. He spent especially enjoyable hours with Robert Sands and Gulian Verplanck. Meeting at the comfortable Sands home in Hoboken, New Jersey, directly across the Hudson River from Manhattan, the three friends would embark on walking excursions to the picturesque meadows, coves, and promontories surrounding the town. Bryant's "A Scene on the Banks of the Hudson," included in the 1828 edition of the *Talisman*, the first of three Christmas gift books that the three men edited and published from 1827 to 1829, reflects the poet's fondness for this pastoral retreat:

> Cool shades and dews are round my way,
> And silence of the early day;
> Mid the dark rocks that watch his bed,
> Glitters the mighty Hudson spread,

Unrippled, save by drops that fall
From shrubs that fringe his mountain wall;
And o'er the clear still water swells
The music of the Sabbath bells.
All, save this little nook of land,
Circled with trees, on which I stand;
Suspended in the mimic sky—
Seems a blue void, above, below,
Through which the white clouds come and go;
And from the green world's farthest steep
I gaze into the airy deep.

Loveliest of lovely things are they,
On earth, that soonest pass away.
The rose that lives its little hour
Is prized beyond the sculptured flower.
Even love, long tried and cherished long,
Becomes more tender and more strong
At thought of that insatiate grave
From which its yearnings cannot save.

River! in this still hour thou hast
Too much of heaven on earth to last;
Nor long may thy still waters lie,
An image of the glorious sky.
Thy fate and mine are not repose,
And ere another evening close,
Thou to thy tides shall turn again,
And I to seek the crowd of men.

Bryant echoes Blake and Freneau, but employs innovative four-foot iambic lines and strikingly plain diction to freshen conventional notions of roses and fleeting beauty.

Planning the *Talisman* as they hiked along the Hudson, the trio would return to the Sands house and, late into the evening, reduce the ideas generated by their rambles to manuscript form. One of Sands's sisters recalled that the house would shake with laughter, readily heard by neighbors when the warm weather kept the windows open, as the threesome also hatched literary hoaxes that Bryant would slip into the *Evening Post*. As Sands dutifully recorded their thoughts, they and other friends composed poetry, fiction, memoir, humor, and criticism for the *Talisman*. With illustrations by Cole, Durand, and other artists, a lavish first edition of the *Talisman* was published in December 1827, in time for Christmas.

Back in the city, the three urban archaeologists often searched for historical landmarks during their rambles, intrigued by the history of old New York. Under the pseudonym "Francis Herbert," Bryant and Verplanck wrote a collaborative essay, "Reminiscences of New York," which appeared over two issues of the *Talisman*. The essay offered a guide through old New York, "a sort of thoroughfare of the world; a spot where almost every remarkable character is seen once in the course of his life, and almost every extraordinary thing once in the course of its existence." Bryant and his friends highlighted living history everywhere in Gotham. At Wall Street, they found the exact spot where Washington had been inaugurated. Likewise, they discovered the house in Stone Street where James Oglethorpe, the founder of Georgia, first stayed on landing in the New World. A two-story structure on Cedar Street held memories of Jefferson's conversation with Talleyrand. Then there was the glorious wooden building with a portico at the corner of Varick and Charlton streets where Lord Amherst had lived, where John Adams entertained ministers and other dignitaries, and where Aaron Burr once resided. Along the North River, the friends followed the original trail that once had been paced by Jonathan Edwards who, temporarily assigned to the Wall Street Church, was already conjuring visions of sinners in the hands of an angry God. Despite ambivalent feelings about urban life, Bryant found tonic in his growing circles of friends and in the cosmopolitan scene. Gotham's variegated pleasures were a respite from what Dana warned were "blackguard squabbles" threatening to overwhelm Bryant at the *Evening Post*.

Actually, Bryant, the child of rural New England, had adjusted to metropolitan life. In "Spring in Town," published in the April 1827 issue of the *Review*, he praised his new home:

> Within the city's bounds the time of flowers
>   Comes earlier. Let a mild and sunny day,
> Such as full often, for a few bright hours,
>   Breathes through the sky of March the airs of May
> Shine on our roofs and chase the wintry gloom—
> And lo! our borders glow with sudden bloom.

For the wide sidewalks of Broadway are then
   Gorgeous as are a rivulet's banks in June,
That overhung with blossoms, through its glen,
   Slides soft away beneath the sunny noon,
And they who search the untrodden wood for flowers
Meet in its depth no lovelier ones than ours.

In seven subsequent stanzas, Bryant weaves his conceit of the lovely urban "flowers" he encounters during his daily strolls in New York. He offers a playful, sensuous catalog, presaging Whitman, of the alluring women—from "Italy's brown maids" to "Gascon lasses" to "fresh Norman girls"—who line the city's streets. An enchanted observer of the urban landscape, Bryant revels in the scene: the "soft voices and light laughter," the "twinkling feet," the "crowd of beauty" that he experiences. The poet prefers the Broadway scene to the pastoral pleasures of Ossining or "the shores of Tappan Bay." Spring and the season's darling "buds" captivate the poet.

Bryant had shed any remaining rural mannerisms and was becoming an urbane New Yorker. He hobnobbed with the city's writers and artists, educators and journalists, lawyers and bankers, and merchants and politicians. Infected with the restless energy of the city, he was propelled by a uniquely urban need to be compulsively on the go and in search of new prospects. His metropolitan persona was energetic and self-reliant.

Bryant's metropolitan world also had acquired an international flavor. On March 1, 1828, the Bryants moved from Mrs. Tripler's boardinghouse on Broadway to a boardinghouse on Hubert Street run by Adelaida de Salazar, the wife of a Spanish businessman. Bryant saw a chance to improve his Spanish. Just as he had refined his French while residing with the Evrards, Bryant conversed with the Salazars in their native language. As his versions of Hérédia's "The Hurricane" and "Niagara" confirm, he became a fluent translator of Spanish poetry. By May, when the Bryants moved with the Salazars to new quarters at 92 Hudson Street, near St. John's Park, the two families enjoyed a growing intimacy. The Bryants and Salazars would live together for three years.

Bryant also enjoyed the companionship of a fellow boarder at the Salazar house, the English botanist Ferdinand E. Field, who became one of Bryant's most devoted walking companions and a correspondent for forty years. They covered the city and its environs; some years later, in 1837, they would hike from West Point to New York. Field claimed that

Bryant was "the most indefatigable tramp" he had ever "grappled with"; the poet happily put up with "a baker's biscuit and a few apples" and "the rude fare of wayside inns and laborer's cottages." Bryant knew as much about American flora as did Field, having studied the discrete particulars of the natural world since childhood. He would visit Field in England several times, and in 1869 found a New York publisher for Field's *The Green-House as a Winter Garden: A Model for the Amateur*, for which he wrote the preface.

Bryant was an indefatigable walker to the end of his life. For fifty years, he daily tramped three miles from various lodgings to the *Evening Post* in downtown Manhattan and then three miles back. Alone or with friends, he would walk up the Hudson for miles or, taking a ferry, wend his way through Brooklyn, Staten Island, or the New Jersey countryside. (Whitman recalled that he had strolled through Flatbush with Bryant, munching on bread and sausage.) One day, Bryant walked to Haverstraw and then returned—a total of forty miles; at a party he attended that same evening, he apologized for his mild exhaustion.

At the *Evening Post*, Bryant promoted the work of his friends and increased the paper's coverage of literature and the arts. In a lengthy editorial review, he praised Catharine Sedgwick's novel, *Hope Leslie*. The novel, Bryant wrote, captured the early history of New England in magnificent fashion. "The writer, we are happy to say, diligently studied the spirit of this extraordinary period, and we believe her delineation of it certainly is striking." Sedgwick reciprocated by sending Bryant little notes about the doings of the various social circles she moved in, starting an epistolary exchange that the two maintained until Catharine's death.

Bryant reviewed other notable books, printed poetry by writers he considered worthy of public acclaim, and reported on the theater and opera, signing reviews with a telltale "Q." New York now boasted several playhouses: the New York Theatre on the Bowery, the venerable Park Theatre on Park Row (where the "Kean Riot" had occurred in November 1826), the Chatham Theatre, and the New York Theatre, among them. The tragedian Edwin Forrest, who would become Bryant's close friend for a time, made his American debut at the opulent Bowery Theatre in May 1826. (In 1829, when Forrest offered a prize for the best play on an American theme, Bryant headed the committee that selected John Stone's *Metamora* for the award.) With Bryant as its booster and most perceptive critic, Manhattan was turning into the drama capital of America.

Light opera was also popular with the city's theatergoers. An *Evening Post* reviewer, in all likelihood Bryant, was smitten by the leading lady in *The Siege of Belgrade*, which played at the Park Theatre in the winter of 1826: "We cannot resist our strong inclination to speak once more of the very interesting and highly gifted female stranger who has lately made her debut on our boards. On Thursday evening, Mrs. Knight made her fifth appearance. . . . Her playing was marked, as it always is, with a naivete, life, and graceful action, that left the spectator nothing to wish for."

Bryant had constructed a multifaceted persona for himself—a complex self-image that never could have been forged in rural New England. He roamed a city filled with English and Dutch merchants and bankers, South American and European expatriates, French dancing masters and Italian singers, and immigrants from Ireland and as far away as China. He also met foreign visitors while boarding with the Evrards and Salazars. Among them was Lorenzo da Ponte, the eccentric émigré literary critic, translator, and librettist for Mozart, with whom Bryant would strike up a friendship. (Da Ponte would translate Bryant's poetry into Italian.) Bryant's emerging idea of America (unlike those of his friends Morse and Cole) included immigrants and people of all classes.

Bryant's cosmopolitanism led to expanded coverage of international news and cultural matters in the *Evening Post*. Under the assistant editor, the *Evening Post* started to cover the opera. The paper sadly concluded that Manhattan was not ready for this Old World art form: "Now, New York has always a large population, either settled or migratory. She is still however, more like Liverpool than London—more like Bordeaux than Paris. The pursuits of her wealthy citizens are in closer connexion with the counting house than the coteries of fashion."

Bryant was leading a hectic metropolitan life. If he had any reservations about it, he masked them with humor, just as his protective reserve with strangers masked his warm inner self. Writing to Dana, he outlined the dilemma of his cluttered days: "There are three classes of things to be done; or at least I divide them so. In the first place there are things that must be done immediately. These I contrive to do. In the second place there are things which must be done soon. These I put off as long as I can, and in some instances I believe I have missed doing them at all. In this class I put writing answers to letters, writing articles for my journal, &c &c. The third class consists of those things which may be done at any time. These for the most part I never do at all." Bryant placed Dana's poems in the second class, but promised to read and edit a new sheaf he had received from his friend during an anticipated "interval of some leisure."

Bryant was variously amused and overwhelmed by the demands placed on him by a public life. Yet he took his editorial role seriously. As a moral and political guide, civic and social commentator, and aesthetic expert speaking to the readers of the *Evening Post*—the democratic masses—he was constructing a uniquely authoritative voice. Bryant still was not a ubiquitous presence in the public sphere. However, his poetry and editorials were making him a recognizable celebrity in the cultural life of the nation.

5

JACKSON DEMOCRAT

And let our festive halls this day
Re-echo Jackson's fame.
—"Ode to Jackson," 1828

I

With the presidential election of 1828 approaching, Coleman aligned the *Evening Post* squarely behind the candidacy of Andrew Jackson. In the popular imagination, the hero of New Orleans had become a symbol of nineteenth-century democracy. Rival party newspapers, especially *The American*, the mouthpiece of the National Republicans, were launching scurrilous attacks on Jackson's character. The *Evening Post* set out to extol Old Hickory, praising his long public service, his courage, and his expansive vision of democracy. With the Jackson presidential candidacy, Bryant fashioned a new version of himself as a red-blooded American democrat.

Bryant warmed to the presidential battle. He admired Jackson's simplicity of manners, honesty, and sense of justice. Coleman would have supported anyone other than John Quincy Adams, but Bryant had become attuned ideologically to Jackson's views on democracy. He subscribed to Jackson's advocacy of a lower tariff and shared the Old General's contempt for Clay's American Plan for internal improvements. Moreover, Bryant disliked Adams's secretary of state, "never having much respect for Mr. Clay's principles nor a high estimate of his political knowledge." Jackson espoused a people's government, and Bryant saw himself as a poor wanderer from the New England backcountry, a fellow democrat. He would devote his energies to making the *Evening Post* the city's major Democratic newspaper.

During the campaign, Bryant was notably adept at dissecting the crude, poorly written assaults on Jackson by the opposition press. In one editorial, he ridiculed the weakness in a rival paper's journalistic style. The newspaper's semiliterate attack was "not remarkable for the profundity of its observations." No Adams propaganda sheet, he lectured, should have the temerity to criticize Jackson's grammar. "No man should raise an outcry about improprieties of expression who is continually committing them himself."

Bryant also offered his literary talents to the presidential campaign. He composed an ode (unavailable to previous biographers) to the Old General at the Jackson Day celebration held at Masonic Hall in Washington on January 8, 1828. Verplanck read the poem, "Drink to Those Who Won," with what he told Bryant was "due emphasis, and a little theatrically," capturing a public voice so different from Bryant's pastoral elegies:

> Not for a realm o'erthrown,
>   Bowed to receive the chain;
> We raise the song of victory—
>   A loud, exulting strain:
>
> But for a City saved,—
>   Its streets from slaughter free:
> And those who rushed to smite its sons,
>   Driven back into the sea:
>
> Backward, with blood and death,
>   Driven from the rescued strand:
> On the proud day whose memory gilds
>   The records of our land.
>
> Pure drops from woman's eye,
>   And grateful tears of age,
> And those of childhood's tender lids,
>   Shall consecrate the page.

Then drink to those who won
  That meed of deathless fame,
And let our festive halls this day
  Re-echo Jackson's name.

Writing to Bryant the next day, Verplanck described the audience's enthusiastic response to the ode: "Vice President Calhoun nodded approbation. Van Beuren [*sic*] was in ecstasies, so was the Speaker, and Kremer shouted glamorous delight. . . . The company . . . shouted and clapped, the music brayed, the cannons fired, and Colonel Hayne swore that the Jackson cause had all the poetry as well as all the virtue in the land." Replying to his friend, Bryant said he was "wonderfully delighted" to learn of his poem's reception.

Bryant's embrace of Jacksonian democracy did not extend to utopian movements. His treatment of Frances Wright reveals the limitations of his reformist impulses as well as his cavalier views about women. Fanny Wright had been raised in privileged surroundings in Glasgow and Devonshire. A self-proclaimed atheist and rationalist, a foe of slavery but no fan of abolitionism, an anti-marriage and free-love advocate, she had fascinated the nation prior to Bryant's career at the *Evening Post*.

Wright had first come to the United States from Glasgow in 1818. She traveled widely, meeting notable people including President Monroe, and producing the euphoric *Views of Society and Manners in America* (1821). Wright was an acclaimed enthusiast of the American system, and her tribute to the new nation, so unlike other more critical assessments by foreign visitors, became a best-seller in England, the United States, and France.

Wright and her sister Camilla joined Lafayette's entourage when the Revolutionary War hero toured the United States one last time in 1824 and 1825. In 1828 she visited the nation's major cities—St. Louis, Louisville, Baltimore, Boston, and Philadelphia—before settling in New York. She purchased an abandoned Baptist church in upper Manhattan and converted it into the Hall of Science. From her rationalist pulpit, Fanny Wright—tall, attractive, with brown hair curling naturally over her shoulders, and possessing a mesmerizing contralto voice—presented visionary, hopelessly impractical ideas for the new nation.

In her autobiography, Wright claimed that she had tried to solve "the grievous wrongs which seemed to prevail in society," but Bryant considered many of her solutions to be extreme. He could not abide Fanny Wright's fanciful ideas—for example, her plan to eliminate the evils of class stratification by having all children raised by the state. More pragmatic than utopian in his commitment to social change, Bryant was cautious in his ideas about the roles of women in American society. He had little "taste," as he termed it, "for female expounders of any kind of doctrine."

Unlike Bryant, Wright had gravitated to the far fringes of socialist thought during the ferment of the Jackson era. She had met Robert Owen, who was struggling to establish his communal settlement at New Harmony, Indiana, and fell under the spell of his utopian experiment. Taking a page from Owen, she and Camilla purchased three thousand acres of land near Memphis in order to set up a slave-freeing community, which they named Nashoba. The Wright sisters believed that abolition was impractical; rather, slaves should be purchased from their owners and gradually emancipated after seven years of indenture. This utopian scheme foundered quickly. The problems and scandals at Nashoba, which became known as "Fanny Wright's free love community," soon doomed the experiment, and Wright retreated to New Harmony to continue her communitarian crusade.

With her arrival in New York City in late 1828, Fanny Wright, now known as the "red harlot of infidelity," was ripe fodder for city's dailies. From Charles King's scandal-mongering *New York American* to the *New-York Evening Post*, she was ridiculed for her lecture style, her ideas, and her "tall, ungainly . . . masculine proportions." Bryant aligned himself with Wright's detractors, warning theater owners that they were risking riot and even fire by scheduling her popular lectures:

> Suppose the singular spectacle of a female, publicly and ostentatiously proclaiming doctrines of atheistical fanaticism, and even the most abandoned lewdness, should draw a crowd from prurient curiosity, and riot should ensue, which should end in the demolition of the interior of the building, or even in the burning it down—on whom would the loss fall?

He also wrote a satiric ode to Wright, steeped in Bryant's self-schooling in Dryden and Pope, that was published in the *Evening Post*'s January 17 issue:

Thou wonder of the age, from whom
Religion waits her final doom,
Her quiet death, her euthanasia,
Thou in whose eloquence and bloom
The age beholds a new Aspasia!

Colonel William Stone's *Commercial Advertiser* initially had supported
Wright, giving Bryant an opportunity to ridicule a competitor:

O 'tis a glorious sight for us,
The gaping throng, to see thee thus
The light of dawning truth dispense,
While Col. Stone, the learn'd and brave,
The press's Atlas, mild but grave,
Hangs on the words that leave thy mouth,
Slaking his intellectual drouth,
In that rich stream of eloquence,
And notes thy teachings, to repeat
Their wisdom in his classic sheet.

Published anonymously, the ode to Fanny Wright was attributed initially to Bryant's friend Halleck, who several years earlier had published
in the *Post* a series of poems satirizing the foibles of New York's notables under the pseudonym "Croaker." Bryant delighted in the sub-
terfuge, writing to Verplanck that his ode had "passed for Halleck's
among the knowing ones."

By mid-1829, Stone had recanted, and no city newspaper editor supported Wright. Only Walt Whitman, who in later years attended her
speeches along with thousands of other workingmen, was captivated by
Wright's alluring presence and scandalous ideas. To the end of his days,
Whitman would remember the dazzle she brought to public discourse.
"I never felt so glowingly towards any other woman," the bard of Cam-
den recollected near the end of his life: "she possessed herself of my body
and soul."

Fanny Wright did not possess Bryant's soul. To him, Fanny Wright
and her libertarian ideas about the sexes exposed elements of excess
that were inimical to human relationships and damaging to social
norms. Bryant had been raised among stern New Englanders who were

conservative in their family values; even his amorous adventures once he left Cummington as a young man had been relatively tame, despite Dr. Bryant's worries about his son's behavior. To Bryant, Fanny Wright symbolized the wretchedness of political extremism and human desire.

II

William Coleman died following a stroke on July 13, 1829. He had imparted to Bryant a dedication to Jackson democracy. At the same time, he warned Bryant to be suspicious of Wright, Owen, and other utopian dreamers who gravitated to Wright's Hall of Science and its newspaper, the *Free Enquirer*. While steering a liberal course through Jacksonian waters, Bryant would not permit the *Evening Post* to tilt toward the quixotic fringes of American thought. More a liberal democrat than a radical reformer like Wright, Bryant inherited his mentor's newspaper along with Coleman's political philosophy.

With Coleman's death and Bryant's immediate ascent to the editorship, a move approved by Mrs. Coleman and Michael Burnham, who were now the *Evening Post*'s principal owners, Bryant found himself at the head of what arguably was the most influential newspaper in the United States. Bryant wrote a eulogy to his mentor that reveals as much about himself as it does about Coleman. The new editor praised Coleman for his "acuteness in controversy" and "disinterestedness." Bryant added: "He might commit errors, but they never arose from any sordid motive. No person was ever more ready to retract a mistaken opinion, when convinced of the mistake, no person was ever more happy to do justice to those whom he had unintentionally wronged, and never did it with better grace. He seemed to have an utter disdain of that false and foolish pride which, veiling itself under the notion of consistency, refuses to retract an error, or repair an injury."

At age thirty-four, Bryant was occupying the editor's chair of the chief Jackson newspaper in the country. In a remarkably brief time, he had turned into an inflexible Jackson loyalist, an ardent free trader, and a promoter of humanitarian reform. As much as he valued order in his personal life, his desk groaned under a mountain of documents that awed his staff. Carving a bit of space for himself among two-foot-high stacks of books, manuscripts, political pamphlets, economic treatises, correspondence, and *Evening Post* sheets, Bryant labored over his daily editorials, penning his opinions on the backs of envelopes, rejected manuscripts, and other waste paper. He was formal and deferential to his staff members; they in turn learned quickly not to bother "Mr. Bryant" when he was crafting an editorial for the day. After all, here was the great poet at labor, a slight, amiable model of equanimity who needed just a little bit of space to oversee the paper and complete his daily contribution to the *Evening Post*.

As editor in chief, Bryant now could offer the *New-York Evening Post*'s readership a singularly powerful voice. From the outset of his tenure, this was a voice blending reason with emotion—the centerpiece of his theory of poetry and his own poetic craft. In his series of lectures on poetry for the New York Athenaeum in 1825, Bryant had argued that the emotions raised by poetry could guide readers to the springs of moral conduct. Just as poetry could be a social and moral force, prose could serve as the voice of culture and democracy. First as Coleman's assistant and now as editor, Bryant transferred poetic theory to the craft and aims of the editorial. He perfected the art of the passionate but well-reasoned, elegantly cadenced editorial designed to prompt feelings of moral conduct and patriotism in the *Evening Post*'s readers. For fifty years, his editorials would offer a guide to the progress of American democracy.

To assist him in this "crusade" (a word that Jackson loyalists popularized) to forge a more militant tone for the *New-York Evening Post*, Bryant recruited the fiery poet and journalist William Leggett as his assistant. The editor valued Leggett for his "large and comprehensive views of public policy, his ardour in the cause of truth, his detestation of oppression . . . and the manly, unstudied eloquence which riveted the attention and persuaded the judgment of the reader." Leggett had been court-martialed out of the navy in 1825 for insubordination and verbal attacks on his ship's commander, whom he had insulted by reciting abusive verses from Byron. At his trial, Leggett had continued his ferocious assault on his commander, prompting John Quincy Adams to observe that this "continuing invective . . . ought not to have passed without reprehension and rebuke." Leggett's tempestuous behavior might have reminded Bryant of a volatile element in his own psyche that he struggled to suppress.

Leggett had published two volumes of poetry, *Leisure Hours at Sea* and *Journals of the Ocean*, and had founded a short-lived literary magazine, *The Critic*, before accepting Bryant's invitation to join the *Evening Post*. Eight years younger than Bryant and a man-about-town, Leggett at first disavowed any interest in writing political commentary. Nevertheless, Bryant confided to Frances, "I like Leggett, so far, very much. He seems to be an honest man, of good principles, industrious, and a fluent though by no means a political writer." Leggett, who found fault with most people, also liked Bryant: "In person, Mr. Bryant is rather above the middle size; his face is of a pleasing character, and his eyes are lighted up with an expression of great intelligence. His manners are easy and urbane; his disposition open, generous, and sincere; his habits those of a gentleman; his pursuits those of a scholar; and his principles those of a man of honour." Soon enough, Bryant would prick Leggett's disinterest in politics. Maligned by the *Evening Star*, a rival anti-Jackson newspaper, as "the Chaunting Cherubs of the *Post*," Leggett and Bryant would write some of the most powerful and eloquent defenses of democratic principles during the Age of Jackson.

III

Even as New York City was becoming the nerve center of Jacksonian reform, it was experiencing new patterns of sociability and civic interaction. Bryant did not associate with the workingmen he would soon defend in the *Evening Post* or with the Astors and other Manhattan bluebloods. Instead, he joined a coalition of writers, artists, businessmen, and professionals committed to the promotion of metropolitan culture. Upwardly mobile, eminently sociable, Bryant fit in easily with this cultivated society. Even as he was redefining American democracy in his editorials for the *Evening Post*, Bryant was enjoying an active civic life.

In 1829, Bryant joined with several new friends to found a literary and artistic gathering known as the Sketch Club. A successor to Cooper's old Bread and Cheese, the Sketch Club or "Twenty-One" as it was called in recognition of its limited membership, included Cole, Morse, Dunlap, Durand, and Verplanck as charter members. These men rounded out the prescribed membership with other artists, writers, and patrons. Twenty-One met weekly at members' homes on a rotating basis, the time and place announced cryptically in the obituaries of the *Evening Post*.

The Sketch Club members based their drawings on topics derived from incidents in the works of Lord Byron, Oliver Goldsmith, Washington Irving, Sir Walter Scott, and other literary figures. But there was nothing unduly serious or lofty about the meetings. On February 20, 1829, the club's minutes recorded that it was "a most abominable night, prolific only in wind, snow, colds, coughs, and frozen ears," producing "no Drawing but of corks." Essentially, the Sketch Club was an excuse for convivial social intercourse and general amusement. At Thomas Cole's house on May 29, 1829, the recording secretary John Inman wrote: "Subject an Indian (from Amer Khan & other poems by Miss Somebody Somebody) in the act of jumping into the sea—probably in an excess of puerile fever."

At Sketch Club gatherings, Bryant was at the hub of a new group of kindred spirits. He was an amiable participant in high-toned literary games that often distracted the artists from their sketch books. (Morse was an excellent writer; while Bryant's drawings reveal a fine eye for line and detail.) One favorite gambit was to invent an elaborate poetry contest, typically on a lofty subject that was to be treated humorously and often daringly, in which participants had to match earlier end rhymes as their turns in the contest came up. Thus, at one meeting, Bryant, Sands, and Inman were instructed to write on "Character," with the group settling on Xantippe, the wife of Socrates. Twenty-six stanzas of pure doggerel were produced, with Bryant's contributions as banal as any of the other spontaneous creations:

> BRYANT
> She was cursed with a very bad character
> A thing which was sadly unlucky;
> SANDS
> Though for modest pretences a fair actor
> When her spouse with a gimlet she struck he.
> SECRETARY [John Inman]
> The doctor was summoned but came not
> Because of her bad reputation;
> BRYANT
> Says her husband, your gimlet I blame not
> But I hate your damned vociferation.

Occasionally an impish Bryant would be fined and forced to perform penance for tardiness and various improprieties contrived by his friends.

The Sketch Club continued to hold its spirited meetings for decades, with the members frequently inviting guests and dignitaries, including an occasional female. Bryant's warm personal and creative association with New York's most important artists would be memorialized in Asher B. Durand's monumental painting of Bryant and Cole, *Kindred Spirits*

(1849), a canvas embodying two friends who viewed America as a spacious realm of democratic promise.

Thomas Cole, who had hosted the first "regular meeting" of the Sketch Club, departed for Europe in 1829. Having painted sublime landscapes of the Hudson River and the Catskills, Cole wanted to seek inspiration in the Old World. Bryant had a message for his friend, offered in "Sonnet—To Cole, the Painter, Departing for Europe":

> THINE eyes shall see the light of distant skies:
>   Yet Cole! Thy heart shall bear to Europe's strand
>   A living image of thy native land,
> Such as upon thy own glorious canvas lies.
> Lone lakes—savannas where the bison roves—
>   Rocks rich with summer garlands—solemn streams—
>   Skies, where the desert eagle wheels and screams,—
> Spring bloom and autumn blaze of boundless groves.
> Fair scenes shall greet thee where thou goest—fair,
>   But different—everywhere the trace of men,
>   Paths, homes, graves, ruins, from the lowest glen
> To where life shrinks from the fierce Alpine air.
>   Gaze on them, till the tears shall dim thy sight,
>   But keep that earlier, wilder image bright.

Bryant relies on a pattern of contrasting imagery to project a tension he sensed in American culture. Cole's true place, Bryant contends, is in the expansive landscape and culture of American democracy that already was stretching toward distant western regions that the poet could only imperfectly imagine. (Savannahs teeming with bison is an admittedly audacious conceit.) By contrast, the picturesque terrain of Europe is "fair" at best; the Old World "shrinks" when matched against the "wilder image bright" heralding American civilization.

Bryant did not have to seek inspiration in Europe for his own verse. He was writing poetry in 1829 that remained attuned to the "wilder image" in the American landscape. In "The Evening Wind" and "To the Fringed Gentian," two lyrics composed in Manhattan that year, he capitalized on natural elements to convey an implicit message to Cole and other artists who might seek inspiration beyond America's shores. The breeze in the musical lyric "The Evening Wind" comes off the sea and sweeps into the city to be inhaled by "a thousand bosoms round"; it then moves into "the vast inland stretched beyond the sight."

The sensuous play of the wind over the American landscape and the simple moral sentiments expressed in "The Evening Wind" appear in more compelling fashion in "To the Fringed Gentian." Composed as an elegy, "To the Fringed Gentian" frames human action in the context of nature. If writers and artists seek a theater to meditate on one's passage through life, they should look to the visionary native landscape. Meditating on the American scene typified by the fringed gentian, a solitary sentinel presaging winter, the artist finds intimations of immortality in the flower: "Blue—blue—as if that sky let fall / A flower from its cerulean wall." For Bryant, a late autumn walk in America serves to articulate both the melancholy passage of human life and the promise of a heavenly realm.

As the decade ended, Bryant, who had lived in New York City for only five years, occupied a unique position of authority that would not be repeated in the history of American letters. He was already the foremost poet in the nation—the first American poet to appear in a school textbook in 1826. He enjoyed a growing reputation in England and France as well. A certain "Mr. Jones" in England had even plagiarized one of his stories, prompting an offended Bryant to inform Verplanck of his intention to "expose the robbery."

As editor in chief of the *New-York Evening Post*, Bryant had reinvented himself as an intrepid advocate of Jackson democracy. He thanked Verplanck for his "oracular hints" about events in Washington, adding, "The President's message has been very favorably received here." Bryant wasn't happy with Jackson's cautious comments on tariff reduction but heartily approved of the president's criticism of the private Bank of the United States. As for the opposition press's weekly predictions that Jackson's health was so precarious that he would soon be dead, Bryant offered a pithy response: "We should all think it very unkind of him, after all the trouble we have been at on his account. Besides, you know that everybody is in an agony of curiosity to know whom he will put into his cabinet. If he should slip off to another world without solving this riddle, we should never forgive him." Bryant was sufficiently independent to be critical of Old Hickory's first cabinet, which, he told Verplanck, was bad—with the exception of Van Buren, who had been appointed secretary of state.

Bryant's life in New York was generally placid, his circle of friends expanding, and his financial circumstances improving. He could only wonder at these five whirlwind years in the city. Just before coming to New York, he had composed a poem capturing the abiding tension in his life:

I broke the spell that held me long,
The dear, dear witchery of song.
I said, the poet's idle lore
Shall waste my prime of years no more,
For poetry, though heavenly born,
Consorts with poverty and scorn.

I broke the spell—nor deemed its power
Could fetter me another hour.
Ah, thoughtless! How could I forget
Its causes were around me yet?
For wheresoe'er I looked, the while,
Was nature's everlasting smile.

Still came and lingered on my sight
Of flowers and streams the bloom and light,
And glory of the stars and sun;—
And these and poetry are one.
They, ere the world had held me long,
Recalled me to the love of song.

The poet of nature and New England, by temperament shy and reserved, would never be wholly reconciled to urban life or to his role as a public celebrity. He had been born into a new nation that lacked great poetry and was largely devoid of a coherent national literature. Poetry, as he mused in "I broke the spell," was the vital part of his genius and identity. Yet his life's path seemed to be luring him away from poetry and toward the political currents of the nation and the public life of the journalist. He acknowledged grudgingly that "the vocation of the newspaper editor is a useful and indispensable, and, if rightly exercised, a noble vocation." Poetry—that bewitching art—would always tug at his mind and heart like the very pull of the sun and the moon on nature. But the affairs of the city and the nation were conspiring to hold him fast.

Poetry and politics merged for Bryant when he had to contend immediately with Jackson's plan for Indian removal. In his message to Congress on December 7, 1829, the president established removal of the tribes east of the Mississippi to dedicated land westward as a priority. Bryant admired the self-made, plainspoken old Indian fighter and already supported the president's policies in foreign affairs, the tariff, internal improvements, and the national bank. Thus he readily endorsed the administration's Indian removal policy. On Indian matters, Bryant considered himself to be, like Jackson, a commonsense Democrat.

In his message to Congress, Jackson emphasized the "impending doom" facing the southern tribes as whites surrounded them and destroyed their resources. Unless something was done, he warned in his message, the Choctaw, Cherokee, and Creek tribes would face the same extinction as the Mohegans, Narragansetts, and Delawares. "Humanity and national honor," Jackson argued, "demand that every effort should be made to avert so great a calamity." The solution that the president proposed was to set apart "an ample area west of the Mississippi, outside the limits of any state or territory now formed, to be guaranteed to the Indian tribes. . . . There they can be Indians, not cultural white men."

From January through May, Bryant wrote a series of carefully reasoned editorials supporting the Indian Removal Act that was before Congress. He reprinted long extracts from studies recommending removal and assessed the state of Indian culture against that of early European civilizations. He attacked the Georgia legislature for trying to bring the Cherokees under state jurisdiction in contravention of national treaties and constitutional principles. Instead, extolling the "liberality" of President Jackson's plan for Indian removal, Bryant urged "that Congress should set aside a tract of land, to be guaranteed to the Indians as long as they should choose to occupy it, and thither all might emigrate who preferred to live under their own government to yielding obedience to the laws of Georgia."

We might be shocked by Bryant's editorial policy, for it is hard to focus on the forces at play in the 1820s and 1830s that led otherwise liberal and progressive intellectuals to support the Indian Removal Act. Yet as news coverage in the *Evening Post* and other newspapers of the period reveals, there were constant attacks and killings of white settlers and travelers passing through Indian lands in the South. These accounts, combined with the rabid fever for land among speculators and restless white settlers, made the removal of the eastern tribes to lands west of the Mississippi seem not only "universally commended for its humanity and justice," as Bryant wrote in one editorial, but also historically inevitable.

The seeming disparity between Bryant's muscular editorials supporting the Indian Removal Act and his idealized treatment of the continent's indigenous peoples in his poetry is misleading. True, he had composed two sentimental verse narratives, "An Indian Story" and "Monument Mountain," that had been published in the *Gazette* in 1816 and that capitalized on the fondness of American readers for romantic and tragic tales of noble savages. Like Cooper and Longfellow, he sought native subject matter, local lore and legend, to craft a distinctively American literature. The primary image of the Native American appealed to his poetic imagination.

Early in the 1820s, Bryant had confessed to Dana that he was obsessed with Native Americans: "You see my head runs upon the Indians—The very mention of them once used to make me sick—perhaps because those who undertook to make poetical use of them have made a terrible butchery of the subject—I think however, at present, a great deal might be done with them." Bryant was dismissing the weak poems on Indian themes written by predecessors like Philip Freneau, Joel Barlow, Timothy Dwight, and Sarah Morton. With his letter, he enclosed a poem about Indians that Dana titled "A Walk at Sunset" and printed in *The Idle Man*. It was the first of five poems on Indian legends that Bryant would write between 1821 and 1828.

"A Walk at Sunset" reflects an unwavering view of history and civilization that Bryant enunciated in his poetry as well as in his editorials. Bryant believed that history moves in cycles—a concept he had first introduced in "The Ages"—and that nations and civilizations are susceptible to the forces of ascent and decline. In "A Walk at Sunset," his romantic conflation of the image of the Indian warrior with the setting sun is a trope capturing the historical cycle of rise and fall that he believed was the inevitable fate of Native American culture:

> So, with the glories of the dying day,
> Its thousand trembling lights and changing hues,
> The memory of the brave who passed away
> Tenderly mingled.

For Bryant, the "red man," as he describes him in "A Walk at Sunset," represents a static state of civilization that had not progressed beyond the hunting stage. Here he was reflecting a sentiment common among a majority of Americans that white settlers, skilled in farming and other domestic activities, had a greater claim to the land than did Native Americans. As Bryant wrote in an editorial, "The nature of the Indians' title to their lands is not reconcilable to the principles of tenure as regulated among civilized nations." That the Cherokees and other members of the South's five tribes had become farmers, were formulating an alphabet, soon would have a printing press, and were embracing Jefferson's agrarian ideal were facts that Bryant ignored.

In "A Walk at Sunset" and the subsequent poems—"An Indian at the Burial-Place of His Fathers," "The Indian Girl's Lament," "An Indian Story," and "The Disinterred Warrior"—Bryant asserts that North American Indian culture has run its course—that white civilization has already superseded it. The powerful and unnerving image of the white farmer's plough striking "the white bone" of a dead Indian in "A Walk at Sunset" leads to a coda about the course of civilization in the final stanza where the "thronged city" greets the wandering warrior's ghost:

> States fallen—new Empires built upon the old—
> But never shalt thou see these realms again
> Deadened by boundless groves, and roamed by savage men.

The poetry about Native Americans that Bryant wrote in the 1820s is filled with imagery and symbolism of darkness, decay, and death. Despite the romantic aura he conveys in his poetry about Native Americans, Bryant presents the extinction of Indian civilization as inevitable.

Given Bryant's belief in the cyclical nature of history, it is difficult to locate deep personal or cultural guilt about the fate of Native Americans in his poetry and editorials. His tendency to sentimentalize Native Americans masks a more abiding belief that white civilization was predestined to supplant Indian culture. At best, his red men, as he calls them, are heroic but lamentable figures caught in the warp of history, as he writes in the last stanza of "The Disinterred Warrior":

> A noble race! but they are gone,
>   With their old forest wide and deep,
> And we have built our homes upon
>   Fields where their generations sleep.
> Their fountains slake our thirst at noon,
>   Upon their fields our harvest waves,
> Our lovers woo beneath their moon—
>   Then let us spare, at least, their graves!

Bryant overlooked the fierce opposition to the removal act by politicians on both sides of the aisle and by Christian groups, as well as the implications of the razor-thin approval of the Indian Removal Act by the House of Representatives that enabled Jackson to sign the bill into law on May 28. Instead, as he had in past editorials, Bryant commended his hero—"To General Jackson only belongs the praise"—and, in another column, stressed "the advantages which those tribes who have emigrated to the west of the Mississippi possess over those who remain to the east of that river."

It was natural for Bryant to present the *Evening Post* as an unshakable supporter of Jackson's Indian removal policy because the editor's personal views on the matter coincided with the old Indian fighter's. Moreover, his firm, measured support of Jackson's solution to the nation's Indian problem was a logical outgrowth of the ideas about progress governing Bryant's Indian poems. The act of creation that had produced his cycle of Indian poems had turned into extravagant editorial claims that Bryant's president could do no wrong.

6

YANKEE BRAWLS

I am sick of the strife of politics—not that I ever liked the quarreling much, though I was always something of a politician—but I have had enough of it, and if I have any talents, they are talents for other things.
                    —Bryant to Richard H. Dana, April 22, 1834

I

"While I was shaving this morning at eight o'clock," Philip Hone recorded in his diary for April 20, 1831, "I witnessed from the front windows an encounter in the street nearly opposite between William C. Bryant, one of the editors of the *Evening Post*, and William L. Stone, editor of the *Commercial Advertiser*. The former commenced the attack by striking Stone over the head with a cowskin; after a few blows the parties closed and the whip was wrested from Bryant and carried off by Stone."

The brawl, which occurred on Broadway opposite City Hall, was "a disgraceful affair," according to Hone. The conservative merchant and unreconstructed Federalist was no admirer of the more liberal Bryant. Hone's diary offers a biased account of the episode. Leggett, who had been walking with the poet when the fight erupted, attests to the fact that the poet-editor offered fair warning to Stone before the two men squared off.

Bryant's fight with Stone, who had called him a liar in the *Commercial Advertiser*, was typical of the acrimony that the city's editors felt toward one another. Bryant had ridiculed Stone in his poem satirizing Fanny Wright that had appeared in the *Evening Post* in 1829:

> While Colonel Stone, the learn'd and brave,
> The Press's Atlas, mild but grave,
> Hangs on the words that leave thy mouth,
> Slaking his intellectual drouth. . . .

The vilest verbal attacks filled rival editors' papers, mirroring their occasionally vicious confrontations in public. The truly irascible Leggett spat upon and attacked handsome, pompous James Watson Webb of the *Courier and Enquirer*. Colonel Webb thrashed a rival who had once worked for him—"an ill-looking squinting man" as described by Hone—a universally disliked newcomer named James Gordon Bennett who would found the New York *Herald* in 1835. Bennett in turn called the sensational and wildly popular New York *Sun*, founded by Benjamin Day, "a sneaking, driveling nigger paper" produced by "the garbage of society."

Bryant's attack on Stone was the culmination a series of back-and-forth barbs that Bryant had initiated when, in a lighthearted editorial, he ridiculed National Republican newspapers for having reprinted in full a turgid speech made by Senator Tristram Burgess of Rhode Island at a dinner given in his honor by the city's Adams and Clay supporters. In an editorial a week later, Bryant alluded to a toast proposed at the dinner, which he implied had been offered by Stone, in which the city's two leading Democratic newspapers had been vilified: "The Evening Post and Courier and Enquirer—stupidity and vulgarity." Stone sent notes to Bryant disclaiming authorship of the insult, but Bryant refused to accept the explanation. Stone then published his second note to Bryant in which he gave the charge "a solemn denial under our own signature, and leaving the brand of a significant word spelt with four letters, which it would outrage polite ears to repeat, to blister upon the forehead of William C. Bryant if a blister can be raised on brass." When Bryant, smarting from being called a liar, ran into Stone on Broadway, the fight ensued.

Bryant rationalized the unseemly but justifiable thrashing of Stone. He argued that "the most outrageous possible insult had been offered me, and if I submitted to it, it would probably be soon repeated." He offered a perfunctory apology to the *Evening Post*'s readers: "In conclusion, I feel that I owe an apology to society for having, in this instance, taken the law into my own hands. The outrage was one for which the law affords no redress."

Leggett refuted the *Commercial Advertiser*'s charge (at odds also with Hone's account) that Bryant had attacked Stone from behind:

On arriving opposite to the American Hotel, Mr. Bryant called out to Stone, who immediately turned about and faced him, the gentleman who was with him turning round also. Mr. Bryant then took off his hat, drew forth a cowskin, and replacing his hat on his head advanced towards Stone, who raised his cane on seeing his opponent. As the parties met, Stone struck with his cane at Bryant, who received the blow on his left arm, and at the same time applied the cowskin on Stone's shoulders. The attack, as near as I can tell, was simultaneous on both sides.

According to Leggett, Bryant struck the cane from Stone's hand before "three stout men" finally intervened to wrest the whip from Bryant. Leggett, for his part, threw Stone's brother-in-law, who also was involved in the brawl, to the pavement, while the "piteous cries of Stone" were pleading for assistance.

Bryant was chagrined by his brawl with Stone. The episode was an unwelcome sign, all too public, that he was prone to the same base impulses seen in the behavior of other city editors. The encounter was an unwelcome glimpse into the inner man. Bryant resolved never again to lose control in public. It would be better for him to convert dark impulses into elegant, well-reasoned attacks on the opponents of Jacksonian democracy.

II

The decade had started peacefully enough. "Another year has passed away," Bryant editorialized, "and we have entered upon the busy scenes of the new under favorable auspices and with cheerful hearts. Our country is prosperous and happy, and there is nothing in prospective which does not indicate a continuance of this blessing. The mild temperature of yesterday, almost resembling the softness of a summer's day, drew out our citizens in immense crowds. The streets were thronged at an early hour with the old and the young, the gay and fashionable, to greet their friends with the compliments of the season."

With residual strains of Puritanism in his blood, Bryant was especially pleased to see that New Yorkers had dispensed with their traditional habit of offering "sickening and intoxicating" concoctions like whiskey punch and nouveau to New Year's Day guests. The trend was in favor of hot coffee, thereby eliminating the chances of "riots or disorderly scenes of any magnitude." Bryant feared the extremes of human behavior.

The 1830 census revealed that Bryant was one of the city's 242,278 inhabitants. Record numbers of immigrants from Europe, upwards of forty thousand annually, were now arriving at Whitehall and the Battery. Bryant told Dana that "The great city keeps on growing a little every year, and filling up with adventurers from all lands." These newcomers jostled with the old Dutch aristocrats clustered in fine houses surrounding shady Bowling Green. Around Park Place, the homes of wealthy grain brokers, shipping magnates, land speculators, and contract-labor managers testified to the city's growing reputation as America's Commercial Emporium. Newly constructed brick homes and storefronts stretched across fields and farms north of Canal Street. "The growth of the city which lies above Canal Street," Bryant observed, "is astonishingly rapid, and the new edifices for the most part are handsome permanent structures." Gotham seemed to be caught in a process of perpetual reinvention.

The *Evening Post* had a daily circulation of 1,728, roughly half that of a rival Democratic newspaper, the *Courier and Enquirer*, edited by the vain, choleric James Watson Webb. Much to Bryant's anger and disappointment, Webb's paper had received the contract to print all of the state's legal advertisements. He was dumbfounded by the slight: "This patronage the establishment of the Evening Post has earned by a long course, we believe we may say without vanity, of diligent attention to the duties of commercial advertising." Even without Albany's patronage, the *Evening Post* was a prosperous newspaper. Bryant, as one-fourth owner, found himself the head of a paper that would earn net profits of $13,466 in 1830, up from $10,544 the previous year.

Still published at 49 William Street and now set in six columns, the *Evening Post* devoted three of its four pages to a colorful array of commercial advertisements and announcements. These advertisements publicized money to loan, lectures on numerous cultural improvements including elocution and dance, and sales of an intoxicating range of commodities—cotton bales, whale oil, Lackawanna coal, naval staves, carriages and gigs, ornamental hair works—all testifying to the variety and vitality of New York's economy. The city was growing prodigiously and was rapidly becoming the leading manufacturing and commercial center in the country.

Bryant filled the second page of the *Evening Post* with local, national, and world news. With growing frequency, he reprinted items from European and American newspapers and reports filed from Albany and Washington. His trenchant editorials addressed a broad range of topics. He supported the city's mechanics—"a class of highly respectable citizens"—and advocated the passage of lien laws to protect their labor from unscrupulous individuals. At the same time, he found fault with the newly established Workingman's Party, which had attracted Fanny Wright and the fiery Workie agitator Seth Luther. He wrote approvingly of the iron workers testifying in Congress against the tariff on raw materials and railed against tariffs in general. Apprehensive about the growing furor over states rights, he printed complete transcripts of the Webster-Hayne debate. Turning to global events, he praised Simon Bolívar, who was leading revolutions in South America and had sailed to England in search of support for his cause. Bolivar, he wrote, "has placed his ambition of his life on giving to his country free institutions and wholesome laws we can no longer doubt."

With Bryant at the editorial helm, readers received expanded coverage of literary and art affairs. He praised the work of his friends Inman, Weir, Morse, Cole, and Dunlap, who exhibited their work at the National Academy of the Arts of Design, and singled out the work of a promising new painter: "A dancing scene by Mount, a very young artist, a pupil of the Academy of Design, exhibits much promise." He wrote glowingly of the new novel, *Clarence*, by Miss Sedgwick. "Those passages," he informed readers, "which relate to our own city—to its external aspect, its amusements, its fashionable society, and its domestic life among various classes—are managed with great liveliness, and constitute one of the most attractive parts of the book." Distancing himself from European models, he was less enthusiastic about a new work by Coleridge, *Aids to Reflection*: "The metaphysics of Coleridge have always appeared to us not a little misty. We admire the grandeur of his poetry, and the occasional eloquence of his prose, and the ingenuity and originality of reflection found in the works of this extraordinary man, while, in some parts of his speculation, we confess our inability to discover anything like meaning." America did not have to look abroad for literary or artistic models. Cultural life in New York—typified by the Academy of Fine Arts—was flourishing. Americans did not have to submit to the cultural authority of Europe.

With his demanding editorial responsibilities, Bryant found little time to nurture the bewitching art. In fact, "Hymn to the City" is the only attributable lyric Bryant composed in 1831. Consisting of five stanzas, the poem is a deistic assertion of a Creator present in nature and the metropolis:

> Even here do I behold
> Thy steps, Almighty!—here, amidst the crowd
> 　　Through the great city rolled,
> With everlasting murmur, deep and loud—
> 　　Choking the ways that wind
> 'Mongst the proud piles, the work of human kind.

The Deity permeates the "inner homes" and stores of the city's inhabitants, "[q]uickening the restless mass that sweeps along" and offering comfort to the "vast and helpless city while it sleeps." The poem prefigures the semimystical invocations of New York City by Whitman and Harte Crane.

Near the end of the year, a curious submission, "The Buckwheat Cake," a poem composed expressly "for the Evening Post," appeared. Consisting of three stanzas of more than one hundred lines running down the left side of the *Evening Post*'s editorial page, the poem offers a tribute to the "resistless theme" of a humble dish that might nevertheless "please an epicure":

> The Buckwheat cake! my passion when a boy
> And still the object of intensest love—
> Love lasting, full to overflowing, though
> Unsated yet. My benison on thee
> Thou glorious plant! That, in life's gloomy wane,
> Not only yield me the lively *taste*
> But furnishest the means of happiness . . .

The intricate mock heroic form, supple stylistic and metrical variations, learned allusions to Greek and Roman mythology, and careful attention to the discrete particulars of the lowly buckwheat cake suggest strongly that Bryant wrote this poem. (Leggett, an inferior poet, could not have brought it off.) The comic description of the entire process of preparing the buckwheat cake—harvesting the corn, assembling the ingredients, preparing the pancake—captures Bryant's ebullient frame of mind. (His share of the paper's annual profits amounted to more than three thousand dollars, enabling the family to finally "keep house.") "The Buckwheat Cake" was Bryant's editorial in verse, his paean to plain, wholesome, healthy food fit for a growing nation of democrats.

Bryant's hymn to the lowly buckwheat cake offered brief relief from the need to grapple daily with the affairs of the Republic. As he conceived it, the core crisis confronting the nation was the clash between emerging capitalist realities and liberal democracy. Could capitalism be reconciled with democratic ideals, or were the two forces in eternal conflict? Bryant had been preoccupied with this issue during the last years of the previous decade, warning that the Industrial Revolution had achieved its prosperity in England at the expense of factory workers, the degradation of thousands, and the unhealthy concentration of wealth in the hands of a new industrial class.

Bryant's opinions on the working class had evolved rapidly. At first, he had been suspicious of the Workingmen's Party, which had been formed in 1829 in the wake of labor unrest in Paterson, New Jersey, and attempts by New York factory owners to lengthen the workday. He was alarmed by the party's strong showing in municipal elections that year, worrying that the party, influenced by Wright, Thomas Skidmore, and other radicals, was a threat to small business owners, private property, and "all social relations." Soon, however, Bryant concluded that New York's workingmen were not radicals or revolutionaries but rather a politically conscious group struggling to preserve a system of petty capitalism. Small enterprises, he believed, produced "an active and industrious community." Ever the democrat and individualist, Bryant championed "the plainer part of the community, respectable mechanics and tradespeople" who were the economic bedrock of his ideal society. The "plainer part" validated American democracy.

Bryant feared that Clay's American System, with its Hamiltonian preferences for a strong centralized government, a protective tariff, a national bank, and government subsidies for roads and canals, threatened his ideal society. To Bryant, the opposition resembled a "bee in a tar barrel"—doggerel satire he composed for the *Evening Post*:

I heard a bee, on a summer day,
Brisk, and busy, and ripe for quarrel—
Bustling, and buzzing, and bouncing away,
In the fragrant depths of an old tar-barrel.

Do you ask what his buzzing was all about?
Oh, he was wondrous shrewd and critical.
'Twas sport to hear him scold and flout,
And the topics he chose were all political

"'Twas a crime to fill the land with groans,
"'Twas a deed," he said, "most foul and ugly,"
To turn out poor unfortunate drones
From the public hive, where they lodged so snugly.

The American System's most insidious weapon was the use of tariffs
to protect and strengthen the nation's industry. Bryant railed against a
report to Congress in defense of tariffs, labeling it "jejune and ill-rea-
soned," and vilified the American System in a series of vigorous editorials. In one leader, he offered an extended poetic conceit, asking if a rose
by any other name would smell as sweet:

> [C]all a rose a skunk cabbage, and two thirds of the world
> would turn up their noses at it. . . . Every species of tyranny,
> ecclesiastical or civil, has made its approaches under the veil of
> a name. Tell our people that they are restrained in their industry,
> deprived of their usual market, and taxed heavily on the neces-
> sities of life for the sake of the "American system," and they
> submit without a murmur to a course of infringements on their
> liberty, which if it went by its more appropriate appellation of
> British system, would call out the whole population with guns
> on their shoulders to resist it.

Pondering the Southern states, Bryant predicted that the tariff issue
could threaten the very fabric of the Union. He had worried about the
growing nullification movement in South Carolina, where planters had
suffered through a collapse in cotton prices and were angered by Jackson's promise to reduce tariffs. Bryant thought that the foremost villain
propounding the doctrine of nullification was John C. Calhoun, "the
candidate of the nullification party," whom he described as looking as if
"the fever of political ambition had dried up all the juice . . . of his constitution." The nullification threat was a monster capable of dividing the
nation: "The quarrel between the friends and enemies of the tariff, between the enthusiasts of internal improvement and their adversaries, are
amicable differences in comparison with that which now divides the citizens of South Carolina."

The South, Bryant discovered, was beset by another specter—slave
revolts. In an August editorial, "Insurrections of the Blacks in Virginia,"
he recorded his initial impressions of the rebellion led by Nat Turner,
observing with some naiveté that "there is some probability that the facts

are exaggerated." In subsequent issues of the *Evening Post*, Bryant reprinted excerpts from the *Richmond Whig, Richmond Compiler, Baltimore Gazette*, and other Southern newspapers, speculating that whites might have helped organize the revolt. "Although it appears beyond a doubt that some horrible and bloody outrages have been committed, the motives and objects of the blacks are not yet discovered."

By September, with slave insurrections occurring in other parts of the South, Bryant became more alarmed. Covering the insurrection in Wilmington, North Carolina, he offered his most extended opinion to date:

> There does not, at the present time, seem to exist any very good ground for anticipating a concerted and general insurrectionary movement among the slave population of the South; but the contemporaneous display, in different and distant parts of the Southern country, of a disposition among the slaves to plot and mutiny, naturally excites apprehensions, and should have the effect not only to place our brothers and sisters on their guard, but cause the people of the more northern states to be ready, in case of need, to extend to them ample assistance in men and munitions.

In his July 4, 1820, oration at Stockbridge, Bryant had decried slavery as an evil, but he was not yet prepared to argue for abolition. Taking a more guarded approach, he found merit in the Colonization Society's efforts to return freed slaves to Liberia.

III

Even as national politics preoccupied him, Bryant had new domestic responsibilities. His mother, Sarah, and youngest brother, John Howard Bryant, had visited the Bryants' new home at Fourth Street and Broadway in March. In June, Sarah, Frances, and Fanny returned to Cummington. Frances was pregnant, and their second daughter, Julia, was born in Cummington on June 29. Meanwhile, John Bryant decided to emigrate to Illinois, joining another brother, Peter, as a homesteader on the west-central prairie near Jacksonville. In late July and August, Bryant spent several weeks with his expanded family in Cummington; he returned alone to New York City in late summer, finding the weather dreadfully hot. Not feeling well, a condition he ascribed to not having the new quarters "properly aired," he stayed with Reverend Ware for a week while the new home was "properly scoured and cleaned and sprinkled with chloride of lime."

Bryant congratulated his brother John, now settled in Illinois, on having become "a landed proprietor." While cautioning against a hasty marriage, he offered advice on finding a good wife who, "along with a proper degree of industry and economy, possesses a love of reading and a desire of knowledge" and who is not susceptible to religious fanaticism. Ever the astute critic, Bryant urged his brother, who also wrote poetry, to "study *vigor* and *condensation* in your language and originality of your ideas. Your blank verse might also be improved by greater variety in the pauses." He concluded his letter by mentioning that he intended "to visit Washington this winter to look at the old General and his cabinet."

Before embarking on journeys that would take him to Washington, the Midwest, and Europe over the next three years, Bryant prepared his first major volume of poems for publication. He was thirty-seven years old and had published some ninety poems in various magazines and gift books. His reputation as a poet was unrivaled. One reviewer, writing in the *New-England Magazine*, stated categorically that Bryant stood "by common assent at the head of the list of American poets," while another critic writing for the New York *American* declared that "Mr. Bryant stands forth the first living poet in the language." His poetry—and the poet—had become a metaphor for America.

Poems appeared in early 1832 in an edition of one thousand copies; half were sold at the relatively high price of $1.25 within four months. Its publication thrilled Bryant's admirers. William Ellery Channing in the *American Monthly Review* called Bryant "one of the great poets of our age," while the influential critic Hugh Swinton Legaré, writing in the *Southern Review*, found the volume "the most faultless, and we think, upon the whole, the best collection of American poetry which we have ever seen." Legaré predicted that Bryant's name would "go down to posterity as one of the first, both in time and excellence, of American Poets." Even more cautious critics found much to praise; writing in the *North American Review*, William J. Snelling did not find Bryant to be "a first-rate poet," but nevertheless admitted that he "has great power, and is original in his own way." His poetry had become a force in the construction of American culture.

Fellow writers hoped that Bryant would not spend his life drudging for a newspaper. Emerson, on meeting Bryant's brother Cyrus in Northampton a year earlier, had conveyed his concern over "your man's folly in leaving poetry, in the hope that it m[igh]t reach him that his verses have ardent and all unprejudiced admirers." Similarly, young John Greenleaf Whittier complained of Bryant's "daily twaddle" at the *Evening Post*:

> Men have looked up to thee, as one to be
>   A portion of our glory; and the light
> And fairy hands of woman beckoning thee
>   On to thy laurel guerdon; and those bright
> And gifted spirits, whom the broad blue sea
>   Hath shut from thy communion, bid thee, "Write,"
> Like John of Patmos. Is all this forgotten,
> For Yankee brawls and Carolina cotton?

To Whittier's consternation, Bryant was thriving on "Yankee brawls." In fact, local and national political events offered the frustrated poet an outlet for suppressed emotions. Even as he was studiously preparing *Poems* for publication, Bryant continued to engage in vitriolic attacks on Clay, Calhoun, and others. When Henry Clay proposed a plan to tax imports, Bryant lost no time in excoriating him: "Mr. Clay's speech contains some singular instances of feeble reasoning." Perhaps Clay's age, Bryant suggested, had "affected his mental faculties."

Bryant did not flatter himself about his celebrity or about the practical compromises that literary people had to make to survive in the new Republic. The preface he wrote to *Poems* expresses his gratitude to a loyal public:

> The favor with which the public have regarded them, and of which their republication in various compilations seemed to the author a proof, has induced him to collect them into a volume. In preparing them for the press, he has made such corrections as occurred to him on subjecting them to a careful revision. Sensible as he is that no author had ever more cause of gratitude to his countrymen for the indulgent estimate placed by them on his literary attempts, he yet cannot let this volume go forth to the public without a feeling of apprehension, both that it may contain things which did not deserve admission, and that the entire collection may not be thought worthy of the generous and partial judgment which has been passed upon some of the separate poems.

Bryant's final revisions for *Poems* were actually quite minor, for as Tremaine McDowell first explained, the poet subjected his verse to numerous drafts before committing them to print. Writing a poem, Bryant would change words, alter meter, and rewrite lines and entire stanzas. The final published version of a poem reflected an arduous process of composition and revision; therefore, Bryant did not have to alter any poem significantly as he prepared *Poems* for publication.

While readying *Poems* for American release, Bryant also explored prospects for publishing the collection in England. In late December 1831, he wrote to Washington Irving, who was residing in Newstead Abbey, the former home of Byron, asking for assistance in locating a "respectable bookseller." Irving replied on January 26, 1832, that he was "delighted" to have "a collection of your poems, which, separately I have so highly admired," and promised to find a suitable publisher on his return to London. Three weeks later, Irving was happy to report that he had placed the book with a Bond Street publisher named Andrews, "who has agreed to divide with you any profits that may accrue. The work is now going through the press, under my eye, and I shall do every thing in my power to launch it successfully."

Irving changed a line in "The Song of Marion's Men" so as not to offend British sensibilities over the Revolutionary War, and he wrote a generous introduction to the English edition of *Poems*, which was published in March. He praised Bryant's precise descriptions of the American landscape, which he likened in power to those of Cooper: "His close observation of the phenomena of nature and the graphic felicity of his details, prevent his descriptions from ever becoming general and commonplace; while he has the gift of shedding over them a pensive grace that blends them all into harmony, and of clothing them with moral associations that make them speak to the heart."

Deeply appreciative of Irving's help and attention to his poetry, Bryant thanked Irving for his kindness:

> I have received a copy of the London edition of my poems, forwarded by you. I find it difficult to express the sense I entertain of the obligation you have laid me under, by doing so much more for me in this matter than I could have ventured, under any circumstances, to expect. Had your kindness been limited to procuring the publication of the work, I should still have esteemed the favour worthy of my particular acknowledgments, but by giving it the sanction of your name, and presenting it to

the British public with a recommendation so powerful as yours on both sides of the Atlantic, I feel that you have done me an honor in the eyes of my countrymen and of the world.

Bryant was generally pleased by the reception of *Poems* in Great Britain. English reviews were, with one or two exceptions, favorable. John Wilson in *Blackwood's Edinburgh Magazine* declared Bryant "a genius of very high order," while perfunctory praise also appeared in the *Athenaeum*, the *Literary Gazette*, and other weekly journals.

However, in a letter to Dana, Bryant struck his typically lachrymose note about the fate of the American poet: "As for the lucre of the thing on either side of the water; an experience of 24 years, for it is so long since I first became an author, has convinced me that poetry is an unprofitable trade, and I am very glad that I have something more certain to depend upon for a living." Bryant was becoming an enlightened capitalist.

IV

Never having traveled beyond New England, the Hudson River Valley, and New York, Bryant was eager to see more of America and the world. With his friends Verplanck and Churchill C. Cambreleng representing New York City in Congress and urging him to visit Washington, he embarked for the capital in January 1832. Bryant had written that winter to his brother John Howard, who had joined another brother, Arthur, in the Sangamon Valley in spring 1831, that he hoped "to look at the old General and his Cabinet." Bryant also was seeking a permanent Washington correspondent for the *Evening Post*. With the election of 1832 looming, the *Evening Post*'s editor planned to take the pulse of Congress about the important issues—nullification, Indian removal, the tariff, and the fate of the United States Bank—that promised a contentious session.

Bryant described his exciting ten-day trip to Washington in long, colorful letters to his wife. He set off on Thursday, January 19, and for three days traveled some two hundred miles "by land over bad roads, and thirty miles by water over a rather rough sea from New York to Amboy." As usual, the boat trip sickened him, and his vertigo persisted as the stagecoach carried him into Philadelphia. From there, feeling better and suddenly invigorated by the journey, Bryant moved through the slaveholding states of Delaware and Maryland, noting of the latter that the "greater number of slaves are owned in the southern part of the state." Carried by ferry across the Chesapeake Bay, he took dinner across from Havre de Grace. "Two blacks (slaves of course) waited on the table, a man and a little girl six or seven years old, very attentive, and as silent as cats."

Bryant had been acquainted with African Americans since childhood. During the harvest season, his father had employed black workers who had taken meals with the family. Moreover Bryant, a compulsive walker in the city, came into daily contact with some of the more than fourteen thousand freed black people now inhabiting New York. But this was Bryant's first encounter with black slaves outside of New York. He did not reveal to Frances the sort of moral revulsion over slavery that in time would animate his editorial writing. In fact, just before leaving New York for Washington, he had composed a lengthy editorial alluding to the "lamentable tragedy" surrounding the events of Nat Turner's rebellion in Southampton, Virginia, and applauding the "laudable" efforts of the Colonization Society to "rid the country of a great national misfortune." But slavery had become, as he acknowledged by the end of the month, "an important and perplexing question."

Bryant reached Washington on Saturday and took up lodgings at the Gadsby Hotel. He found the capital to be "a shabby place" filled with "a great many wretched buildings some of which appear not to be tenanted." With Verplanck and Cambreleng organizing his schedule, he was introduced to Washington's "fashionable society," as he described it in a letter to his brother John. He dined with cabinet members and congressmen and visited the House and Senate, where he heard speeches by Henry Clay, Robert Hayne, Daniel Webster, Edward Everett, and John Quincy Adams. One bitterly cold evening, he went with Cambreleng, who was majority leader of the House of Representatives and close to the president, to visit Old Hickory at the Executive Mansion. Bryant found the president to be "a tall white haired old gentleman, not very much like the common engravings of him. He received us very politely and after about three quarters of an hour in which he bore his part very agreeably in the conversation we took our leave." On his last day in Washington, Bryant dined with the president, concluding a journey that cemented the editor's reputation as a trusted spokesperson for Jackson's party. Aligned with Jackson, he had achieved centrality in the political life of the nation.

Once back in New York, Bryant looked on his adopted city with renewed fascination and pride. New York had become "the great center of commerce. . . . Its relations with all parts of the United States are

more various, general and numerous than those of any other city."
Gotham was both great and magnanimous: it had just eliminated fees
for public education, resulting in truly free schools "open to the poorest
class in the community." The arts were flourishing: his friend Edwin
Forrest, who had loaned Bryant money to increase his share of the
Evening Post, offered a stunning performance of *Othello* at the Park
Theatre. And the National Academy of Design had received two wonderful paintings from Cole, one of them "the largest and most finished
piece he has ever painted." This was one of the monumental canvases
constituting Cole's *Course of Empire*, intended, Bryant observed, as "a
series of a History of Landscape, as well as an epitome of man's progress
from barbarism to civilization."

Bryant loved the "newness" of New York:

> Here, every year, new streets are opened, new ranges of
> houses built up, the old hills leveled, the ponds filled up, the
> brooks taught to flow in subterranean canals, and acre after acre
> recovered from the waters of the bay, and made into firm land
> for the habitation of man. . . . Even the ancient burial grounds
> have not been able to withstand the process by which all old
> things have become new in the city. Thorburn raises tulips from
> the dust of the Quakers, the graveyard of the Huguenots is
> excavated for cellars, and that great cemetery, the Potter's Field,
> is turned into a parade ground.

Bryant recommended that Dana come to New York to "shake off
the bile of which you complain." Visitors reviled Bryant's city at their
peril. When Mrs. Trollope criticized American theater audiences for their
lack of manners, Bryant reprinted an article from a London journal
attacking the "coarseness and brutality" of London theatergoers.

In earlier editorials, Bryant had tracked the worldwide progress of
cholera, a pestilence that had killed fifty million people, from Asia to
Europe. To prepare for the epidemic's inevitable appearance in North
America, the editor urged New Yorkers to engage in exercise. Noting a
change of address for Fuller's Gymnasium, he wrote in April, "The season is approaching when the sedentary will do well to fortify themselves
by morning exercise, against the debilitating effects of the heat, and, perhaps against the cholera." Anticipating the arrival of the epidemic in the
city, Bryant took precautions by finding a residence to board at across
the Hudson River in Hoboken, close to his friend Sands. The Bryant

family moved to Mrs. Bostwick's house on May 1, and they boarded there for a month and a half before finding permanent lodgings of their own. By mid-June, cholera was reported in Quebec and Montreal; by the end of the month, the New York Board of Health reported eleven deaths in the city from the epidemic.

Meanwhile, Bryant had planned to visit his brothers in Illinois, and in late May he set out for the Midwest by coach and steamboat. In good health, he delighted even in the hardships of travel. Once again, he wrote long letters, addressed invariably to "My dear Frances," recounting his progress by stagecoach to the Ohio and then down that river to the Mississippi and on to the Missouri and Illinois by steamboat. He was entranced by the scenery and people encountered during his eight-week adventure.

During this western journey, Bryant cultivated a new image of himself as an insatiable traveler and cultural commentator. America's cities—Baltimore, Cincinnati, Louisville, St. Louis—stretched away from the settled East Coast in an urban string that prompted "a vague desire" in Bryant "to wander further," as far as the Mississippi River and its tributaries could take him, perhaps, he surmised, all the way to the Yellowstone. Along the way, he warmed to fellow travelers, recorded local manners that might amuse Frances, and commented on the vagaries of the American character. Leaving St. Louis by steamboat, he encountered a passenger, Mr. Burton, who was victimized by New Orleans sharpers:

> Yesterday they got Mr. Burton to try his luck at cards and after playing all day and a part of the night they stripped him of all the money he had and all he could borrow. Having squeezed him dry about the middle of the night they took passage for New Orleans in a steamboat which we met on her way from Louisville. This morning the unfortunate gentleman who lost the money was endeavoring to solace himself with playing on the fiddle. He complained that it had but three strings. I told him of Paganini who played better on a single string than any other fiddler on four. He had never heard of Paganini.

Gazing from steamboat railings, Bryant saw hardscrabble farmers and settlers carving lives out of the wilderness. On land, he stayed with fellow travelers in rude taverns and log cabins, eating cornbread and hominy, and sharing space with "brawny hard-breathing fellows," up to twenty men and women in the same room. "Shall I confess the truth to you," he confided impishly to Frances, "and suffer you to judge whether I am not what the French call *un homme a bonnes fortunes*? Have I not slept in an apartment with two young ladies?" Bryant was curious about local customs and manners; when a Cincinnati lady invited him to dinner, he was struck by the fact that supper, unlike the more lavish protocol in New York, "consisted of but two dishes." Letters of introduction smoothed his passage westward. Arriving in St. Louis, he met William Clark, who had explored the Pacific Northwest with Meriwether Lewis, served as the governor of Missouri, and was now federal superintendent of Indian affairs.

Bryant was transfixed by the western landscape. His letters to Frances reveal a naturalist's delight in the region's untrammeled forests and prairies. Proximity to this natural world rekindled an element in his character that the years in New York City had suppressed. Here were endless miles of woods, some of them, especially along the Ohio, reminding him of his ancestral home. "The appearance of the woods is more like that of the Berkshire woods, than those of any other part of the country I have seen. They consist of oak sugar maple, hickory buckeye which is a kind of horse chestnut, the tulip tree, the button wood and sometimes the cotton wood which appears to be a gigantic poplar, and other trees common at the eastward, except evergreens of which there are none." During their courtship, Bryant and Frances had studied botany with the famous naturalist Amos Eaton, author of the *Manual of Botany for the Northern States* (1817). He knew that his wife would enjoy his descriptions of the western landscape.

Soon after arriving in Jacksonville, Illinois, Bryant set off on horseback with his brother John to explore a new wonder of the "great west," as he called it, the American prairie. "I carry my plunder in a pair of saddlebags, with an umbrella lashed to the crupper, and for my fare on the road I shall take what Providence pleases to send." Cullen and John slept where they could, often in dingy dwellings with other travelers, where food consisted of coffee, bacon, and lettuce with bacon grease poured over it. Bryant didn't mind the rigors of the trip or the wildness of the topography. In fact, while passing through the fertile area around Pleasant Grove, he began to think about purchasing land in Illinois. The following fall, he would buy a tract near Princeton where his brothers John and Cyrus had settled.

Bryant recorded the distinctive flora and fauna of the American prairie—the wild plums and gooseberries, May-apples, and "strawberries now in their perfection." His botanist's eye uncovered "a large scarlet flower" called the painted cup, which would result in a poem by that name after his second visit to Illinois in 1842. Writing to Dana later in 1832, Bryant described his experience of the level land and sweeping vistas of this distinctive part of the Great West:

> These prairies, of a soft fertile garden soil, and a smooth undulating surface, on which you may put a horse to full speed, covered with a high thinly growing grass, full of weeds and gaudy flowers, and destitute of bushes or trees, perpetually brought to my mind the idea of their having been once cultivated. They looked to me like the fields of a race which had passed away, whose enclosures and habitations had decayed, but on those vast and rich plains smoothed and leveled by tillage the forest has not yet encroached.

Bryant's words, images, and musings prefigure a major poem that he would compose and revise for more than a year, "The Prairies."

Bryant hinted at the emotional and philosophical impact of the prairies: "What I have thought and felt among these boundless wastes and awful solitudes I shall reserve for the only form of expression in which it can be properly uttered." In "The Prairies," Bryant returns to a theme that he had expressed in "The Ages" as well as his personal favorite, "To the Past": the cyclical nature of history and existence. He begins this long poem, composed in supple blank verse, in an incantatory style:

> These are the gardens of the Desert, these
> The unshorn fields, boundless and beautiful,
> For which the speech of England has no name—
> The Prairies. . .

From the outset, the poet adopts a prophetic voice, likening the American prairies not to England but to the Fertile Crescent. The American prairie is a promised land, wild and boundless, filled with New World phenomena and suggestive of a special earthly paradise.

Yet historical disruptions can compromise even a New World paradise. Bryant returns to his Indian theme in "The Prairies," deepening it to include mysterious mound builders he had surmised during his travels to represent an older vanished race. "[W]arlike and fierce" Native Americans had displaced these mound builders. The "red man" in turn had been removed from "the blooming wilds he ranged so long" by white settlers. Bryant, the apologist for Jackson's Indian Removal Act, is unsentimental about this dispossession of the Indian from a pastoral landscape. According to Bryant, the epoch of the mound builders had been an agrarian interlude. Now the prairies echo to the sounds of white settlers—"the laugh of children, the soft voice / Of maidens, and the sweet and solemn hymn / Of Sabbath worshipers." This is the way of the world, the violent overthrow of earlier civilizations by new ones ordained by "the quickening breath of God."

Returning to New York on the twelfth of July, Bryant discovered that the cholera epidemic was at its peak. Everyone with any means—upwards of one hundred thousand people—had deserted the city. In Bryant's absence, Leggett noted that the roads were lined with "well-filled stage coaches, livery coaches, private vehicles and equestrians, all panic struck, fleeing from the city, as we may suppose the inhabitants of Pompeii or Reggio fled from those devoted places, when the red lava showered down upon their houses." Bryant had anticipated the exodus with his removal to Hoboken, where the family, while suffering "premonitory symptoms" that affected Bryant, his wife, and infant daughter, survived the more lethal consequences of the epidemic. To the editor of the *Sacred Offering* who had requested a contribution from the poet, Bryant responded: "the cholera, just then, made us all sadly unpoetical." Nevertheless, he offered "The Journey of Life," a "little poem" of three stanzas that captures the funereal mood of the moment:

> Beneath the waning moon I walk at night
>   And muse on human life—for all around
> Are dim uncertain shapes that cheat the sight
>   And pitfalls lurk in shade along the ground,
> And broken gleams of brightness, here and there,
> Glance through, and leave unwarmed the death-like air.

From Hoboken, Bryant commuted by ferry to his office at the *Evening Post*. Every morning, he wrote to Dana, he was "witnessing the same melancholy spectacle of deserted and silent streets and forsaken dwellings, and every day looking over and sending out to the world the list of the sick and dead." From his editor's chair, he lamented the horrible consequence of the plague on the pulse of the city:

The absence of so many of our citizens at this time from New York gives the place an air of unworldly gloominess. So many houses are shut up, so many warehouses and ships are closed, so many familiar faces are missed in the streets, and such a quiet permeates the places of business, that we hardly recognize the gay, bustling, noisy city of two months ago.

Hearses couldn't keep up with the death toll, which ultimately would claim 3,513 lives. Corpses littered the gutters, especially in Five Points and poorer areas of the city, while recently buried victims festered in shallow graves at Potter's Field.

Bryant inveighed against the city's filth—in cellars, backyards, vacant lots, and other places—that had contributed to the malignity of the disease. His editorials prompted a crusade led by the Board of Health to clean out a decade's accumulation of waste and to spread lime in dwellings, alleys, docks, and cellars, while burning the clothes and bedding of the sick and dying. "It is to be hoped," Bryant wrote, "that the measures which have been adopted for purifying the city, will be actively and perseveringly followed up." As quickly as it had arrived, the epidemic departed, working its way westward along the canal and river towns of western New York, the Ohio, and the Mississippi. By the end of August, medical authorities declared that it was safe to return to the city.

With "the sweetness and purity of its atmosphere" having returned to New York following the departure of the cholera epidemic, Bryant devoted many of his editorials to the controversy over the Bank of the United States. Bryant now turned his stylistic powers—at times with cool logic and at other times in white heat—to a defense of Jackson's plan to destroy the bank. When in August the president vetoed the renewal of the bank's charter by both houses of Congress, Bryant wrote the first in a year-long series of editorials supporting Jackson's decision to dismantle this "mighty pecuniary institution." He sensed correctly that the upcoming presidential election would be "little else than a battle between the United States Bank and the friends of the administration." Bryant had inherited from William Coleman a skeptical attitude toward banks in general. Banks were proliferating in the city and state—in 1826 alone New York City received twenty-seven applications for bank charters—and Coleman had resented these new-fashioned money-making establishments, believing that the spread of banks fed a fever of speculation that in turn produced periodic financial panics. Banknotes, whether held by big institutions or small, in the city or in the country, were not actually money defined as legal tender. They were simply "promises to pay," and as such they were the principal form of currency used by Americans for financial transactions. For good or bad, banks governed the nation's credit system. And when the Bank of the United States, located in Philadelphia and led by the shrewd and arrogant patrician, Nicholas Biddle, mobilized its powerful political and commercial supporters to renew its charter, which would not expire until 1836, the "Bank War" erupted.

Even as the Bank War was heating up, the nullification crisis continued to roil the nation. Jackson had dealt sternly with South Carolina when it attempted to abrogate the tariff of 1828, looking Calhoun squarely in the eye at an 1830 Jefferson Day dinner and offering a toast: "Our Union—it must be preserved." Bryant echoed Jackson's sentiment in his editorial for August 29, 1832, striking a note of militancy that was to characterize his evolving thoughts on the nullifier's threat to the Union. South Carolina, he charged, was engaging "in nothing short of rebellion" in its advocacy of nullification and was threatening civil war and the dissolution of the Union over the tariff issue. When South Carolina issued its ordinance of nullification in December, Bryant labeled it an act of "madness." Jackson sent General Winfield Scott and a naval force to Charleston, issued a proclamation declaring that disunion by armed force was treason, and threatened to hang Calhoun, thereby forestalling the threat of secession and giving Henry Clay time to forge a compromise on the reduction of the tariff—a solution that Bryant, still the ardent free trader, begrudgingly endorsed.

Bryant had become the nation's most formidable political journalist, cultivating in the *Evening Post* a representative and authoritative American voice capable of capturing the democratic promise of the new nation. He had stepped out of the comfortable role as America's foremost poet to deal with the tangled issues of the era. He was a rare intellectual authority in a democratic age. Alexis de Tocqueville, who spent the first six weeks after his arrival in 1831 in Manhattan, thought that the question of authority was a seminal issue. Within the rhetoric and reality of democracy, Tocqueville asked in the second volume of *Democracy in America*, how could one establish authority? "[T]he question is," writes the aristocratic Tocqueville, "not of knowing whether an intellectual authority exists in democratic centuries, but only where it is deposited and what its extent will be. . . . Men who live in times of equality are therefore only with difficulty led to place the intellectual authority to which they submit outside of and above humanity." Tocqueville, who thought that America had not produced a single poet of note, might have found both a poet and an intellectual authority in Bryant. To Bryant, the editorial was was an especially empowering mode of authoritative discourse. His broad editorial project was to advance the complex, ever-evolving genius of American democracy.

Bryant struggled to balance his daily editorial duties and his affection for the literary life. Along with his next-door neighbor Sands and their friend Gulian Verplanck, Bryant planned a collection of stories, *Tales of the Glauber Spa*, at the request of Harper Brothers. He wrote two stories for the collection, "The Skeleton's Cave" and "Medfield," while Catharine Sedgwick, Leggett, and James Kirke Paulding contributed additional tales. In Hoboken, a new acquaintance, the South Carolina poet William Gilmore Simms, joined Bryant and Sands for strolls through the village and along the congenial banks of the river.

Bryant hailed the return of Thomas Cole and Samuel F. B. Morse from their European sojourns with an editorial reminding his friends and the *Evening Post*'s readers that America possessed "mountains and clouds, earth and skies as fitted to inspire the poet or the painter as Italy can boast." But the year ended sadly when Sands died unexpectedly of a paralytic stroke. His last words were, "Oh Bryant, Bryant!"

V

Bryant was so alarmed by the dangers of sectional conflict caused by the specter of nullification that he reluctantly accepted the Compromise Tariff of 1833. But he considered it "a clumsy piece of legislation," an assertion that led to charges by one rival Democratic newspaper, the *Standard*, that the *Evening Post* was not a loyal "party print." To this charge Bryant readily assented, vowing that his paper would never be "a mere *party hack*—it is not a pipe for politicians' fingers to sound what stop they please." Bryant in fact was close to the wellsprings of Democratic power and largesse in the city; when he had the chance to acquire a one-third interest in the *Evening Post*, he received a seven thousand dollar loan from Congressman Churchill Cambreleng.

Fears of sectional conflict impelled Bryant to write several 1833 editorials attacking the nascent abolitionist movement whose center was shifting from Boston to New York. Bryant had opposed slavery, as his denunciation of the Missouri Compromise had demonstrated more than a decade earlier. His poetry, especially the lines written in defense of Greek liberation, was filled with the rhetoric of freedom for all peoples, while "The African Chief" specifically exposed the tragedy of black enslavement:

> Chained in the market-place he stood,
>   A man of giant frame,
> Amid the gathering multitude
>   That shrunk to hear his name—
> All stern of look and strong of limb,
>   His dark eye on the ground:—
> And silently they gazed on him,
>   As on a lion bound.

The poem, a colloquy between the African chief and his captor, ordains his fate as "the Christian's slave / In lands beyond the sea."

But while personally and ideologically opposed to slavery, Bryant was not prepared to embrace the abolitionist cause, warning the *Evening Post*'s readers against Northern interference in the affairs of the South. He was intrigued by the platform espoused by the American Colonization Society, although leading New York blacks and former white supporters like Arthur and Lewis Tappan denounced the organization.

In April, Bryant attacked William Lloyd Garrison and "a small party of enthusiasts" who were, he argued, trying to incite the South against Northern agitators for the abolition of slavery. His reasoning was curiously detached from the horrors of slavery or "right or wrong, the prejudices which separate the white and coloured races." Instead, he worried that the comity between the North and South created by the tariff compromise was being eroded by a fringe band of emancipators who were advocating a congressional ban on slavery. He doubted that Boston's *Liberator*, founded by Garrison in 1831, or *Freedom's Journal*, which had been launched in 1827 in New York as the nation's first black newspaper, represented the thinking of mainstream Americans.

Bryant's animus toward William Lloyd Garrison was in keeping with his suspicion of other radicals—the Robert Owenses and Fanny Wrights of the period—whose schemes for political reform, he feared, endangered national unity. When Garrison sailed for London to seek support for his antislavery campaign, Bryant took a swipe at him, "in the capital of the British empire holding forth in public lectures against American slaveholders." England abolished slavery in September, and Garrison, once back in the United States, joined with Tappan and others to launch the New York Anti-Slavery Society on October 2 at Clinton

Hall. Whipped up by Webb's racist editorials in the *Courier and Enquirer*, a mob of fifteen hundred New Yorkers arrived at Clinton Hall that night, only to discover that the small band of abolitionists had shifted their meeting uptown to the Chatham Street Chapel, conducted business, and escaped through the back door.

Throughout the year, the *Evening Post* warred against the advocates of abolition. Bryant seemed unaware that New York City, quickly supplanting Boston, had become the center of abolitionist activity. New York had emancipated its slaves in 1827. Moreover, Arthur Tappan, a prominent evangelical who had become disillusioned with the American Colonization Society, launched the *Emancipator*, a newspaper devoted to abolition that was distributed to the clergy. On December 4, 1833, sixty black and white delegates organized the American Anti-Slavery Society, making Gotham the hub of antislavery agitation.

For his part, Bryant stuck to his opinion that the antislavery crusade was misguided and a threat to the Republic. In a lengthy editorial in August, he wrote:

> We have strong doubts whether the efforts of the *Telegraph* and other prints of the same kidney will be successful in producing a belief that the people of the north are determined to emancipate the slaves of the southern states. That the existence of slavery in the Union is regretted by the great mass of the population of the non-slave-holding states, we believe to be true; but that there is the slightest disposition to interfere in any improper and offensive manner, except among certain fanatical persons, and those few in number, we regard to be as well settled as any fact in relation to public opinion ever discussed in public journals.

Only certain "crack-brained enthusiasts" in the North and their nullification counterparts in the South who dreamed of a unified confederacy wished for a cause that could lead to the dissolution of the Republic.

A full decade before Walt Whitman expressed similar sentiments, Bryant criticized the indifference of the abolitionists to the threat their campaign posed to national unity, and predicted that their activities would spawn an earthquake of apocalyptic proportions. "They are regarded as advocating measures which, if carried out, would most assuredly deluge the country in blood, and the mere discussion of which has a tendency to embroil the south with the north, and to endanger those relations of good will which are so essential to the duration of the Union."

The turbulence of American political life was testing Bryant's equanimity. He disdained the "love of meddling with agitating subjects" that characterized the behavior of certain New Yorkers. He refused to bow to pressure from the city's business community to moderate the *Post*'s unwavering support for Jackson's plan to destroy the United States Bank, leading to a brief decline in his paper's advertising revenue. He lashed out at the anti-Jackson press, "the contemptible bank tools in the city," attacking editors like Mordecai M. Noah, who recently had started the *Evening Star*, for their vulgarity and venality. He indulged in hero worship when Old Hickory visited the city in June, writing ecstatic editorials describing the tens of thousands of cheering partisans who lined the streets, the lavish receptions, and the accolades showered on the president as he campaigned to end the power of the "Monster," the national bank.

Personal friendships inevitably suffered. Verplanck had voted with the majority to renew the bank's charter and as a consequence had lost his seat in Congress. When he subsequently ran for the state assembly in 1833 on an anti-Jackson platform, Bryant sorrowfully declared that his old friend had joined "an odious monied monopoly." Bryant was aware that the Verplanck family was part of New York's commercial elite: Gulian had recently joined with John Jacob Astor and other prominent businessmen to borrow two hundred thousand dollars from the Second Bank's city branch to start the New York Life Insurance Company. Nevertheless, Bryant distrusted the partisans of the United States Bank as well as the power wielded by financial institutions, convinced that the bank deliberately precipitated a recession in late 1833 by calling in loans.

Still, Bryant did not want to lose a friend like Verplanck. In early January 1834, he went out of his way to remind Verplanck of a meeting of the Sketch Club: "Did you not see in the Post of last night an advertisement of a meeting of the Sketch Club at my House at 2 o'clock P.M.? . . . I hope you will be there—we are to have a long walk and a long talk, and I wish to have a special conversation this week about certain matters." But he was disturbed when his friend, who had been among the first New Yorkers to praise Bryant's poetry, ran for the mayoralty of New York City on the newly established Whig ticket.

Verplanck's desertion of the Democrats served to crystallize Bryant's own commitment to the masses. He immersed himself in the affairs of New York's "mechanics and labouring classes," as he called them, supporting workingmen's causes against the arrayed might of the rich. Although he had been suspicious of the Workingmen's Party, he now defended the right of workers and mechanics to protest the firings of fellow workers who supported Jackson. A free speech advocate, he was wary of "the domineering spirit of a purse-proud aristocracy" that threatened to discharge men for their opinions, pointing to the free environment at the *Evening Post*, where he did not know or care about his thirty employees' political opinions.

Defending the working class, Bryant kept up a steady drumbeat against the reactionary forces—Whigs, National Republicans, and Independent Republicans—arrayed against the Democratic candidate for mayor, the banker Cornelius W. Lawrence. It was obvious to Bryant that the city's aristocracy was using the election to foment class warfare; thus the campaign had become "one of the rich against the poor; the idle against the industrious; of the spending and earning classes of this community; of those who contribute everything, and those who contribute nothing to the wants and the comforts of society." The three days of voting that began on April 8, the first election in which the mayor and city council were chosen by popular vote, turned into a battleground, with Tammany forces, including toughs from the Sixth Ward and recently arrived Irish immigrants, fighting pitched battles with Whig defenders. When the votes were counted, the *Evening Post* reported that Lawrence had eked out a slim victory over Verplanck by a tally of 17,573 to 17,393, but the Whigs had won control of the Common Council.

Shortly after the election, Bryant confessed to Dana a degree of disillusionment with his professional life. "I am sick of the strife of politics—not that I ever liked the quarreling much, though I was always something of a politician—but I have had enough of it, and if I have any talents, they are talents for other things." He was in remarkably good health, which he ascribed to "a diet principally vegetable, a bowl of milk and bread made in my house of unbolted wheat flour, at breakfast, and another at noon, and nothing afterwards." But he needed to collect his thoughts "for some literary enterprise of a kind in which I shall take some satisfaction." For some time he had wanted to turn affairs at the *Post* over to Leggett and get away. He was planning, he told Dana, to sail for Europe.

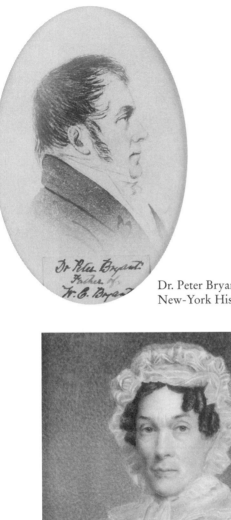

Dr. Peter Bryant. Collection of The
New-York Historical Society. 1910.17.

Sarah Snell Bryant. Collection of The New-York
Historical Society. 1910.18.

Frances
Fairchild
Bryant.
Collection of
The New-York
Historical
Society.
1910.21.

Bryant's Home-
stead. Print
Collection,
Miriam and Ira
D. Wallach
Division of Art,
Prints, and
Photographs,
The New York
Public Library,
Astor, Lenox,
and Tilden
Foundations.

Catharine M.
Sedgwick ca.
1832. Copyright
by James
Herring.
Library of
Congress.

James Fenimore
Cooper. Engrav-
ing by O. Pelton
from the painting
by M. Mirbel.
Library of
Congress.

William Cullen Bryant by Samuel F. B. Morse, 1825. Print Collection, Miriam and Ira D. Wallach Division of Art, Prints, and Photographs, The New York Public Library, Astor, Lenox, and Tilden Foundations.

Samuel F. B. Morse ca. 1845.
Library of Congress.

Washington Irving at the age of 27.
Library of Congress.

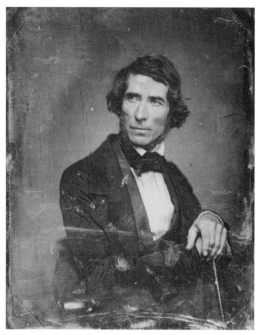

Asher Brown Durand. Library of Congress.

Thomas Cole. Library of Congress.

Washington Hotel ca. July 1833. Library of Congress.

Richard Henry Dana. Print Collection, Miriam and Ira D. Wallach Division of Art, Prints, and Photographs, The New York Public Library, Astor, Lenox, and Tilden Foundations.

Andrew Jackson. Library of Congress.

Frances Wright, 1831. Library of Congress.

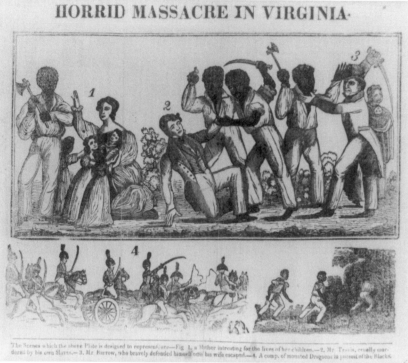

"Horrid Massacre in Virginia." Library of Congress.

"A Gone Case," 1836. Library of Congress.

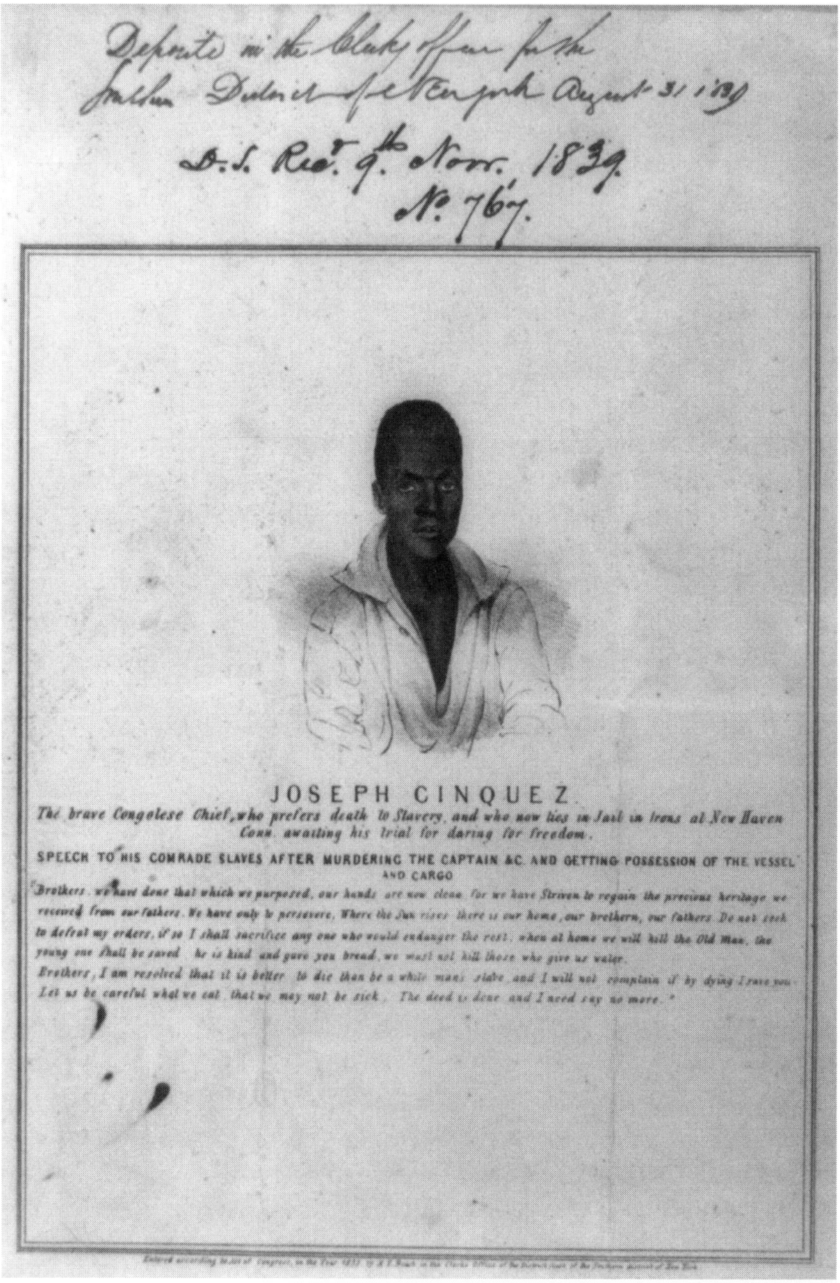

Joseph Cinquez. Library of Congress.

Broadway, 1836. Library of Congress.

Parke Godwin. Print Collection, Miriam and Ira D. Wallach Division of Art, Prints, and Photographs, The New York Public Library, Astor, Lenox, and Tilden Foundations.

Henry Wadsworth Longfellow. Library of Congress.

Bryant, 1830s. Library of Congress.

7

MY NATIVE COUNTRY

I am tempted to ask what I am doing so far from my native country.
                    —Letter to Julia Sands, Florence, October 12, 1834

I

Bryant sailed for Europe on the packet ship *Poland* on June 24, 1834. He was planning to stay abroad for at least one year. Travel, he had discovered during his trips to Washington and the West, offered an escape from politics, a respite from the strain of running the *Evening Post*, and relief from the turbulence of city life. Overseas travel also was a way for nineteenth century writers to enhance their cultural authority. With the exception of Poe, Whitman, and Dickinson, virtually every major American writer from Washington Irving to Henry James would treat overseas travel as a vital part of their literary experience. By visiting the Old World, Bryant could burnish an image of himself as a self-reliant adventurer while testing his democratic American impulses against European otherness.

Bryant yearned for escape from daily routine, the excitement of travel, and especially the counterforce of the artist's creative existence that he imagined Europe would provide. However, he would not find solace or inspiration in Europe. Aside from his travel accounts, whose popularity would enhance his cultural authority, and a few poems, Bryant would not discover on this or future overseas adventures the major "literary enterprise" that he dreamed the ambience of the Old World promised.

Perhaps, on the day of his departure from the United States, Bryant's stomach was trying to tell him something. By mid-afternoon on June 24, as the ship cleared Staten Island and moved into the Atlantic, he had become "as sick as the heart could wish." Frances Bryant would recall that her husband "suffered unmercifully all the way," as he would during almost all nautical voyages over the next forty years. Leaving America was always an occasion of gastric distress. Nevertheless, Bryant sensed that one way to broaden a writer's cultural authority was to transcribe the overseas tour for an American public enthralled by travel writing. Irving and Cooper had already recorded the rituals of travel to sustain their literary reputations. Bryant, with the pages of the *Evening Post* at his disposal, would write lengthy letters—carefully composed articles—celebrating his own mixed experience of Europe.

Bryant's discomfort lasted until he reached Le Havre three weeks later, frustrating his plan to keep an extensive journal of the voyage. He was able to record descriptions of the colorful fellow travelers aboard the *Poland*, including the notorious Madame La Laurie, "the same who committed such horrible cruelties upon her slaves last winter in New Orleans." Madame La Laurie had avoided the wrath of local citizens by escaping in men's clothes; she was now returning to France with her husband.

The beauty of the ocean inspired him to poetic rapture: "Sea smooth and fair—I was able to walk a little on deck. In the evening I witnessed a most beautiful spectacle, the luminous appearance of the sea. The waves broke before the bow of the vessel in sheets of fire; the foam shone on the top of every wave; the ocean seemed full of beacon lights; and in the extreme distance they formed a luminous ring on the edge of the horizon." Like Irving's avatar Geoffrey Crayon and Emerson in his 1833 travel diary, both of whom found inspiration in the physical sensations of the Atlantic crossing, Bryant anticipated pleasure and creative renewal once he arrived in the Old World.

Landing at Le Havre on the fifteenth of July, Bryant was struck almost immediately by the stark contrasts between the Old and New Worlds. Europe truly was ancient, as he had imagined in "The Ages" and "The Greek Boy," the latter a lyric extolling Greek independence while lamenting the passing of an epic age:

> Gone are the glorious Greeks of old,
>   Glorious of mien and mind;
> Their bones are mingled with the mould,
>   Their dust is in the wind;

The forms they hewed from living stone
Survive the waste of years, alone,
And, scattered with their ashes, show
What greatness perished long ago.

Europe, despite the charm of its antiquities and richness of the arts, was not necessarily superior to the American experiment. Just as literary visitors like Frances Trollope in her *Domestic Manners of the Americans* had been critical of and condescending toward the New World, Bryant's transatlantic journey confirmed for him the superiority of political and cultural life in the United States.

Bryant dutifully noted the beautiful and fertile country on the trip from the seacoast to Paris but typically qualified his observations with critical commentary. He was awed, he informed the American portrait painter John Rand, by the magnificent cathedral at Rouen. Bryant noted "the traces of preceding ages which have met me at every step since I entered this country, ancient customs, ancient modes of dress yet preserved among the peasantry, buildings of antique architecture, the ceremonials of an ancient and pompous worship, and the vestiges of power and magnificence which have passed away." Europeans, however, were also "vexatious" in their bureaucratic behavior, were dishonest, and were notably adept at cheating Americans. Bryant was ambivalent about Europe, awed by its civilization but unwilling to accept its cultural authority.

Bryant spent three weeks in Paris, but the city did not appeal to his deepest needs and instincts. The city's monumental architecture did confirm the ancient power and magnificence of France. And Paris afforded him time to practice his French, a language that had intrigued him for years. (In letters to his daughter Fanny, he often had inserted passages in French; moreover, Bryant had translated passages from the Provençal poets in a lengthy scholarly essay.) Parisians, however, seemed to be blissfully unaware of their heritage; they preferred to "make love and quiz the priests." Parisians were pleasure seekers, often fiddling and jigging until early morning hours in the street by the Tuileries, where the Bryants had taken lodgings. Even the Pere Lachaise and Montmartre cemeteries struck Bryant as bizarre: they were joyful rather than somber habitats for the deceased, reminding him not so much of departed ancestors as "gay multitudes" enjoying an eternal party.

After listening to late-night *chansons* for three weeks, Bryant had had his fill of Paris and was ready to head south toward Italy. He was not enamored of the unfolding countryside, he confessed in a letter to the *Evening Post*: "Monotonous plains, covered with vineyards and wheat-fields, with very few trees, and those spoiled by being lopped off for fuel—sunburnt women driving carts or at work in the fields—gloomy, cheerless-looking towns, with narrow, filthy streets—troops of beggars surrounding your carriage whenever you stop." Marseilles intrigued him—primarily because it reminded Bryant of New York: "I found its streets animated with a bustle which I had not seen since I left New York. . . . Marseilles is the most flourishing seaport in France; it has already become to the Mediterranean what New York is to the United States, and its trade is regularly increasing." In his most acute moments of perception, Bryant would measure his European experience against America and find Europe wanting.

Ann Douglas in *The Feminization of American Culture* examines the "contiguity of travel and writing" and concludes that most nine-teenth-century travel authors "built their professions on a form of eva-sion—of their country, of their own identity, and of their occupation itself." Bryant might have succumbed to these forms of evasion had he not retained a healthy skepticism toward his Old World wanderings. In a letter to the *Evening Post*, Bryant asserted that Europe's sordid politi-cal realities strengthened his patriotism:

> I think I shall return to America even a better patriot than when I left it. A citizen of the United States traveling on the continent of Europe finds the contrast between a government of power and a government of opinion forced upon him at every step. He finds himself delayed at every large town and at every frontier of a kingdom or principality. . . . He sees everywhere guards and sentinels armed to the teeth. . . . He sees the many retained in a state of hopeless dependence and poverty, the effect of institutions forged by the ruling class to accumulate wealth in their own hands.

Unlike Washington Irving, Bryant was not predisposed to be a senti-mental traveler concocting romantic and visionary accounts of Europe. Bryant's critical impulses were more attuned to those of his friend Feni-more Cooper, who censored European monarchy and aristocratic preten-sion even as he imagined that every remark by an Englishman conveyed a latent insult.

Arriving in Florence on the twelfth of September, Bryant continued to measure the antiquity of Europe against the newness and vitality of America. To William Ware he observed that Florentines were "as indolent and effeminate as their ancestors of the republic were hardy and enterprising" and that modern Florentines were scarcely interested in their illustrious history. The local exhibitions, he claimed, were inferior to those offered by the Academy of the Arts of Design in New York. The American sculptor Horatio Greenough, whom Bryant had met in New York in 1828 and who now had a studio in Florence, agreed with the poet's severe assessment of contemporary European art. Bryant did admire the fine hues of the Florentine evening skies, but again they only served to remind him of "Cole's fine little landscape taken from the bridge over the Arno close to the lodgings which I occupy. . . . It presented a view of the river traveling off towards the west, its banks shaded with trees, with the ridges of the Apennines lying in the distance, and the sky above flushed with the colours of sunset." (Bryant was alluding to Cole's *View of the Arno*.)

Bryant offered his impression of the Florentine landscape in "To the Apennines," a lyric in which he wrestled with his ambivalence about the Old World. The poem proceeds from a pristine description of the untrammeled upper reaches of the Apennines, its peaks bathed in "the soft light of these serenest skies," to a more somber panorama of the historical cycles played out around the mountain's base:

Ages of war have filled these plains with fear;
   How oft the hind has started at the clash
Of spears, and yell of meeting armies here,
   Or seen the lightning of battle flash
From clouds, that rising with the thunder's sound,
Hung like an earth-born tempest o'er the ground!

Asian hordes, Libyans, Scythians, Gauls, and later generations of "beleaguering foes" dramatize the need to seek wisdom in the sublime—the "noiseless air and light" around the mountain's heights. But in the eighth and last stanza, Bryant responds to these contrasts between the natural and human worlds with somber but subtle intelligence:

In you the heart that sighs for freedom seeks
   Her image; there the winds no barrier know,

Clouds come and rest and leave your fairy peaks;
   While even the immaterial Mind, below,
And Thought, here wingèd offspring, chained by power,
Pine silently for the redeeming hour.

The lofty peaks of the Apennines reminded Bryant of freedom, but the "eternal peace" of the mountainous landscape contrasted with the vicious struggles of the Italian states. Only the upper ranges of the Apennines, where Europeans couldn't degrade the landscape or scar it with centuries of conflict, offered towering renditions of the picturesque that could match the purity and freedom of the untrammeled parts of the American landscape.

II

Bryant's poetic musings during his first European journey returned persistently to the splendors of the American scene. In 1830 he had written the prospectus, preface, and commentary for an illustrated chapbook, *The American Landscape*. The volume included views of Weehauken, the Catskill Mountains, Fort Putnam, the Delaware Water Gap, the Falls of the Sawkill, and Winnipiseogee Lake—all engraved by his friend Asher Durand from paintings by Durand, Cole, and W. J. Bennett. In *The American Landscape*, Bryant compared landscapes at home and abroad, suggesting that "Nature is not less liberal of the characteristics of beauty and sublimity in the new world, than in the old." Now the sight of the Apennines confirmed Bryant's earlier supposition that America's "far-spread wildness, a look as if the new world was fresher from the hand who made it," was far superior to the "tamings and softenings" found on the Continent.

    To Julia Sands, the sister of his deceased friend Robert Sands, Bryant confessed that he was not identifying with the European scene. "I am tempted to ask what I am doing so far from my native country. If one wants to see beautiful or majestic scenery, he needs not go out of the United States; if he is looking for striking and splendid phenomena of climate . . . he needs not leave the United States; if he delights in seeing the great mass intelligent, independent, and happy, he <u>must</u> not leave the United States." Nevertheless, Bryant would satisfy his curiosity about the rest of Europe.

In late autumn, Bryant uprooted his family and left Florence for Pisa. Frances had been increasingly unhappy with their lodgings in Florence, writing to her friend Eliza Robbins, "We had our apartments on the south side of the Arno, looking to the North, and exposed to the tramontane winds. . . . The chilly air penetrated our rooms through the crevices of the doors and windows, which were numerous, and we found it impossible to keep ourselves warm." Concerned about his wife's health, which often was fragile during their European wanderings, Bryant thought that Pisa's temperate winter climate would be more beneficial to her.

Compared to Florence, Bryant informed readers of the *Evening Post*, Pisa was "the very seat of idleness and slumber." A typical day in Florence, which Bryant described comically, was a carnival of human follies and delights—an unending procession of tourists, farmers with their livestock, men and women in exotic costumes, pompous priests and black-shrouded Brothers of Mercy, extravagant carriages and dress of the Florentine nobility. Pisa, on the other hand, was "all stagnation and repose."

Bryant looked skeptically upon the indolence of Pisa's inhabitants, so unlike the cosmopolitan ferment and commercial energy infecting Manhattan's citizens. He was especially critical of the lax morals of the "higher class." Pisa's married ladies had their *cavaliere servante* and carried "their gallantries to lengths which in any other country would be deemed extraordinary." Bryant's continental vision was steeped in the morality of his Calvinist forebears.

Bryant did enjoy the mild winter months that he and the family spent in Pisa. The Arno flowed through the city between massive and lofty houses. "I have my lodgings," he told Austin, "consisting of seven furnished rooms, besides the kitchen which is also furnished, comprising the entire floor, for which I pay twenty eight crowns a month" (about thirty-five dollars). Ever the naturalist, he described the lush winter landscape: a profusion of flowers, along with peach and plum trees, were in full blossom in February; crops were ready for winter harvesting; and a plenitude of deciduous trees and conifers enhanced the landscape. "Orange and lemon trees grow in the open air, and are now loaded with ripe fruit. The fields in the environs are green with grass nourished by abundant rains, and are spotted with daisies in blossom. Crops of flax and various kinds of pulse are showing themselves above the ground, a circumstance sufficient to show that the cultivators expect nothing like what we call winter." Landscape divorced from Europe's violent history, oppressive traditions, and vulgar cultural habits could offer Bryant consolation.

But Bryant could not escape the violent contours of European civilization. While staying in Pisa, he composed "The Knight's Epitaph," a eulogy for a forgotten Italian buried in "a sepulchral vault" of St. Catharine's Church. The lyric apostrophizes the knight's chivalry while lamenting Pisa's decline:

> "He lived, the impersonation of an age
> That never shall return. His soul of fire
> Was kindled by the breath of the rude time
> He lived in. Now a gentler race succeeds,
> Shuddering at blood; the effeminate cavalier,
> Turning his eyes from the reproachful past,
> And from the hopeless future, gives to ease,
> And love, and music, his inglorious life."

Europe had become decadent. To Bryant, ever the proponent of a cyclical view of history (stated elegically in "The Prairies"), European civilization was in decline.

Bryant wrote "The Knight's Epitaph" on commission. Before his departure, he had contracted with George Pope Morris's weekly *New-York Mirror* for twenty poems to help defray his travel expenses. He had outstanding loans at the *Evening Post*, which Leggett was dutifully paying from the poet's share of the newspaper's profits. Moreover, a commission from the American secretary of state to carry confidential papers to Europe had never materialized, placing a further strain on Bryant's resources during his European sojourn. To help cover expenses, he had eventually agreed for "small compensation" to have the fifteen-year-old son of a friend, the wealthy New York textile merchant Saul Alley, accompany the family as they toured the continent. And he could earn a few extra dollars by churning out poetry for the *Mirror*.

To Horatio Greenough, who had completed a bust of Bryant when the two friends were residing in Florence (and who introduced him to Walter Savage Landor), Bryant lamented what he feared was a decline in his creative talents: "My *labours*, as you are pleased to term them are not worth inquiring about. I am occupied with nothing of importance—but I am only trying in my active interests to recover what I nearly unlearned in the course of several years, thinking and writing on political subjects;

namely, the modes of thought and mechanism of languages which belong to poetry."

Before leaving the United States, Bryant had completed the second edition of *Poems*, published at Boston by Russell, Odiorne & Metcalf in 1834. However, the second edition contained only three new poems, "The Prairies," "Sonnet, from the Portuguese of Somedo," and "The Journey of Life." Edgar Allan Poe regretted in the *Southern Literary Messenger* that a poet "of uncommon strength and genius" should languish "probably for want of that due encouragement, which to our shame as a nation be it spoken, has never been awarded to that department of literature." Bryant would not complete the twenty poems he had agreed to send to the *Mirror* (several forwarded to Leggett apparently were lost), but one poem that he did compose demonstrated that his poetic powers had not diminished.

"Earth," among Bryant's strongest and most mature poems, is an extended meditation in five long stanzas of free verse on the mutability of the natural world and human history. At the start of the poem, Bryant, the earthbound philosopher, positions himself in the "midnight black" of the European landscape, a world of "vast brooding shadow." He ends the first stanza with the lines "And sands that edge the ocean, stretching far / Into the night—a melancholy sound," prefiguring Matthew Arnold's "Dover Beach" as he seeks to read history in "the breast of the Earth."

Bryant achieves a stately, self-assured style in "Earth," a varied and measured awareness of transience. He first started to compose the poem in rhyme but "found it convenient," he states in a note, to abandon this scheme after seven stanzas of forty-two lines, starting over with a second version that relied on the more fluid rhythms of blank verse. As he contemplates the earth of the Old World, Bryant remains the unsentimental tourist: he employs a chilly lyricism to catalog the exploitation of Europe's natural beauty and the vicissitudes of the continent's history. The "vales of Italy" where the poet rests are filled with memories of "tremendous warfare," of "old dungeons yawning now / To the black air," of vanished nations and shackled peoples.

For almost one hundred lines in "Earth," Bryant is critical of the Old World. However, in the final stanza, he offers a guarded vision of a brighter day:

> What then shall cleanse thy bosom, gentle Earth,
> From all its painful memories of guilt?

The whelming flood, or the renewing fire,
Or the slow change of time?—that so, at last,
The horrid tale of perjury and strife,
Murder and spoil, which men call history,
May seem a fable, like the inventions told
By poets of the gods of Greece. O thou,
Who sittest far beyond the Atlantic deep,
Among the sources of thy glorious streams,
My native Land of Groves! a newer page
In the great record of the world is thine;
Shall it be fairer? Fear, and friendly Hope,
And Envy, watch the issue, while the lines,
By which thou shalt be judged, are written down.

There are limited virtues in the European landscape, as he had warned in the sonnet to his friend Cole before the artist's departure for Europe. As in the earlier sonnet, but this time with greater stylistic assurance and richness of evocation, Bryant looks to America as the emblem of a brighter world.

Bryant's thoughts persistently returned to America as he contemplated the course of European civilization. Personal news from home also drew his thoughts back to his native land. While residing in Pisa, he learned from Austin, the only brother still living in Cummington, that he and their mother had decided to sell the family farm and join the rest of the family in Illinois. "I cannot help a feeling of regret," he wrote Austin, "at learning that you had parted with the farm in Cummington, but I have no doubt that the step will be for the advantage of your children." Through his wife, Bryant asked his brother about the books in their father's library, volunteering to buy them rather than having them sold to others. He told Austin that soon they would depart for Rome, then Naples, planning to be in Germany by midsummer.

Bryant seemed to be measuring time, eager to see what the rest of Europe offered but tiring of the Grand Tour. The nine-day journey from Pisa to Rome was agreeable, as Bryant wrote to the widow Susan Renner, a new English friend whom the Bryants had seen much of in Pisa. After staying at the Hotel Franz on the Via Condotta for a week, they took lodgings at 57 Via Pontifici, having their dinners sent up from a trattoria for fifty cents a day. But Bryant found Rome to be a filthy place, making it hard to appreciate the intoxicating array of antiquities, museums, churches, fountains, and gardens. "It is a magnificent old city," he informed Leggett, "but terribly infested with fleas." He was pleased to see his friend Edwin Forrest, who "came but went away in a day or two" and who also was writing letters to the *Evening Post* describing his European travels.

By the time Bryant reached Naples on May 1, he had had his fill of monuments to antiquity. While staying at 267 Strada Chiaga for three weeks, he wrote to Leggett: "I have strolled through the streets of Pompeii, dived into the darkness of Herculaneum, and climbed to the smoking crater of Vesuvius." If these ancient ruins impressed him, Bryant did not reveal it. Writing to Julia Sands, he described Naples as "populous, lively, as noisy as New York and inexpressibly dirty—that whoever visits either that place or Rome must lay his account in being eaten up alive by fleas—that the farther you go south of Tuscany the greater cheats you find the people, and that half at least of the pleasure you take in looking at objects of curiosity is counterbalanced by being plagued by swarms of beggars ragamuffins and rogues of all sorts who come upon you at every turn and keep a perpetual din in your ears." Moreover, he told Leggett, the brutish aspects of Italian political life bothered him: "In Sardinia, capital executions for political causes are frequent, and long and mysterious detentions are resorted to, as in Lombardy, with a view to strike terror into the minds of a discontented people. The royal family of Naples kill people by way of amusement."

Bryant was now prowling Italy like a bourgeois tourist eager to see everything at breakneck speed: he went back to Rome and Florence and on to Bologna, Ferrara, and Padua. Bryant must have worried that Europe was not providing the deep creative stimulus he had anticipated. On June 20, Bryant checked into the Albergo dell'Europa hotel in Venice—a city that, with certain reservations, he actually enjoyed. Bryant found Venice to be "a city which realizes the old mythological fable of Beauty born by the sea." He liked the clean canals filled with gondolas, the immense square of St. Mark, and the "watery and oceanic" aspect of the city's architecture. The Venetian palaces reminded him of stalactites and icicles. "The only thing needed to complete the poetic illusion," he informed Leggett, "is transparency or brilliancy of colour, and this is wholly wanting, for at Venice the whitest marble is soon clouded and blackened by the corrosion of the sea air." Despite its political decline, Venice was the "most pleasing of the Italian cities which I had seen." Still, he remained of two minds about his time in Italy. To William

Ware he concluded, "I was glad to get out of Italy—and yet I had a most vehement hankering to stay. Italy is a most beautiful woman no better than she should be, and her suitors must feel the alternate admiration and disgust usual in such cases."

III

Bryant's unending quest for "some literary project" of import took the family to Germany in late June. The Bryants left Venice and traveled through the Tyrols, descending the Brenner in a snowstorm before reaching Innsbruck. From there, they "climbed and crossed another Alpine ridge scarcely less wild and majestic in its scenery than those we had left behind," before the vagabonds reached Munich on June 30. Bryant wrote to Mrs. Renner that he and Frances were "glad to repose in a cool climate with such a place as the English Garden close at hand for our daily walks." After a brief stomach illness, his wife's health improved; she felt better than she had during their Italian sojourn. Little Julia delighted in speaking Italian and what she insisted was "American," getting into a "high dudgeon" whenever anyone called her English; while Fanny was happy to take piano lessons with a German instructress. Bryant, meanwhile, set out to master the German language, "a crabbed kind of tongue after all, and very obstinately peculiar in prescribing the order of words in a sentence." Germany was all that Italy was not—clean, plain, orderly—and the culture sparked brighter spirits than had Italy.

Having few acquaintances in Munich and wary of its variable winter climate, Bryant decided to move to Heidelberg. He carried introductions from Susan Renner's many friends—along with information on her own anticipated arrival after a lingering illness—and these promised a more active social life. Leaving Munich on October 2, the Bryants reached Heidelberg four days later. They stayed at the King of Portugal for a month and then took up housekeeping at 266 Freidrichstrasse. They expected to settle into life and society at Heidelberg. Perhaps here Bryant could find inspiration for a major literary project.

Bryant was sorry to learn that Susan Renner would not be joining them, but his disappointment was alleviated by the arrival on December 15 of a young poet from America whose verse Bryant had long admired. He had never met Henry Wadsworth Longfellow, but their careers were intertwined. Their poetry—Longfellow's "Thanksgiving" and Bryant's two sonnets "Mutation" and "November"—had appeared on the same page of the *United States Literary Gazette* of November 15, 1824, and Bryant had published three poems by "H. W. L." the following year in the *New-York Review*. Longfellow had reached Heidelberg barely two weeks after the death of his young wife, Mary Peter Longfellow, during what he had planned as a lengthy study tour of Europe. He was accompanied by one of his wife's companions, Clara Crowninshield. Learning that the Bryants were residing in the city, Longfellow immediately sought them out.

Bryant and his new friend got along famously. They spent considerable time together over the next six weeks, often practicing their German together and taking long walks over the hills around Heidelberg. Longfellow liked his older companion "exceedingly," while Clara felt that she had "always known" the Bryant family. Little Julia captivated Longfellow: at four years of age she was already a multilingual wit. The two poets anticipated many cordial winter months together. However, news from New York brought Bryant's plans to remain in Germany until the following spring to an abrupt end.

At first Bryant didn't realize how precarious the situation at the *Evening Post* had become during his absence. In early December, he received a letter from his business manager, Michael Burnham, Jr., who had assumed his father's position, that William Leggett had developed a "bilious fever of a high grade" and might not recover. Everything, however, was under control: Theodore Sedgwick, Jr., had agreed to provide lead editorials, and Dr. Henry Anderson, Bryant's friend and associate from the *New-York Review*, would "furnish something every day on political economy." However, by the middle of January, Bryant informed Longfellow and Clara Crowinshield that he had received several letters that required his immediate return to America.

Because of adverse weather conditions, Bryant was detained at Le Havre for seven days and at Plymouth for another week before sailing for America. The passage took fifty days across rough Atlantic seas, once again rendering him ill, he informed Frances stoically, "the greater part of the time." Bryant arrived in New York on March 26, had his luggage sent to the American Hotel, and set out to appraise the situation at the *Post*. To his surprise, Michael Burnham, Jr., had left the newspaper in the wake of his father's death. Leggett, whom he saw the following morning, was "sallow, dark emaciated with an expression of pain and anxiety in his countenance." Bryant sensed that Leggett was unlikely to return to work with his former "vigor of constitution." He notified

Frances that he would have to remain in America and resume management of the paper.

Bryant's friends flocked to the returned voyager. Miss Sands, the Wares, and the Sedgwicks were delighted to see him. A new acquaintance, the English journalist and economist Harriett Martineau, who talked "agreeably and with considerable sprightliness," paid her respects. Ware insisted that Bryant stay with his family, but another friend, the lawyer Thatcher Payne, prevailed. That week, two dozen notable New Yorkers, including Washington Irving, Asher Durand, Fitz-Greene Halleck, Samuel Morse, James Kirke Paulding, Henry Inman, Robert Sedgwick, and Gulian Verplanck, proposed a dinner to celebrate Bryant's return to his native land and to express their "high sense" of his "literary merits and estimable character."

Bryant was flattered but declined the invitation. "I cannot but feel . . . that although it might have been worthily conferred upon one whose literary labours abroad had contributed to raise the reputation of his country, yet that I, who have passed the period of my absence only in observation and study have done nothing to merit such distinction." While overseas, he had never found his literary project of consequence, concluding that—unlike Irving and Cooper, who had been productive while living abroad—he had done nothing to merit their tribute. Moreover, he had neglected affairs at the *Evening Post* for almost two years; he now had to attend to business and more conventional forms of textual production than travel writing.

8

LEGGETT'S LEGACY

His love of truth, too warm, too strong
For Power or Fear to chain of chill,
His hate of tyranny and wrong,
Burn in the breasts he kindled still.
—"In Memory of William Leggett"

I

Europe had not inspired Bryant to literary production. However, the authoritarianism and decadence he had witnessed during his wanderings on the continent had intensified his love of freedom and hatred of oppression in the United States. By the time he returned to New York, he was susceptible to the radical opinions of the man he had left in charge of the editor's desk, William Leggett. In Bryant's absence, Leggett had alienated readers, advertisers, and the Democratic establishment with his militant editorials. Leggett had been read out of the party; the *Evening Post*'s revenues were in precipitous decline as offended merchants withdrew their advertisements from the paper.

Scarcely had Bryant departed for Europe in 1834 when Leggett denounced the white mobs that had attacked a largely black group that had assembled at the Chatham Street Chapel on July 7, 1834, to celebrate New York's emancipation of its slaves seven years earlier. In fiery editorials, he reviled handsome, temperamental James Watson Webb, the reactionary editor of the morning *Courier and Enquirer*, whom Leggett had spat on and trounced a year earlier on Wall Street. Equally detestable to Leggett was William Leete Stone of the *Commercial Advertiser*. Both

133

Webb and Stone engaged in wildly anti-Negro and Nativist diatribes that precipitated disturbances throughout the month of July. Leggett labeled the anti-Negro and anti-Catholic mobs that rampaged through the city "a motley assemblage of infuriated and besotted ruffians, animated with a hellish spirit," whose leaders should "be shot down like dogs."

In lengthy, impassioned editorials Leggett defended the rights of Negroes, abolitionists, immigrants, and Catholics. He also repeatedly denounced banks and "monopolists," political corruption, and cronyism. On December 6, 1834, he became the first editor of a major American newspaper to support the rights of workingmen to form unions. In the summer of 1835, he attacked the Jackson administration while denouncing Postmaster General Amos Kendall, who had issued instructions to the postmaster of Charleston, South Carolina, permitting the censorship of abolitionist literature. As a result, Tammany and the federal post office canceled their advertising contracts with the *Evening Post*, joining many members of New York's commercial elite who, fearful of alienating their Southern friends, had canceled their advertising as well.

Instead of repudiating Leggett's radical editorial opinions, Bryant embraced them. He had to bolster finances at the *Evening Post*, for profits for the six months ending May 16, 1836, had declined from $6,605.80 a year earlier to $3,517.98. Nevertheless, he embarked on a series of editorials on the very issues that had driven Leggett to such fury and had contributed to the deterioration of his health.

Leggett's biting editorials against bankers and monopolists, an "order of American Barons" inimical to municipal equality and working class well-being, had contributed to the founding of the Equal Rights or "Loco Foco" Party. Not strictly a labor or union party, and consisting largely of journeymen, small manufacturers, shopkeepers, and professionals, the Loco Foco Party embraced the rights of journeymen, artisans, and mechanics to organize in order to protect their interests. Bryant was immediately sympathetic to the platform. Galvanized by Leggett's denunciations of the monopolists, he devoted one of his first editorials following the resumption of duties at the *Evening Post* to a defense of workingmen's unions or "combinations."

Writing with intellectual poise and in a plain, forceful style, Bryant demonstrated how government regulation of the economy produced inequalities in working conditions that in turn had led to a wave of strikes as New York's workers tried to keep up with rocketing inflation. Without "unconditional free trade," inequalities in working conditions were inevitable. Moreover, "absurd legislation" permitting a flow of paper money made it impossible to fix the value of labor:

> But when Congress takes upon itself to paralyse the great preserver and equalizer of the standard of value among nations—when, enabled by this mad experiment, to bid defiance to the laws of trade, the states engage in a course of correspondent folly, and turn panders to speculators and stock gamblers—when, in consequence of this prostitution of the high powers of legislation, money is made to depreciate one half in the space of a few years—when the price of labour, having become fixed by custom, is, in consequence of the impracticability of a sudden change in occupation, unable to fluctuate with the same facility as that of merchandise—when, taking advantage of this very inability of the labourer, his employer refuses to fix his wages at a price corresponding with the enhanced value of every other commodity, we say the only effectual and justifiable remedy is COMBINATION.

Combinations, Bryant asserted, were a means of self-preservation. If employers could fix the wages of workers without any restraint, the resulting situation, the editor concluded, was tantamount to slavery.

Bryant's political convictions, influenced by the autocratic conditions he had witnessed in Europe, had become more radical, changing even as the very look of New York City had altered during his absence. The great fire that had roared through downtown Manhattan on December 16 and 17, 1835, consuming more than thirteen acres and 674 buildings (but taking, miraculously, only two lives), had resulted in what Bryant thought was a dramatic change in the city's commercial district. "I found New York much changed," he wrote Frances, "the burning of one of the finest quarters of the city, and the building of many elegant new houses, churches, and other public buildings have given it quite a new aspect. Astor's new hotel is a noble edifice of massive granite, and the new University, in the Byzantine style of architecture, is the finest public building in the city." The city's transformation had also produced a mess: "You cannot think what horrid confusion there is here—the burnt district is rebuilding, streets are widening, whole rows of buildings and numerous single ones are demolishing, and one can scarcely pass in some parts of the city for the dust and rubbish."

Chained to the oar, as he complained to Dana, arriving at the *Evening Post* at seven in the morning and working steadily until four in the afternoon, Bryant had little time for poetry. He hastily prepared a third edition of *Poems*, which included a dozen new selections that, with the exception of "Catterskill Falls," had been published in the *New-York Mirror*. Harper's agreed to produce twenty-five hundred copies, for which Bryant would be paid $625 outright and twenty-five cents for every book sold. Bryant wrote to his friend, the artist Robert Weir, with a request: "Can you oblige me so far as to design a vignette for the third edition of my poems which Harpers are about to publish? I want an illustration of my little poem entitled 'Inscription for the Entrance to a Wood.'" In 1834 Bryant had been instrumental in obtaining a teaching position for Weir as instructor of drawing at the United States Military Academy at West Point, and the artist was happy to oblige. Bryant liked Weir's vignette for the title page—"a wild forest with a brook flowing through it, fallen trees lying on the ground, rocks &c." It was the first illustration to appear in an edition of Bryant's poems, and it was accompanied by lines 5 and 6 of "Inscription for the Entrance to a Wood": "—enter this wild wood / and view the haunts of Nature."

Soon after the publication of the third edition of *Poems* in August, Edgar Allan Poe proclaimed in the January 1837 issue of the *Southern Literary Messenger* that "Mr. Bryant's poetical reputation, both at home and abroad, is greater, we presume, than that of any other American." Poe found fault with certain word choices in "The Past" but acknowledged that Bryant was unexcelled in the art of versification and the use of trisyllabic feet. He generally liked the poet's recent productions, praising the "fine imagination" and "noble conception" apparent in "The Prairies" and "Earth." Poe also singled out "Thanatopsis," "To a Waterfowl," and "A Forest Hymn" for their excellence; above all he admired "Oh, Fairest of the Rural Maids," which attained for the critic "the very loftiest order of true Poesy." Still, while Bryant was the first poet of America, Poe concluded that he lacked those spiritual qualities that might place him in the first rank occupied by Shelley, Wordsworth, Coleridge, and Keats.

The *Mirror* reprinted Inman's portrait of Bryant with the caption that his poems "have long since won for him an imperishable name wherever poetry is read." Bryant didn't care for the likeness; for his part, he was uncertain about the future of poetry in America. The world, he feared, was turning away from poetry and preferred novels. He read Miss Sedgwick's *The Linwoods*, which he found to be "interesting but not the best of her works in point of talent." Then there was the Southern novelist William Gilmore Simms, who had been introduced to Bryant in 1832 and who dropped by the *Evening Post* to say hello and ask about a boarding school for his daughter in Northampton; Simms was in New York to oversee publication of *Mellichampe: A Legend of the Santee*. And his friend William Dunlap had just published *Thirty Years Ago; or, Memoirs of a Water Drinker*, which Bryant had not read.

Abandoning his pursuit of the Muse save for an occasional poem like the patriotic "The Green Mountain Boys," written for the ever-obliging *Mirror*, Bryant refined his radical opinions on the nation's major political controversies. To Bryant, the country had become a cauldron of competing interests. At the heart of these controversies was the growing schism between an "aristocracy of wealth" and ordinary citizens. Corrupt congressmen and state legislators, in league with the political aristocrats and other "desperate gamblers," were a danger to American democracy.

With a clear head, serene mind, and perfect digestion, as he boasted to his wife, who was still in Europe, where she was an increasingly irritated witness to the affair between Longfellow and Clara Crowninshield, Bryant resolved to make the *Evening Post* the conscience of the country. Bryant prefaced his editorials with bold type supporting Martin Van Buren for president and Richard M. Johnson for vice president in the upcoming elections. He visited Van Buren at the Astor Hotel, coming away with a renewed appreciation of the political wiles of the Little Magician who was, as Bryant concluded after Van Buren was elected that fall, "a solid and consistent democrat."

Inspired by Leggett, who was slowly recovering from various ailments in May and June, Bryant now took a keen interest in the plight of New York's workingmen. When twenty tailors were convicted of forming an association or "conspiracy" to resist low wages offered by their employers—a "combination" deemed injurious to trade and commerce and therefore a punishable offense—Bryant was outraged. It was a "monstrous doctrine that any two persons may be sent to prison for agreeing together what price they shall set upon their labor." The editor recommended the abrogation of "such a tyrannical and wicked law." His editorials were now a form of cultural performance, a literary stage upon which he could validate the drama of American democracy.

Bryant treated journalism as militant textual production, a self-assertive tool for instructing and molding society. He was appalled by Judge Edwards's imposition of high fines on the workingmen, suggesting that the judge be tried by the same standards. He implied that Edwards was guided by dislike of aliens: "It is somewhat remarkable that Judge Edwards should have supposed that the only persons who dissent from the doctrine he was laying down were a few emigrants from other countries, when the fact is that the Trades Union comprises thousands of native born Americans. But this is not extraordinary in one who in addressing twenty men, of whom eleven were native Americans, told them that they were almost all foreigners."

In several editorials, Bryant equated the law forbidding combinations with European forms of servitude and with American slavery, pointing out its logical absurdities. "Can any one be so weak as to dream of realizing, in the State of New York, and in the nineteenth century, the resurrection of the services of feudal villenage?" Bryant exulted when fellow journeymen collected funds to pay the tailors' fines, while attacking once again the "base and barbarous" law under which the tailors had been convicted. "They were condemned because they had determined not to work for wages that were offered them! Can any thing be imagined more abhorrent to every sentiment of generosity or justice, than the law which arms the rich with the legal right to fix, by assize, the wages of the poor." He exulted when, in July, striking shoemakers in Hudson, New York, were acquitted of similar charges.

Bryant had become a Loco Foco. Starting one editorial in typically droll fashion, he ridiculed the Albany *Argus*, which like Spanish nurses trying to frighten children with tales of goblins, attempted to terrify readers with tales of Loco Focos who possessed horns, claws, and monstrous tails. In fact, Bryant asserted, the antimonopoly party in the city had "excellent principles, upright intentions, and disinterested conduct," and it would be a formidable force in local politics. The opposition press hated Bryant's figurative style and mordant wit. "Every editorial of Bryant opens with a stale joke and closes with a fresh lie," sniped one jealous Whig. But Bryant argued from a position of literary and intellectual dominance. No other editor could match his cultural authority.

II

The *Evening Post* moved to 43 Pine Street on May 1, and shortly thereafter Bryant cautioned against the premature admission of Texas into the Union. He realized that there were forces scheming to admit Texas as a slave state. Southerners, speculators, owners of Texas land, and other "sordid types" were joining with members of Congress to achieve independence for Texas and its admittance into the Union. It was absurd, Bryant wrote, to hear of Americans anxious to rush to Texas to defend Texans against the depredations of Santa Ana. It would be better, he declared, if those impassioned adventurers turned their "martial ardour" to fighting in the Creek and Seminole wars.

The central argument over the admission of Texas as a state centered on the contest between slavery and free soil, a subject that Bryant had addressed more than fifteen years earlier. In May, when John Quincy Adams, now an outspoken Congressman, was defeated in his effort to guarantee the reception of abolitionist petitions, Bryant railed against this "gag" rule designed to "shackle the expression of opinion." With his experience of European political culture still fresh in his mind, he condemned the "tyrannical doctrines and measures of Mr. Calhoun":

> It is too late an age to copy the policy of Henry VIII; we lie too far in the occident to imitate the despotic rule of Austria. The spirit of our people has been too long accustomed to freedom to bear the restraint which is sought to be put upon it. Discussion will be like the Greek fire, which blazed the fiercer for the water thrown upon it; and if the stake be set and the faggots ready, there will be candidates for martyrdom.

Bryant was sounding like an abolitionist. In June, he advocated the end of slavery in the District of Columbia. Soon he would excoriate his friend Van Buren, after the Little Magician's election to the presidency, for his pledge to veto any attempt to abolish slavery there. Early in August, when a Cincinnati mob numbering between four and five thousand people smashed the press of abolitionist James G. Birney, Bryant rushed to his defense, castigating the "noisy fanatics" who had trampled on freedom of expression and a free press. "We are resolved that the subject of slavery shall be as it ever has been, as free a subject of discussion and argument and declamation, as the difference between Whiggism and democracy, or as the difference between the Arminians and the Calvinists."

Bryant was not deceived by the Whigs, whom he viewed as a motley collection of conservatives masquerading as the "People's party." At the outset, the Whigs were a loose assemblage of factions rather than a party unified by any coherent ideology other than a fierce dislike of President Jackson. Hudson River patricians, unreconstructed Federalists, powerful merchants such as Philip Hone and Cornelius Vanderbilt, Antimasons,

Nativists, pro-tariff businessmen, and western New York farmers demanding internal improvements formed the core of the Whig movement in the city and state. Influential Whigs included the jovial Albany editor and political operative Thurlow Weed and a young, ungainly, and tempestuous newspaperman, Horace Greeley, who had worked briefly at the *Evening Post* until Leggett had fired him because of Greeley's unkempt condition. Now the publisher and editor of his own weekly paper, the *New Yorker*, at this stage in his career the homely Greeley was a Whig enthusiast, opposing the antislavery movement and workingmen's combinations. The controversial Greeley would change his opinions and political allegiances repeatedly. Bryant would never like or trust him.

When the *American*, a conservative city daily, questioned the *Evening Post*'s patriotism, Bryant summarized his case against the Whigs, who had polled strongly in the city elections of 1834 and who, in the wake of the April 1836 election, shared control of the city council with Tammany Democrats:

> Who stirred up the genteel mob of this city to break up the meetings of the Anti-Slavery Society, and to make its principal members flee for their lives? The conductors of whig prints—the men who are "ready to defend the liberty of the press with their heart's blood." Who inflamed the Cincinnati mob to break open the office of the Philanthropist, destroy its types, throw its press into the river, and hunt its editor as if he were a wolf? The instigators of that infamous mob comprehended some of the leading whigs of the city. Who introduced in Congress the gag law—the law of censorship by means of the Post Office—a measure so arbitrary and tyrannical as to shock even many of his own artisans? John C. Calhoun, the vile leader of the southern whigs. Who have clamoured the most loudly for penal laws to be passed in the northern states, compelling the press to silence on the subject of slavery? The southern whigs—the defenders of the liberty of the press at the price of their "heart's blood."

Bryant predicted that the conservative forces building locally and nationally could lead the nation to ruin.

To Bryant, William Henry Harrison, the Whig candidate for the presidency, was another sad commentary on reactionary America. In editorials leading up to the November election, Bryant lambasted the General for his "incapacity . . . pretensions . . . imbecility and weakness."

Even Bryant's friend Morse, who had run for mayor as the candidate of the American Nativist Party, had succumbed to reactionary dogma that was at odds with the democratic ideals Bryant promoted. Bryant exulted when Van Buren was elected to the presidency, carrying New York State by 28,000 votes and winning 170 national electoral votes against a total of 124 for his three opponents. The editor praised the Little Magician as "a sound and consistent democrat."

Despite Van Buren's election, Bryant worried about the nation's feverish economic condition. Soon after his return from Europe, Bryant sensed that an overheated real estate market, a proliferation of unregulated local and state banks, wild speculation in currency and commodities, and runaway inflation were creating the conditions for an economic collapse. "When will the bubble burst?" he wondered. "When will the great catastrophe which the banks have been preparing for us actually come about?" In October, Bryant claimed in an *Evening Post* editorial that the "financial storm" already was out of control. Predicting a monetary panic, he warned that the growing economic storm would spawn "a tornado over the land," leaving "wreckage scattered in its path." This parlous state of affairs was not the fault of the Jackson administration's economic policies, as opposition papers and their foolishly inept supporters implied. True, Jackson had destroyed the Bank of the United States, resulting in a proliferation of unregulated state and local banks. Moreover, that July the president had proposed and Congress had passed the Specie Circular, decreeing that the government would accept only gold and silver in payment for western lands, which did little to dampen inflation or discourage speculation. The financial condition of the nation, Bryant warned in a succession of editorials, was ominous.

Leggett, who along with a " drunken and saucy clerk" named Hannah had caused many of the *Post*'s financial problems, had returned to the newspaper in September. Bryant took the opportunity to get away from political battles for a week to travel to Great Barrington with William Gilmore Simms, who had come from South Carolina to see the poet. Simms enjoyed his walks with Bryant through the Berkshires countryside. They rambled along the banks of the Green River, reminding Bryant once again, as he had written more than a decade earlier, that fate had not left him "free / To wander these quiet haunts." They climbed Monument Mountain, overlooking the valley of the Housatonic, whose "shaggy and wild" precipice had prompted Bryant to tell a sentimental tale of an Indian girl who had thrown herself from the steep rock out of "unlawful" love of a cousin.

Bryant's vacation, as well as Leggett's return to the *Evening Post*, was short-lived. On November 1, the paper announced that the partnership between Leggett, Bryant, and Mrs. Coleman had been dissolved. Leggett issued a prospectus for his own newspaper, *The Plaindealer*. Two days later, Bryant wrote a tribute to Leggett and his eight-year association with the paper: "The readers of the *Evening Post* have admired, on a multitude of occasions, his strong sense, his large and comprehensive views of publick policy, his ardours in the cause of truth, his detestation of oppression and unjust restraint in all their forms, his perspicacity in discovering abuses and his boldness in exposing them without regard to personal consequences, and the manly, unstudied eloquence which riveted the attention and persuaded the judgment of the reader."

Leggett's penchant for vituperation and editorial excess reflected in the first issues of the *Plaindealer* almost caused an awkward rupture in Bryant's friendship with Washington Irving. The two writers were not close friends, owing to Irving's seventeen-year residence abroad, but they respected each other. Leggett, however, charged that Irving had meddled with Bryant's poetry during the London publication of *Poems*, which Irving had been so instrumental in promoting. In the January 14 issue of the *Plaindealer*, Leggett wrote that it was "contemptible" that Irving had changed a line in "Song of Marion's Men" from "The British soldier trembles" to "The foeman trembles in his camp" so as not to offend English sensibilities. Such alteration, Leggett charged, revealed an "unmanly timidity which is afraid to let the public see the truth."

Irving, who had returned to America in 1832 and was living quietly at his estate in Tarrytown, north of the city, was shocked by Leggett's charge of "literary pusillanimity." He also suspected that Bryant must have known about his "bosom friend's" accusations and might even have approved them. Replying to the charges in a January 28 letter to the *Plaindealer*, which Leggett published with a note absolving Bryant of any knowledge of the editor's criticism, Irving justified his decision to alter "Song of Marion's Men" in order to prevent any "prejudice against the work." In fact, Irving had written to Bryant in 1832 to tell him of the alteration: "I have taken the . . . liberty of altering two or three words in the little poem of Marion's Men—since they might startle the pride of John Bull in your first introduction to him." Bryant was also shocked by this unpleasant contretemps, and in a letter to the *Plaindealer* he indicated that although he would not have made the alterations himself, he had never complained of the changes made by

Irving to the poem extolling the exploits of the "Swamp Fox" of Revolutionary War fame. At the same time, Bryant expressed surprise that his "particular friend and literary associate" had suspected that he had been party to Leggett's intemperate criticism. Irving closed the controversy with apologies to Bryant that were printed in the *American*, regretting that he had made the changes, because "it is difficult to alter a word without marring a beauty."

The controversy with Irving was an unsought and upsetting distraction, but Bryant had more important matters to deal with as a new year began. Frances, Fanny, and Julia had returned from Europe in November, and Bryant's old buoyancy resurfaced. Moreover, another boarder at the house on Fourth Street, a twenty-year-old "briefless barrister" named Parke Godwin, offered intelligent conversation during their evenings together. In characteristically slanted language reflecting the difficult relationship that would develop between the two men, Godwin described his future father-in-law at the time of their first meeting:

> He was of middle age and medium height, spare in his figure, with a clean-shaven face, unusually large head, bright eyes, and a wearied, severe, almost saturnine expression of countenance. One, however, remarked at once the exceeding gentleness of his manner, and a rare sweetness in the tone of his voice, as well as an extraordinary purity in his selection and pronunciation of English. His conversation was easy, but not fluent, and he had a habit of looking the person he addressed so directly in the eyes that it was not a little embarrassing at first. A certain air of abstractedness in his face made you set him down as a scholar whose thoughts were wandering away to his books; and yet the deep lines about the mouth told of struggle either with himself or with the world. No one would have supposed that there was any fun in him, but, when a lively turn was given to some remark, the upper part of his face, particularly the eyes, gleamed with a singular radiance, and a short, quick, staccato, but hearty laugh acknowledged the humorous perception. It was scarcely acknowledged, however, before the face settled down again into its habitual sternness. . . .

Needing assistance at the *Evening Post* when an employee, Henry Ulshoeffer, announced that he was leaving because of poor health, Bryant offered Godwin a position at the paper as a reporter.

III

As the Panic of 1837 took hold, Bryant watched a city and nation spiraling downward. In New York City, the price of flour tripled over 1834 levels, while the cost of pork doubled. Grain, coal prices, and rents were also skyrocketing. Gotham's citizens, abetted by penny papers like the *Herald* and the *New Era*, suspected that "monopolists" were hoarding produce in order to drive up prices. In February, with snow and ice covering the city's streets, Loco Foco leaders called a public rally at City Hall to proclaim their grievances. Posters announced "BREAD, MEAT, RENT, FUEL! THE PRICES MUST COME DOWN!" Bryant's *Evening Post*, along with the *Herald*, urged participation in the rally.

Monday the thirteenth was the coldest day of the winter, but some five thousand New Yorkers braved whipping winds to show up for the rally at City Park. Loco Foco leaders warmed the crowd with fiery speeches denouncing everything from paper currency to ferry monopolies. Other speakers attacked merchants whom they charged were hoarding foodstuffs in order to drive prices even higher. When the final speaker, unknown to Loco Foco organizers, inflamed the crowd with a call to march on Hart and Company's flour store on Washington Street, a riot ensued. The mob broke through the barricade that had been hastily erected around the building and ransacked the counting room. Hundreds of barrels of flour and sacks of wheat were thrown out windows to the crowd below before the mob next marched to the South Street store of E. and J. Herrick, which it spared when a company official convinced the rioters that the firm was selling flour at low prices. Onward the mob surged to S. H. Herrick and Son at Coenties Slip, where more destruction occurred. Not until nine o'clock that night, after Mayor Cornelius Lawrence had called out the militia, was the flour riot suppressed.

The next day, Bryant excoriated the rioters. The "scene of disorder and violence" that took place, which a "feeble" police force did little to suppress, brought dishonor to the community. Moreover, the *Courier* and the *Express*, whose editors insinuated that the *Evening Post* was responsible for the riots by having recommended that New Yorkers attend the meeting, were unethical and misinformed. Never, he insisted, had the *Post* recommended "illegal violence of any kind," which could not be said of the opposition press.

In his editorial for Thursday, February 16, Bryant returned to the controversy, criticizing "corrupt journalists" working for the *Commercial Advertiser* and other "kindred prints" for having caused the abolitionist riots and the heightened hostility to workers. Papers contributing to a culture of popular violence would "gather in the harvest of the tempest. The beast of prey which was uncaged to destroy an adversary, having tasted blood, turns to attack those who, in their folly, let him loose."

Bryant, feeling like a "draft horse harnessed to the wain of a daily paper," was in a sour mood about the state of his city and nation. To Dana, his closest literary confidant, he wrote that "the affairs of the republic give me no little trouble. You cannot imagine how difficult it is to make the world go right." The Whig victory in the mayoral and Common Council elections that spring demonstrated that even inept fools when united could defeat a divided opposition. "We have only to thank our own folly," Bryant lamented in a censorious editorial. At times it was hard to promote the democratic ethos.

To Bryant, the plight of the city was epitomized in its Whig mayor, Aaron Clark, a bigoted party hack who attacked immigrants despite his own poor command of English. The "nonsense" and "falsehood" as well as the sheer ungrammaticality of Clark's hostility toward the city's burgeoning immigrant population suggested to Bryant both a childish mind and party bigotry. "Mr. Clark has wronged the character of the emigrants from Europe, by the sweeping misrepresentation that they are a class of paupers; his accusation that they are a race of felons and incendiaries, who have caused all the disturbances of the peace which have taken place in this country, is grossly untrue." Immigrants were building the canals and railroads and engaging in every species of labor necessary to construct a great nation. If they could not find employment in New York City, then sensible plans should be made to transport them to the fertile soils of the West. After all, "Those who complain of the multitude of emigrants daily arriving on our shores should not have forgot that it is ourselves who have invited them over."

Surveying the national scene, Bryant was disturbed by a grotesque convergence of political forces consisting of "Websterists," partisans of General Harrison ("who is so tickled with the idea of having been made a candidate once that its is said he is determined to try it again"), adherents of Clay, and supporters of that arch nullifier, Calhoun. Bryant was amazed by the contradictions inherent in such a political alignment. "The states' rights party are to be made to support an advocate of the extreme doctrines of free construction—the enemies of the tariff are to be persuaded to vote for the friend of a high tariff . . . the opposers of internal improvements are to be won over to a champion of high internal improvement doctrines—in fine, the whole south and west are to be brought to accept a candidate of the most peculiar northern and eastern school." Such a marriage of political opposites could not succeed.

Bryant composed a droll editorial suggesting that Americans were witnessing the decline—at least in Whig eyes—of Calhoun. "The other day he towered to a height like that of Milton's arch-fiend," but now he is "shrunk to size no larger than that of the same personage whom he lay 'squat at the ear of Eve.'" Warming to his subject, Bryant likened Calhoun to a fallen colossus before moving to the anecdote of a hunter who, having caught a rabbit, thought that the hare would taste good prepared any number of ways—before the rabbit escaped, leaving the hunter to charge that it was only a "dry-meat animal." Likewise, Mr. Calhoun "was once good in a speech, good at a report, good in defence, particularly good in an attack." But now, supporting the Van Buren administration on at least one salient issue, he had become for the Whigs a "good-for-nothing dry-meated animal." Bryant's rhetorical flourish reinforced his authority.

The Whigs and their sympathizers were proving themselves fools on so many fronts that Bryant could find a sense of the comic in their follies. Yet the excesses of such political marriages of convenience could be dangerous. Especially vexing to Bryant were the continuing demands of Southerners and other states' rights partisans for the admission of Texas to the Union. The Texas project was "a great evil, a great misfortune, and a monstrous anomaly" threatening to convulse the Republic. There was a heightened public anxiety and disturbance in the air that worried Bryant. To William Ware, who had resigned his Unitarian pastorate in New York and retired to a literary life in Brookline, Massachusetts, Bryant confessed that the world his friend had left was "noisy and agitated still, but with the working of fiercer though not stronger passions."

These passions erupted in November when the abolitionist editor Elijah P. Lovejoy was murdered by a proslavery mob attacking his press in Alton, Illinois. Bryant immediately wrote a ringing condemnation of the "atrocious violence" and destruction of the *Observer*'s premises and press. To Bryant, freedom of the press was so intimately connected to other liberties in America that to "muzzle the press by the fear of violence" could only lead to despotism and anarchy. Such a "bloody outrage" could not be countenanced in a free, open society.

Shortly after the Alton, Illinois, incident, a Whig mob smashed the office of the Democratic *Aurora* in Norwich, Connecticut, injuring its editor. Bryant readily signed a petition proposing a meeting to demand an end to Congress's gag rule and defending freedom of the press. Replying

to a correspondent, he reiterated that "liberty of the press, and the repro-
bation of unlawful violence—matters concerning which one would think
there could be but one opinion,—and yet recent events, not merely the
death of Lovejoy, but others, like the attack on the newspaper press at
Norwich, admonish us, that it is time for the friends of liberty, law and
peace to give a decided and emphatic expression to the light in which they
regard them." Bryant attended the meeting of 150 New Yorkers that was
held in Clinton Hall on January 28, 1838. The participants approved and
sent to Congress, which had renewed the gag rule in December despite
furious opposition from Northern lawmakers, a petition affirming that
"the liberty of the press, of speech, and the right of petition, are among
the greatest blessings and proudest prerogatives of a free people."

As 1837 drew to a close, Bryant saw signs of a more hopeful year
ahead, but he reminded readers of the financial tempest that had swept
the nation and of the rise in public violence. "Over all the world a change
is going on favorable to human liberty; power is diffusing itself from the
center to the masses. Mankind are growing and more democratic in all
civilized nations." Even in Europe, public opinion was turning against
absolute monarchy, preventing rulers like the emperor of Austria from
ruling "like the King of the Ashantees." Bryant's democratic sentiments
were global in reach.

By mid-year Bryant even saw slight improvement in the financial
affairs of the *Evening Post*. The semiannual dividend announced on May
16, 1838, was four hundred dollars more than that of the previous
November, a modest increase that was encouraging during hard times.
Bryant was still deeply in debt—some twenty thousand, he confided to
Rand in a letter—and was working long hours at the newspaper. Friends
and family worried about his health. Frances wrote to Mrs. William
Ware: "You cannot think how distressed I am about his working so
hard." Leggett, burdened by his failing newspaper enterprises and in
poor health himself, found time to write a confidential letter to Van
Buren suggesting that the president quietly provide government assistance to the *Evening Post*.

Bryant, unaware of Leggett's overtures, never heard from Van Buren.
He had assumed a stoical air, reveling in the good health that enabled him
to work so hard. Admitting to a degree of egotism, he wrote Dana, "To
keep myself in health I take long walks in the country for half a day, a day
or two days . . . and I accustom myself to the greatest simplicity of diet,
renouncing tea, coffee, animal food &c. . . . when I am fagged I hearken to
nature and allow her to recruit." Dana was shocked on learning about

Bryant's financial condition: "I had taken it for granted that you had all along been doing well in your paper, and that, if your desires did not enlarge along with your means, you would, in a very few years at farthest, go back into the country, and chime song once more with your own Green River." He told Bryant that he had seen their mutual friend, the artist Washington Alston, who praised "Green River." "That man," Alston declared, "is a true poet, his *heart* is in it." It saddened Dana to think of his friend laboring on the "dusty public highway, and your flower-pot all the while lying waste." Another Bostonian, Ralph Waldo Emerson, also lamented Bryant's preoccupation with public affairs. He wrote to Margaret Fuller after a trip to New York City, "I saw Bryant, but his poetry seems exterminated from the soil not a violet left—the field stiff all over with thistles and teazles of politics."

Bryant confessed as much to Dana: "I have no time for poetry." Chained to the oar, he had found time to write only one poem the previous year, "The Battle-field," which was published in the *Democratic Review* that October. He conceived the lyric as an ode to the fallen patriots of the Revolutionary War. But after four quatrains, the poem veered into a confession of "the harder strife" as Bryant struggled to save the *Evening Post*. Poetry and other literary pursuits had to wait. Bryant the editor was needed in the battle between truth and falsehood then sweeping the nation:

> A friendless warfare! lingering long
>   Through weary day and weary year,
> A wild and many-weaponed throng
>   Hang on thy front, and flank, and rear.
>
> Yet nerve they spirit to the proof,
>   And blanch not at thy chosen lot.
> The timid good may stand aloof,
>   The sage may frown—yet faint thou not.

Resurrecting the mordant imagery characteristic of his verse, Bryant lamented that only death could vindicate his editorial battles. Perhaps, he concluded in "The Battle-field," he would be remembered as a warrior who sought truth in his time—and a "blast of triumph" would echo over his grave.

Bryant's friends in the literary and artistic worlds were scattered, and he felt their absence. Cooper was in Cooperstown but wrote letters

to the *Evening Post* threatening lawsuits against libelous newspaper publishers. Invariably successful in his legal battles, he visited Bryant at the
office whenever he was in town. (Bryant praised Cooper's *The American
Democrat* in an April review, calling attention to its "clearness, acuteness, and perfect independence in the expression of his opinions.")
Morse was off to Europe and, in any case, associating with reactionary
elements. Verplanck, too, had drifted into the Whig camp; the two old
friends saw each other infrequently. Cole was in Catskill on the Hudson,
leaving Bryant to recommend two of his "glorious landscapes" at the
annual exhibit of the Academy of Design. Robert Sedgwick had suffered
an apoplectic stroke that spring and was trying to recover in the Rock-
aways. William Dunlap also was ill: the veteran painter, playwright, historian, and theatrical impresario who had just published a life of Charles
Brockden Brown was very old and very poor. He would die soon after a
benefit organized to assist him that November. The self-styled editor of
"a principle democratic newspaper in the first city of America" was
fighting a lonely battle.

Even the city seemed to conspire against Bryant. Beggars, the tangi-
ble residue of the Panic years, were everywhere. The streets were filthy
during the hot summer months, prompting Bryant to compose a pungent editorial describing the "masses of vegetable and animal offal steam-
ing in the sun." Conditions reminded the editor of Dante's description of
"the most offensive region in the future abode of the wicked." The
Whigs, triumphant once again in fall elections, were "profligate" in their
indifference to declining civic culture and notorious for their bribery.
Whigs were "essentially gullible," much like young crows who, when
leaving their nest for the first time, would eat anything—just like the
readers of Whig newspapers.

Certain Whig newspapers like the *Evening Star* were even making
feeble attempts to compose editorials in "blank verse." Bryant reprinted
nine lines from a *Star* editorial, offering his jaundiced assessment: "Very
appropriately this is called blank verse. It is blank of rhythm of course.
In the second place it is blank of meter. Thirdly and lastly it is blank of
meaning. It is therefore entitled to the appellation of blank verse by a
triple right, being utterly and absolutely blank of all the attributes which
constitute verse."

More to Bryant's liking than inane poetic editorials were volumes of
verse published by John Greenleaf Whittier and William Gilmore
Simms. In a review for the *Evening Post*, Bryant praised the "flowing
and spirited" tone pervading Whittier's *Poems* and reprinted Whittier's

"The Moral Warfare." According to Bryant, the Quaker emancipationist wrote poetry designed "to kindle a warlike courage in the minds of his countrymen." Poetry could be cultural performance, assisting the cause of democracy.

Simms, by contrast, was a poet of southern landscapes whose descriptive powers often wandered "into a shadowy metaphysical region, whither it is not always easy to follow him." Still, poems like "The Edge of the Swamp," printed in entirety in the *Evening Post*, and "Indian Village" offered "a striking delineation of the peculiar scenery of the south."

As for Bryant, his entire production for the year had been a translation from the Latin of a fragment in memory of a dead dog that he had inserted into the *Evening Post* and a five-quatrain poem, "The Death of Schiller," published in the *Democratic Review*. Like Schiller on his deathbed, Bryant was yearning to "wander forth wherever lie / The homes and haunts of humankind"—sailing to Rome, Egypt, "Hindoo caves," or even the New World's forest streams. But the poet was obliged by his incessant editorial responsibilities, as he wrote to William Ware, "to write more than he cares for." The poet was trapped in the harder strife.

IV

"The sky now begins to brighten," Bryant wrote to his brother Cyrus at the beginning of 1839. Confessing to hard times after his return from Europe and the perilous state of the *Evening Post* that might have forced him "to discontinue the paper and go into the world again loaded with debt," Bryant now felt that he had weathered the storm. The newspaper's dividends for the year ending November 16, 1838, had totaled $5,013.13, an increase of nearly $2,800 over the previous year. But the effort to restore the paper's solvency had absorbed all of Bryant's energy, and Frances lamented that her husband's only writing during this period had been editorials for the *Evening Post*.

Although the *Evening Post*'s circulation in its daily and semiweekly papers was modest when matched against the penny and twopenny sheets of James Gordon Bennett's *Herald*, Benjamin Day's *Sun*, or Horace Greeley's new *Tribune*, influential Americans now viewed its editor as not only the country's most famous poet but also a formidable voice in national affairs. With his best editorials—allusive, inventive, and beautifully cadenced—readers could detect traces of the poet. Bryant revealed a poet's talents in his New Year's message to the *Evening Post*'s readers on Friday, January 4. In his editorial, Bryant composed a hymn to the Republic—a tribute to a new nation that resembled a "spectacle" and reflected "some elements of the sublime." The poet-editor depicted the United States as a "living flood," rolling across varied and pictur-esque lands, nurturing communities, and moving inexorably toward the Pacific where, before the end of the century, Americans would fashion new cities. Finally abandoning his extended metaphor to acknowledge the violence and dissension of the past year, Bryant ended his editorial by claiming that these political disruptions would ultimately yield to the enlightened and peaceful spirit of the American people.

But before that utopian future could be achieved, Americans would have to refine their tastes, communities—especially New York City—would have to attend to their problems, and politicians would have to improve their ethics. Scarcely had the new year started when Bryant made a plea to readers not to let George Catlin take his collection Indian artifacts and his own artwork, on exhibit in the city, to England. If kept in the United States, the collection could form the basis of an "Aborigi-nal Museum." In a similar vein, Bryant scoffed at the public's reaction to his friend Fenimore Cooper's critique of the American character in his latest work, *Home Is Found*. Only thin-skinned and shortsighted people worried about how people overseas might respond to Cooper's "ani-madversions on American manners." Great reformers, preachers, and satirists throughout the ages, Bryant reminded his audience, never wor-ried about public responses to their work.

Turning to the local political scene, Bryant composed a series of edi-torials accusing the city's Whig mayor, Aaron Clark, and the Common Council of "monstrous corruption and profligate expenditures. . . . Let any of our readers take up the report of the Comptroller of this city for the present year and observe how three millions and a half of the public money, part raised by taxes, part obtained by selling Water stock, and part received from the sale of property belonging to the city, are parceled among certain favored members of the whig party." The mayor, commis-sioners of the Alms House, the superintendent of buildings, the chief engineer, street commissioners, and the Corporation attorney: all were scoundrels engaged in "generous confidence and magnanimous indul-gence." With the victory of the Democrats in the April elections, Bryant congratulated New Yorkers for their common sense in electing a new mayor, Isaac Varian, who was noted for his "honesty, sense and humanity," and in installing new members of a Common Council who were pledged to reform.

In a hitherto uncollected ode that he composed for the semicentennial anniversary of the inauguration of George Washington on April 30, Bryant returned to the theme of the nation's potential greatness. The splendid affair was sponsored by the Historical Society and held at the Middle Dutch Church, with a four o'clock dinner at the City Hotel. At the church, Bryant's ode reminded a distinguished gathering that included John Quincy Adams, General Winfield Scott, and the governor of New Jersey of the Republic's origins and its unique destiny:

> Great were the hearts, and strong the minds
>   Of those who framed, in high debate,
> The immortal league of love that binds
>   Our fair broad empire, state with state.
>
> And ever hallowed be the hour,
>   When, as the auspicious task was done,
> In solemn trust, the sword of power
>   Was given to Glory's unspoiled son.
>
> That noble race is gone; the suns
>   Of fifty years have risen and set;
> But the bright links those chosen ones
>   So strongly forged are brighter yet.
>
> Wide—as our own free race increase—
>   Wide shall extend the elastic chain,
> And hold in everlasting peace,
>   State after state, a mighty train.

After Bryant presented his ode, former president Adams, now a venerable member of the House of Representatives, delivered an oration in which he likened the founders of the Republic to the children of Israel on their entrance to the Promised Land. Asked to speak again at the luncheon, Adams alluded to Bryant's earlier poetic presentation of the Revolutionary period as the heroic age in the country's history.

Bryant found fewer heroes populating his own age, but one notable figure of greatness, he felt, was his friend and former partner William Leggett. No one had done more to steel Bryant's sympathies for the working class and the sanctity of free speech than Leggett. Now his friend, practically destitute, was living with his wife in a New Rochelle house purchased for them by Edwin Forrest. Prone to debilitating colic attacks, deeply in debt after the failure of *The Plaindealer* and a second newspaper, *The Examiner*, Leggett depended on loyal friends like Forrest, who paid his debts, and Bryant, who tried to find him work.

Bryant set out to secure a federal appointment for his friend, applying to President Van Buren on behalf of Leggett to obtain a diplomatic post to Guatemala, the capital of the Central American Republic. Writing to the president after learning that Leggett would be appointed a confidential agent, Bryant suggested that the position and pay be upgraded to that of chargé d'affaires. "I write in behalf of a most meritorious individual, in whom a large number of persons in this community take a strong interest, but the ease of whose pecuniary circumstances bears no proportion to his deserts." The president replied that Leggett would receive better financial terms as a confidential agent than as chargé d'affaires, a post that Van Buren did not consider appropriate for diplomatic reasons.

Bryant announced Leggett's appointment as confidential agent to the Republic of Central America in a May 25 editorial. The administration, Bryant wrote, did honor to itself by employing a person of Leggett's merits. Moreover, the *Evening Post* was hopeful that "a sea voyage and a residence for a few months in the benignant climate of Guatemala" would improve Leggett's health. That nation, with its temperate climate and "ancient aboriginal cities" that were "far superior in civilization and the arts to any that existed before the continent was discovered by Columbus," was a worthy destination for a person of Leggett's talents.

Leggett was preparing to depart for Central America when, on the evening of May 29, 1839, he died from an acute attack of colic. He was thirty-nine years old. The following day, Bryant eulogized his friend in an editorial. Commending the force, clarity, and fluency of Leggett's style, Bryant reminded readers of the ways in which his friend used his literary powers for worthy causes. A defender of the most comprehensive equality of rights and liberty for Americans, Leggett warred against opinions and legislative measures designed to foster inequality and distrust. "We sorrow that such a man, so clear-sighted, strong minded and magnanimous has passed away, and that his aid is no more to be given in the conflict which truth and liberty maintain with their numerous and powerful enemies."

Reviled by numerous opponents in his lifetime and criticized even by radical Democrats for his excesses, in death Leggett became the apotheosis of the courageous promoter of the rights of all Americans. Whitman called him "the glorious Leggett," while Whittier extolled the man's "free and honest thought, / The angel utterance of an upright mind." Following the funeral and internment in New Rochelle, Bryant wrote the epitaph that would be engraved on Leggett's monument: that he "loved truth for its own sake . . . and raised his voice against all injustice on whomsoever committed and whoever were its authors." With Theodore Sedgwick, Jr., Bryant selected and arranged Leggett's publications into two volumes, *A Collection of the Political Writings of William Leggett* (1840), in an effort to aid the widow. Forrest purchased Leggett's library with the same aim in mind.

Bryant, who had written a biographical sketch of Leggett for the *Democratic Review* prior to his death, memorialized him in verse. Published in the November 1839 issue of the *Democratic Review*, the four quatrains of "In Memory of William Leggett" offer sentiments that Bryant honored in his capacity as the *Evening Post*'s editor:

> The earth may ring, from shore to shore,
>   With echoes of a glorious name,
> But he, whose loss our tears deplore,
>   Has left behind him more than fame.
>
> For when the death-frost came to lie
>   On Leggett's warm and mighty heart,
> And quench his bold and friendly eye,
>   His spirit did not all depart.
>
> The words of fire from his pen
>   Were flung upon the fervid page,
> Still move, still shake the hearts of men,
>   Amid a cold and coward age.
>
> His love of truth, too warm, too strong
>   For Hope or Fear to chain or chill,

His hate of tyranny and wrong,
    Burn in the breasts he kindled still.

Inspired by Leggett, Bryant would wield his own fiery pen to confront what he was coming to believe was a cold and coward age.

9

POLITICS AND POETRY

It is our belief that Mr. Bryant is not only the very first of American poets, but that, with perhaps one eminent living exception, he is the first living poet in the world.
—Lewis Gaylord Clark, *Knickerbocker Magazine*, September 1842

I

On September 19, 1839, at the start of the *Amistad* case in Hartford, Connecticut, the *Emancipator*, an abolitionist newsletter based in New York City, reprinted Bryant's "The African Chief," which opened with these lines:

Chained in the market-place he stood,
　　A man of giant frame,
Amid the gathering multitude
　　That shrunk to hear his name—
All stern of look and strong of limb,
　　His dark eye on the ground:—
And silently they gazed on him
　　As on a lion bound.

Vainly, but well, that chief had fought,
　　He was a captive now;
Yet pride, that fortune humbles not,
　　Was written on his brow.

157

The scars his dark broad bosom wore
  Showed warrior true and brave;
A prince among his tribe before,
  He could not be a slave.

In early 1839, five hundred African captives had been packed aboard a Spanish slave ship, the *Tecora*. The ship was bound for Cuba in contravention of laws agreed to by Spain that had outlawed the importation of slaves into the New World. Spirited into Havana at night, the Africans were kept in prison and were then auctioned off as if they had always been slaves. In June, Jose Ruiz and his associate Pedro Montes purchased fifty-three Africans from the *Tecora* for $450 each. One of the slaves, a twenty-five year old from the Mende interior of Sierre Leone, was later given the name Joseph Cinqué by the press. Ruiz and Montes planned to take the slaves in a boat, the *Amistad*, to Puerto Principe, another location in Cuba.

On June 30, as the *Amistad* made its way along the Cuban coast, Cinqué freed himself and the other Africans, broke into the weapons storage room, killed the captain and cook, and took Ruiz and Montes hostage. Cinqué then commanded Montes to steer the *Amistad* back to Africa. By day, Montes sailed slowly eastward, but at night he reversed course and sailed northwest, arriving off the coast of Long Island in late August. There the American patrol boat U.S.S. *Washington* captured the Africans, ten of whom had died during their passage, secured the ship, and steered the *Amistad* into the port of New London, Connecticut (a state where slavery was still legal), on August 27, 1839. A federal district judge, Andrew T. Judson, held an inquiry aboard the *Washington* and decided that the Africans would be temporarily held in New Haven and then sent to Hartford, where a grand jury of the United States Circuit Court was scheduled to convene.

Readers readily understood the aptness of Bryant's opening lines: the African chief in his heroic stature resembled Joseph Cinqué. Bryant sympathized with the Africans who had rebelled against their captivity and had been apprehended in American waters.

From the beginning of the inquiry to its resolution two years later before the United States Supreme Court, Bryant took an avid interest in the *Amistad* affair. Theodore Sedgwick, Jr., the son of his good friend, who contributed articles under the pseudonym Veto and helped occasionally with editorials for the *Evening Post*, was one of the three defense lawyers for the captives. Moreover, Bryant had defended the work of the wealthy New Yorker, Lewis Tappan, one of the founders of the American Anti-Slavery Society and a principal in the hastily established *Amistad* Committee, which had been organized to raise money for the Africans' legal expenses.

Bryant's first editorial on the *Amistad* affair, laying out the legal basis for freeing the Africans, appeared in the *Evening Post* on September 4, 1839: "These men it appears were not born in slavery, but were captives newly deprived of their liberty and brought to the island of Cuba, from the coast of Africa." Two points, the *Evening Post* claimed, had to be considered: whether the courts of the United States had any jurisdiction in the matter; and whether the slaves claimed by the Spanish authorities should be given up. As to the first question, it was doubtful that any American court had jurisdiction over a crime that was strictly a Spanish affair. Any answer to the second question was troublesome, stated the *Evening Post*, which then provided a graphic description of the "heinous crime" of the importation of slaves—"to the cruel separation of members of families, and to the most horribly barbarous treatment in their transportation from their native country to America." Nevertheless, despite the repugnance felt by the *Evening Post*, if the owner purchased the men as slaves in Cuba, in all likelihood they must be delivered up—but not before a thorough examination of the case.

The next day, on further inquiry into the *Amistad* affair, Bryant reversed course, arguing that the Africans should not be surrendered to Spanish authorities. He wrote, "we find that the slave trade has been prohibited in Spain and its dependencies since the year 1820. A treaty was entered into between Great Britain and Spain in 1814, by which after 1820 the slave trade was to cease. To carry the prohibition into effect a mixed commission of Spanish and British authorities was established to condemn vessels engaged in carrying on that trade." Employing his legal training to build a case, and probably aided by young Theodore Sedgwick, Bryant argued that the slave trade was unlawful in Cuba, that emerging accounts indicated that the Africans had been unlawfully introduced onto the island, and that therefore they should not be sent back for the execution of the ringleaders and for slavery for the rest.

Other New York newspapers and the Van Buren administration disagreed with Bryant. The *New York Morning Herald* huffed: "The Abolitionists are determined to baffle those desirous of justice," while Bryant's old nemesis, the *Courier and Enquirer*, fulminated that the abolitionists were "making sport of the law and perverting the power of the courts of justice to . . . fanatical ends." In Washington, President Van

Buren and his cabinet were under tremendous pressure from the Spanish government to remand the prisoners to Spanish jurisdiction.

The Circuit Court had decided on September 23 that the United States could not try the prisoners for piracy and murder because the events clearly took place aboard a Spanish ship in Spanish-controlled waters. In anticipation of a more favorable District Court verdict on the question of salvage and property claims, President Van Buren ordered the ship *Grampus* to waters off the Connecticut coast to immediately transport the prisoners to Cuba. Judge Judson was expected to decide that the Africans were lawful property belonging to Ruiz and Montes. On October 17, they had been arrested and jailed in New York City on the charge of false imprisonment of Cinqué.

During the fall and winter months, the *Evening Post* provided periodic reports on the Africans, alerting readers about the legal implications of their case as well as about their perilous state. The *Evening Post* supported the opinion of "Correspondent Veto" that the Africans aboard the *Amistad* were not slaves under Spanish law. Bryant commented that "there assuredly could be no more distressing duty than surrender these poor, ignorant, unfriended Africans, guilty only of having obeyed the sacred law of self defence, to the tender mercies of Spanish slave dealers." In another article, the *Evening Post* reported that the "unfortunate Negroes" had been denied proper clothing to protect them from the onset of winter. "They are kept in close rooms, where they are sickening and dying weekly. Five have already died, and as many more are suffering under severe disease."

Finally Judge Judson ordered the United States Marshall to stop treating the Africans as prisoners, and their condition improved after they were moved to a house outside New Haven. On January 13, 1840, Judson announced his decision: the Africans were not property, but people. They had revolted in order to gain their freedom. Consequently they should be taken back to Africa. In the January 15 edition of the *Evening Post*, Bryant removed articles that already had been typeset in order to reprint the Court's verdict in its entirety, and devoted the editorial to the "principles of great importance" that Judge Judson's decision implied. President Van Buren immediately instructed the government's lawyer to appeal the District Court's verdict. After a series of rejected appeals, the U.S. Supreme Court agreed to hear the case in February 1841.

The *Amistad* affair reminded Bryant of the work that remained in transforming America into a nation of equal opportunity for all its citizens. Both at the local and national levels, Bryant thought that the nation was an unfinished project. The fondness of mercantile New Yorkers for their southern brethren was dangerous. Their lack of support for art and literature was deplorable. Their self-serving capitalism could lead to social instability.

In September 1839, Bryant alerted the public to an exhibit from a "sumptuous work," *Birds of America*, by John Audubon at the Lyceum of Natural History at 563 Broadway. Ever the student of nature and supporter of American artists, Bryant observed that "Mr. Audubon's drawings of birds excel, we believe, in life-like appearance, spirit, and variety of attitude any that have been produced. The bird is never or rarely figured alone, but some picturesque accessory, some beautiful plant which grows in its places of resort, or some striking scene which it haunts, is generally introduced, so that each drawing forms an agreeable composition." Audubon dropped by occasionally to see Bryant; his tall, sparse frame, weather-beaten face, hawklike nose and long white hair impressed the *Evening Post*'s employees. When it became apparent after a month that the exhibit had been scantily attended, Bryant lamented that the disinterest of New Yorkers in great art of the American landscape "reflects the highest discredit upon the taste and intelligence of the community."

The entire community, Bryant felt, was in need of radical improvement. Despite the downturn in the economy and a consequent drop in immigration, New York's population had mushroomed to 391,000 in 1840, a 62 percent increase from the census ten years earlier. The population surge had exacerbated civic ills. Paupers and the unemployed proliferated on every corner of Manhattan, from the compressed area below Fourteenth Street to the wasteland destined to become Central Park. Horace Greeley's admonition in the *New-Yorker* to the city's jobless to flee the city for western lands echoed the common attitudes of publishers, politicians, and the public toward the city's poor and unemployed. In 1838 Mayor Clark had worried that "New York is likely to become the general rendezvous of beggars, paupers, vagrants and mischievous persons" if city relief were not reduced below its already paltry levels. Charitable and evangelical groups, among them the New York Female Moral Reform Society and the New York City Tract Society, found contributions hard to come by and had to curtail their relief efforts.

The general sentiment in Manhattan was that almsgiving and public aid were "unscientific" and counterproductive, a viewpoint that Bryant shared. Metropolitan attitudes toward poverty had been shaped by

Jacksonian ideals of individualism and self-reliance, and the notion that the poor were responsible for their abject condition was strong. In a succession of didactic novels, Bryant's close friend Catharine Sedgwick had exposed the growing chasm between the rich and poor while rendering conventional moral judgment about the need for the poor to reform themselves. Especially in *The Rich Man and the Rich Poor Man* (1837), Sedgwick was harsh on the poor: "It is the poor who fence themselves in with ignorance and press themselves down with shiftlessness and vice."

Bryant departed from conventional wisdom in chastising the city for ignoring the plight of poor women. Such willful failure to protect the truly indigent underscored the contradictory and self-defeating approaches to urban poverty. "Pauperism and mendacity have increased to an alarming extent," he wrote in early February 1840, noting that the infestation of beggars in Manhattan's streets reminded him of the squalid social conditions in European cities. The present system of almsgiving was a bad one, Bryant suggested, for it discouraged able-bodied individuals from finding employment. Perhaps New York City could adopt the system of public relief established in Boston, where the distresses of the truly poor but not the willfully indigent were met. In any case, the "evil" of poverty, as the *Evening Post* termed it, "has now reached such a height, that a reform is indispensable."

Paupers and filthy streets, venal police and obnoxious firefighters, corrupt politicians and self-serving merchants, fractious publishers and rival editors: the metropolis, Bryant felt, was in a sorry state. The city's police were "a virtuous society of rogues and rogue-catchers" whose behavior and self-interest all too frequently coincided. He was especially appalled by the city's volunteer fire department, which consisted of scores of rival hose, engine, and ladder companies whose members, Bryant wrote, were scarcely better than ruffians and blackguards, prone to drinking, fighting, robbery, insulting women, and assaulting men. From 1840 until the elimination of the volunteer system in 1865, Bryant excoriated the outrageous conduct of the men who gravitated to the incendiary world of firefighting and who functioned like gangs preying on law-abiding merchants and citizens. "It is a class," Bryant wrote in an early 1840 editorial, "composed chiefly of young men. Their custom is to assemble nightly in the neighborhood of engine houses to incite their depraved impulses to acts of insolence. Destitute for the most part of education, withdrawn from all meliorating influences, and mutually corrupting each other, they indulge in obscene conversations, and by loud laughs and licentious jests, fit themselves for the career of villainy to which they aspire." These depraved young men, Bryant charged, were "banditti" masquerading as firemen.

Even more shocking to Bryant than the city's ills was the charade transpiring at the national level, where the Whigs were transforming William Henry Harrison into a presidential candidate to run against Van Buren in 1840. General Harrison had lost to Van Buren in the previous election. Bryant launched a series of witty, vicious attacks on Harrison in December 1839 and maintained a drumbeat of satire and invective up to the presidential election the following November. The Whigs, Bryant surmised, had thought they were through with the General after his trouncing in 1836, but here he was again, "come up for a second time as a candidate, like a cat which you thought you saw killed yesterday, looking in at your window with a bloody head, to scare you as you wake in the morning."

Bryant delighted in exposing the travesty of the Whigs' log cabin and hard cider campaign to transform the feeble old Indian fighter on his two-thousand-acre estate near Cincinnati into a hard-drinking man of the people. Ranging over the course of Western civilization, making allusions to the history of wine, cider, and other potions that revealed the playfully encyclopedic knowledge he enjoyed bringing to his editorials, Bryant exposed the Whigs' pretense that Harrison was a common man. Could the Whig establishment, like Medea saving Jason from the last stages of decrepitude, restore Harrison to youth "by soaking him in hard cider, transform him into a Nestor, the subtlest of men"? Was it possible, the editor mused, to "make a statesman out of a barber's block by putting it into a pickle of hard cider?" Bryant was doubtful. Warming to his subject, employing fresh figurative ammunition in his editorials, Bryant likened voting for Harrison to accepting a pig in a poke, marrying a woman in a mask, and buying a horse with patches and plasters. The Whigs were keeping Harrison under wraps, thereby preventing him from having to articulate positions on issues of the day; Bryant took to calling the candidate "William Henry the Silent" and "General Mum." Log Cabin rallies were little more than "regular drunken follies" attracting slothful, vicious mobs. Exposing their egalitarian pretenses, the editor labeled the Whigs the "anti-democratic party."

Surmising that the public held the Van Buren administration responsible for the Panic of 1837 and the lingering economic downturn, Bryant was fatalistic about the triumph of the Whigs in the November 1840 election. Announcing the ascendancy of Harrison to the presidency, he concluded morosely: "The time for a 'change' has at last arrived; the time when the people, in order to be convinced of the benefits of a democratic policy, must try a taste of the opposite." At least Van Buren had carried New York by an even greater majority than he had in 1836. And the editor found a bright spot in the country's naturalized Irish American voters who had overwhelmingly supported Van Buren. Indeed the "wild Irish," as they were called, could be "neither coaxed nor driven to vote against their consciences." The Irish were, Bryant avowed, eternally lost to the Whig party because their "democratic instinct" was too strong.

When Harrison died in April 1841, barely a month after having assumed the presidency, Bryant did not waste false sympathy on the president's passing. Instead he wrote that Old Tippecanoe had been snatched from life before he had been able to do any good or evil as president. "An inaugural speech, the formation of a cabinet, a considerable number of removals from office for the sake of appointing his friends, and many promises of other removals and appointments—these are the sole monuments which remain of his brief career, and some of these are perhaps destined to pass away almost as speedily as the breath of life has passed from his own lips." Defying journalistic custom on the death of illustrious people, Bryant refused to turn the column rules in the *Evening Post*, which he considered a form of "typographical foppery," instead using a heavy rule to alert readers to Harrison's death. Philip Hone, never a Bryant enthusiast, was outraged, writing in his diary that "The newspapers were clothed in mourning, all but the *Evening Post*, whose malignant, blackhearted editor, Bryant, says he regrets the death of General Harrison only because he did not live long enough to prove his incapacity as President." The Whig press labeled the poet-editor of the *Evening Post* a "vampire" and "ghoul."

Bryant initially took a cautious approach to the accession of Vice President John Tyler to the presidency. After all, the tall, refined statesman had been a Democrat before being elected to the vice presidency as a Whig. Moreover, to Bryant's delight, Tyler soon was at odds with Henry Clay over the senator's support for a national bank. In appointing scurrilous types to high office, Tyler might have revealed himself as "a treacherous and unprincipled partisan," but in August he partially redeemed himself in Bryant's eyes by vetoing Clay's bill to establish a national bank. "Departed this Life," Bryant exulted, "at eleven o'clock, on Saturday morning, after a lingering illness, the United States Bank.

The patient was originally of weak constitution, but succeeded by a course of high living to give itself an appearance of florid vigor."

II

With the fortunes of the *Evening Post* improving, Bryant had been able to get away from the city for one of his favorite activities. In June 1840, Cole proposed that the two friends embark on a Catskills excursion: "There is a valley reported 'beautiful' in the mountains a few miles above the [Kaaterskill] Clove—I have never explored it & am reserving the delicate morsel to be shared with you—Let me know that you can come & that quickly for if possible I would explore the Platte-Kill valley before the waters are low—If report says true there is a beautiful little Lake with a cascade tumbling into it—If you can leave the city for a few days *now* come!" Bryant joined the painter near the end of the month at Cole's house in Cedar Grove, just north of Catskill, and the two men set off on their rambles.

Often walking from dawn to dusk, the painter and poet traipsed through the Catskills—Pine Orchard, Plattekill Cove, Schoharie Creek, and the Plattekill River. Both delighted in the details of the landscape, and Bryant, trained in his youth by his father in Linnaean botany, was able to identify most of the plant species they encountered. In 1848, delivering the eulogy in honor in Cole, Bryant would recall that they ranged "over scenes of wild grandeur peculiar to our country, over our aerial mountain-tops with their mighty growth of forest never touched by axe, along the banks of streams never deformed by culture, and into the depth of skies bright with the hues of our own climate."

Bryant and Cole shared an affinity for nature's teachings, for the meditative and spiritual elements inspired by raw landscape. As he explored the Catskills, Vermont, and New Hampshire, Cole found the force of nature to be most profound at twilight and sunset. At this moment, nature seemed to be poetic, mysterious, and transcendent. The painter especially liked the view of North Mountain seen from Catskill Creek, and he depicted this scene in *Sunset, View on the Catskill* (1834), in which a solitary fisherman gazes at the mountain across the water at twilight.

The images that leap from Cole's canvas resemble those invoked by Bryant in the opening stanzas of his poem "A Walk at Sunset," which he had published in Dana's *Idle Man* in 1821. The poem echoes Keats and demonstrates the range of Bryant's lyric voice:

When insect wings are glistening in the beam
    Of the low sun, and mountain-tops are bright,
Oh, let me, by the crystal valley-stream,
    Wander amid the mild and mellow light;
And while the wood-thrush pipes his evening lay,
Give me one lonely hour to hymn the setting day.

Oh, sun! that o'er the western mountains now
    Go'st down in glory! Ever beautiful
And blessed is thy radiance, whether thou
    Colorest the eastern heaven and night-mist cool,
Till the bright day-star vanish, or on high
Climbest and streamest thy white splendors from mid-sky.

Painter and poet sought the sublime in nature. As Cole wrote in his 1836 "Essay on American Scenery," a person gazing on a sunset scene experiences "the pure creations of the Almighty, he feels a calm religious tone steal through his mind."

Writing of their trip in the July 24 issue of the *Evening Post*, Bryant stated that he and Cole had been transfixed by a scene on a ridge at the source of Schoharie Creek and the Plattekill. Here they gazed with fascination on "a grand mountain ridge, indented by deep notches, in one of which, a dark ravine called Stony Clove, the ice of winter remains unmelted throughout the year." Their mutual friend Asher B. Durand must have learned from either Bryant or Cole about the supernal beauty of this unique spot; in *Kindred Spirits*, the canvas commissioned for Bryant in gratitude for his eulogy at Cole's funeral, Durand reproduces the scene, with the poet and painter standing on a towering ledge commanding the mountainous scene. These three men—who shared the same social circles in New York, were members of the same clubs, and were frequent guests at one another's homes—believed that nature, especially the landscape of the New World, was a sacred place that could prompt great art.

Stimulated by his Catskills excursion, Bryant took his wife to Pennsylvania to tour the area around the Moravian settlement at Bethlehem in July. "It is situated on the Lehigh," he wrote Dana, "a rapid and most beautiful river, with an island in the midst shaded with old oaks and elms and drooping birches whose twigs hang down to the water." Bryant liked the simplicity and orderliness of the Moravians, their passion for music, and their plain lifestyle.

In August, Bryant embarked on a yet another trip, this time alone. He traveled to New Milford, Connecticut, by steamboat and railroad and then commenced a walking excursion through Connecticut and Massachusetts. Never happier than when he was a solitary wanderer, Bryant walked some fifty miles along the Housatonic River to Great Barrington. Whether walking in heat or rain, Bryant found the trip exhilarating. If the heat was too oppressive, he tarried in the shade of a tree and read Goethe's *Tasso*. If it rained, a tidy inn awaited the tired traveler. With huckleberries and milk for supper and breakfast, he was in high spirits by the time he reached Great Barrington and greeted his daughters, who were spending the summer there. From Great Barrington, Bryant then traced in reverse the course of his youth and childhood, traversing on foot much of Hampshire County: first to Worthington, where he had studied law, then on to Cummington, where he visited the grave of his father in the cemetery adjoining his Grandfather Snell's farm high in the Berkshire hills.

Bryant yearned for both rural pleasures and the literary life; he stole time from his daily labors at the *Evening Post* to sustain both. He corresponded with fellow writers and artists, attended Sketch Club meetings, and participated in cultural events in Gotham. When Dana had come to town in late January 1840 to give a series of eight lectures on Shakespeare at the Stuyvesant Institute, Bryant put him up at his boarding house on Carmine Street. One evening, Bryant hosted Dana, Longfellow (who was lecturing in the city on Dante and Molière at the Mercantile Library Association), and Fitz-Greene Halleck at a lively dinner.

For more than a year, Bryant had been making strenuous efforts to find a publisher for *Two Years Before the Mast*, which had been written by Dana's son, Richard Henry Dana, Jr. "I like the book extremely," he wrote to the elder Dana, praising its "picturesque simplicity" and powerful account of life before the mast. Several publishers rebuffed Bryant's queries, but he finally was able to report to Dana that Harpers had accepted the book. Following the publication of *Two Years Before the Mast* in September, Bryant wrote an unsigned notice in the *Democratic Review*: "It is a new thing in our literature," he announced. "Not only is the description graphic and striking, but you feel as you read it, that nothing is overcolored or exaggerated." Bryant surmised that young Dana's harrowing account of the hardships endured by American sailors would result in a call for improved naval conditions.

Buried in the common strife, as he called it, Bryant nevertheless found time for literary pursuits. When Harpers engaged him to edit an anthology, *Selections from the American Poets* (1840), he included verse by numerous friends—Sands, Dana, Longfellow, Simms, Halleck, Sigourney, and Whittier—as well as six accomplished sonnets by an unknown poet, Jones Very. Bryant did not contribute any new poetry of his own to the anthology, only four older selections—"The Past," "The Prairies," "The Rivulet," and "Earth's Children Cleave to Earth."

Compiling *Selections from the American Poets*, Bryant felt a special need to include "The Rivulet," which he had published in the *United States Literary Gazette* in 1824 just before coming to New York City. It must have struck Bryant that the stream of life was pushing him away from his literary calling. "The Rivulet," a lengthy lyric composed in rhyming couplets and notable for its sonorous cadences, describes the stream that ran along the boundary of the Snell farm in Cummington:

> This little rill, that from the springs
> Of yonder grove its current brings,
> Plays on the slope awhile, and then
> Goes prattling into groves again,
> Oft to its warbling waters drew
> My little feet, when life was new.
> When woods in early green were dressed,
> And from the chambers of the west
> The warmer breezes, travelling out,
> Breathed the new scent of flowers about,
> My truant steps from home would stray,
> Upon its grassy side to play,
> List the brown thrasher's vernal hymn,
> And crop the violet on its brim,
> With blooming cheek and open brow,
> As young and gay, sweet rill, as thou.

From this opening stanza, Bryant traces the advancing years and changes in his life, the transitory images set against the unchanging permanence of the stream. In this lyric, the poet strikes a mood of tender nostalgia for the passage of life from infancy to old age. The rivulet, "singing down thy narrow glen," outlasts humanity and mocks "the fading race of men."

Energized by his previous excursion to the Berkshires and the return to family haunts, Bryant set off in May 1841 to see his mother and brothers in Illinois. His wife and Fanny accompanied him; Julia was left with Frances's sister in Great Barrington. Their itinerary traced once again the route taken by Bryant in 1832—first to Philadelphia and Pittsburgh, then by steamboat down the Ohio and up the Mississippi and Illinois rivers, and finally by carriage to Princeton, where Bryant found his mother well and his brothers prosperous. The beauty and bounty of the West, Bryant felt, had rewarded his intrepid New England family.

In letters sent back to the *Evening Post*, Bryant told readers about the wondrous western world that awaited emigrants and visitors. Traveling outside Princeton into the prairies, Bryant described the natural history of the region and the traces of Indian culture seen in old Indian mounds and ancient trails furrowed in the grass. Only the depredations of unsavory white men, horse thieves and murderers subject to summary lynch law, marred the beauty of this world. In the northwestern region of the state around Rock River, the West remained pristine. To Bryant the unfenced prairie was splendid, a grassy paradise stretching to the horizon and teeming with wildlife—turtledoves, plovers, quail, rabbits, wild turkeys, prairie hawks, bald eagles, wolves, mink, and more.

Ever the botanist, Bryant was inspired to write about an indigenous plant, the painted cup. In a note appended to his collected verse, the poet offered a description of the flower: "The Painted Cup—*Euchroma coccinea*, or *Bartsai coccinea*—grows in great abundance in the hazel prairies of the Western States, where its scarlet tufts make a brilliant appearance in the midst of the verdure." The poem itself playfully invites putative poets not to construct fairy tales about this flower but to attend to its natural beauty:

> Call not up,
> Amid this fresh and virgin solitude,
> The faded fancies of an elder world;
> But leave these scarlet cups to spotted moths
> Of June, and glistening flies, and humming-birds,
> To drink from, when on all these boundless lawns
> The morning sun looks hot. Or let the wind
> O'erturn in sport their ruddy brims, and pour
> A sudden shower upon the strawberry plant,
> To swell the reddening fruit that even now
> Breathes a slight fragrance from the sunny slope.

If the poet, Bryant suggests, lacks discrete knowledge of the natural world, then at least invoke the Manitou, from native Indian rather than European lore, to capture the beauty of the painted cup. Nearing fifty,

Bryant could still create the lofty sentiments, fresh imagery, and brilliant metrical cadences found in the best verse of his earlier years.

Bryant's two-month sojourn in the western states and briefer excursions during the summer of 1841 had been temporary respites from local and national political battles. The fall, however, found him embroiled in an emerging local conflict over public funding for the city's Roman Catholic public schools. The priest John Hughes, putative leader of New York's Catholic congregation, was demanding public funding for parochial education. Hughes, an Irish immigrant who was held in awe by his parishioners and was known as "Dagger John" for his combative skills, had been sent from Philadelphia in 1838 to assist the elderly bishop, John DuBois, who suffered a paralytic stroke two months after Hughes's arrival. Hughes himself would become bishop in 1842 following DuBois's death. A skillful politician, he threatened to break Tammany's hold on the city's Irish Catholics and take them into the Whig fold over the issue of funding Catholic schools. To fortify his threat, Hughes aligned himself with Governor William Seward, who in 1840 introduced a bill in the Albany legislature recommending public funding for church schools.

As a radical Democrat and a persistent critic of anti-immigrant nativists, Bryant found himself in a delicate position. On the one hand, he did not want to see New York's Irish Catholics desert the party over one issue; nor did he want to find himself inadvertently in the nativist camp. On the other hand, he believed in the separation of church and state. Bryant's first editorial on the subject on October 28, 1841, presented a judicious opinion: "The community will not consent to be taxed that children may be educated according to certain religious distinctions, any more than they will consent to be taxed for the religious instructions which grown men receive from the pulpit." Bryant was joined in his opposition to public support of church schools by another journalist, Walter Whitman, who at twenty-three had assumed the editorship of a new twopenny newspaper, the *Aurora*.

Bryant's position on the school issue reflected the ethos of the *Evening Post*, which on November 11, 1841, announced the start of a weekly edition. "In politics, it will embrace the democratic side, but it will be more devoted to the spread of sound political principles than to the support of a party." Having expanded from seven to eight columns the previous year, the weekly edition of the *Evening Post* would now be better able to command a national audience.

III

In early 1842, the nation greeted Charles Dickens with an enthusiasm unmatched by any foreign visitor since Lafayette. American readers lined up at the docks in Boston, New York, and Philadelphia demanding the latest installments of his novel, while publishers pirated earlier editions and sold them cheaply to a mesmerized public. In fact, Dickens had embarked in part on his American tour to argue for an international copyright law. He would find a partner in this crusade in William Cullen Bryant.

During the first week of February, Bryant devoted several issues of the *Evening Post* to Dickens's reception in Boston. Dickens's phenomenal popularity had been acknowledged by the *Evening Post* in early 1839 with publication of the successive installments of *Nicholas Nickleby*: "His humor is frequently broad farce, and his horrors are often exaggerated, extravagant, and improbable; but he still has so much humor, and so much pathos, that his defects are overlooked." Speaking at a public dinner in Boston, Dickens alluded to the many letters he had received from Americans captivated by Little Nell, acknowledging the enthusiasm that had greeted his work. Dickens talked repeatedly about his desire to see Bryant, but certain partisans of the press told him to be more circumspect: "I speak of Bancroft, and am advised to be silent on that subject, for he is a 'black sheep—a Democrat.' I speak of Bryant, and am entreated to be more careful, for the same reason."

Dickens left Boston in the second week of February and came to New York City. "Where is Bryant?" he is said to have asked after checking into the Carleton House. Plans had been made for a great Boz Ball on February 14. The Park Theatre was converted into a ballroom in which corners would be decorated in the fashion of the Old Curiosity Shop and other niches would illustrate scenes from Dickens's novels. Bryant made two attempts to see Dickens at the Carlton House without success, prompting the English celebrity to send a note on February 14:

> My Dear Sir: With one exception (and that's Irving) you are the man I most wanted to see in America. You have been here twice, and I have not seen you. The fault was not mine; for on the evening of my arrival committee-gentlemen were coming in and out until long after I had your card put into my hands. As I lost what I most eagerly longed for, I ask you for your

sympathy, and not for your forgiveness. Now, I want to know when you will come and breakfast with me: and I don't call to leave a card at your door before asking you, because I love you too well to be ceremonious with you. I have a thumbed book at home, so well worn that it has nothing upon the back but one gilt "B," and the remotest possible traces of a "y." My credentials are in my earnest admiration of its beautiful contents.

Bryant finally caught up with Dickens for their breakfast, where they were joined by Fitz-Greene Halleck and Professor Charles Felton of Harvard. Bryant also entertained the novelist in his house at 326 Ninth Street, where the family had resided since 1840.

Bryant was among the twenty-five hundred New Yorkers who attended the Boz Ball held to honor Dickens—in the words of Philip Hone "the greatest affair of modern times." The *Evening Post* concurred that the event at the Park Hotel was "one of the most magnificent that has ever been given this city. The gorgeousness of the decorations and the splendor of the dresses, no less than the immense throng, glittering with silks and jewels, contributed to the show and impressiveness of the occasion." Three days later, the Boz Dinner for 230 guests was held at the City Hotel, presided over by Washington Irving, who gave a halting toast to Dickens. In turn, Dickens offered a tribute to Irving, referred to Bryant and Halleck, and concluded with a toast to American literature.

Following his departure from New York, the *Evening Post* reported on the triumphal reception of Dickens in Philadelphia, Washington, and elsewhere. Bryant continued to applaud this young visitor from England who "without birth, wealth, title, or a sword, whose only claims to distinction are in his intellect and heart, is received with a feeling that was formerly rendered only to conquerors and kings." Above all, Bryant approved of the novelist's sympathies for the masses, "that class with whom American institutions and laws sympathize most strongly."

Bryant also sympathized with Dickens's attempts to promote an international copyright law. Dickens had devoted much of his speech at the Boston dinner in his honor to this subject, much to the consternation of several Boston and New York journals. Bryant defended the novelist in the *Evening Post* on February 11: "When we deny a stranger the same right to the profits of his own writings as we give to our citizens," he wrote, we commit an injustice. Dickens touched on the subject at the New York dinner, and on May 9 the *Evening Post* reprinted a letter in which the novelist repeated his appeal from Niagara Falls. He also enclosed a longer letter "to the American People" that had been signed by Carlyle, Bulwer-Lytton, Tennyson, Leigh Hunt, and others arguing for an international copyright agreement. Bryant responded with an editorial that drew an inspiring picture of American letters and the benefits that would accrue to writers like Irving, Cooper, Catlin, Prescott, and Bancroft if they could enjoy worldwide royalties for their work. In the summer of 1843, the efforts of Bryant, Verplanck, and others to curtail literary piracy by equalizing native and foreign copyrights would result in the formation of the American Copyright Club. At its founding meeting on August 23, 1843, the members elected Bryant as their first president.

Buoyed by Dickens's appearance, his own creative juices once more flowing, Bryant forged ahead with plans to assemble a new volume of poetry. The previous November, he had written to his brother John, "I am thinking of putting my own verses such as have not been collected, into a little volume and publishing them this winter." The result was *The Fountain and Other Poems*, published in New York and London by Wiley and Putnam in July 1842.

Bryant was in high favor with American readers, and his reputation and cultural authority increased with the publication of *The Fountain and Other Poems*. The flourishing Mercantile Library Association at Clinton Hall hailed Bryant as "the Genius of American verse." Alluding to Wordsworth as Bryant's only equal, Lewis Gaylord Clark of the *Knickerbocker* declared: "Mr. Bryant is not only the very first of American poets, but, . . . with perhaps one eminent living exception, he is the first living poet in the world." Writing in the *North American Review*, Charles Felton of Harvard was both pleased and astonished that Bryant could move so easily from the invective of his editorials "to the smiling fields of poetry." Felton could "scarce believe the poet and politician to be the same man."

The Fountain and Other Poems consists of fifteen pieces that Bryant had written since his return from Europe. One, "An Evening Revery," had been published in the January 1841 *Knickerbocker* with the subtitle "From an unfinished poem." Bryant's note to *Poems* (1876) adds, "This poem and that entitled 'The Fountain,' with one or two others in blank verse, were intended by the author as portions of a larger poem, in which they may hereafter take their place." Two other poems in the new collection written in blank verse, "The Painted Cup" and "The Old Man's Counsel," a richly detailed evocation of the natural world introduced to young Bryant by his Grandfather Snell, suggest that Bryant might have had an epic of the New World landscape in mind, but in the absence of any specific hints among the poet's manuscripts, this is conjectural.

Dana had persistently encouraged his friend to grapple with a longer poem, but Bryant knew instinctively that his talent was for the shorter lyric. Indeed, "The Painted Cup," "An Evening Revery," "The Old Man's Counsel," and "The Fountain," while advancing overlapping themes on the beauties of nature and the passage of history and human life, stand on their own as examples of Bryant's poetic strength at middle age. Taken together, these four poems present a panorama of the national landscape, a sort of field guide to American flora and fauna. Each of these poems reveals the attention to detail that Bryant's artist friends found painterly, as does this stanza from "The Old Man's Counsel":

> I listened, and from midst the depth of woods
> Heard the love-signal of the grouse, that wears
> A sable ruff around his mottled neck;
> Partridge they call him by our northern streams,
> And pheasant by the Delaware. He beat
> His barred sides with his speckled wings, and made
> A sound like distant thunder; slow the strokes
> At first, then fast and faster, till at length
> They passed into a murmur and were still.

Each of the selections in *The Fountain and Other Poems* has a separate identity, but if there is a single theme underlying the four poems in blank verse, the clue to this unity—the possibility that Bryant might have had the makings of a longer poem in mind—lies in the title poem. "The Fountain," originally published in the April 1839 issue of the *Democratic Review*, is unlike such earlier poems as "The Ages" that had optimistically traced the course of civilization. In the signature poem of Bryant's new volume, the world exists in Manichean tension, with the symbolic fountain originating in "red mould and slimy roots" and emerging from its "dark birthplace" to coexist in a world poised between "the dark and foul, the pure and bright."

As with "The Past," time, culture, and civilization flow steadily through "The Fountain." Indian, huntsman, and settler depict the stages in the American experience. Progress, however, is at best provisional. Bryant offers an alternative vision in the last stanza:

Is there no other change for thee, that lurks
Among the future ages? Will not man
Seek out strange arts to wither and deform
The pleasant landscape which thou makest green?
Or shall the veins that feed thy constant stream
Be choked in middle earth, and flow no more
For ever, that the water-plants along
Thy channel perish, and the bird in vain
Alight to drink? Haply shall these green hills
Sink, with the lapse of years, into the gulf
Of ocean waters, and thy source be lost
Amidst the bitter brine? Or shall they rise,
Upheaved in broken cliffs and airy peaks,
Haunts of the eagle and snake, and thou
Gush midway from the bare and barren steep?

There is no easy affirmation of divine or cosmic progress, no connective tissue linking nature to the Almighty, in the concluding stanza. Instead dark images and primal eruptions portend environmental or geological disaster. As in his earlier "A Winter Piece," Bryant looks at nature with a cold gaze and confronts the prospect that life might end in dissolution.

Bryant's cold gaze had turned inward a few weeks before the publication of *The Fountain and Other Poems* when his youngest daughter, Fanny, now twenty, married Parke Godwin, who was six years older. There is virtually no mention of the marriage in Bryant's correspondence, save for a cryptic sentence in a letter to Dana: "You gave the true interpretation to my silence on another subject, so that there is no need of making any further explanation." Bryant did not approve of the marriage. Godwin, outgoing, gregarious, and enthralled by socialist causes, was the polar opposite of Bryant in personality. Moreover, in contrast to his typically warm letters to Julia, Bryant's correspondence with Fanny, although couched in tender moralizing tones, noted faults in his first daughter: her shaky spelling and diction, her tendency toward boredom and frivolity, her failure to write to him at any length. Despite the rigorous education he had given his girls, it is probable that Bryant thought that Fanny was immature and not ready for marriage.

A month after the wedding, Fanny and Godwin moved out of the comfortable two-story house on Ninth Street, and Godwin left the *Evening Post.* With six thousand dollars advanced to him by his father-in-law, Godwin announced the start his own paper, the *New York Morning Post*. Then he abruptly dropped his plans to launch a new paper and purchased the Democratic *New Era*. Bryant wished the new editor well, trusting that Godwin would conduct himself "with fidelity to the loftiest standard of political morality." He was less certain of Godwin's personal ethics, for Godwin apparently had kept his courtship of Fanny secret from her parents.

IV

On February 5, 1843, Bryant wrote to his brother John: "Congratulate me! There is a possibility of my becoming a landholder in New York! I have made a bargain for about forty acres of solid earth at Hempstead Harbor, on the north side of Long Island." Since the previous fall, Bryant had been negotiating with Joseph Moulton to buy his farm, which was situated roughly twenty miles east of the city. With the *Evening Post* "steadily prosperous" and in fact "flourishing," as he boasted in his New Year's editorial, Bryant looked forward to becoming a country gentleman.

For several years, Bryant had enjoyed his rambles on the north shore of Long Island. On one occasion, he hiked from Oyster Bay to Lake Ronkonkoma, a distance of more than thirty miles, and then walked to Smithtown to spend the evening before returning to New York the next day. Long Island, Bryant informed *Evening Post* readers, offered a wonderful opportunity for people "to leave the close and sultry towns on pedestrian excursions. The deep harbours running far into the island, the bold woody heights stretching far into the sound, the rich vegetation, the deeply embowered roads and paths, the beautiful alternation of hill and valley, make this altogether one of the most picturesque tracts in the vicinity of New York."

In the summer of 1843, the Bryants moved into an old Quaker farmhouse on the property in the village of Hempstead Harbor. (In 1844, local residents renamed their village Roslyn.) After eighteen years of renting in New York City, Bryant and his wife finally had a permanent home. Bryant initially called his property "Springbank." Then he changed the name of the farm, which hugged the shoreline, contained a natural pond, and was graced by towering trees, to "Cedarmere." For more than thirty years, Cedarmere would be Bryant's preferred residence. He kept lodgings in the city in order to supervise affairs at the

Evening Post, but relished weekends and more extended summer interludes at his Roslyn retreat.

Shortly after the purchase of the property at Hempstead Harbor, Bryant and Frances, acting on an invitation from William Gilmore Simms to visit his plantation, Woodlands, in South Carolina, embarked on a tour of the South. Departing on the evening of February 24, their first stop was Washington, D.C., where Bryant visited both houses of Congress. He lamented the decline of courtesy and decorum among the members of these illustrious bodies. In a letter to the *Evening Post*, he wrote: "I visited the Senate Chamber, and saw a member of that dignified body, as somebody calls it, in preparing to make a speech, blow his nose with his thumb and finger without the intervention of a pocket-handkerchief. The speech, after this graceful preliminary, did not, I confess, disappoint me." Bryant used his travel writing to champion improved standards of taste and refinement.

As he traveled through Virginia and into the Old South, a six-week odyssey that would end in St. Augustine, Bryant offered little commentary on the institution of slavery. Perhaps the generosity and grace of his hosts induced him to suppress an untoward mention of the South's peculiar institution. In his mind's eye, he was a guest among the South's aristocracy, all of whom received him with great warmth, admiration, and respect. Southerners invariably received Bryant as a privileged and influential guest.

Bryant didn't seem disturbed by the sight of eighty slaves working in a tobacco warehouse outside Richmond, preferring to mention their penchant for singing hymns as they labored at their arduous tasks. He treated his contact with black slaves as a window into the folkways and local color of the South. Writing from Charleston, South Carolina, in late March about the hospitality of the planters, who were "very agreeable and intelligent men," Bryant informed readers that he had "been out on a raccoon hunt; been present at a corn shucking; listened to negro ballads, negro jokes, and the banjo; witnessed negro dances; seen two alligators at least, and eaten bushels of hominy."

A fascinated observer of the South's rituals and customs, Bryant devoted much of his March 29 letter to an extended description of slave culture. He concluded: "The blacks of this region are a cheerful, careless, dirty race, not hard worked, and in many respects indulgently treated." True, he warned, there was a dangerously symbiotic relationship between planter and slave: "The master has power of punishment on his side; the slave, on his, has the invincible inclination, and a thousand expedients learned by long practice." The result was a compromise in which "each party yields something and a good-natured though imperfect and slovenly obedience on one side, is purchased by good treatment on the other."

Moving inland from Charleston, the Bryants arrived at Woodlands, where they spent three weeks with Simms and his young wife. Simms was of humble origin, having been a drugstore clerk before training for the law. On the death of his first wife, Simms had married the daughter of a rich planter who owned seventy slaves and had transformed himself into a southern aristocrat. Tall, handsome, and vigorous, the South's self-proclaimed poet laureate was inordinately fond of Bryant and looked after his famous Northern guest with great affection and respect. Before Bryant left Woodlands, Simms provided him with letters of introduction to some of the most distinguished people in Savannah and St. Augustine, thereby effectively shielding Bryant from the darker contours of Southern life.

Bryant liked Simms and his amiable friends. The warm weather and the kindness of the plantocracy that wrapped itself around Bryant as he traveled from Woodlands to Savannah and finally to St. Augustine shielded the poet from moral dilemmas about slavery. Impressed by the refined manners of the South's aristocrats and fascinated by the lush landscape, Bryant felt compelled to compliment his hosts. Writing to Simms a year after his trip, he said, "I remember my visit to the South as one of the pleasantest periods of my life. It gratified a strong curiosity which I had always felt in regard to that region and it left me a favorable impression and a most friendly recollection of its inhabitants." Soon, however, Bryant's tolerance of the South, fondness for its citizens, and fascination with the folkways of its peculiar institution would change dramatically. Colorful travel accounts could not alter Bryant's conviction that slavery was antithetical to democracy.

10

AMONG THE FIRST
IN THE WORLD

Sometimes, walking across the Park in New York, or along
one of the thoroughfares of the city, you may meet a plainly
dressed man of middling size, considerably beyond the
younger age of life, with rather a bloodless complexion, sparse
white hair, and expressive grey eyes. Of this description is
William Cullen Bryant—a poet who, to our mind, stands
among the first in the world.
—Walter Whitman, *Brooklyn Daily Eagle*, 1846

I

As he entered the fifth decade of his life, William Cullen Bryant was
America's most famous poet at home and abroad and a source of cultural authority. His *Evening Post* editorials raising fundamental questions about the character of American democracy had made him a
respected social and political voice. Fenimore Cooper, often in town to
pursue his libel suits against Whig editors, said it best: "I place the name
of Bryant as near the top of American literature, as any man has yet
attained. In my view, he is not only one of the noblest poets, but one of
the best prose writers of the age. . . . This is not the opinion of a political
partisan either, for while I think generally with Mr. Bryant, on political
subjects, we are widely separated on many essentials."

Among Democratic editors, only Bryant had given newspaper space to Cooper's responses to attacks by Whig partisans James Watson Webb of the *Courier and Enquirer*, William L. Stone of the *Commercial Advertiser*, and Horace Greeley of the *Tribune*. When the influential politician and journalist Thurlow Weed persistently made scandalous remarks about Cooper in the *Albany Evening Journal*, Cooper sued Weed for libel five times. Bryant worried about his friend's penchant for litigation, but after seeing Cooper on one occasion he told Dana: "every body allows that the manners of the newspaper-makers are much mended since he took them in hand."

Another of Bryant's friends from Bread and Cheese days, Samuel Morse, had revolutionized the collection and distribution of news when, in 1844, his electric telegraph transmitted the news of James K. Polk's nomination for the presidency from Baltimore to Washington, D.C. Thanks to Morse's invention, the center of the newspaper world was shifting from Washington to New York City, where Bryant continued to position the *Evening Post* as the foremost newspaper championing liberal democracy. With the newspaper enlarged to nine columns of reduced type in order to accommodate a surge in advertising, Bryant boasted that the *Evening Post* was now competitive with the largest papers in the city.

Bryant was an influential voice of liberal democracy among the nation's editors, and the weekly edition of the *Evening Post* was now the party's most widely distributed newspaper. With the change in administration on March 4, 1845, the *Post*'s editor tried to mediate between warring Democratic political camps. New York State's Democratic party had split into two factions: the radicals or "Barnburners," as they soon were called, who were committed to free soil and free labor; and the conservatives or Hunkers. Bryant aligned himself with the radical camp but struggled to maintain a conciliatory editorial policy toward the entire Democratic Party.

Relieved that the patronage-scarred Tyler administration was ending, Bryant congratulated James Polk, the dark horse Democrat from Tennessee, on his ascendancy to the presidency. "We think we can perceive somewhat a purification of the political atmosphere; we are beginning already to respire a purer air." Bryant praised Polk's "tone of modesty, understanding and dignity." The new president's "impartiality, the fairness of intention, and the magnanimous elevation over party views" appealed to the editor of the *Evening Post*.

II

Strapped for cash after subsidizing Parke Godwin's failed journalistic venture, and involved more than ever in the life of the city and nation, Bryant had not thought about revisiting Europe. In September 1844, he had written to his friend and walking companion Ferdinand Field: "Would that I could have accompanied you in your visit to Stonehenge and other old places in your walking excursions! But these are dreams: the probability is that I shall never visit England nor you come to New York. I shall go on a mere journalist until I am worn out." But in early 1845, Charles Leupp, a wealthy young Sketch Club member and an associate in the management of the American Art Union, proposed a six-month journey abroad to Bryant. Leupp, who was a partner and son-in-law of the prosperous leather dealer Gideon Lee, offered to cover all expenses. Bryant could not resist the opportunity of returning to Europe—and of seeing England for the first time. Travel, as always, was a way to break away from the daily journalistic routine and escape metropolitan life. More significantly, travel enabled Bryant to redefine himself and, from a European vantage point, interrogate the idea of America.

Settling his family at Roslyn and leaving the *Evening Post* in charge of his friend Charles Elbert Anderson, Bryant and his patron set sail for England aboard the packet ship *Liverpool* on April 22. Handling the rock and swell of the ocean as best he could while waiting off Sandy Hook, Bryant told his wife in several notes that he anticipated a prosperous voyage. He had a stateroom to himself. Moreover, "the passengers," he informed Frances, "appear like civil people." With the days calm and pleasant, Bryant was able to read, talk with passengers, and play shuffleboard on deck. His seasickness was "as little troublesome as possible," as it would be throughout the unusually placid voyage.

His only preoccupation was the state of affairs at his new estate in Roslyn. Do not forget, he reminded Frances, to plant several plum trees on the hill in the orchard. Landscape design was one of Bryant's passions, and this was the start of the decades-long process that would transform Cedarmere into a horticultural showplace. Already he missed his new home and his wife: "It seems strange to travel without you—and the strangeness is not an agreeable one I assure you."

Although he wrote that he "never felt perfectly right" during the twenty-eight-day voyage from Sandy Hook to Liverpool, Bryant held up tolerably well during the trip and even managed to eat with "something of an appetite." On May 26, the ship docked in Liverpool, where Bryant and Leupp found their way in rain and fog to the Adelphi Hotel. Bryant, a resilient traveler, found the lodgings to be "very comfortable." Unlike other American tourists who described Liverpool as ugly and uninspiring, Bryant liked the city's sturdy looks, its massive buildings and, especially, the Zoological Garden. At the same time, he wondered whether he had not embarked too hastily on the journey. He confided to Frances, "To leave so many objects of interest and affection, and to purchase five or six months of fatigue at the expense of a month of misery, which besides for all profitable purposes was almost a blank seemed to me little short of madness."

Aside from the sight of the mainland from Plymouth Harbor, where he had waited a week for favorable winds during his return from Le Havre in 1836, Bryant had never seen England, which most nineteenth-century American tourists perceived through nostalgic lenses. Irving had created the prototype of the sentimental American tourist in England with his hugely popular *Sketch-Book of Geoffrey Crayon* (1820). In his letters to the *Evening Post*, Bryant would pay more modest homage to Mother England than had Irving; the nation of his ancestors did not inspire sublime feelings. In fact, he told readers of the *Evening Post*, Liverpool engaged his fancy in large part because its bustling, prosperous energy reminded him of New York. Even the azaleas in the countryside had finer American counterparts. When Bryant visited the walled town of Chester, which so many American tourists found to be the apotheosis of romantic Old England, he was not inspired to write glowingly about it. Still, at a time when Americans found travel accounts popular, Bryant offered the *Evening Post*'s readers graphic descriptions of England—its countryside, byways, manners, and oddities. Bryant's luminous descriptive powers, intelligent observations on the British character, and plain, clear style led one Whig critic to declare in the Philadelphia *North American* that the poet's letters from Europe were "the most interesting productions of their sort we have ever read."

In letters to his wife and the *Evening Post* and in diary entries for 1845, Bryant dutifully recorded his travel impressions without ever claiming that England was a unique source of cultural authority. Unlike Emerson, who had gone to England in 1833 largely for his health; Margaret Fuller, who visited England on a sentimental journey; or Nathaniel Hawthorne, who would accept a consulship in Liverpool in 1853 in order to have a steady income, Bryant was neither an innocent abroad nor an impoverished American writer. He would never lament, as

Hawthorne did in his preface to *The Marble Faun*, the paucity of American cultural experience: "no shadow, no antiquity, no mystery, no picturesque and gloomy wrong." Bryant was self-assured and influential, and he was sufficiently aware of his cultural authority.

The British generally perceived Bryant as the bard of America, the sage of a democratic nation. English writers and critics were inclined to view him as a unique cultural icon—America's only significant poet, its leading journalist, and its most distinguished civic leader. His friend Harriet Martineau, whom he had met in 1834 through Catharine Sedgwick and her family, exempted Bryant from her dour cultural comments in *Society in America* (1837), introducing him to the English public as America's preeminent writer. Martineau argued that although there was a "nonexistence of literature" in the United States, the Americans "did have a poet" in Bryant. "Those of his poems which are the best known, or the most quoted," she wrote, "are smooth, sweet, faithful descriptions of nature, such as his own imagination delights in." Martineau praised "The Evening Wind" for its "most delicious" sensations drawn from nature, along with "Thanatopsis" and "The Past" for their "higher degree of power." Sharing with Dickens a disdain for the American press, Martineau exempted the *Evening Post* from her blanket condemnation.

Bryant's arrival in England had been preceded a year earlier by an anonymous evaluation of American poetry in the *Foreign Review Quarterly* that probably was composed by John Foster, a confidant and literary adviser of Dickens. During Dickens's twenty-two days in New York City in 1842, the novelist had seen Bryant on at least eight occasions. "I like him hugely," Bryant had told Dana; Dickens in turn had been impressed by the American poet, conveying this high regard through Foster. Echoing Martineau's assessment of American literature, Foster asserted that Bryant was the only American poet worthy of the title. "We have been all looking out for a purely American poet, who should be strictly national in the comprehensive sense of the term. The only man who approaches that character is William Cullen Bryant. . . . Out of this national inspiration he draws universal sympathies."

Bryant's reputation and his letters of introduction to English luminaries from the worlds of literature, art, commerce, and politics thus made him a notably distinguished American visitor. In Liverpool, he dined with Harriet Martineau's brother John, a prominent Unitarian minister and scholar; the two men enjoyed a delightful conversation about Unitarianism in England and notable Unitarians in America—Dewey, Ware, Parker, Furnace, and Hedge. In London, where he stayed from June 4 to June 23, Bryant breakfasted twice with the elderly English poet and patron Samuel Rogers, to whom Irving had dedicated the London edition of Bryant's poems, and also met Thomas Moore, Leigh Hunt, and other famous writers, scholars, and artists. The Field family, including Bryant's friends Ferdinand and Alfred and their brother Edwin, a prominent lawyer and patron, entertained Bryant on several occasions. Edward Everett, the American minister to England, invited him to a literary breakfast, where he saw Samuel Rogers, Thomas Moore, and R. Monckton Miles. His American friends Edwin Forrest and John Rand took Bryant to the theater and opera and introduced the poet to their many acquaintances. Bryant visited the unfinished Houses of Parliament, the Reform Club, the London docks, Barclay's Brewery, and other public sites.

Bryant was impressed by London's extensive park system. Unlike Manhattan, which had scarcely 170 acres of parkland, London was a pastoral paradise. Bryant sent a letter to the *Evening Post* regretting the shortsightedness of Manhattan's planners: "your sultry summers, and the corrupt atmosphere generated in hot and crowded streets, make it a cause of regret that in laying out New York, no preparation was made ... for a range of parks and public gardens along the central part of the island or elsewhere, to remain perpetually for the refreshment and recreation of the citizens during the torrid heats of the warm season." As early as 1833, Bryant had deplored "a deficiency of public squares in the lower part of the city for the purposes of health and refreshment." London's parks reinforced Bryant's conviction, which he had enunciated clearly in his July 1844 editorial "A New Public Park," that New Yorkers deserved space for public pleasure.

London's parks might be edifying, but its exhibitions were not. Touring an exhibition of paintings by the Royal Academy, Bryant "saw nothing in it to astonish one who has visited the exhibitions of our Academy of the Arts and Design in New York." Several new impressionistic paintings by Turner—admittedly "a great artist, and a man of genius"—struck Bryant as abstract and strange, composed of "mere blotches of white paint with streaks of yellow and red, and without any intelligent design." Once again Bryant distanced himself from European experience, reminding American readers of their own independence and cultural authority.

Bryant, an American of consequence, was at ease among English celebrities and intellectuals. Attending a rally of the Anti-Corn League at Covent Garden with the Forrests, he was introduced to the huge audience, several members of which, he recounted, leaned forward "to get a peep at the Yankee poet"; and he heard lines from his "Hymn to the City" quoted by a speaker to applause. At Cambridge he met the historian Henry Hallam; the distinguished mathematician and master of Trinity College, William Whewell; and the geologist and dean of Westminster, William Buckland, who entertained the poet at breakfast in his home. Invited to the annual meeting of the British Association, Bryant heard Adam Sedgwick, a Cambridge geologist and past president of the Geographical Society, propose a toast to the health of "Mr. Bryant, of New York," to which the American poet made a gracious response, complimenting the "great and generous British nation."

Chief among the celebrities that Bryant wanted to see was William Wordsworth. Bryant had been nurtured in childhood on English poetry, including Wordsworth's verse. However, Wordsworth was only one in a gallery of figures in his father's well-stocked library, which included, according to Bryant, "most of the eminent English poets": Shakespeare, Milton, Dryden, Pope, Johnson, Goldsmith, Thomson, Burns, Southey, Cowper, Byron, and Coleridge. Along with the hymns of Watts, several of which he memorized and recited often to family and friends, Bryant's favorite had not been Wordsworth or any other Romantic poet but rather Pope; he had spent many winter evenings reading Pope's translations of Homer.

Among the cult of nature poets in England, Bryant had been drawn more to Cowper with his concentration on the beauty and innocence of nature than to Wordsworth and his mystical preoccupation with nature as a spiritual inspiration and guide to conduct. Perhaps the closest Bryant came to the author of "Tintern Abbey" and Wordsworth's incomparable mysticism was "A Forest Hymn," with its mildly deistic conception of nature:

> Thou art in the soft winds
> That from the inmost darkness of the place
> Comes, scarcely felt; the barky trunks, the ground,
> The fresh moist ground, are all instinct with thee.
> Here is continual worship;—Nature, here,
> In the tranquility that thou dost love,
> Enjoys thy presence. . . .

Although Bryant echoes Wordsworth's ideas in "A Forest Hymn" in his line, "The groves were God's first temples," he sees in nature's beauties only a "visible token" of the Creator rather than seeing the actual presence of God in the landscape. Nevertheless, Bryant held Wordsworth in esteem and probably had learned more from the English poet in style and phrasing, if not substance, than he admitted. The closest he came to acknowledging his debt to Wordsworth was his description of his pleasure when first reading *Lyrical Ballads*: "A thousand springs seemed to gush up at once into my heart and the face of Nature, of a sudden, to change into a strange freshness of life."

Bryant and Leupp visited Wordsworth at Rydal Mount on a rainy day in July, carrying with them a letter of introduction from the diarist Henry Crabb Robinson, an intimate of Wordsworth, Coleridge, and Southey. The Wordsworths, having heard from friends in London about the Americans' itinerary, were expecting Bryant and his travel companion. Although Bryant did not mention his time with the Wordsworth family in his letters to the *Evening Post*, he provided an account in correspondence with his wife. He found Wordsworth "in the garden in a broadbrimmed, low-crowned white hat looking like a southern planter. He appears much younger than Mrs. Wordsworth, his stature is rather tall, his forehead prominent, bald, with long white hairs on the temples; his face is finer and more expressive than the common engravings give him, and the features larger; his nose is high and morbidly enlarged at the nostrils, and the chin small." Bryant was charmed by the old poet's love of his grounds, interest in horticulture, and modest demeanor. Wordsworth led his two guests to the spot on Rydal Lake where Henry Inman had painted the scene. Again and again, Wordsworth spoke fondly of Inman, declaring that he thought the American artist's portrait of him was the best ever made.

Bryant spent several hours with Wordsworth, finally departing so that the older poet and his wife could greet other guests; he returned at six o'clock, finding the poet engaged in ornamental gardening. The two men shared a fascination with laying out grounds, and Bryant was pleased to see that his host "piques himself on understanding particularly well, and his own little place is a good example of his skill." Wordsworth apparently appreciated the visit of the Yankee poet. Writing to Crabb Robinson, Mary Wordsworth observed that of the many strangers besetting them that summer, "among those we liked best was the Poet Bryant. He was an agreeable modest person—& my husband enjoyed his society."

Bryant did not spend much time in the Lake District. Learning from Wordsworth that Miss Martineau lived nearby and was anxious to see him, Bryant called on her on July 11, finding her "apparently full of life and vigor," still a lively and vivacious talker, and just "as positive and dogmatical as ever." Afterwards, Bryant and Leupp quickly passed through the border country to Edinburgh.

Although the magnificent physical setting of Edinburgh made it "the finest city" he ever saw in the English isles, Bryant deplored the reality of a "wretched and squalid class" of people constituting a majority of its citizens. After visiting Roslin, "an ugly Scotch village" outside Edinburgh, the poet told Frances that it "looks no more like Roslyn on Long Island than A. looks like an Ampersand." Glasgow was little better. Despite its substantial population of three hundred thousand people and its relative prosperity, the city contained "an extraordinary large proportion of plain women—indeed it was rare to see one who was not so." Britain might have its satisfactions—its countryside and urban parks, imposing monuments and magnificent buildings, and haunts of famous writers like Shakespeare, Scott, and Byron—but Bryant maintained an independent and often critical judgment.

The two Americans continued by steamer across the channel to Belfast, then by carriage to Dublin, which they reached on July 25. Dublin received little comment from Bryant, who by now was complaining to Frances that she was not writing to him with any regularity. Before leaving Yorkshire, he had confessed to his wife: "If I had five minutes to spare from trotting about and looking at new sights—if in short, I were not kept busy every minute as a dog in an Orange County china mill I think I should be homesick."

After spending two days in Dublin, Bryant and Leupp sailed for Liverpool and from there returned to London, arriving on July 26 in order to prepare for a trip to Paris. Before leaving London, Bryant saw the Forrests, with whom he attended the opera; and Rand, who was in good spirits, anticipating that his invention, an Eolian attachment to the piano forte, would have widespread appeal. Bryant also visited the Lunatic Asylum at Hanwell, writing to the *Evening Post* that the humane and progressive treatment of the inmates by its director, Dr. John Conolly, had created an environment of relative tranquility for the facility's residents.

On July 29, Bryant and his young companion left London for Brighton, where they crossed the Channel en route to Paris, which Leupp had never seen. They passed through Dieppe and Rouen, where Bryant had just enough time to "peep into the cathedral" before continuing to the French capital by railway. Bryant found Paris "somewhat altered" since he was there with his family some ten years earlier. "The streets are kept cleaner, in many of them side walks have been made. . . . The Boule-vards have been furnished with a smooth broad *trottoir* of asphaltum, and they are as lively as ever." With Leupp in tow for the ten-days stay in the French capital, Bryant diligently showed his benefactor the city's high-lights—the Louvre and the Luxembourg, the Jardin des Plantes, Ver-sailles, and countless churches including the venerable Notre Dame Cathedral. Fascinated by cemeteries, the poet visited Pere Lachaise, "now crowded with monuments" and teeming with funerals. He also walked by the central morgue on two occasions, viewing two corpses that had been pulled from the Seine on his second visit. The French apparently did not share the poet's mordant imagination. Parisians were as lively as ever, thronging the boulevards and parks, crowding the opera and theaters, and dancing till midnight on Sunday evenings.

Bryant regretted that Frances was not with him and that he was not receiving letters from her. Leupp had received "a great pile of letters" in Paris, but there had been none from Frances. "You may imagine my vex-ation," he wrote her, "by supposing that you were yourself in a strange land, that I were in America, that steamers were passing to and fro every fortnight or oftener, and that I had neglected to write to you for two months." The weather in Paris had turned rainy and muddy, comple-menting Bryant's leaden spirits.

Bryant's travels to this point scarcely had been leisurely, but now he seemed frantic to complete his travels and get back to America, his family, and work. The "solitariness" of the journey without his family tinged his letters to the *Post*. Belgium, the Netherlands, Germany, Prague, and Vienna were scarcely more than a blur of recollection as Bryant and his companion went "zig zagging through Europe" that summer, as he wrote Frances, often moving so swiftly that "the recollection of the different places I have seen do not always come in their proper order."

In his diary, Bryant catalogued the points on his European tour—Graz, Trieste, Venice, Padua, Ferrara, Bologna, Florence—as if they were cities any dutiful traveler had to experience. True, there were some mem-orable sites: the cathedral in Trieste, the crowds in Piazza San Marco, the university at Padua. Bryant's health was good; there were no complica-tions. At Florence he saw his friend Horatio Greenough and fellow American artists Hiram Powers, Henry Peters Gray, and George Loring Brown. Their talent and projects seemed superior to those of European artists, whose work he viewed at Florence's annual exhibition at the Academy of the Fine Arts. Aside from two landscapes reminding him "somewhat of Cole's manner," Bryant found most of the exhibition to be "decidedly bad; wretched landscapes; portraits, some of which were absolutely hideous, stiff, ill-colored, and full of grimace."

Disturbing news awaited Bryant when he reached Rome on September 30. His business partners William G. Boggs and Timothy Howe had fired Charles Anderson and had turned the editorial post over to Parke Godwin. Bryant was upset by this development. In a conciliatory letter to Anderson, he wrote, "I certainly did intend that you should hold in the editorial management of the paper the same place which I held and that you should have the editorial control and responsibility of its columns." The few issues of the *Evening Post* that Bryant had seen in Europe had impressed him with their discretion and relative firmness on such issues as the Texas question. Bryant told Anderson that he could not assess his friend's complaint from afar. However, he suspected Parke Godwin's role in the matter, for within a year Bryant would rid the *Evening Post* of his son-in-law's services.

Although he confessed to Frances that time was "dragging heavily," Bryant nevertheless decided to visit other parts of Europe that he had come to see. After touring Italy—Tivoli, Naples, Pompeii and Herculaneum, Sorrento, Genoa, Milan—he dragged Leupp up the Alps and down into the Rhone valley, visiting Byron's castle and Edward Gibbon's former house in Lausanne, where they had breakfast. In Geneva, Bryant ran into his friend Henry Anderson, learning more from him about his brother Charles's problems at the *Post*. Returning to Paris, he saw Samuel Morse, in France to promote his telegraph; and John L. O'Sullivan, editor of the *Democratic Review*. Crossing the Channel, he stayed in London for three days, seeing Rogers twice, moved by the old poet's lament that he probably would never see Bryant again. On November 4, 1845, Bryant departed for Liverpool, boarded the steamship *Britannia* for a rough sixteen-day passage to Boston, and from there rushed back to New York.

III

After six months wandering through Europe, Bryant found Cedarmere to be the closest thing to heaven. To Dana he wrote that his country retreat in Hempstead Harbor was almost as dear to him as one of his own children. "My heart yearned after it during the whole of my absence in Europe. I used to beguile the qualms of seasickness as I lay in my berth with thinking over my little plans for its improvement, such as planting a fruit tree here and a shade tree there and clearing away the growth of shrubs about some fine young pear trees that had sprung up in a corner of my field."

But Gotham and the *Evening Post* beckoned, and Bryant quickly found suitable winter accommodations in the city. At the invitation of William T. McCoun, who was vice chancellor of the New York Court of Chancery and president of the newly formed New York Prison Association, Bryant took rooms with him and his daughter Mary in their house at 30 Warren Street. "Amidst a thousand interruptions"—dining one evening with Alfred Field and another night with Orville Dewey and dealing with the "kind proffers of hospitality" from many other friends— Bryant immediately resumed editorial control of the *Evening Post*. One of his first steps was to demote Parke Godwin to the position of news assistant.

The news that winter was dominated by rumors of war with Mexico over the Texas question and growing tension with England over the status of the Oregon territory. Bryant thought that the crisis with Mexico could be resolved amicably, especially in light of President James Polk's offer of five million dollars for the purchase of New Mexico and twenty-five million for the purchase of California. Polk's special envoy to Mexico, John Sidell, had instructions to defuse the confrontation over the Texas boundary dispute. War, Bryant thought, could be averted. He was especially pleased by Polk's first message to Congress, in which the president stated that the issue over Texas should be resolved early in the session.

Bryant was less sanguine about his country's dispute with Britain over the Oregon territory. Already more than five thousand Americans, fueled by "Oregon fever," were in the territory below the Columbia River at the 49th parallel—the line established by the two nations in 1818 and reaffirmed for an indefinite period in 1827. On assuming office, President Polk had offered to partition the Oregon territory, which stretched northward into half of British Columbia, at the 49th parallel, but the British minister in Washington had summarily rejected the proposal without submitting it to London. Now, in his annual message to Congress, Polk took a more aggressive stance, suggesting that the United States look John Bull "straight in the eye" and assert a claim to all of Oregon.

A week before Polk's annual message to Congress, Bryant had claimed in an editorial that the United States should assert its claim to the Oregon territory even at the risk of war. "If we were to yield what we believe to be our just title to the northwestern coast of our continent," he wrote on November 28, "on so slight and shadowy a menace of danger as that which exists, we should deserve to be classed with the most cowardly and abject races of men that ever lived." In subsequent editorials Bryant would temper his martial fervor with more cautious comments advocating a peaceful resolution of the dispute. Nevertheless, he concurred with his friend John L. O'Sullivan's credo, which the Jacksonian journalist advanced in a December editorial in the *Morning News*, affirming "the manifest design of Providence in regard to the occupation of this continent."

In 1846, the Oregon controversy prompted Bryant to compose "Oh Mother of a Mighty Race," a poem obliquely attacking England and other European powers for their incursions into the New World. Over seven six-line stanzas, Bryant personifies the American nation as a source of inspiration for "down-trodden and opprest" peoples fleeing the "elder dames" and "haughty peers" of Europe:

> They know not, in their hate and pride,
> What virtues with thy children bide;
> How true, how good, thy graceful maids
> Make bright, like flowers, the valley-shades;
> > What generous men
> Spring, like thine oaks, by hill and glen;—
>
> What cordial welcomes greet the guest
> By thy lone rivers of the West. . . .

Europe, Bryant implies in militant tones, was an oppressive power whose "baffled hounds" should not try to pursue territorial claims in Aroostock County and Oregon.

During his first voyage to Europe, Bryant had searched fruitlessly for inspiration in Old World landscapes. He had given little thought to writing poetry during his second visit to the Continent, concentrating instead on composing thousands of words of travel narrative for the *Evening Post*. But now, back in New York, he set out to revise and prepare his poetry for an illustrated edition that the Philadelphia firm of Cary & Hart would publish.

On December 4, 1845, Bryant wrote to Dana, the one person he trusted for literary advice, asking if he would be willing to offer serious criticism of Bryant's poetry. Bryant implored his friend, who had been his mentor when he prepared his first small volume in Cambridge in

1821, to offer an unbridled assessment of his poems: "In looking at them again you will be very apt to remember how they struck you at first, without taking the trouble to read them over a second time. If your former impression was unfavorable in regard to any one of them you will counsel me of course to omit it." A month later, Bryant sent Dana "an English cheap edition which has all my poems that have been published in a single volume. . . . You shall have something better than this shabby pamphlet when Cary & Hart's edition is out."

Dana apparently read and reread every poem Bryant had published, writing two long letters—the first running to twenty pages—that offered detailed advice on altering metrical lines, substituting words, and improving imagery and sense. Reading "The Ages," Dana questioned the lines "Europe . . . / too is strong, and might not chafe in vain / Against them, but shake off the vampire train / That batten on her blood, and break their net," objecting to the vampire imagery. Bryant was chagrined: "Such nonsense I could hardly believe I had written." For the new edition, he changed the offending lines to: ". . . / Against them, but might cast to earth the train / That trample her, and break their iron net." Dana offered similar suggestions for improving dozens of other selections. But on the whole, Dana was awed by Bryant's verse. He closed his first letter with high praise: "Let me say in plain honesty, and without any mere wish to please you, that my looking over your poems afresh has served to raise you higher than ever in my mind. The truth of your language, the felicities of phrase, the eye and feeling from nature, the tenderness and exceeding beauty, were always present with me. But I am more than ever before impressed with the *number* of the pieces that ascend into grandeur of thought, into the *higher* order of powers." In his second letter, Dana expressed relief that Bryant would follow his advice and not omit, as Bryant had contemplated, any poems from the new edition. "It is quite delightful," Dana wrote, "to find fault with you, you take it so patiently, thou least sensitive, or, more definitely, least touchy, of poets."

Bryant had high expectations for the new edition of his poetry, hoping that it would be as attractive as the one that Carey & Hart had produced late in 1845 for Longfellow with Daniel Huntington's illustrations. In January, he wrote to Longfellow to tell him how much he liked the embellished edition, *The Belfry of Bruges and Other Poems.* The quality of Longfellow's verse seemed "more beautiful than on former readings, much as I admired them then. The exquisite music of your verse dwells more agreeably than ever on my ear, and more than ever am I affected by their depth of feeling and the spirituality and the creative power with which they set before us passages from the great drama of life."

Bryant found true merit in his friend's verse, but he was also defending Longfellow against Edgar Allan Poe's attacks in the *Broadway Journal*, in which Poe called Longfellow "a determined imitator and a dextrous adapter of the ideas of other people." Poe had become a sensation with the publication of "The Raven" in the New York *Evening Mirror* of January 29, 1845, and of his volume *The Raven and Other Poems* later that year. Bryant received a reply from Longfellow within a week in which his friend, perhaps subconsciously echoing Poe's attack, acknowledged a profound debt to his mentor: "In return, let me say what a staunch friend and admirer of yours I have been from the beginning, and acknowledge how much I owe to you, not only of delight, but of culture. When I look back upon my earlier poems, I cannot but smile to see how much in them is really yours."

One feature of the new project worried Bryant: the quality and appropriateness of the illustrations by Emanuel Leutze, whom he had seen in Düsseldorf when the artist was completing his canvas, *Washington Crossing the Delaware*. Bryant suspected that the German-born artist, who had emigrated to America and called Philadelphia his permanent home, had an imperfect understanding of his poetry and an idiosyncratic approach to illustrating specific selections. Leutze for his part complained to the publishers about the project: "It is difficult to find any but landscape subjects in his works. I do not understand him so well as Longfellow—but I will do my utmost."

Bryant would have preferred Huntington or John G. Chapman as an illustrator for the new edition and was unhappy with Leutze's final designs. While admiring the "genius" of Leutze and the fine work he accomplished for certain poems like "Catterskill Falls," Bryant did not think the artist had captured the purpose of "Fairest of the Rural Maids." Moreover, he was appalled by the artist's illustration for "The Greek Boy," in which one leg of the image seemed grotesquely elongated. Bryant was profoundly indebted to Dana for the "great service" he had rendered in helping to correct a "thousand faults" that were embedded in the poems, but he confessed to his friend that he did not take much delight in the engravings. "I think very well of the talents of Leutze who makes the designs, but what can be expected of an artist who works to order in that way? What sort of verses should I make if I were to sit down to put his pictures into verse? Worse than I make now I fear."

IV

Poetry was a welcome distraction from Bryant's crusade to make the *Evening Post* the leading voice of liberal democracy. Central to the editor's creed was his belief that the "best course for the democratic party" was to place right above expediency and to identify always "with the permanent interests and sympathies of the mass of the people." Philip Hone, as usual, despised Bryant's enunciation of the *Post*'s principles, calling the opinions "virulent and malignant as are usually the streams which flow from that polluted source." But young reporter Walter Whitman, still using his full first name, embraced Bryant's editorial ethos: "It is an honor and a pride to the Democratic party that it has such a man to conduct one of its principal newspapers—to be an expounder of its doctrines, and act as one of the warders to watch the safety of the citadel."

To Bryant, the safety of the citadel seemed precarious in 1846. That spring, the *Evening Post*'s editor did not think it prudent to place "twenty thousand rifles beyond the Rocky Mountains" in defense of the Oregon territory and was pleased to see a peaceful resolution of the dispute. But he was distressed by the course of events concerning the Republic of Texas, which had been annexed by the United States on December 29, 1845, and now was subject to increasingly bellicose behavior by the Mexican government. Clashes between Mexican and American forces broke out on April 25, 1846, prompting President Polk to declare before Congress on May 11 that a state of war existed and to request the enrollment of fifty thousand volunteers. In a May 13 editorial, Bryant urged caution, contending that a "prodigious army could only be employed for the purpose of invading the territory of the enemy."

The conflict with Mexico was more complex, but Bryant continued to urge caution. Only when it became clear that war was inevitable did Bryant offer a bland endorsement of "such demonstrations of vigor as shall convince Mexico that we are in earnest." Aware that many of his friends and acquaintances in New York and New England, including fellow poets Emerson, Whittier, and Lowell, were hostile to the war with Mexico, and doubtful about the rightness of the conflict himself, Bryant dutifully reported on military operations while maintaining a low editorial profile. He saw to it that the *Evening Post* offered ample coverage of the war, which was provided by correspondents in the field. However, he refused to join six other New York newspapers—the *Sun, Tribune, Herald, Journal of Commerce, Courier and Enquirer*, and *Express*—in sharing the costs of procuring Mexican War updates by telegraphy. Bryant's editorials on the Mexican War were few and far from militant. When General Zachary Taylor—"Rough and Ready" as his troops called him—captured Monterey that fall, Bryant wrote hopefully that "Mexico should desire a peace."

Bryant was more militant when considering the issue of the territories—especially California—that might be wrested from Mexican control. Lowell's cracker-barrel Yankee, Hosea Biglow, offered a prediction that echoed Bryant's own fears:

> They jest want this Californy
> So's to lug new slave-States in
> To abuse ye, an' to scorn ye,
> An' to plunder ye like sin . . .
> Chaps that make black slaves o'niggers
> Want to make a slave o' you.

Bryant stated the matter in more elegant terms: "California, if acquired, shall be acquired for the west, and not for the south . . . the institution of slavery, which operates as an exclusion of that class of emigrants who carry with them only their families and their own strong arms, shall be prohibited forever."

Unlike Whitman, who ranted in the *Brooklyn Eagle* that "Mexico must be thoroughly chastised," Bryant maintained a subdued editorial posture as the war progressed. In a rapid sequence of victories, General Winfield Scott—"Old Fuss and Feathers"—took Vera Cruz and Mexico City; Colonel Stephen Kearny occupied Santa Fe; and Commodore John Sloat raised the American flag over Monterey, claiming all of California for the United States. Perhaps it was manifest destiny at work, but Bryant, while nominally supporting President Polk's policies, wrote remarkably few editorials on the Mexican conflict.

In July 1846, Bryant once again escaped the city and the *Evening Post* to enjoy a summer vacation, this time to visit his mother and brothers in Illinois, spending about a week in Princeton in the middle of his travels. Instead of retracing the 1841 itinerary, Bryant, accompanied by Frances and Julia, traveled by Great Lakes steamboats, seeing the major cities—Buffalo, Cleveland, Detroit, and Chicago—and the towns and wilderness settlements along the shores of Lakes Erie, Huron, and Michigan.

Writing to the *Post*'s readers, Bryant offered a colorful critique of frontier life and America's expansion into the old Northwest. He observed that Buffalo, with its burgeoning population, was not an especially attractive city, and that Detroit, as a fellow traveler warned, might very well be filled with thieves. On the other hand, Cleveland was "a thriving village yet to grow into a proud city of the lake country." And Chicago had undergone a remarkable transformation since he had seen it on his return trip from Illinois in 1841: "Anyone who had seen this place, as I had done five years ago, when it contained less than five thousand people, would find some difficulty in recognizing it now when its population is more than fifteen thousand. . . . The slovenly and raw appearance of a new settlement begins in many parts to disappear."

Although his ideas about the nation's Native American population had not changed significantly, Bryant felt compelled to relate the pernicious influence of white Americans on the remnants of the Chippewa and Pottawatomie tribes who resided on both sides of the border between the United States and Canada. Visiting a Chippewa village that the Canadian government had constructed in an effort to bring white culture to the tribe, Bryant learned that the experiment was a failure: the Indians refused to adapt to farming and instead spent their time hunting and fishing and in general idleness. At another village outside the settlement at Sault de Ste. Marie, Bryant and his party encountered Indian and half-breed men and woman, almost all of them drunk on whiskey. Even in the few settlements, usually run by missionaries, where there were congregations of productive "good Indians," Bryant heard from a local missionary that the population was in precipitous decline. "Such appears to be the destiny of the red race while in the presence of the white," Bryant concluded in a letter published in the *Post* on August 24, "decay and gradual extinction, even under circumstances the most favorable to its preservation."

Soon after returning to New York in late August, Bryant ran into Maria Clemm, the mother-in-law of Edgar Allan Poe, who informed him that "her son-in-law is crazy, his wife dying, and the whole family starving." The Bryants had known Poe and his family since 1837, when they had lived near each other on Carmine Street in Greenwich Village. More recently, Bryant and Poe occasionally saw each other at the homes of the writer Caroline Kirkland and the aspiring poet Anne Charlotte Lynch, who ran two of New York's most popular salons. Parke Godwin recalled seeing the two men at an evening party hosted by Mrs. Kirkland "when they talked together for a long time." Slim and neatly dressed, Poe approached Bryant "as some Grecian youth might be imagined to approach an image of Plato—with a look and attitude of the profoundest reverence; and during the whole time of their conversation he preserved this expression."

Bryant's old friends Miss Sedgwick, Caroline Kirkland, Halleck, and the Reverend Orville Dewey often attended the evening parties on the upper floor of the Lynch house on Waverly Place—the ladies elaborately coiffed and elegantly dressed and the men wearing formal black. Margaret Fuller and other younger writers who knew and admired Bryant also attended these gatherings. Along with many of Poe's literary acquaintances, Bryant provided aid to Poe during the poet's harrowing last years, when his family was living in a small cottage in Fordham, just outside New York, and his wife, Virginia, was dying of tuberculosis.

Poe was one of Bryant's most astute critics and admirers. In a review appearing in the April 1846 issue of *Godey's Lady's Book*, Poe offered a defense of the older poet against the increasingly popular work of younger poets and critics like Longfellow and Lowell. Poe declared that Bryant might not possess that "genius of a higher order" associated with Shelley, Coleridge, Wordsworth, and Keats, but that he was "a man of high poetical talent, very correct, with warm appreciation of the beauty of nature and great descriptive powers." Bryant's unique form of genius, which "tranquilizes the *soul*," could be seen in poems like "June," in which Bryant expresses the wish that he should die in this lovely month:

> I gazed upon the glorious sky
> And the green mountains round,
> And thought that when I came to lie
> At rest within the ground,
> 'Twere pleasant, that in flowery June,
> When brooks send up a cheerful tune,
> And groves a joyous sound,
> The sexton's hand, my grave to make,
> The rich, green mountain-turf should break.

"The thoughts here belong to the highest class of poetry, the imaginative-natural," Poe claimed, "and are of themselves sufficient to stamp their author a man of genius."

Poe described the poet in middle age:

> He is now fifty-two years of age. In height, he is, perhaps, five
> feet nine. His frame is rather robust. His features are large but

thin. His countenance is sallow, nearly bloodless. His eyes are piercing gray, deep set, with large projecting eyebrows. His mouth is wide and massive, the expression of the smile hard, cold—even sardonic. The forehead is broad, with prominent organs of ideality; a good deal bald; the hair thin and grayish, as also are the whiskers, which he wears in a simple style. His bearing is quite distinguished, full of the aristocracy of intellect. In general, he looks in better health than before his visit to England. He seems active—physically and morally energetic. His dress is plain to the extreme in simplicity, although of late there is a certain degree of Anglicism about it.

Sharing an interest with Bryant in the popular science of phrenology, Poe insisted that the older poet's countenance should not be taken as a sign of frigidity: "The peculiarly melancholy expression of his countenance has caused him to be accused of harshness or coldness of heart. Never was there a greater mistake. His soul is charity itself, in all respects generous and noble."

For his part, Bryant did not know what to think of Poe and his unconventional lifestyle. Bryant's moral sense had been formed by his New England origins and the legacy of Puritanism that he never completely filtered from his identity. Even though Bryant professed the gentler, more humanistic tenets of Unitarianism, he was suspicious of people like Poe, who obviously had fallen from social norms if not from grace. Bryant was not alone in his opinion of Poe. Whitman called Poe "morbid, shadowy, lugubrious." The young poet and critic James Russell Lowell ridiculed him, while fellow New Englander Ralph Waldo Emerson famously labeled Poe "the jingle man." Bryant was ambivalent, but Poe's dissolute lifestyle clearly was an impediment to a close friendship.

In any case, Bryant, who had scores of close acquaintants and friends, was not seeking friendship. Writing to Dana, he confessed, "The three things most irksome to me in my transactions with the world are to owe money, to ask a favor, and to seek an acquaintance. The few excellent friends I have, I acquired I scarcely know how, certainly not by any assiduity of my own." He was self-sufficient and self-contained to a fault, and there was even a bit of bourgeois smugness in his remark. But Bryant's "transactions with the world" had resulted in metropolitan success, and in a very real sense America and the world had befriended him. To many, his fame as a poet and his worldly success were the essence of what Emerson called the "complete man."

11

KINDRED SPIRITS

There is Bryant, as quiet, as cool, and as dignified,
As a smooth, silent iceberg, that never is ignified . . .
—James Russell Lowell, *A Fable for Critics*

I

On a hot August evening in 1846, a portly young Democratic member of Congress from northern Pennsylvania introduced an amendment to a bill in the House of Representatives appropriating two million dollars toward the purchase of territories from Mexico. David Wilmot adapted language from the Ordinance of 1787, applying to the western territories the same principle that Jefferson had designed for the lands northwest of the Ohio. Wilmot stipulated that "as an express and fundamental condition to the acquisition of any territory from the Republic of Mexico . . . neither slavery nor involuntary servitude shall ever exist in any part of said country." The Wilmot Proviso, as it became known, ignited a national firestorm.

Wilmot was a man after Bryant's own liking—a proponent of the rights of workingmen, of hard currency, and of such social reforms as the abolition of imprisonment for debt. It was irrelevant that this "mischievous and foolish amendment," as President Polk termed it, would fail repeatedly in the Senate. With the Wilmot Proviso, the nation became polarized over the issue of slavery or free soil for the new territories. The South would secede rather than submit, Senator John C. Calhoun threatened. A fearful die had been cast.

Bryant rode the tempest created by the Wilmot Proviso toward an increasingly militant position on the issue of slavery or free soil. In late January, titling a leader "Slavery in California," Bryant asserted the rights of American settlers, who already were streaming toward the Pacific, to carve their own destiny—an outcome that he predicted would result in California's admission "into the bosom of the Confederacy, a free state." Bryant carefully and logically set forth the doctrine of free soil, arguing against the proposition that new territory admitted to the Union should be divided equally between free and slave states. When Calhoun submitted four resolutions declaring that legislation barring slavery in the western territories would violate the Constitution, the editor answered sharply: "We thank Mr. Calhoun for playing so bold and open a game," commenting on the senator's "manly" inclination to treat other men as "merchandise." Compounding Calhoun's assault on free soil was the Virginia legislature's resolution, which Bryant thought clearly treasonous, to disregard federal laws prohibiting slavery in the territories to be claimed from Mexico: "A plainer and more direct threat of organized and forcible resistance to the laws, even to the extent of dissolving the Union, could not be made."

Calhoun had become Bryant's bête noire, an adversary provoking the editor's deepest thought on the issue of slavery and free soil. In March, Bryant summarized the dispute:

> A man who does not approve of slavery in the abstract may tolerate it where it exists, from the want of constitutional authority to extinguish it, or from regard to the actual conditions of society, and the difficulties of change; but how can he justify himself in instituting it in new communities, unless he believes with Mr. Calhoun, that it is in itself a "great good"? . . . The federal government represents the free as well as the slave states; and while it does not attempt to abolish slavery in the states where it exists, it must not authorize slavery where it does not exist. This is the only middle ground—the "true basis of conciliation and adjustment."

II

In the midst of the growing political battles over slavery and free soil, personal matters were weighing heavily on Bryant. His daughter Fanny had given birth to the Godwins' first child; the Godwins were now living in a two-story brick cottage near the pond below the main house at Cedarmere. Parke Godwin, chafing under the editorial control of his father-in-law, had left the *Evening Post*, forced out by Bryant after Godwin inserted articles on Fourierism into the paper. Relations between Bryant and Godwin had become notably cool. Godwin had written to Charles A. Dana the previous December, complaining that the "association with Bryant, who is a cold, irritable and selfish man (*entre nous* all this) was distasteful" and that the situation at the *Post* was "intolerable." Bryant in turn thought that Godwin's flirtation with socialism and other communitarian movements, all the rage in certain intellectual quarters, was fatuous and impractical.

Suddenly in need of an assistant, Bryant surmised that a young man he had met after both took rooms in May 1847 at a new house at 4 Amity Place was an attractive prospect. But John Bigelow, a lawyer who had contributed articles on political reform to the *Evening Post*, was not prepared to give up his practice unless Bryant could offer him a stake in the paper. Only after purchasing the shares of his partner Boggs in December 1848 would Bryant be able to offer Bigelow, who was then thirty-two, the partnership he demanded.

Around the same time, Bryant learned from his brother John that their mother, Sarah Snell Bryant, had died on May 6 at the age of seventy-nine. She had broken her hip during the winter and then declined rapidly. As Bryant reflected on his mother's death, he recalled her "blameless and useful life, which it pleased Providence to prolong to so late a period." Sad but prudential, he was certain that his mother had assured her salvation and that even her physical suffering in the last months of her life "had its uses in fitting her for that new state of being on which she has entered." Two years later, Bryant would compose "The May Sun Sheds an Amber Light" as a tribute to his mother. It ends:

> That music of the early year
> Brings tears of anguish to my eyes;
> My heart aches when the flowers appear;
> For then I think of her who lies
> Within her grave,
> Low in her grave

In this short lyric, Bryant revealed a greater emotional loss over the death of Sarah Snell Bryant than in the more diffident tone of his correspondence.

Following a brief summer sojourn in Boston, New Hampshire, and Maine, Bryant returned to New York City and more political skirmishes in the fall of 1847. Replying to an important but unidentified correspondent (perhaps Van Buren, who was still a force in Democratic politics), he wrote, "Your praise would make me vain of my conduct of the Evening Post, if I had not known its defects, and if I were at proof on that question. As a journalist I have no ambition. It is merely my determination to fulfil its duties conscientiously and to do no mischief if I can do no good. It is a contentious kind of life and though I take great interest in questions of public policy, constant debate is ungrateful to me."

In November, the state Democratic Party, irretrievably split between the Barnburner and Hunker factions, suffered a shattering defeat at the hands of the Whigs. It was evident to Bryant that, with events in Mexico exacerbating the political scene, critical choices awaited his party and the nation.

By early 1848, new political storms were roiling the nation and also erupting in Europe. While agonizing over the statewide defeat of his party in the previous fall's elections and the absence of a unifying party leader after the death of Silas Wright, Bryant pondered prospects for new political alignments in the wake of the war and the issue of slavery in the new territories that would be wrested from Mexico. In February, he explained the disarray in the state's democratic party to his brother John. Nevertheless, he predicted, "No man pledged against the prohibition of slavery in the territory, or supposed to be hostile to it, will be able to get the vote of the state of New York. Any separate organization would come to nothing. All parties formed for a single measure are necessarily short-lived and are as much subject to the abuses and vices of party as any other."

Bryant's prediction was wrong, but he quickly changed his opinion about the need for new political alignments as the Mexican War drew to a close. At the Democratic Convention in Baltimore on May 27, the United States senator from Michigan, General Lewis Cass, a leading proponent of popular sovereignty for the territories, was elected on the fourth ballot as the party's presidential candidate. He had been fiercely opposed by the radical faction and especially the Barnburners, who now decided to act independently of the party. New York's Barnburners had been excluded from the convention and had been supplanted by a rival set of Hunker delegates, prompting Bryant to charge in the Evening Post that the nomination of Cass was "spurious." He warned: "We ourselves have been formally excommunicated and anathematized" by the state's

Democratic Party "without finding our standing in the party at all affected by it." By late summer Bryant had changed his mind about the need for a third party, finding a "strong and compelling reason" for bolting the party and creating a new political entity united "for a single measure"—the prevention of slavery in the new territories.

When the Whigs nominated General Taylor for the presidency and Millard Fillmore for the vice presidency at their June 7 convention in Philadelphia, Bryant was fatalistic about the outcome of the fall elections. He had predicted that Taylor would sweep the South from Cape May to Key West and from the Ohio to the Rio Grande and would run strongly in the Northern states as well. Nevertheless, Bryant threw his reputation and the *Evening Post* behind the decision of New York Democrats to advance their own candidates, which they accomplished later in the month at Utica, nominating Martin Van Buren for president and General Henry Dodge of Wisconsin as vice president.

Regretting the regional composition of the Utica meeting, Bryant worked behind the scenes with prominent Barnburners—among them John Van Buren, Samuel J. Tilden, and John Bigelow—to hold a national convention of antislavery dissidents. On August 9, ten thousand anti-slavery representatives from the Barnburner, Democratic, Liberty, and Whig parties, along with radicals unaligned to these factions but united in their hatred of slavery, assembled in Buffalo for a national convention of free soilers.

Bryant was pleased when the assemblage—an emergent Free Soil Party—nominated Van Buren for president and Charles Frances Adams, a Conscience Whig from Boston, as his running mate. "We have candidates," he wrote in the *Evening Post*, "with whom we are satisfied, whom we can trust—in electing whom we cannot be deceived, and for whom we are not obliged to invent or imagine a creed suited to the latitude in which we live." When Taylor achieved a landslide victory in November, Bryant found solace in the substantial Free Soil vote, which was "large enough to show that a powerful anti-extension party has been formed." At the same time, pondering the election of 1848, he asked whether the Republic would "no longer be known as the home of the free and the asylum of the oppressed, but as the home of the slave and the oppressor of the poor."

More than ever before, Bryant was devoting the pages of the *Evening Post* to the slavery issue, offering space to some of the most articulate opponents of the South's peculiar institution. From New York, the young attorney Samuel Jones Tilden, who was opposed to Cass, wrote in support of the Barnburner revolt. Connecticut journalist Gideon Welles contributed powerful essays on the need to bar slavery from the new territories. Likewise, the deeply religious Salmon P. Chase of Ohio assailed slavery while supporting the Free Soil Party. Charles Frances Adams offered Bryant extracts from his father's private diary. "Ever since meeting of the Buffalo Convention," he told Bryant, "I have been favored with the receipt of your daily *Evening Post* and have been gratified by reading what seems to me the best daily journal in the United States."

While hammering at the reactionary forces he detected in the American grain, Bryant reminded readers of the revolutionary political conflicts erupting in Europe during the fateful year of 1848. News of the February uprising in Paris had quickly reached America by ship, and Bryant threw the prestige of the *Post* behind the rebellions against monarchy that were breaking out from Ireland to Russia. In April, he exulted over the fate of tyrannical European governments whose thrones were being "rooted up from [their] foundation and prostrated in a moment by a whirlwind." The ideals of liberty, equality, and fraternity, he claimed, were notions that his own nation should take to heart. "Let Conservatism and Privilege," the *Post*'s editor warned, "wherever to be found in this country, take reasonable warning from its fate in Europe."

A month later, in a letter to Ferdinand Field, Bryant again alluded to the turmoil in Europe: "Our leveling is already done; Europe has hers yet to do. You nations of the old world are so full of fluctuation and change, putting up and pulling down your institutions! For quiet, and tranquility, and freedom from troublesome innovations, you must come to the United States." Bryant spun an extended metaphor involving his "poor" friend Audubon who, now in his mid-sixties, had lapsed into "a state of mental imbecility," forced to leave to his sons John and Victor the task of completing the magnificent *Quadrupeds of America*: "Well, your old world is the old Audubon—fidgety, uneasy, and uncertain in its projects; and we of the new world are the young Audubons—staid, sober young men, who keep on in the good old track."

III

Bryant was concerned about the health of his friends. Audubon, whose exhibitions and work, especially *The Birds of America*, he had praised in various editorials, was declining mentally. Bryant and Audubon shared a love of nature that their mutual acquaintances were quick to detect. Bryant's Unitarian friend and pastor, Orville Dewey, recalled that on one occasion when he and Bryant visited the elder Audubon at his home in upper Manhattan, the artist paid the poet an endearing compliment: "Seating himself before the poet, Audubon quietly said, 'You are our flower,'—a very pretty compliment, I thought, from a man of the woods."

Even as Audubon's gradual decline was on his mind, Bryant had to deal with the death of another artist—his close friend Thomas Cole. On February 11, 1848, Cole had died suddenly of pleurisy at the age of forty-seven. The editor praised his friend as a pioneer in portraying in art "the wild magnificence" of the American landscape, investing nature with "a moral interest." Accepting a unanimous request from the artists of the National Academy of Design, Bryant gave the memorial address for Cole at a tribute on May 4. He spent considerable time composing the funeral oration, working through what he admitted to Dana was "deep grief." Bryant's oration was the first in a series of memorial discourses that the poet would be asked to deliver as close friends—Cooper, Irving, Halleck, Verplanck—passed from the American scene.

That New York's artists selected Bryant rather than one of their own to deliver the eulogy on Cole underscored the poet-editor's celebrity. The popular novelist Elizabeth O. Smith, herself a famous lyceum lecturer, saw the qualities that made Bryant such a dominant presence in New York City's cultural scene and a force in local and national politics. He was, according to Mrs. Smith, "the most genial and companionable of men." She and her husband, the humorist Seba Smith (better known as Jack Downing), had met Bryant in London in 1845 and subsequently visited the Bryants at Cedarmere. Mrs. Smith found Bryant to be "playful and cordial"; above all, she admired him as "a contemner of shams, pretenses, and affectations of every kind."

To judge by his letters and by contemporary accounts, Bryant had a full social life despite his editorial responsibilities. He was still a Sketch Club denizen and a charter member of its spin-off association, the Century Club, which he had helped to found at a meeting in the rotunda of the New York Gallery of Fine Arts in January 1847. Guests descended on him at Cedarmere, staying briefly like Catharine Sedgwick or remaining for weeks, as did Dana on several occasions. Other friends and solicitors visited the editor in his cramped office in the *Evening Post*'s dilapidated building at 18 Nassau Street, where the famous man scratched out his editorials amid frequent interruptions, using the backs of letters and manuscripts for paper. The Homoeopathic Society, the Burns Club, the American Art Union, and a host of other civic organizations competed for his time.

Evenings in the city involved a round of visits: Bryant, often accompanied by Frances, attended Anne Lynch's Saturday evening receptions for artists, writers, and cognoscenti at her home on East Ninth Street. He enjoyed Gotham's social swirl. On a typical evening in September 1848, he visited a Mr. Sherwood's house, where he saw some Barrington acquaintances. Then he dined at the home of his friend Dr. Samuel Dickson, the founder of the Medical College of South Carolina and a professor at New York University; among the guests were Colonel Braxton Bragg, a hero of the Battle of Buena Vista, and Ashbel Smith of Texas, formerly minister from that republic to the United States. Close friends and more distant acquaintances dropped their problems on his doorstep, including Edwin and Catherine Forrest, who were on the verge of separating and soon would be engaged in a sensational divorce trial.

If Bryant realized that he had become a celebrity—part of the texture of American life—he did not trumpet his lofty cultural eminence. When his friends in the art world asked to paint his portrait or sculpt his form, requests that now came with increasing frequency, he quietly submitted without any sense of self-importance. William Page painted an oil portrait of Bryant in 1848; the next year Henry Kirke Brown made a marble bust of the poet. Asher Durand began a striking series of landscapes based on Bryant's poems, including *The Fountain* (1848), *Green River* (1849), *Scene from 'Thanatopsis'* (1850), and *Monument Mountain* (1853). The influential art critic Henry Tuckerman stressed Bryant's profound influence on Durand: "Set Durand's 'The Beeches' alongside certain verses by Bryant . . . and in spirit you will find they are identical."

Following the memorial service for Cole in May 1848, the wealthy and influential art patron Jonathan Sturges, who worked closely with Bryant in the management of the American Art Union and who had been impressed by Bryant's oration, commissioned Durand to paint a picture of Bryant and Cole in the Catskill Mountains, where the two friends had so often wandered together. The following February, Sturges presented the painting to the poet, remarking in an enclosed note that the canvas was "a token of gratitude for the labor of love performed on that occasion. . . . I requested Mr. Durand to paint a picture in which he should associate our departed friend and yourself as kindred spirits."

slaves. Bryant let him know his own negative opinion of slavery. Bryant then visited a textile mill that employed "crackers"—poor white girls given an opportunity to improve their economic condition. "I have since learned that some attempts were made at first to induce the poor white people to work side by side with the blacks in these mills," an effort that apparently failed. Bryant was far more critical of the South than he had been during his first visit.

After visiting the Simms family, Bryant returned to Charleston and boarded the steamer *Isabel* for Cuba, reaching the island in four days. Cuba had been an imaginary destination for Bryant for a quarter of a century. While boarding with the Salazars during the late 1820s, he had met their many Cuban guests. Bryant also had translated "The Hurricane" by the great Cuban poet José Maria Hérédia and had composed "A Story of the Island of Cuba" for the 1830 volume of the *Talisman*. He looked forward to seeing Cuba close up.

Once in Havana, where he felt the languor of the tropics, Bryant found it hard to compose letters to the *Evening Post*: "I feel a temptation to sit idly, and let the grateful wind from the sea, coming in at the broad windows, flow around me, or read, or talk, as I happen to have a book or a companion." Bryant thought that Cubans, living so much in open air, were a handsome people. He especially liked the amplitude of Cuban women: "they have plump figures, placid, unwrinkled countenances, a well-developed bust, and eyes, the brilliant languor of which is not the languor of illness." When not peering through open windows to gaze on the languorous lives of Cuba's inhabitants, Bryant observed the curious rituals of Holy Week. He also visited the public cemetery, observed a cockfight, and attended a masked ball in the Tacon Theatre.

In his travels outside Havana, Bryant discovered a dimension of Cuban life that was neither romantic nor picturesque. In his last letter from Cuba to the *Evening Post* on April 22, Bryant described the execution of a slave who had killed his master. The slave's death by the *garrote*, "an instrument by which the neck of the criminal is broken and life extinguished in an instant," horrified Bryant, turning his thoughts to the practice of slavery in Cuba and the illicit slave trade that still brought fresh bodies from Africa despite the ban forty years earlier. "The truth is, that the slave-trade is now fully revived; the government conniving at it, making a profit on the slaves imported from Africa, and screening from the pursuit of the English the pirates who bring them." The importation of Indian slaves from Yucatan and indentured Asians, who for all practical purposes were treated as slaves, added to Bryant's shock. Aware that

Southern planters were eager to seize Cuba to add to their slaveholdings, and recalling President Polk's unsuccessful attempt to purchase the island from Spain in 1848, Bryant warned that an American takeover would ensure the "perpetuity of slavery" on the island. After returning to Havana for three days, Bryant and Leupp sailed for Charleston on April 22 and reached New York on the 28th.

Shortly after his return to the city, Bryant witnessed the catastrophic Astor Opera House disturbances between the supporters of Edwin Forrest and the British tragedian William Charles Macready, resulting in the killing and wounding of more than 150 rioters by the Seventh Regiment on the evening of May 10. These two actors were long-standing rivals. At one time the rivalry had been sufficiently cordial for the two tragedians to enjoy dinner together, including a supper in the fall of 1843 that Bryant, Mr. and Mrs. Longfellow, Fitz-Greene Halleck, and Henry Inman attended. Macready liked Bryant enormously, but was distressed when the *Evening Post* was sharply critical of Macready's acting in *Macbeth* at Philadelphia during his third tour of America in 1848–1849. The bombastic Forrest was the favorite of the American masses, an actor with a Bowery touch. The more refined Macready, polished and professional in acting technique, was beloved by Anglophiles and Broadway's "uppertens" or aristocrats.

With the newly opened Astor Opera House situated precisely at the convergence of Broadway and the Bowery, the probability of confrontation between the rival supporters of the actors was high. During the second week in May, the *Evening Post* covered the heated rivalry. Forrest's adherents disrupted Macready's performance of *Macbeth* on May 7, while Forrest, competing in the same play at the Broadway Theatre, brought the working-class audience to its feet with wild applause. At the urging of forty-seven of the city's most prominent citizens, the newly installed Whig mayor Caleb S. Woodhall called out 350 policemen and militia soldiers to prevent a similar disturbance at the Astor on the night of May 10.

When almost ten thousand native-born and anti-English Irish immigrants assembled outside the Astor and attempted to break in, the police and militia forces opened fire, immediately killing eighteen protestors. James Watson Webb of the *Courier and Enquirer* celebrated the triumph of order over chaos, inviting "the Capitalists of the old world" to send their money to the United States, which offered a safe haven from "red republicanism, or chartists, or communionists [*sic*] of any description."

On May 14 Bryant sent a note to his wife: "All is quiet here. The mobs are over."

V

Cuba had whetted Bryant's appetite for even more travel. After only three weeks in New York, and with cholera appearing once again in the city, he and Leupp escaped on June 13 for Europe aboard the steamer *Niagara*, landing in Liverpool on June 23. It was a quick, pleasant voyage, Bryant informed his wife, who had stayed behind at Cedarmere.

Now a seasoned travel writer, Bryant spent a week in London, which he found to be an "overgrown city" that "spreads like a great cancer and if it goes on at this rate will cover the whole island at last." There was that old ambivalence: Bryant was drawn to Europe by its civilization but compelled to assert his own cultural authority over it. He passed pleasant hours with the historian George Bancroft, who had been appointed American minister to Great Britain by President Polk in 1846 and was waiting to be relieved by Abbott Lawrence, appointed by President Taylor. He also called on Samuel Rogers; the old poet was now in his eighties and was delighted to see Bryant once again, telling him, "You look hearty and cheerful, but *our* poets are losing their minds."

Instead of traipsing around London, Bryant concentrated on art collections and exhibitions, finding much to admire in English miniatures, watercolors, and historical painting. But the annual exhibition at the Royal Academy was a disappointment: "Upon the whole I did not see any thing in the exhibition to make it compare very favorably with that of our own Academy of Design." Bryant presented himself as a nationalist for the *Evening Post*'s readers: to him, Manhattan was the center of artistic excellence (as well as democratic opinion).

The wild and picturesque Orkney and Shetland islands, which he and Leupp visited in July, elicited some of Bryant's most vivid and forceful travel writing. Hiking through the mist in the high country around Bressay, Bryant was transfixed by thousands of sea birds and a tapestry of flowers—"daisies nodding in the wind, and the crimson phlox, seeming to set the cliffs on flame; yellow buttercups, and a variety of other plants in bloom." Climbing through low clouds, bracing themselves against a stiff wind, the companions ascended to the very top of a mountain—the Noup—where they could look out at "the green island summits around us, with their bold headlands, the winding straits between, and the black rocks standing out in the sea."

Aberdeen, Inverness, Glasgow, and Edinburgh and other sites in the Scottish Highlands did not hold as much personal pleasure for Bryant as the wild islands he had visited. On July 28 the travelers started southward, making the standard tourist's pilgrimage to Melrose Abbey and Sir Walter Scott's home, Abbotsford. There Bryant encountered a tipsy fellow and a flushed woman who would not let them enter; but they were able to view Scott's tomb at Dryburgh Abbey and his boyhood home at Sandy-Knowe. After three days in Birmingham with Ferdinand Field, Bryant returned to London, where he dined twice with Rogers and met several new people, including the naturalist William Benjamin Campbell and the artist Charles Eastlake. One evening after dining with Rogers, the eighty-six-year-old poet rushed to catch up with Bryant, accompanying him across St. James Park to his hotel on Grosvenor Street.

Bryant's travel writing is at its best when he can appropriate from his European experience a sense of contrast with American democracy. Crossing the Channel on August 9, Bryant and Leupp discovered an armed continent in the wake of the 1848 revolutions. Arriving in Paris, Bryant described a repressive scene for his readers: "Whoever should visit the principal countries of Europe at the present moment, might take them for conquered provinces, held in subjection by their victorious masters, at the point of the sword." To Frances, he wrote, "The words, liberty, equality, fraternity are inscribed in staring letters on the churches, but soldiers with fixed bayonets are marching before them, and every where you see armed men, the signs of a government of force." Everywhere he and Leupp traveled over the next weeks and months, Bryant found the cities crowded with soldiers. Heidelberg "had a strange air," with the streets filled with drunken Prussian troops; while his beloved Munich, where Bryant, Frances, and the children had spent enjoyable days some fourteen years earlier, made him feel sad. He hated the state of siege he found throughout Europe, "the perpetual sight of the military uniform." His spirits picked up only when he crossed Lake Constance to Switzerland on August 25: "I could almost have kneeled and kissed the shore of the hospitable republic," he confessed to readers of the *Evening Post*.

But his remarks to his daughter Fanny were more optimistic: "The political condition of France is bad enough, but the friends of liberty are not discouraged. They see that if they can but keep the *form* of government as it now is the *substance* of liberty will be obtained at last."

Once again, he was measuring Europe against the democratic essence of America.

Arriving in New York on October 20, Bryant rushed to Cedarmere. He found Frances in a state of depression, for she did not enjoy residing at Roslyn by herself. Bryant confided to Leonice Moulton, with whom he had exchanged several witty letters while in Europe, about "the disconsolateness of the *Frau.*" He had "hoped to pass many pleasant days" at Cedarmere. He set out to reconcile Frances to the place, succeeding so successfully that "she passed a whole day with me in planting and transplanting trees shrubs and roses."

Bryant rented pleasant rooms at 263 Greene Street near Eighth Street in the city, and Frances, enjoying the diversions and social life that she had missed during her solitary months in Roslyn, returned to normal. One of their first guests at the Greene Street quarters was Dana, who urged Bryant to collect his travel letters for publication in book form. Bryant acknowledged that the *Post*'s readers had received them "in a rather friendly manner" and agreed to consider republishing them.

Bryant's trust in Bigelow had been rewarded; the *Evening Post* was prospering. Despite the cholera epidemic that claimed more than a thousand lives, revenue from advertising, circulation, and the job-printing department had increased. Bigelow had hired new reporters and correspondents while replacing the inefficient Timothy Howe with a new business manager, Isaac Henderson. With thousands of people rushing to California after gold had been discovered in January 1848, Bigelow commissioned two new "extras" for California, Oregon, the Sandwich Islands, and Central America, with a "full chronicle of European and domestic news of peculiar interest to the inhabitants of the Pacific." Bryant was proud that the *Evening Post*, which never sank to the sensational level of twopenny dailies like Bennett's *Herald*, was doing exceptionally well for a sixpenny paper. He had come back from Europe "a little stouter and a good deal stronger." Enjoying a "stock of health," he was ready for the new year.

Walt Whitman, 1849 or 1850. Library of Congress.

Edgar Allan Poe. Library of Congress.

Ralph Waldo Emerson. Library of Congress.

James Russell Lowell. Library of Congress.

John Greenleaf Whittier. Library of Congress.

WILLIAM CULLEN BRYANT, ABOUT 1850.

Bryant ca. 1850. Print Collection, Miriam and Ira D. Wallach Division of Art, Prints, and Photographs, The New York Public Library, Astor, Lenox, and Tilden Foundations.

"Barn-Burners in a Fix," 1852. Library of Congress.

Bryant. Emmet Collection, Miriam and Ira D. Wallach Division of Art, Prints, and Photographs, The New York Public Library, Astor, Lenox, and Tilden Foundations.

Bryant, 1853. Cedarmere Collection, Nassau County Department of Parks, Recreation, and Museums.

John Brown ca. 1859. Library of Congress.

Abraham Lincoln, February 27, 1860. Library of Congress.

Horace Greeley ca. 1865. Library of Congress.

New York Draft Riots. Library of Congress.

NEW YORK EDITORS FOLLOWING THE EXAMPLE OF JAMES GORDON BENNETT.
MUSCULAR JOURNALISM.

"Muscular Journalism." Print Collection, Miriam and Ira D. Wallach Division of Art, Prints, and Photographs, The New York Public Library, Astor, Lenox, and Tilden Foundations.

Bryant by Thomas Nast, 1866. Print Collection, Miriam and Ira D. Wallach Division of Art, Prints, and Photographs, The New York Public Library, Astor, Lenox, and Tilden Foundations.

Gulian Verplanck. Brady-Handy Photograph Collection, Library of Congress.

Julia Bryant ca. 1870. Cedarmere Collection, Nassau County Department of Parks, Recreation, and Museums.

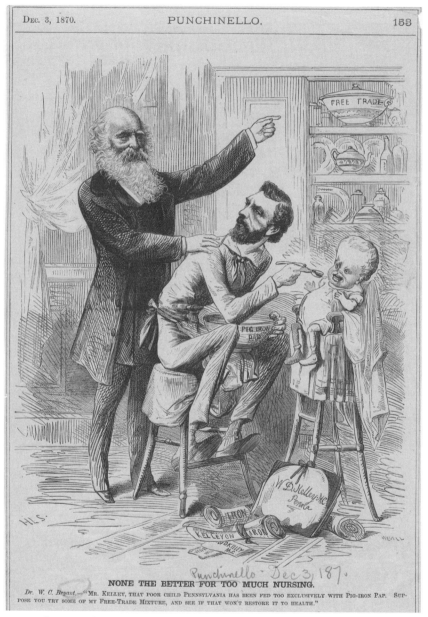

NONE THE BETTER FOR TOO MUCH NURSING.

Dr. W. C. Bryant,—"Mr. Kelley, that poor child Pennsylvania has been fed too exclusively with Pig-Iron Pap. Suppose you try some of my Free-Trade Mixture, and see if that won't restore it to health."

"None the Better for Too Much Nursing," 1870. Print Collection, Miriam and Ira D. Wallach Division of Art, Prints, and Photographs, The New York Public Library, Astor, Lenox, and Tilden Foundations.

William Marcy "Boss" Tweed. Hoxie Collection, Library of Congress.

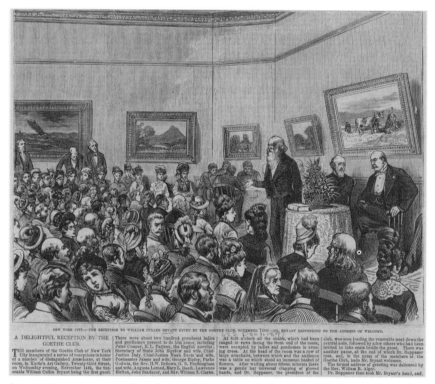

Bryant Reception, Goethe Club, 1877. Picture Collection, The Branch Libraries, The New York Public Library, Astor, Lenox, and Tilden Foundations.

Cedarmere. Print Collection, Miriam and Ira D. Wallach Division of Art, Prints, and Photographs, The New York Public Library, Astor, Lenox, and Tilden Foundations.

Bryant. Brady-Handy Photograph Collection, Library of Congress.

12

OLD TEMPLES AND TOMBS

As I sat among the forest of gigantic columns in the great court of the temple of Karnac, it appeared to me that after such a sight no building reared by human hands could affect me with a sense of sublimity.

—*Letters from the East*

I

New York at mid-century was "fast assuming a cosmopolitan tone," as Bryant's friend, the novelist Caroline M. Kirkland, observed. Mrs. Kirkland, who had spent the summer of 1849 in a rented cottage on Bryant's property in Roslyn, was not certain what this cosmopolitanism portended. Manners and behavior, she thought, were in as much flux as architectural styles; the new rich who were building garish mansions along Fifth Avenue were "emulating the repudiated aristocracy of the old world." Bryant shared Kirkland's disdain for cosmopolitan excess—including the disagreeable particulars of the Forrest divorce case that he had been asked to mediate. But perhaps the vagaries of human behavior were unavoidable in a metropolis that by 1850 had a population of 694,000, a two-thirds increase of humanity, much of it from Europe, in a single decade.

To prepare for the challenges confronting the city and nation in 1850, Bryant moved the *Evening Post*'s offices from its cramped building at 18 Nassau Street to larger quarters on the corner of Nassau and Liberty streets in the spring. The purchase of a new steam-driven Hoe press would enable the editor to print larger sheets with greater daily runs, prompting him and his associates to anticipate increased circulation. The *Evening Post* would never rival the cheaper papers in circulation, but Bryant thought that the amount of news in his sixpenny paper was far more substantial than that appearing in the journals of his competitors and was thus a far better investment.

As he reviewed national and world events at the start of the year, Bryant continued to believe in the ultimate triumph of democratic values. True, the fires of the 1848 revolution—"the Movement" as Emerson called it—had been extinguished. Many famous partisans, among them Karl Marx, Giuseppe Mazzini, and the Hungarian patriot Louis Kossuth, had fled into exile; Giuseppe Garibaldi, for one, could be seen dipping candles on Staten Island. In Washington, talk of secession wafted through Congress. Only the *Evening Post* among all of New York's newspapers remained solidly in the Democratic fold.

On March 7, 1850, Daniel Webster supported Henry Clay's compromise resolutions proposing, among other things, admitting California to the Union as a free state while leaving New Mexico and Utah to the vagaries of popular sovereignty. Bryant and his Free Soil friends responded vigorously, wondering what had become of the Democratic Party and the forces of liberal nationalism. Whittier, expressing his disdain for the Massachusetts senator in verse, hastily penned "Ichabod," lambasting Webster's betrayal: "When faith is lost, when honor dies, the man is dead." (Bryant reprinted Whittier's poem in the *Post* on May 6.) Emerson was equally appalled: "The word *liberty* in the mouth of Mr. Webster sounds like the word *love* in the mouth of a courtesan." Whitman, fired two years earlier from the *Brooklyn Eagle*, now took Northern men with Southern principles to task in his "Song for a Certain Congressman," a poem he published in the *Evening Post*. He also wrote "Blood Money," his first poem in free verse, on the same theme. In one of several articles he wrote for the *Evening Post*, Whitman called for "the young artist race" to band together in "a close phalanx, ardent, radical, and progressive," to create an art worthy of the times they lived in.

When the final language of the Compromise empowered federal marshals to apprehend runaway slaves in Northern states, putting teeth in the largely ineffective Fugitive Slave Act, Bryant reminded Webster of a previous vow to resist any extension of slavery. He accused the flamboyant Massachusetts senator, who could be seen from time to time in New York City dressed in wildly incongruous colors, of having deserted "the cause which he lately defended, deserted it under circumstances which force upon him the imputation of a sordid motive."

Bryant's new associate editor, John Bigelow, shared the editor's disdain of slavery. Bigelow made a trip to Jamaica in January and February, returning to write twelve articles for the *Evening Post* on the conditions of blacks on the island sixteen years after their emancipation. Bigelow also created a column, "John Brown, Ferryman," in which his fictive mouthpiece overhears the political conversations of his passengers, passing along inside information that in fact was provided by Bigelow's friends Charles Sumner and Samuel Tilden and other Free Soil advocates. Sumner, whom Bryant had known since 1841 and who was running for the Senate with the support of Massachusetts Free Soilers and Democrats, was an especially helpful partisan, contributing letters to the *Post* during the spring and summer months.

Even though he was writing very little new poetry at the time, no other American poet rivaled Bryant's stature, and only Longfellow enjoyed as large an audience. In 1850, when Bryant's collected poems were published in London and Liverpool, one critic described him as "the most popular of American poets" in both England and his native country. Bryant could not walk the streets of New York City without being approached for autographs or requests for copies of his poems. Maria Clemm, the mother-in-law of Poe, who had died in 1849, begged Bryant for an inscribed copy of his *Poems*: "There are so many beautiful things in that book which my dear son has so often recited to me." Bryant obliged Mrs. Clemm, who subsequently underlined two poems— "June" and "The Death of the Flowers"—that her son had been especially fond of.

Bryant was the nation's "dear old poet," as the publisher James T. Fields called him when recalling a picnic in the summer of 1850 atop Monument Mountain, overlooking the Housatonic in the Berkshires. It had been a notable gathering, with Herman Melville, Nathaniel Hawthorne, Oliver Wendell Holmes, and the editor and author James T. Fields hiking to the top of the craggy precipice overlooking the river in Great Barrington that had prompted one of Bryant's memorable poems from an earlier time. Fields recalled: "There we all assembled in a shady spot, and one of the party read to us Bryant's beautiful poem commemorating Monument Mountain."

Bryant had written "Monument Mountain" at the height of his poetic powers in 1824. In a note to the blank verse tale, Bryant told of the Indian legend of "a woman of the Stockbridge tribe who killed herself by leaping from the edge of the precipice." This Indian woman "had formed an attachment to her cousin, which according to the customs of the tribe, was unlawful. She was, in consequence, seized with a deep melancholy, and resolved to destroy herself."

Bryant's lines

> She loved her cousin; such a love was deemed,
> By the morality of those stern tribes,
> Incestuous, and she struggled hard and long
> Against her love, and reasoned with her heart,
> As simple Indian maiden might.

set the poet's mature and daring drama of sexuality and forbidden love against the savage spectacle of nature:

> ... It is a fearful thing
> To stand upon the beetling verge, and see
> Where storm and lightning, from that huge gray wall,
> Have tumbled down vast blocks, and at the base
> Dashed them in fragments, and to lay thine ear
> Over the dizzy depth, and hear the sound
> Of winds, that struggle with the woods below
> Come up like ocean murmurs.

Hawthorne, with his penchant for dark tales of sexual sin, and Melville, who may have been inspired by this poem to write *Pierre*, a novel exploring the theme of incest, were especially drawn to Bryant's tale of transgression set against the wild forces of nature. Fields remembered the day on Monument Mountain with fondness: "Then we lunched among the rocks, and somebody proposed Bryant's health, and 'long life to the dear old poet.' This was the most popular toast of the day, and it took, I remember, a considerable quantity of Heidsieck to do it justice."

With or without champagne, Bryant was a source of inspiration to his friends in both the literary and art worlds. At the National Academy, Asher Durand exhibited *Landscape, Summer Morning*—later called *Early Morning at Cold Spring*—after "A Scene of the Banks of the Hudson." In the painting, Durand tried to capture the religious overtones raised by Bryant as he contemplates the bucolic scene:

> Mid the dark rocks that watch his bed
> Glitters the mighty Hudson spread.
> Unrippled, save by drops that fall

From shrubs that fringe his mountain wall;
And o'er the clear still water swells
The music of the Sabbath bells.

Durand also exhibited *Landscape—Scene from "Thanatopsis"* at the Academy of Design, which had relocated the previous year to a new building, paid for largely by Charles Leupp and Jonathan Sturges, on the west side of Broadway south of Amity Street. In the academy's catalogue for the exhibition, nine lines from "Thanatopsis" captured the mournful beauty of Durand's painting and Bryant's poem:

    . . . The hills
Rock-ribbed and ancient as the sun,—the vales
Stretching in pensive quietness between;
The venerable woods—rivers that move
In majesty, and the complaining brooks
That make the meadows green; and poured round all,
Old ocean's gray and melancholy waste,—
Are but the solemn decorations all
Of the great tomb of man.

Bryant, an inveterate stroller on Broadway, recommended the exhibition to friends; he invited his Williams classmate, Orville Dewey, to join him for a private showing.

Early in the year, Bryant assembled his many travel letters to the *Evening Post*—fifty-three articles totaling more than one hundred and thirty thousand words—for publication in book form by George P. Putnam in early 1850. Spanning fourteen years and embracing his trips to Europe, the American South and West, and Cuba, *Letters of a Traveler* fed the popular demand for travel accounts and was an instant success. Bryant sent Dana a copy of the book. "I hope you got it. You are the instigator of its publication, and if it be a bad book must bear your share of the blame. . . . It is a tolerably good book in the bookseller's sense of the phrase, for it sells pretty well." Bryant was pleased that reviewers, among them Henry Jarvis Raymond of the *Morning Courier* (who would cofound the *New York Times* in 1851), "had the magnanimity of commending the style."

By summertime, which descended ferociously on the region, Bryant yearned to leave the city (where, as he told Frances, he often was "fairly parboiled" in his own perspiration) for the restorative scene at

Cedarmere. But work kept him from Roslyn more than he liked, and the "dull summer" weighed heavily. He had managed to get out to Roslyn for the Fourth of July, walking in the garden; picking raspberries, strawberries, and cherries; and luxuriating in the scent of flowers and the odors of the hayfields. Late in the day, he would often sea bathe, for "Dr. Bryant," as he styled himself when offering homoeopathic advice, recommended saltwater to keep people "strong and hearty." Bryant's crops of hay, wheat, corn, and potatoes were progressing nicely. While at Cedarmere, he read Susan Fenimore Cooper's *Rural Hours* with delight, recommending her tribute to the country life to Leonice Moulton. He told Fenimore Cooper that his daughter's book was "the greatest of the season, and a credit to the country."

Cedarmere was proving to be an inspiration for Bryant, and now he was writing his poetry there. One of the lyrics he composed at the time, "The Planting of the Apple-Tree," reveals the hold that Cedarmere had on his imagination. In nine stanzas, each consisting of nine lines, Bryant conceives the life of the apple tree from its planting to old age as an extended metaphor for the passing of seasons, human existence, and the life of the Republic. In the last stanza, he is playfully affirmative and self-reflective in praising the enduring rhythms of nature and poetry:

> "Who planted this old apple-tree?"
> The children of that distant day
> Thus to some aged man shall say;
> And, gazing on the mossy stem,
> The gray-haired man shall answer them:
> "A poet of the land was he,
> Born in the rude but good old times;
> 'Tis said he made some quaint old rhymes;
> On planting the apple-tree."

Here Bryant anticipates Yeats and Frost. He withheld publication of the poem, with its graceful rhythms, decidedly quaint rhyme scheme, and complex construction, for almost fifteen years. By the time it appeared in the *Atlantic Monthly* in January 1864, Bryant had indeed become the quaint old poet of the land.

Like the poet in "The Planting of the Apple-Tree," Bryant was now gray-haired and balding, the enormous forehead and dome of his head becoming more prominent as he aged. But he was also in superb health, fortified by his long walks, outdoor work at Cedarmere, and devotion to homoeopathic remedies—aconite, arsenic, belladonna, mercurius, tartar emetic, sulfur—a host of tinctures and powders he usually ordered from Smith's Homoeopathic Pharmacy at 488 Broadway. He could only ponder the fates and infirmities of his friends. Cole was gone, Poe too was dead, and Audubon would soon follow. Margaret Fuller, her Italian husband, and their infant son drowned in a shipwreck off Fire Island on July 14. Eliza Robbins was in delicate health, beginning a gradual decline that would end with her death in 1853. Charity Bryant, the unmarried sister of his father and the last of that generation of his family, died at Weybridge, Vermont, on October 5, 1851, at the age of seventy-four. William Ware, Bryant's pastor when he first came to New York in 1825, passed away in February 1852. Even the grand old men of the Republic—first Calhoun on March 31, 1851, and then President Taylor himself on July 9—were passing from the national scene.

Of special concern to Bryant was Fenimore Cooper, who had been ill with a liver ailment since the fall of 1850. Bryant saw him the following April when the novelist came to town for treatment: "He has grown thin and has an ashy rather than florid complexion," Bryant lamented. The novelist died in Cooperstown on September 14, 1851. Writing to Rufus Griswold while en route to Illinois to visit his brothers, Bryant apostrophized his friend: "not only the country, but the civilized world and the age in which we live, have lost one of their most illustrious ornaments. It is melancholy to think that it is only when such men are in their graves that full justice is done to their merit." At a meeting in New York City Hall on September 24, Bryant was appointed to a committee organized to plan a suitable tribute to Cooper. As he anticipated with some trepidation, he was asked to deliver the keynote eulogy.

The memorial service for James Fenimore Cooper was held at Tripler Hall on February 25, 1852. Daniel Webster, who had salted the audience with his supporters, gave the opening address. Bryant informed Dana that he found Webster's speech, which the senator delivered in a very low voice, to be "deplorably common place,—poor in thought, and clumsy in expression. The man seemed in a sort of collapse and actually moved my compassion." After Rufus Griswold read letters from sixteen writers and politicians, "Mr. Bryant," as the *Post* reported the next day, "commenced his address at half-past eight, and concluded about a quarter before ten. He was frequently interrupted by the most flattering applause." Bryant offered a warm, balanced, and judicious appraisal of his old friend, claiming that Cooper was "in the highest sense of the word a poet" in his ability to capture the grandeur of the American continent. Acknowledging Cooper's criticism of American society and quarrels with some of its citizens, Bryant defended the proud, independent, and uncompromising spirit that occasionally forced the novelist to confront his fellow men. Cooper had faults as a novelist, Bryant confessed, but his great popularity derived from his ability, even in translation, to "touch the heart and kindle the imagination."

Another death that affected Bryant was that of the young landscape architect Andrew Jackson Downing. Only thirty-seven, Downing perished while attempting to rescue passengers from a steamboat fire on the Hudson River in July 1852. Bryant wrote in the *Evening Post* that Downing "made himself a high reputation in the peculiar walk of art to which he had devoted his life." As early as 1848, Downing had aligned his influential magazine, *The Horticulturalist*, with Bryant in demanding a large public park for New York City.

In an editorial on July 6, 1850, Bryant described New York as lamentably "destined to preserve its reputation of being the dirtiest city in the world" and advocated the creation of a park "to which we may make a temporary escape from the polluted air." In an 1844 editorial, "A New Public Park," Bryant had called for the acquisition of Jones's Wood, launching a campaign that ultimately would result in the creation of Central Park. "The people of New York," Bryant wrote, "are entitled, if the thing be within the compass of possibility and reasonable expense, to open grounds within their own city—to shady walks and a pure atmosphere, gratuitously accessible to themselves and their children."

II

In November 1851, the *Evening Post* celebrated its fiftieth year since its founding by Alexander Hamilton and William Coleman. The semicentennial anniversary prompted Bryant to write a history of the paper for the November 15 issue; it was published simultaneously in pamphlet form by the newspaper's printing office as *Reminiscences of the Evening Post*. Bryant devoted more than ten thousand words to the article, recounting the history of the paper's many battles and tracing its gradual transformation from its Federalist origins into a leading Democratic paper. He also reflected on the vagaries of journalism, which "fills the mind with a variety of knowledge relating to the events of the day, but that knowledge is apt to be superficial, since the necessity of attending to many subjects prevents the journalist from thoroughly investigating any." Journalists, Bryant warned, had to guard as well against a hasty, loose, diffuse style, often filled with "local barbarisms and cant phrases of the day." Above all, Bryant concluded, journalists should not "betray the cause of truth to public opinion," a temptation to which the *Evening Post* "has not often yielded." Reflecting on the next half-century of the *Evening Post* on December 9, Bryant predicted: "We think its past history no unimportant guarantee that the *Evening Post* will continue to battle for human rights in preference to human sovereignties; for the welfare and improvement of the multitude, rather than for exclusive privileges to classes and tribes; for freedom of industry and thought, regardless of the frowns and blandishments of power and wealth."

Soon after offering his strictures on journalistic ethics, Bryant agreed to serve as chairman for a press banquet honoring the Hungarian freedom fighter Louis Kossuth, who arrived from England in December. At a lavish banquet at the Astor House on December 15, the New York press corps paid tribute to Kossuth, who had edited liberation newspapers before Russia intervened in Hungary to crush the revolution. Bryant introduced Kossuth as a man in the tradition of America's own great leaders of the Revolutionary War, believing that he would be "cheered and strengthened with aid from this side of the Atlantic."

Bryant preferred to devote space in the *Evening Post* to celebrating revolutionary heroes like Kossuth rather than provide transcripts of the sensational Forrest trial that began the same month. But to keep up with the twopenny papers and to satisfy his daughter Fanny, who was close to Mrs. Forrest and who faithfully attended the trial, Bryant dedicated seven columns daily to the sordid details. To Bryant's relief, the trial ended in Catherine Forrest's favor: it had been "one of the most disgusting trials that ever was held in this country," the editor observed.

With 1852 an election year, Bryant prepared the *Evening Post* for yet another shift in political endorsements and a brief return to the Democratic Party. The Compromise had become federal law in September 1850, and the consequences of its provision concerning the Fugitive Slave Act were being felt bitterly in the Northern states. Throughout 1851, crowds in Boston, Syracuse, and other towns and cities in the North rescued blacks from authorities attempting to return them to their putative owners. Bryant labeled the Fugitive Slave Law so "offensive" and "revolting" that even law-abiding citizens would find civil disobedience to be inevitable: "The people feel it to be an impeachment of their manhood, to be asked to assist in manacling, for the purpose of reducing to slavery, one who has lived among them the life of an industrious and honest citizen."

Bryant concluded that the Free Soil Party, which boasted thirteen congressional delegates, was a failure. He confided to his brother John in August 1852 that "The Free-Soil Party is now doing nothing. Its representatives in Congress have wasted their time till all chance of repealing or modifying the fugitive slave law is gone by, if there ever was any. . . . A journal belonging to a large party has infinitely more influences than when it is the organ of a small conclave." Reaffirming his paper's opposition to slavery and his resolve to make the Fugitive Slave Law so "odious" that it could not be enforced, Bryant let John know that the *Evening Post* was supporting the Democrat Franklin Pierce for the presidency. Pierce was running against the Free Soil candidate, John Parker Hale, and the Whig nominee, General Winfield Scott, who had been selected over the incumbent president, Millard Fillmore. Bryant endorsed Pierce, a dark horse candidate elected the previous June on the forty-ninth ballot. In June, Bryant wrote that Pierce was "a man who has done nothing to purchase the presidency, retired for the present from political life, and uncommitted on the questions which for the last three or four years have divided the Democratic party."

Just before the Democrats regained the presidency in the November election, Bryant became embroiled in a controversy with Daniel Webster. The Whig secretary of state charged that the *Post*'s editor had unjustly accused him of speculating in guano fertilizer from the Pacific Lobos Islands. The *Times* reported that shortly before his death, Webster said, "I can only hope that when Mr. Bryant stands on the brink of the grave, as I now do, his conscience will be as clear of having performed the duty of justice towards my name." As it turned out, it had been Bigelow, not Bryant, who had met with A. G. Benson, a principal figure implicated in the scheme; Benson attested that the discussion had been fair and proper. Bryant protested the aspersions cast on his name to Henry Jarvis Raymond, the editor of the *Daily Times*: "Mr. Benson is personally unknown to me, and certainly, if the statement in your paper is a sample of his veracity, I desire never to know more of him than I do now." The *Times* issued a tepid retraction.

III

With the election behind him, Bryant planned another overseas adventure—once again with Charles Leupp and this time with the Near East as their final destination. The biblical lands had become all the rage for

Western travelers in the 1850s as well a fascinating topic for armchair-traveler Americans. Dr. Henry Abbott's private museum of Egyptian antiquities on Broadway in New York City—a treasury of mummies, inscribed tablets, gold-encased funerary objects, and papyrus scrolls—drew large crowds, including a mesmerized Walt Whitman. The demand for books on Egyptology was brisk. Bryant was already familiar with *Biblical Researches in Palestine* (1841), written by his friend Edward Robinson. On their way to Liverpool aboard the steamer *Arctic*, which left New York on November 13, Bryant and Leupp read Edward William Lane's *Account of the Manners and Customs of the Modern Egyptians* (1836). While on board, they also met the American naval officer William Francis Lynch, who had just published a report on his expedition to the Dead Sea and River Jordan.

Eager to reach the Near East, Bryant and Leupp did not linger in England. Arriving in Liverpool on November 25, they made a quick trip to London, where Bryant had tea with the publisher John Chapman, meeting there "a blue-stocking lady" who wrote for the *Westminster Review*; he didn't elaborate on his conversation with the writer celebrated as George Eliot. Bryant also wrote a note to the *Post* instructing an assistant, Isaac Henderson, to send a ten-dollar contribution for "the monument they are erecting in England to the poet Wordsworth," who had died in 1850.

From London, Bryant sent a letter to the *Evening Post* providing a vivid account of the constant rains that had been soaking the island for seven weeks: "Such numbers of wet women and children I never saw before; wet wagoners walking by the side of their dripping teams; wet laborers, male and female, digging turnips in the muddy fields; wet beggars in the towns, their rags streaming with water; wet sheep staggering under their drenched fleeces, nibbling the grass in the yellowish-green fields—for the pastures wear, at this season, a sallow verdure—or biting the turnips scattered for them by the farmers in long rows." The *London Weekly News*, lamenting the disregard the English had for famous American visitors, quoted the paragraph, commenting: "There is not in the whole of his exquisite pieces of pastoral poetry a sketch more faithful to fact than this."

Paris, which the two friends reached on December 1 and where they stayed for a week, seemed to have shed the post-revolutionary tension that had struck Bryant on his last visit to the city. Bryant viewed the throngs of Parisians assembled in the Champs Elysees and the garden of the Tuileries to witness the coronation of Napoleon III, noting their total lack of enthusiasm for the new emperor but concluding that the French favored "the present order of things."

The city was filled with foreign tourists, among them some two thousand Americans, "birds of every feather," enjoying the "gayeties of the place." Bryant met John Durand, the eldest son of Asher Durand, who decided to accompany the travelers; and hired a Maltese courier, John Muscat, to serve as the company's guide. Bryant and Leupp had toyed with the prospect of visiting Spain and Portugal but were easily persuaded by Muscat to abandon this plan in favor of quickly reaching the Near East in order to enjoy the temperate season.

It was in the Near East that Bryant could cultivate his most romantic persona, adapting himself comfortably to the role of an American vagabond. He was gradually leaving European civilization and its discontents behind. The passage to Alexandria was not especially pleasant owing to cramped staterooms and a "proportion of ill-bred people" on board who were noisy, drank excessively, and committed "various other acts of petty rudeness." But Bryant was delighted to encounter one passenger, the British botanist Robert Fortune, who had visited China for the Horticultural Society in 1842 and for the East India Company in 1848, sending numerous specimens from his travels back to England. Bryant enjoyed long conversations with Fortune, the two men absorbed in discussions of Chinese, Indian, English, and American flora and the prospects of transplanting exotic Eastern specimens to Western soil. Intrigued by what he learned from Fortune, Bryant would talk about the domestication of Oriental teas, grapes, and palms before the New York Horticultural Society in 1855.

Egypt and the Holy Land were the exotic locales Bryant apparently longed for. Here was the freedom and danger that fulfilled some of his most suppressed emotions. Landing in Alexandria on December 30, he was immediately engulfed by visceral sensation—a threatening mob of donkey drivers vying for his business. Undaunted by the riotous scene, Bryant grabbed the nearest driver by the throat, shoved the startled man out of the way, cut through the crowd, mounted the best donkey he could find, and made his escape. "The good-natured Mussulmans smiled at finding themselves thus unceremoniously handled by an infidel," he wrote in one of the first of his letters from the exotic East that he sent to the *Evening Post*.

Cairo showed no signs of the high culture of Europe or of the commercial glamour of Gotham. The city was alluring, dizzying, threatening. Its crooked streets congested with donkeys and carts, its bazaars and open stalls humming with business, its minarets and monuments, and above all its frenetic noise, made Cairo a metropolitan world that Bryant had never before encountered. The ancient city was "still almost as soft and elastic as a Turkey carpet" and was populated by a tapestry of humanity: swarthy, bearded men "in turbans or close caps of every color," water carriers, barefoot women with jugs on their heads and their "more opulent sisters," some astride donkeys and accompanied by servants. Above all was the "perpetual noise, not of the clanking and humming of machinery, and the rattling of carriages, and the striking or iron hoofs on the pavement, as in our cities; but of human voices, greeting, arguing, jesting, laughing, shouting, scolding, cursing, praying, and begging, mingled with the bleating of camels, the braying of asses, and the barking of innumerable dogs."

Whereas Bryant could assert a uniquely American identity during his European travels, Egypt would force him to construct a deeper persona, more primal and more attuned to antiquity's rhythms. To begin the transformation, he decided to stop shaving. On a glorious winter day, Bryant and his companions escaped the city's pandemonium for a trip along the Nile to the pyramids of Giza. He climbed to the top of the Great Pyramid, measuring it against a familiar metropolitan norm: "From the summit of this vast pile of hewn stones, which would cover all Washington Square with its base, we looked over the green Delta, stretching north, with dark groves spotting it like broad shadows of clouds." A day or two later, the party visited the vast cemetery at Saqqara, where the French archaeologist Auguste Mariette treated them to a private tour of the tomb of Apis. The party also traveled to Memphis—"the once great city to which Martial attributes the building of the pyramids, those miracles of barbaric art, *barbara miracula*, as he calls them."

Bryant and his party had hired a dragoman to convey them across the Little Arabian Desert—today the Sinai—to Jerusalem. However, they postponed their departure when the opportunity to visit Upper Egypt arose. The government had just outfitted a steamer for this purpose, and on January 12, Bryant joined a party of fifteen for the sixteen-day excursion from Cairo to Aswan. "The weather was monotonously fine," he wrote Frances. All of the passengers were amiable, "and I believe we had seen old temples and tombs to our hearts' content." Bryant and his companions stopped at Thebes, Dendera, Idfu, Isna, and Kom Ombo before reaching Aswan, Elephantine Island, and the temple at Philae. Of these ancient monuments, the temples at Luxor and Karnak struck Bryant as the grandest: "As I sat among the forest of gigantic columns in the great court of the temple at Karnac, it appeared to me that after such a sight no building reared by human hands could affect me with a sense of sublimity." Egypt was working its magic on him. "My health is good," he told Frances, "and no fatigue that I meet affects me."

Bryant was shedding both his American identity and his experience of Europe as he departed Cairo for Jerusalem, now as the head of a caravan. The Bryant caravan consisted of thirteen camels tethered to each other in a row, with a nasty Nubian monkey, not quite tamed, perched on one of them. Guiding the group was a dragoman, Emanuel Balthas, a choleric Athenian who, in addition to Greek, spoke Romaic, Italian, Turkish, Arabic, and tolerable French and English. The guide, whom Bryant thought was a bit too hasty in flogging his four Arab assistants, had been engaged for the price of one Napoleon a day from each member of the party. A cousin of Balthas, a cook "who plucked chickens as he sat on a camel," and their courier John Muscat completed the colorful entourage as it moved away from Cairo until the minarets of the mosque of Mohammed Ali gleamed on the western edge of the horizon.

After he switched from an unruly camel to a more tractable one, Bryant took to the desert like a Bedouin. He found the desert, with its surprising wealth of flora and fauna, its graves and potsherds hinting at previous civilizations, to be fascinating. Often during the two-week passage, Bryant would dismount from his camel and walk beside it in order to observe the insects, animals, birds, and plants more closely. Bryant astonished his companions, as Durand recalled later, with his ability to identify innumerable species: a heron rising from brackish waters, herds of gazelles racing gracefully across the sands, jackals on hillocks, the *retem* or "bloom of the desert" with its beautiful white flowers veined with purple. Nothing escaped his wonder, not even the mosquitoes, venomous snakes, black beetles, lice, and centipedes that shared their tents and bedding. It was as if Bryant was experiencing an exotic landscape so intensely that he became one with it.

As the caravan curved around northern Egypt and western Syria, following the Mediterranean, Bryant was mesmerized by the exotic panorama unfolding before him. Pilgrims returning from Mecca, caravans loaded with spices, fierce Bedouin camel riders, sheikhs demanding *baksheesh* (tribute), the daily striking of tents and loading of camels, even a five-day quarantine at Khan Yunis and Gaza—all were part of the incredibly picturesque journey that Bryant described avidly for the *Evening Post*'s readers. His white beard was growing; he was beginning to resemble a Muslim.

After a tedious journey across the bare hills and bleak tableland of Judea, the travelers finally "came in sight of the walls, the towers, and the domes of the Holy City. The ancient metropolis of Palestine, the once imperial Salem, had not lost all its majesty, but still sat like a queen in her place among the mountains of Judea." In his diary, Bryant recorded a trip on horseback to the Mount of Olives and visits to Jericho and Bethlehem. He bathed in the Jordan and swam in the Dead Sea. Bryant's sense of fulfillment was almost erotic.

No danger bothered Bryant. In Nablus, he encountered women and children preparing to stone the travelers, but Bryant assuaged the angry crowd by blowing kisses at them. His needs had become visceral: at the Convent of Lebanon on Mount Carmel, he ate an excellent dinner and drank a copious amount of wine. He galloped horses along the beach near Tyre and bathed in the Mediterranean. His self-indulgence amazed him.

As the travelers moved out of Lebanon to Damascus and Constantinople, Bryant gradually started to shed his astonishing desert persona. Politics—the current Western conflicts—intruded. He assessed the impending conflict along the Bosporus and Golden Horn, noting the weakness of the Turkish Empire and the intrigues of the great powers of Europe. "The Russian negotiators are the ablest and wiliest of Europe. Now, when they are just on the point of becoming by superior dexterity winners in the Turkish question, England tosses a sword upon the chessboard, and breaks up the game." The Crimean War was about to start.

Athens, Corinth, and Venice held little interest for Bryant, sated as he was with his Middle Eastern adventures. Arriving in Rome on May 8, he still seemed to be vicariously wandering in the desert with his "broad-brimmed white hat and long beard of the same color." One evening at a masquerade party hosted by the artist John Chapman, the guests dressed in Damascus costumes. With his long palmer's beard, Bryant was decidedly the most authentic of the faux Arabs. In Paris, he had a daguerreotype made of himself.

Suddenly Bryant yearned for Broadway and the summer pleasures of Cedarmere. On June 8, he boarded the steamer *Humboldt* for Manhattan. During the voyage, Bryant cared for his wife's goddaughter, the future wife of Frederick Law Olmsted, who was traveling with a small baby and was overcome with seasickness. Nearing sixty, the bearded traveler was hearty and refreshed. He especially enjoyed the company of William J. Stillman, who would become coeditor with John Durand of the art journal the *Crayon* and later an art editor for the *Evening Post*.

Just before docking in New York on June 22, Bryant and Stillman toasted the captain with champagne.

With his flowing white beard and sun-blasted face, Bryant was amused that a clerk sent by the *Evening Post* to meet him and assist with the luggage failed to recognize him. Bryant enjoyed the ruse so much that he repeated it: "I went down to my place on Long Island, put on a Turkish turban and gown, and had a long conversation in broken English with a young lady, our next-door neighbor, who thought that I was an oriental." Travel for Bryant would never again approach the intensity of his experience of the Orient. Bryant's beard became the symbol of his amazing, transformative odyssey.

13

TUMULTS OF THE
NOISY WORLD

Our public men want stiffer backbones. A weakening of the
spine is epidemic amongst them. Not one in a hundred stands
straight.

—*The Evening Post*, February 27, 1854

I

Bryant's seven-month overseas sojourn had been delightful, but he
soon found himself "grinding at the mill," lamenting his "dull
work" at the *Evening Post* to Dana. He had to deal immediately with
the threat of excommunication from the Democratic Party by its official
organ, the Washington *Union*, which accused the *Evening Post* of abolitionist tendencies. Bryant coolly dismissed the threat, offering a dozen
good reasons why the *Evening Post* was truly committed to democratic
principles and represented "the party of the people," whereas the *Union*
was merely a "party hack" serving proslavery interests. The drift toward
proslavery policies under the Democratic administration of Franklin
Pierce prompted Bryant to consider a final break with his party.

Not even the Crystal Palace Exhibition, which opened in New York
City on July 14, 1853, with a parade reviewed by President Pierce, could
brighten Bryant's mood or obscure the dark drama over slavery that was
unfolding in the nation. Bryant, along with Theodore Sedgwick III,
August Belmont, and members of other patrician New York families—
the Schuylers, Livingstons, and Hamiltons among them—had been

231

instrumental in erecting this Exhibition of the Industry of All Nations. With its massive iron beams, glittering enameled glass panes, and 123-foot dome, the Crystal Palace heralded the birth of a new American era in science, technology, and the arts. The massive complex covered four acres on Sixth Avenue between Fortieth and Forty-Second streets on land that would become Bryant Park early in the next century.

The Crystal Place transformed Forty-Second Street, making it what the journalist George Foster called "the Sedgwickean center of the metropolis." Omnibuses—often painted in garish yellows, reds, and blues—now operated past Houston and Madison Square to the Crystal Palace, conveying tens of thousands of Americans to the site. One visitor, seventeen-year-old Sam Clemens, found the site to be a "perfect fairy palace—beautiful beyond description." Bryant's friend and associate Theodore Sedgwick III was serving as the exhibition's president, and Bryant had been invited to the grand opening and the banquet the following day, but as he informed Eliza Robbins he did not attend the festivities: "I like more space than you get at such places. I like air and elbow-room, as you find them about the Pyramids, as at Thebes and Baalbec." (Robbins died at Cambridge, Massachusetts, on July 18 at the age of sixty-nine, prompting Bryant to write a graceful obituary celebrating "one of the most eloquent and witty persons we have known.")

II

By fall, Bryant concluded that the Democratic Party had become a feeble version of its former self and that the Pierce administration, riddled with patronage and proslavery sentiment, was on a downward course. Then on January 4, 1854, Stephen A. Douglas, the ambitious Democratic senator from Illinois who chaired the Senate Committee on Territories, repudiated the Compromise of 1820 by proposing a bill that would separate the Nebraska territory into two states, Nebraska and Kansas, allowing each state to determine the future of slavery for itself. Bryant was outraged. The editor accused Douglas, whose squat form and bull-like head had earned him the sobriquet the Little Giant, of being "a convenient agent when any game of petty cunning is to be played." Bryant labeled the Kansas-Nebraska bill an evil instrument that would result in "Africanizing the heart of the North American continent." Pierce was complicit, declared the *Evening Post*, in a "mad and wicked adhesion to the Nebraska perfidy" and serving as the "tail of Senator Douglas's kite."

The Kansas-Nebraska bill prompted some of Bryant's most virulent and sustained editorials against slavery and the men endorsing its expansion into the territories. During the winter and spring, as the bill worked its way through Congress toward eventual passage, Bryant inveighed against "the Nebraska fraud." On January 25, he reprinted a manifesto prepared by former Free Soilers Salmon P. Chase, Charles Sumner, Joshua Giddings, and others urging opposition to the measure. He also signed a proclamation calling for a mass meeting on January 30 to protest the Douglas bill, and he shared the platform as one of the honorary vice presidents.

Bryant attacked Congress in a series of editorials, writing sharply in one: "It is mortifying to witness the general feebleness which has characterized the opposition in Congress to Senator Douglas's bill of abomination. Our public men want stiffer backbones. A weakening of the spine is epidemic amongst them. Not one in a hundred stands straight." Typical of these spineless representatives was the Whig senator Edward Everett, a "polished icicle" who with his "effeminate, and soft, flattering voice" betrayed the will of his Massachusetts constituency. In rhetorically powerful cadences, Bryant lashed out at such feeble politicians while offering lyric praise of the masses: "It is not a few ranting abolitionists—it is not a few noisy brawlers who constituted the opposition to Judge Douglas's unholy, treacherous and monstrous proposition. It is the masses—the honest masses—the masses, all lovers of liberty, with backbones stiff and straight—it is the masses, almost without exception, who are opposed to it. If there are for these any more orators, with clear voices and stiff backbones, let them speak soon."

In a rare sign of editorial comity, New York newspaper editors who normally were at one another's throats opposed the Kansas-Nebraska bill. Mercurial Horace Greeley, who soon would desert his Whig allies to help found the Republican Party; wily and influential Thurlow Weed; and even the vain, bombastic James Watson Webb joined Bryant in denouncing the perfidy being perpetrated in the nation's capital. After the Senate passed the resolution on March 3, Bryant warned: "The President has taken a course by which the greater part of this dishonor is concentrated upon the Democratic Party. Upon him and his administration . . . and upon the Democratic Party who gave the present executive his power of mischief, the people will visit this great political sin of the day." Later in March he lashed out with Calvinistic fury: "Wherever slavery goes, the whole brood of evils which naturally appertain to the accursed institution will follow in its train." When the House passed the

Douglas bill on May 22 and President Pierce signed it into law three days later, just before Bryant's departure for Illinois with Frances to visit his family, the editor concluded: "If it should become the custom of the long-flourishing republic of the United States to erect statues to the authors of the abolition of slavery, the first should be erected to the authors of the fugitive slave bill, and the second to the authors of the Nebraska bill."

While Douglas, wounded and angered by the attacks by the Northern press, railed against "Abolitionism . . . Niggerism," Bryant cast about for Free Soil support. But where could he look? The Whig party was devoid of ideas, preferring equivocation to firm principles and well on its way to dissolution. The Democratic Party was split hopelessly into factions: Southern slaveholders, Ohio valley farmers, Northern free soil spokesmen. Bryant despised the anti-immigrant and anti-Catholic new American or "Know-Nothing" Party, which would elect nine state governors and more than one hundred congressmen in 1854. He took some solace in the lone voices—old Jackson loyalist Thomas Hart Benton of Missouri, who filed occasional reports with the *Post* and published much of his memoir *Thirty Years' View* in it; magisterial and moralizing Salmon P. Chase of Ohio; and radical, uncompromising Charles Sumner of Massachusetts—who denounced the Kansas-Nebraska bill and possessed the collective backbone that Bryant had called for. Such men might constitute the moral center of a dissident movement. Perhaps a new alignment out West composed of Conscience Whigs, Free Soilers, and antislavery Democrats and calling itself "Republican" was the answer, but Bryant held off on endorsing a new national party.

Bryant joined antislavery Whigs and radical Democrats in planning an "Anti-Nebraska" convention to be held in August 1854 in Saratoga Springs, New York. Part of a four-member Committee of Correspondence that included John Jay, the grandson of the nation's illustrious statesman and chief justice, Bryant presided as a vice president at a mass meeting in the park at City Hall that attracted thousands of citizens. The meeting adopted a resolution "that slavery shall be no longer allowed in an existing territory or new state." Under the banner "No More Slave States," Bryant announced in the *Evening Post* on August 15 that the goal of the Saratoga convention opening the next day would be to organize a new party and select candidates to run for statewide office on an antislavery platform.

But the Saratoga meeting, while formally renouncing the Kansas-Nebraska Act, was unable to agree on forming a new state party and broke up in discord. The fall gubernatorial election reflected the muddled condition of New York State politics when the fanatical temperance Whig Myron H. Clark eked out a victory over the incumbent Democrat Horatio Seymour, who lost because of the strong showing by the Know-Nothing candidate Daniel Ullman. Bryant was dismissive of the Know-Nothings, who in raising the "hobgoblins, Popery and Foreign Influence" were in "conflict with the principles of democracy. . . . The children of the 'aliens' of this generation," Bryant prophesized, "will be native Americans in the next." Soon after the election, Bryant warned that there was a "popular dissatisfaction with the way in which the old parties have been managed by mischievous and place-seeking office-holders."

III

By the middle of 1855, violence in the Kansas territory presaged the greater war that soon would overwhelm the Union. Two rival territorial legislatures—one proslavery and the other antislavery—had installed themselves in Kansas. Pierce sided with the proslavery legislature, dismissing the "informalities of the election" that had enabled hordes of Missourians to vote in Kansas. Bryant thundered: "Informalties! Where did Mr. Pierce learn English? By what authority does this man, who has got into the executive chair, presume to tell us who may settle in Kansas?" By the end of the year, the *Evening Post*, strongly endorsing the activities of the Emigrant Aid Society in its efforts to transport free soil settlers to Kansas, declared, "Every liberal sentiment—the love of freedom, the hatred of oppression, the detestation of fraud, the abhorrence of wrong cloaked under the guise of law—every feeling of the human heart which does not counsel cowardly submission and the purchase of the present safety as the price of future evils, takes part with the residents of Kansas."

In May 1856, President Pierce sent a federal marshal to arrest two free state leaders in Lawrence. The marshal's posse of some five hundred men hailing largely from the South and Missouri made the arrests, sacked the town, and killed one resident. The crisis in "Bleeding Kansas" confirmed Bryant's suspicion, expressed earlier, that the Democratic Party had "ceased to serve the cause of freedom and justice."

Even as the *Evening Post* lamented the sacking of Lawrence, the paper covered an equally electrifying episode unfolding in Congress. In mid-May, Senator Charles Sumner of Massachusetts delivered a two-day speech that he subsequently entitled "The Crime against Kansas." The handsome, hirsute bachelor, who at six feet three inches was one of the few statesmen who could stand eye to eye with Abraham Lincoln, was a complex man. Skilled in five languages, a friend of Longfellow and other literary celebrities, often dignified and courteous, Sumner also could be arrogant and cruel toward opponents. A hero in New England for his fierce abolitionism, Sumner took special pleasure in insulting Southern politicians. He probably was the most hated man in the Senate.

Sumner's heated speech, filled with pedantry and rhetorical excess in its condemnation of "the rape of a virgin state" by the "harlot, Slavery," was notably insulting toward Andrew P. Butler, the kindly, patriarchal senator from South Carolina whose conscientious work and refined manners had earned him the goodwill of his colleagues. When Senator Butler's nephew, Preston Brooks, who was serving his second term in the House, learned of Sumner's rebuke, he plotted revenge. Entering the nearly empty Senate chamber on May 22, intent on defending his uncle's honor and that of South Carolina, he found Sumner alone at his desk. After accusing Sumner of libel, Brooks raised a gutta-percha cane and rained a series of hard blows down on the senator's bare head. The attack was so severe that it incapacitated Sumner for three and a half years; he was reelected almost unanimously by the Massachusetts legislature, but his Senate seat remained empty—a stark reminder of the horrifying event—until his return in December 1859.

Bryant had written to Sumner when he was first elected to the Senate in 1851 as a Free Soiler: "Allow me to add my congratulations . . . on your success. I am glad that my native state is once more worthily represented in the United States Senate." Sumner in turn had asked John Bigelow to obtain Bryant's autograph. The senator admired Bryant's poetry and politics, as well as his address on Fenimore Cooper, which he called "a truthful, simple & delicate composition." Appalled by the "base assault" on Sumner, Bryant explained the origin of this "cowardly brutality":

> Violence reigns in the streets of Washington . . . violence has now found its way into the Senate chamber. Violence lies in wait on all the navigable rivers and all the railways of Missouri, to obstruct those who pass from the free States into Kansas. Violence overhangs the frontiers of that territory like a storm-cloud charged with hail and lightning. Violence has carried election after election in that territory. . . . In short, violence is the order of the day; the North is to be pushed to the wall by it, and

this plot will succeed if the people of the free States are as apathetic as the slaveholders are insolent.

Bryant was a principal speaker at a meeting on May 30 that drew five thousand indignant New Yorkers to the old Broadway Tabernacle to protest the Sumner outrage. The "deafening cheers that rose at his appearance," lasting for more than a minute and forcing him to wait in embarrassment before he could read the impressive list of vice presidents nominated for the meeting, testified to Bryant's celebrity.

Sumner's horrible beating also prompted a satiric poem by Bryant—"Brooks's Canada Song"—that appeared in the July 24, 1856, issue of the *Evening Post*. In the aftermath of the Sumner travesty, Anson Burlingame of Massachusetts had insulted Brooks, provoking a challenge to duel with rifles. The two men selected Canada as the site, but Brooks never appeared. In six stanzas, Bryant paints a devastating portrait of a bully and coward who offers reasons why he cannot journey to Canada, as in these lines:

> "There are savages haunting New York Bay,
> To murder strangers that pass that way;
> The Quaker Garrison keeps them in pay,
> And they kill at least a score a day.
>   And I am afraid, afraid, afraid,
>   Bully Brooks is afraid.
>
> "Beyond New York, in every car,
> They keep a supply of feathers and tar;
> They daub it on with an iron bar,
> And I should be smothered ere I got far.
>   And I am afraid, afraid, afraid,
>   Bully Brooks is afraid."

Portentous events had propelled Bryant and his newspaper into the camp of the "Black Republicans." The *Evening Post* led the *Tribune*, *Times*, and *Courier* into the new party, throwing its weight behind the candidacy of John Frémont in the 1856 presidential election. Bryant ridiculed the Democrats, who had nominated James Buchanan of Pennsylvania as their candidate, calling them "bucaniers" (a word that he subsequently spelled "Buchaneers"). The *Evening Post* praised Frémont as a man of "unshaken courage, perfect steadiness of purpose, and ready command of resources." The newspaper offered readers two hundred dollars in prizes for the best campaign songs, while Bigelow serialized his biography of Frémont in the paper. Supporters hoped that the new party's catchy slogan—"Free Speech, Free Press, Free Men, Free Labor, and Frémont"—would catapult General Frémont to victory.

When the votes were counted, Buchanan had defeated Frémont by a vote of 1,838,189 to 1,335, 264, while the candidate of the American Party, Millard Fillmore, trailed with 874,534. The Whigs had disappeared from the national scene. To Bryant, "one mighty stream"—the Republican Party—had been called forth from a "thousand rivulets." The editor predicted: "We have at least laid the basis of a formidable and well-organized party, in opposition to the spread of slavery—that scheme which is the scandal of the country and the age."

IV

Now in his sixty-first year, still walking briskly along the streets of Manhattan, Bryant was well known to New Yorkers. Walt Whitman, who in 1855 had published *Leaves of Grass*, a curious book of poetry that many found scandalous, recalled Bryant at this time as one with a "dry, spare, hard visage" sporting "a huge white beard of somewhat ragged appearance," striding along the streets of the city "regardlessly and rapidly, a book in his hand, a thought—and more too—inside his head, a most rustical straw hat outside of it, turned sharp up behind and down before, like a country boy's, and a summer coat streaming flag-like from his shoulders." Burdened by the destiny of his great country, Bryant had started to look like Father Time.

Bryant might have been "surfeited with politics," as he confessed to his brother John, but this was the price of being at the hub of the city's intellectual and cultural affairs. He still faithfully attended Sketch Club meetings, enjoying the diverse company of local friends and visitors who attended the club's sessions—Verplanck, Halleck, George Bancroft, Catharine Sedgwick, Ralph Waldo Emerson, and William Makepeace Thackeray among them. The artists Frederick Church, Jaspar Cropsey, Thomas Hicks, John Kensett, and William S. Mount also appeared at the club's biweekly meetings; along with Bryant's older friends Durand and Leutze, they held the poet in high esteem. Martin Van Buren was among the prominent politicians, businessmen, and industrialists who were guests at Sketch Club gatherings. But the former president, who had angrily cancelled his subscription to the *Evening Post* after its editor renounced the Democratic Party, no longer viewed Bryant as a reliable friend.

Buffeted by fierce political winds and needing respite from the buzz and hum of civic affairs, Bryant retreated to Cedarmere whenever he could, seeking comfort and inspiration from country life. The few poems that he published during the tumultuous fifties—"The May Sun Sheds an Amber Light," "The Voice of Autumn," "The Snow-Shower," "A Rain-Dream," "Robert of Lincoln," "The Twenty-Seventh of March," and "An Invitation to the Country"—capture the rural pleasures that he found at his country retreat. In "A Rain-Dream," he hinted at the dark political clouds from which he had to escape from time to time:

These strifes, these tumults of the noisy world,
Where Fraud, the coward, tracks his prey by stealth,
And Strength, the ruffian, glories in his guilt,
Oppress the heart with sadness. Oh, my friend,
In what serener mood we look upon
The gloomiest aspects of the elements
Among the woods and fields! Let us awhile,
As the slow wind is rolling up the storm,
In fancy leave this maze of dusty streets,
Forever shaken by the importunate jar
Of commerce, and upon the darkening air
Look from the shelter of our rural home.

In "An Invitation to the Country," Bryant urges his daughter Julia (who would never marry, serving as her father's companion in his later years) to leave "the gloomy city" in order to enjoy early summer's pleasures:

Come, Julia dear, for the sprouting willows,
The opening flowers, and the gleaming brooks,
And hollows, green in the sun, are waiting
Their dower of beauty from thy glad looks.

Bryant, who never brought the *Evening Post*'s business home with him, was happiest at Cedarmere. Caroline Kirkland, who occupied one of Bryant's cottages, captured the lure of the poet's "haunt" in *The Homes of American Authors* (1852): "The house stands at the foot of a woody hill, which shelters it on the east, facing Hempstead harbor, to which the flood tide gives the appearance of a lake, bordered to its very edge with trees, through which, at intervals, are seen farm-houses and cottages, and all that brings to mind that beautiful image, 'a smiling land.'" For Kirkland, it was the sight of Bryant clearing woodland paths, laboring in his gardens, and pruning trees that captured the essence of the man—"a simplicity of character and habits," as she called it in her astute portrait. "It is under the open sky, and engaged in rural matters, that Mr. Bryant is seen to advantage—that is, in his true character. It is here that the amenity and natural sweetness of disposition, sometimes clouded by the cares of life and the untoward circumstances of business intercourse, shine gently forth under the influences of nature, so dear to the heart and tranquillizing to the spirits of her child. Here the eye puts on its deeper and soft luster, and the voice modulates itself to the tone of affection, sympathy, enjoyment."

Bryant's major concern both at Cedarmere and in the rooms they had taken at 53 Lexington Avenue in the city, was the precarious state of his wife's health. In late 1856, doctors had diagnosed Frances's condition as rheumatic fever. After Frances had recovered somewhat by the following spring, doctors advised a change of climate and scene. Perhaps, Bryant hoped, a sea voyage and a six-month tour of the Continent would restore his wife to sound health. Bryant resolved to embark on the trip in May, accompanied by Julia and her cousin Estelle Ives.

On May 2, the Bryant entourage left New York for Le Havre aboard the *William Tell*. They reached the port city after occasionally rough seas by the end of May. Not since 1834 had Frances and Julia been on the Continent, and Bryant planned to revisit their favorite sites—Paris and Heidelberg—before striking out for the Low Countries, crossing Switzerland and France into the Pyrenees, and descending into Spain, where he wanted to spend most of his time.

Bryant found Paris much changed, generally for the better, with the city's narrow alleys and derelict buildings being razed to make way for Baron Haussmann's grand boulevards, constructed under the edict of Napoleon III. The family found elegant rooms at the Hotel des deux Mondes on Rue d'Antin, close to the Tuileries and the Louvre. While the ladies replenished their wardrobes, Bryant toured the city's museums and galleries. He talked with Sumner, who was traveling in Europe and recuperating slowly. Bryant found the senator "looking exceeding well—too fat, rather; in fact, he had lost something of the intellectuality of his expression, which was exchanged for a comfortable, well-fed look," Bryant informed Julia Sands.

The two men had long talks on American politics. Sumner "seemed highly gratified to learn that everybody was dissatisfied with the decision in the Dred Scott case, and, although the court had declared negroes not to be citizens, nobody at the North but a few old bigots to judicial infallibility acknowledged the decision to be law." Bryant surmised correctly that Sumner still had a long period of convalescence before he could return to the Senate.

Prior to his departure, the Dred Scott decision had confirmed Bryant's conviction that the government in Washington could not be looked to for leadership on the question of slavery. In March 1857, two days after President Buchanan's inauguration, the Supreme Court had ruled that Scott, a former slave who had claimed his freedom because he had been transported to a free state, was not a citizen and consequently could not sue in federal courts. Scott had to be returned to his owner. Moreover, Chief Justice Roger Taney's court ruled that the Missouri Compromise was unconstitutional and consequently that slavery had to be permitted in any territory of the United States. In eight successive editorials, Bryant subjected Taney's decision to scrutiny, claiming that the chief justice's reasoning was so "superficial and shallow" that it resulted in a deliberate misreading of the Constitution. Bryant charged that the outright perfidy of the Court's decision had reduced the United States to a "Land of Bondage; hereafter, wherever our jurisdiction extends, it carries with it the chain and the scourge—wherever our flag floats, it is the flag of slavery."

Bryant looked for signs of progress and enlightenment as he steered his family through Europe in sweltering summer weather. He informed the *Evening Post*'s readers, who could now purchase the paper at the reduced price of three cents, that he was much impressed by the pauper colonies in northern Holland. The houses in the colonies were clean; the people were neatly dressed and productive in the fields and at their looms; and a school, closed temporarily for repairs, offered rudimentary education for the children. Bryant stressed that religious teachers were provided for the colony in a most ecumenical manner—"a Protestant, a Catholic, and a Jewish Rabbi." Europe might not be experiencing the epochal transformation in human experience at the heart of the American experience, but it was making progress nevertheless.

Bryant filed a letter to the *Evening Post* extolling Swiss ingenuity in manufacturing, carpentry, taxidermy, and virtually every aspect of human endeavor. To Orville Dewey, he highlighted the marvelous changes that had occurred in Geneva: "Shallows of the lake filled up; rows of stately houses, with broad streets between, built on the level space, thus usurped for the water; massive quays and breakwaters, advancing into the lake, form a spacious port for the skippers; old fortifications of the town utterly demolished, and converted into public grounds and building lots, and Geneva overflows into the fields. I could hardly believe my eyes. The emancipated Catholics are building themselves a magnificent church on the west side of the Rhone, and priests, in cocked hats and long black skirts, go hobbling about in the city of Calvin."

By the time the vagabonds reached Bagneres-de-Luchon in the French Pyrenees in late August, Bryant sensed a decided improvement in Frances's health. She had surmounted mountains on donkeys, climbed the hills around Heidelberg, and conquered Mount Rigi in Switzerland in a sedan chair. Bryant wrote to a family friend, the Scottish American teacher Christiana Gibson, whose mother had established a school for girls on Union Square in the early 1830s: "My wife I am glad to be able to say is on the gaining hand. She makes some little expedition every day, and is stronger than when we left home." The most daunting part of their trip, however, lay ahead.

"Spain is a backward country," Bryant wrote to Charles Leupp, "following the rest of Europe at some distance—Spain is like the tail of a snake a good way from the head but dragged along after it nevertheless." After all the "renovation and repair" that he had seen on the Continent, Bryant found Spain, which the group entered in early October, to be a reactionary world resistant to progress. The country was dirty and the people often ragged. Accommodations ranged from fetid rooms where the servants' faces were quite literally black with dirt to immaculate quarters in monasteries. Jolting roads and primitive customs contrasted with the magnificence of Spain's architecture and its museums. Fleas and mosquitoes made the group's three-week passage from the northern border of Spain to Madrid a trial—more so for the women than Bryant, as he jauntily informed Leupp: "The young ladies with me complain of being nearly eaten up by fleas on the road, but I can assure you, that you and I found a hundred fleas in Palestine to one that I find in Spain."

Bryant also encountered warmth and civility among the Spanish people: on the whole he found them kind and generous. It helped that Bryant was carrying letters of introduction and knew enough Spanish to navigate the culture. As he and his little band of ladies traveled south toward Madrid, America's most famous poet was passed from one admiring host to another, each of whom placed his house at Bryant's disposal. At Burgos, he marveled at the Gothic convent perched on a hill overlooking the city and was impressed by the austere cells that the Carthusian monks showed him. The asceticism of the monk's lives contrasted with the bloody spectacle that Bryant witnessed at the city's bullfight. On the last day of the season, a frenzied crowd of six thousand seemed to Bryant to be transported by the blood sport, cheering the attack dogs and horses sacrificed to the bulls in order to weaken them. One bull impaled a horse on its horns "and laid him on the ground, ripping open his bowels. I then perceived, with a sort of horror, that the horse had been blindfolded, in order that he might not get out of the way of the bull." After witnessing the dispatch of four more horses and the deaths of two bulls in a gory, drawn-out ritual involving picadors, banderilleros, and matadors, Bryant and Estelle went to the cathedral to compose themselves. Frances and Julia had declined to witness the spectacle.

A different level of society awaited Bryant when, on October 17, he reached Madrid, where he would stay for a month. His fame had preceded him. After the hazards of the road, Bryant and his party found themselves in demand by American diplomatic and consular representatives. The American ambassador, Augustus Dodge, and his wife entertained Bryant on a daily basis—even advancing Bryant money until his funds could be replenished. Madrid's cultural arbiters were aware of Bryant's presence as well: an article appearing in the *La Discusion* praised him as "one of the greatest poets in the world today, and without doubt the first among Anglo-American poets."

Assisted by the secretary of the university, Bryant moved into comfortable quarters near the Puerto del Sol and set out to enjoy his time in Madrid. He quickly developed a passion for the Royal Museum, visiting it on numerous occasions and describing the place to Mrs. Kirkland as "a Museum of pictures of which I am not sure that it may truly be said that it is the best in Europe." Describing the museum for readers of the *Post*, he expanded on his intoxication with the thousands of paintings—including works by "the gentle and genial" Murillo, sixty-four paintings by Valasquez, fifty-eight by Ribera, and exquisite canvases by Raphael, Titian, and Veronese: "I wanted to enjoy all this wealth of art at once, and roamed from hall to hall, throwing my eyes on one great masterpiece after another, without the power of fixing my attention on any. It was not till after two or three visits, that I could soberly and steadily address myself to the contemplation of the nobler works in the collection."

Adding to the pleasure of his sojourn in Madrid was the presence of Carolina Coronado, the wife of Horatio Perry, the former secretary of the American Legation whom Bryant met at the Dodge home. A poet-novelist known as La Carolina ("Little Crown"), the vivacious and romantic Mrs. Perry presided over one of Madrid's most popular salons. Thirty years Bryant's junior, Carolina set out to charm the famous white-bearded poet, who visited her often. On one occasion, she received him in her boudoir in an "elegant wrapper," as Bryant described the scene in his diary.

During his visits to the Perry home, Bryant was introduced to some of the most distinguished politicians, writers, philosophers, cabinet ministers, historians, and editors in Spain, including Emilio Castelar y Ripoli, destined to become the first president of the Spanish republic. But he was mainly attracted to "the pretty poetess" who, as an anonymous New York letter writer revealed, had "taken possession of Mr. Bryant." He read his hostess's poetry and on his return to the United States would translate "The Lost Bird" ("*From the Spanish of Carolina Coronado de Perry*") for the *New York Ledger*. The title was apt, for the poem's six stanzas, as translated by Bryant, trace the course of unrequited love:

> For only from my hand
> He takes the seed into his golden beak
> And all unwiped shall stand
> The tears that wet my cheek,
> Till I have found the wanderer I seek.

Before Bryant left Madrid for the south of Spain, Carolina gave him a picture of herself, vowing tearfully, "I am going to learn English in order to read your writings." Frances was not amused. After an evening at the Perrys', Julia wrote in her diary: "Mother pronounced it stupid while Father greatly enjoyed his chat with the poetess."

In mid-November, armed with a new set of introductions, Bryant set off for Alicante on the coast. When the roads beyond the railroad terminus at Almansa became too arduous, the women boarded a steamer at Almería for Cartagena, while Bryant continued overland. Bryant found Alicante to be "a decayed town of great antiquity." Cartagena was little better—"a dull, dreary town" redeemed somewhat by the excellence of its flavorful grapes and pomegranates. Grenada also was "ugly . . . gloomy . . . nasty" and overrun by beggars and "gipsees." Only the town's "Moorish splendor"—and the beauty of Andalusian women—

relieved the dullness. To Bryant the Alhambra, despite its ruinous condition, was a symbol of the great Arab dominion over Andalusia, reflecting a Moorish "sense of the beauty of nature." A letter from Archbishop Hughes in New York to the archbishop of Grenada enabled Bryant and his party to visit the vault of Ferdinand and Isabella in the cathedral. Mordantly fascinated by burial sites, Bryant descended through a trap-door into the deepest and darkest regions of the cathedral to view the lead caskets containing the royal remains.

Eager to show Italy to Julia and Estelle, on December 12 Bryant boarded the steamer *Normandie* at Malaga, bound for Marseilles by way of African ports. The striking beauty of Algiers impressed the poet, who composed an impressionistic portrait of the city "rising from the water up the hill-side, a vast cone of flat-roofed houses, as white as snow, so compact as to look like a gigantic beehive, with not a streak, or path, or shade of any other color between them; not a red roof nor a shrub to break the uniform whiteness." Bryant speculated that the surge of French and Spanish immigrants to Algiers and Oran would someday make the entire North African coast a European domain.

V

The Bryant party reached Marseilles on Christmas Eve, but Julia and Estelle were sick with the grippe, and they had to wait until New Year's Eve to take passage aboard the steamer *Capri* for a three-day trip down the coast to Naples. Despite the hospitality of the American minister Robert Dale Owen and his wife, Bryant disliked Naples: the weather was cold and damp, beggars proliferated, and disease—smallpox and rheumatic fever—was rampant. Within two weeks, Frances became perilously ill, and for the next three months she was bedridden. A homoeopathic physician, Dr. Rocco Rubini, attended to Frances daily, while Bryant and Julia kept anxious vigil over her day and night.

During the worst stage of Frances's illness in February, when Bryant feared he was losing her, he returned to composing poetry for solace. In the first poem he wrote, "The Night-Journey of a River," Bryant develops the conceit of an archetypal body of water coursing through all history from Rome to the present and embracing all stages and conditions of life from birth to old age. Intimations of disease, dissolution, and death pervade the poem:

... A dimmer ray
Touches thy surface from the silent room
In which they tend the sick, or gather round
The dying; and a slender, steady beam
Comes from the little chamber, in the roof
Where, with a feverous crimson on her cheek,
The solitary damsel, dying, too,
Plies the quick needle till the stars grow pale.

Still, Bryant ends the poem on a cautious note of optimism, praying that a "mysterious force" will restore the polluted night river to "The crystal brightness of thy mountain-springs."

In a second poem, "A Sick-Bed," Bryant assumes the persona of his dying wife. The speaker implores the poet to move her from her sickroom:

Yet here I may not stay,
    Where I so long have lain,
Through many a restless day
    And many a night of pain.

But bear me gently forth
    Beneath the open sky,
Where, on the pleasant earth,
    Till night the sunbeams lie.

Heeding the doctor's advice, in late April Bryant moved his family to Castellammare, a resort south of Naples, where Frances began to slowly recover. The imagery and tone of Bryant's verse now reveals the cautious hope that the poet would not lose his wife. In "A Day-Dream," he imagines sea nymphs from deep in the Bay of Naples beckoning "Love-stricken bards" and other artists to capture their beauteous form. And in "The Life That Is," Bryant welcomes his wife back, if somewhat provisionally, to the world:

To this grand march of season, days, and hours,
The glory of the morn, the glow of eve,
    The beauty of the steams, and stars, and flowers;

Bryant exults in his good fortune:

Twice wert thou given me; once in thy fair prime,
    Fresh from the fields of youth, when first we met,
And all the blossoms of that hopeful time
    Clustered and glowed where'er thy steps were set.

And now, in thy ripe autumn, once again
    Given back to fervent prayers and yearnings strong,
From the drear realm of sickness and of pain
    When we had watched, and feared, and trembled long.

Preoccupied with last things during his three-month vigil at Frances's bedside, Bryant made a momentous decision. Although he had been a regular churchgoer at Unitarian services, he had never formally joined the church. When the Unitarian minister Robert Waterston, whom Bryant had met in Heidelberg, arrived in Naples with his wife and seventeen-year-old daughter Helen in late April, Bryant asked him to perform the rites of baptism and communion. Waterston later recalled that the poet, living "in that twilight boundary between this world and another, over one more precious to him than life itself, the divine truths and promises had come home to his mind with new power."

VI

His wife, Bryant observed, had been reduced by a third during her illness, but by mid-May she was well enough to travel with the family to Rome. Bryant was convinced, as he informed his brother John, that "the gentle methods of the new system" of homoeopathy had saved Frances; the allopathic method would not have brought her out alive. Bryant's friend, the artist John Gadsby Chapman, had reserved pleasant rooms for the party at the Hotel d'Europe. After the noxious atmosphere of Naples, where upwards of four hundred people perished each day, Bryant found Rome to be clean and convenient. Some even claimed that the residents had grown more intelligent, but Bryant thought any increase in intelligence was vitiated by the French occupation and their exclusion from civic affairs.

During his two-week stay in Rome, Bryant called on Sophia and Nathaniel Hawthorne on the evening of May 20. Two days later, at the invitation of the sculptor William Wetmore Story, he joined the Hawthornes for breakfast. Bryant left no detailed record of the meetings, but Hawthorne recalled that the two men had met briefly ten years earlier, when Bryant, traveling in the Berkshires with one or two Sedgwicks, had stopped by Hawthorne's house in Lenox. Bryant had consistently provided favorable notices of Hawthorne's work in the *Evening Post* and had decried his sacking from the Salem Custom House in 1849 after Zachary Taylor had won the presidency: "An act of wanton and unmitigated oppression by the Whigs," the *Evening Post* charged.

In *Passages from the French and Italian Note-Books*, Hawthorne writes that he found the "venerable" poet to possess a Yankee simplicity and plainness of manner, not at all affected or self-conscious, but wanting in passion. He detected "a weary look in his face, as if he were tired of seeing things and doing things." When Hawthorne raised the subject of Kansas, the novelist sensed a kind of "bitter keenness" in Bryant as the editor analyzed the recent defeat of free soil advocates. Hawthorne concluded that Bryant "uttered neither passion nor poetry, but excellent good sense . . . a very pleasant man to associate with, but rather cold, I should imagine, if one should seek to touch his heart with one's own."

Two weeks later after arriving in Florence, Bryant saw the Hawthornes again at Casa Guidi, the villa of Elizabeth and Robert Browning. That evening, Hawthorne observed that Bryant was unusually deferential toward Elizabeth, a petite, sprightly invalid much taken with spiritualism. The handsome Hawthorne, with his fine eyebrows and nose but with a mouth that often betrayed a sneer, did not find the conversation to his liking: "that disagreeable and now wearisome one of spiritual communications, as regards which Mrs. Browning is a believer, and her husband an infidel." Hawthorne, who was considered by many to be reserved and unfriendly, surmised that Bryant "appeared not to have made up his mind on the matter, but told a story of a successful communication between Cooper the novelist and his sister, who had been dead fifty years." Hawthorne coldly predicted that Bryant would soon experience "a great loss" because Frances could "hardly live to reach America." Sophia Hawthorne herself was a notorious invalid, but the novelist had little empathy for either Elizabeth or Frances. Hawthorne, perhaps experiencing competitive jealousy, wrote in his notebook that Bryant probably had no special appreciation of Elizabeth's or Robert's verse, while the Brownings, he mused, probably disliked the work of America's first poet.

By mid-July, after passing through Bologna, Venice, Milan, and Turin, Bryant reached Paris and began to make preparations for a return to the United States. He was pleased to discover that the Brownings were next-door lodgers. Bryant saw them on several occasions, and Robert Browning provided a list of hotels in central London. Sumner was also in Paris, having regressed somewhat following surgery to correct his injured spine. While in Paris, Bryant learned from Bigelow that the New York legislature had appointed him a regent of the University of the State of New York, but he wrote back to his partner that he was inclined to decline the honor, expressing an "aversion to any form of public life now." From Isaac Henderson, his other partner, he received the pleasant news that his semiannual dividend was $22,500, the largest ever.

On July 20, Bryant, Frances, and Julia crossed over to England and took up quarters in one of the small hotels that had been recommended by Robert Browning at 41 Jermyn Street in London. Earlier they had booked passage home for Estelle Ives, who was recovering from a painful case of boils, aboard the *Vanderbilt*; she would travel under the care of Henry Loop and members of the Sedgwick family. After a whirlwind of social engagements in London, Bryant traveled to Evesham in Worcestershire to visit his old hiking companion Ferdinand Field. While in Evesham, Bryant learned from Robert Waterston that his daughter Helen had died in Naples of a heart condition; Bryant wrote to his new friend expressing his grief, and also wrote a moving obituary of the seventeen-year-old girl for the *Evening Post*—a sad coda for the trip.

Relieved that Frances had survived the noxious Naples climate that had felled a much younger woman, but chastened by the experience, Bryant set sail for New York aboard the *Africa* on August 20. The return voyage was uneventful. The Bryants arrived in Jersey City on September 2, where Fanny Godwin, her nine-year-old son Willy, and Bryant's partners Bigelow and Henderson met them. They spent the night at the Brevoort House in Manhattan and returned to Roslyn the next day. On the day of their arrival, the *Evening Post* had reported on the second Lincoln-Douglas debate.

14

LINCOLN

Whatever is peculiar in the history and development of America, whatever is foremost in its civilization, whatever is grand in its social and political structure, finds its best expression in the career of such men as Abraham Lincoln.
—*The Evening Post*, May 21, 1860

I

As Bryant boarded the Jersey City ferry that would take him across the Hudson River and back to Manhattan that early September afternoon, he must have marveled at the city unfolding before him, stretching northward and struggling to accommodate almost one million inhabitants. Rows of brick buildings, some six stories high, marched along the island's western shore. Church steeples, anchored by Trinity Church at Wall Street, whose 281-foot spire was the equivalent of twenty-seven stories, dotted the skyline. Hundreds of ships plied the harbor and loaded and unloaded supplies, a forest of masts and yardarms that always amazed visitors to America's preeminent commercial city. Among the flotilla were slavers engaged in lucrative trade with the South. New York's proslavery mayor, Fernando Wood, boasted: "The South is our best customer." The *Evening Post* agreed ruefully: "The City of New York belongs almost as much to the South as to the North."

Just as the conflict over slavery had clouded Bryant's departure for Europe a year earlier, the subject insinuated itself immediately on his return to the *Evening Post*. On his first day back, Bryant read an article in his journal on the second Lincoln-Douglas debate held at Freeport,

Illinois, on August 27. Lincoln, the correspondent for the *Evening Post* wrote, was "awkward" and "ugly," but the candidate for the Senate possessed "the fire of genius" and was "a man of rare power and strong magnetic influence." Bryant followed the remaining five debates as the two rivals clashed repeatedly over the Dred Scott decision, popular sovereignty, the extension of slavery, and the rights of black Americans. After the final debate at Alton, Illinois, on October 16, Bryant concluded that "No man of this generation has grown more rapidly before the country than Mr. Lincoln in this canvas." Although Lincoln lost the senatorial contest to the Little Giant, he had achieved national prominence and had piqued the interest of the *Evening Post*'s editor.

Bryant wasn't ready to endorse the tall, gangly, decidedly unkempt politician from the West who was largely unknown to the Eastern political and newspaper establishments. The conventional wisdom was that New York's former governor and current senator William H. Seward, backed by Thurlow Weed's potent political machine, would be the Republican candidate in the 1860 presidential election and would probably face off against the Democrat Douglas. For his part, Bryant disliked Seward's temporizing politics; he preferred Salmon P. Chase as the Republican's choice, but doubted that the Ohio politician had sufficient national appeal. Nevertheless, a month following his return Bryant was confident that the Republican Party would prevail in the next national election and that the *Evening Post* would be in the vanguard of victory: "The Republican party, which has fought the good fight against countless discouragements, is the party which will soon be called to distribute the political honors of this nation, and no one can complain of our agency in allying them to its fortunes."

Under Bigelow's efficient editorial guidance and Isaac Henderson's business acumen, the *Evening Post* had flourished during Bryant's absence. With daily circulation nearing twenty thousand copies and advertising revenues pouring in, the paper was "prosperous—very prosperous," as Henderson was fond of crowing to Bryant in the early months of 1859. Bryant had to savor the paper's prosperity without Bigelow, who had sailed for Europe with his family the previous November on a trip that would keep him abroad for eighteen months. To assist him in the daily editorial affairs of the paper, Bryant reluctantly rehired Parke Godwin, who needed work, in February and also appointed William S. Thayer, a former Washington correspondent, as managing editor.

Relieved of mundane responsibilities at the *Evening Post*, free now to focus only on lead editorials, Bryant returned to the familiar routines of city life. He informed his brother Cyrus in February, "We are all now in town. I have bought a house for Fanny [at 82 East Sixteenth Street] and we are all with her." Frances's health was gradually improving, a happy turn that Bryant trumpeted in letters to family members and his friends Dana, Dewey, and Bancroft (who had just published the seventh volume of his *History of the United States from the Discovery of the American Continent*). Bryant took time to assemble the correspondence from his recent European visit and prepare a second volume of his travels, which Appleton published in March. When Robert Bonner, the editor of the popular weekly the *New York Ledger*, offered him one thousand dollars for any occasional verse the poet might compose, Bryant sent him his translation of Carolina Coronado's "El Pajaro Perdido."

The members of the Sketch Club and its offshoot, the Century Association, were delighted to have Bryant back in their circle. However, he was a bit overwhelmed by the popularity of the Century, writing to John G. Chapman: "The Century is prosperous and plethoric—it consists of 250 members now and the new place in Fifteenth Street is very convenient and very popular. For me there are quite too many strange figures among them. I begin to find myself a little homesick when I visit it and pine for 'the old familiar faces.'" Artists insisted on reproducing Bryant's iconic face: he sat for portraits by Thomas Hicks, Sanford Gifford, and Charles Ingham, while John Durand engraved his father's portrait of the poet for popular subscription. Matthew Brady, who had photographed Bryant in 1845, captured the poet's likeness once again at the "prince of photographer's" elegant new studio on Broadway and Tenth Street.

Bryant took special pleasure in the progress occurring at Central Park and his association with its superintendent of construction, Frederick Law Olmsted, and Calvert Vaux, who together had prepared the *Greensward Plan* for the park that had been published by William C. Bryant and Company. Fifteen years after he had first proposed it, Bryant's dream of a park for the people was coming to fruition. In mid-April 1859, he visited the area with Frances, Julia, and his brother-in-law Egbert Fairchild, who was part of the engineering team constructing the Croton Reservoir within the park's boundaries. In a letter to Christiana Gibson, Bryant described a scene "in which thousands of men are at work blasting rocks, making roads, excavating, rearing embankments, planting trees—a sight that reminded me of Virgil's description of Dido and her people building Carthage." One result of the financial panic that had taken place in 1857 had been Fernando Wood's shrewd decision to implement a vast public works program, which now employed the thousands of workers swarming over Central Park.

The autumn and winter months of 1859 brought Bryant unsettling news of the deaths of friends. In October, he learned that his erstwhile travel companion and American Art Union friend Charles Leupp, unable to shake a deep depression, had committed suicide in his fifty-second year. Bryant served as a pallbearer at the funeral; he wrote in the *Evening Post* that Leupp "was one of those whom the maxims and habits of trade had never corrupted; a man of open and generous temper, who abhorred every form of deceit and every unfair advantage."

The following month, Washington Irving died at Tarrytown, New York, at the age of seventy-eight. Bryant recalled that he and Irving had been "on excellent terms whenever we met" and that he "was under some personal obligations to his kindness." The two men were linked in the popular mind as pioneers of the American experience in literature; thus it was not surprising that members of the New-York Historical Society contrived for Bryant to deliver the main eulogy on Irving at a commemorative meeting they were planning for the following April.

Other friends and acquaintances—his old "Veto" collaborator Theodore Sedgwick III and, most grievously, his grandson Alfred Godwin, who died in February 1859—were joining that "innumerable caravan," as Bryant had written in "Thanatopsis." Now sixty-five, Bryant was aware also of his own mortality; he intimated in a short lyric, "The New and the Old," that his hold on the upcoming year was provisional:

> What am I doing, thus alone,
>   In the glory of Nature here,
> Silver-haired, like a snow-flake thrown
>   On the greens of the springing year?

Bryant would convey the same elegiac tone of loss in other poems he composed around this time, including "Waiting by the Gate" and "The Constellations." Even his innovative lyric "The Tides" conveyed through impressionistic imagery a desire to escape the pull of cosmic forces:

> Brief respite! They shall rush from that recess
>   With noise and tumult soon,

And fling themselves, with unavailing stress,
    Up toward the placid moon.

In "The Cloud on the Way," yet another lyric cast in an elegiac tone, Bryant might have had been thinking of the delicate health of his wife Frances as well as of the impending storm of civil war:

One by one we miss the voices which we loved so well to hear
One by one the kindly faces in that shadow disappear.
Yet upon the mist before us fix thine eyes with closer view;
See, beneath its silken skirts, the rosy morning glimmers through.

For Bryant, the darkness pervading this lyric was a metaphor for the clouds hanging over the Union, especially in the wake of the John Brown affair. On the night of October 16, 1859, old John Brown of Osawatomie, Kansas, accompanied by nineteen others, including several of his sons, freed ten slaves and seized the federal armory at Harpers Ferry, Virginia, hoping to spark a slave insurrection. The next day, a marine squadron under the command of Colonel Robert E. Lee battered down the armory door. During the skirmish, two of Brown's sons were killed, and Brown was stabbed with a sword and taken prisoner. Brown was summarily tried, found guilty, and hanged six weeks later.

With the nation's newspapers offering sensational accounts of John Brown's raid, Bryant calmly assessed the ultimate causes underlying the old man's "crazy attempt to excite the slaves of Virginia to revolt." The editor reminded readers of the bloody history of Kansas, the saga of Brown's family in the conflict, and the role of proslavery settlers who were "as great fanatics as Brown." Within this bloody tapestry of slavery, Brown was "only a disciple" of the slaveholders who were intent on fomenting conflict.

Bryant was appalled by the haste by which Virginia authorities hurried Brown "to the gallows." Alluding to the "twist in his intellect" that prompted Brown to think that he could provoke a slave insurrection, Bryant urged the Virginia authorities to spare Brown from execution by virtue of insanity. On the day in December that Brown mounted the scaffold, prayers were offered for the abolitionist hero at churches in New York and throughout New England. Emerson was heard to say that Brown's execution "will make the gallows as glorious as the cross," while Longfellow wrote that the men who hanged Brown "are sowing the wind to reap the whirlwind, which will come soon." Hawthorne disagreed: "Nobody was ever more justly hanged." For his part, Bryant found the tolling of church bells and firing of cannon at the moment of Brown's execution to be moving beyond description. Brown's fate, the result of "simple and manly virtues" gone tragically astray, was "an event in our national history which warrants every thoughtful man amongst us in pondering over it deeply." The editor predicted that "History, forgetting the errors of his judgment in the contemplation of unfaltering courage, of his dignified and manly deportment in the face of death, and of the nobleness of his aims, will record his name among those of its martyrs and heroes."

II

February 1860 was cold and snowy in Manhattan. By the end of the month, Broadway had turned into a sea of mud and muck—not an auspicious setting for Abraham Lincoln, who was scheduled to deliver his first speech to an Eastern audience at Cooper Union. Bryant had been a senior advisor to the Young Men's Central Republican Union that invited Lincoln to speak at the massive new red brick building on Seventh Street between Third and Fourth avenues that had opened the previous year. Boasting a great underground hall that could accommodate fifteen hundred people, Cooper Union had been chosen as the site for Lincoln's speech as a replacement for Reverend Henry Ward Beecher's Plymouth Church in Brooklyn. Lincoln, who had checked into the Astor House at the south end of the Broadway's Hotel Row, was surprised to learn of the change in venue, for the Young Republicans had not notified him. He immediately set about making last-minute changes in his speech, which he had researched diligently and composed expressly for delivery to the abolitionist Beecher's audience.

As one of the most influential advisers to the Young Men's Central Republican Union, Bryant was instrumental in bringing Lincoln to New York and catapulting him to national fame. Years after Lincoln's carefully wrought speech before an audience of fifteen hundred, George Haven Putnam recalled a meeting of the executive committee of the Young Men's Republican Committee in Bryant's office at the *Evening Post*. Bryant ended the bickering among the participants by endorsing the invitation to Lincoln: "I can but think that Mr. Lincoln has shown a better understanding of the policy and spirit of the Republican Party and of the conditions under which is to be made the coming Presidential fight, than has been shown by any other political leader in the country, not excepting even our own Seward." With Bryant's benediction, the group sent the invitation to Lincoln, promising him a stipend of two hundred dollars.

On the night of February 27, Bryant waited in the wings of the great hall at Cooper Union with Lincoln and attorney David Dudley Field. Manhattan's most distinguished citizens filled the rows of the Great Hall, and eighteen leading Republican dignitaries mounted the elevated platform to sit facing the audience. The three men walked out on stage at precisely eight o'clock—Bryant first, then Field, and finally the towering Lincoln, who was dressed in a wrinkled black suit and new, ill-fitting boots. Following loud and prolonged applause, Field stepped to the rostrum and quickly obtained unanimous approval for Bryant to serve as chairman of the meeting.

Assuming his position behind the podium, Bryant began by expressing his honor "in introducing to you an eminent citizen of the West, hitherto known to you only by reputation, who has consented to address a New York assembly this evening." The poet-editor praised Lincoln as "a gallant soldier of the political campaign of 1856" and "great champion" of the Republican cause in Illinois who would have gone to the Senate in 1858 if not for an "unjust apportionment law." Bryant's brief introduction was interrupted by applause five times as he explained the importance of "the great West in the battle which we are fighting in behalf of freedom against slavery and in behalf of civilization against barbarism."

"These children of the West, my friends," Bryant continued in an allegorical vein, "form a living bulwark against the advances of slavery, and from them, is recruited the vanguard of the armies of Liberty." Ending his introduction, Bryant invited the audience to offer the "profoundest attention" to the evening's guest. "I have only, my friends, to pronounce the name of"—and here Bryant paused for dramatic effect—"Abraham Lincoln of Illinois." The audience erupted again in applause as Lincoln, the gaunt, gangling giant from the West, delivered an antislavery oration and ringing endorsement of the Republican Party that held the vast assemblage at Cooper Union spellbound for almost ninety minutes. His closing line— "Let us have faith that right makes might"—thrilled the audience. The speech catapulted Lincoln to national fame.

Bryant offered full coverage of Lincoln's "Great Speech" in Tuesday's *Evening Post*. Two columns appeared on the first page, with bold headlines proclaiming the article's organization—"The Framers of the Constitution in Favor of Slavery Prohibition," "The Republican Party Vindicated," and "The Demands of the South Explained"—and two more columns on the fourth page. In his leader, Bryant regretted that the *Evening Post* was not "infinitely elastic" so that even more extensive response to Lincoln's "particularly forcible" speech could be provided. Lincoln had placed "the Republican party on the very ground occupied by the framers of our constitution and fathers of our republic" in "a most logically and convincingly stated" manner. Impressed as much by Lincoln's rhetorical style and strength of argument as he was by the man, Bryant observed "how much truth gains by a certain mastery of clear and impressive statement."

Lincoln left New York the next morning to make speeches throughout New England; he did not have an opportunity to see Bryant's afternoon editorial, but was anxious to know what the *Evening Post* had said about the Cooper Union address. Lincoln held no editor in greater esteem than Bryant; he was pleased when two weeks later James A. Briggs provided him with a copy of Bryant's flattering coverage and editorial. Lincoln declared to Briggs, "It is worth a visit from Springfield, Illinois, to New York to make the acquaintance of such a man as William Cullen Bryant."

Throughout March and into April, Bryant wrote no further editorials on Lincoln, preoccupied as he was with the eulogy for Washington Irving. He confessed to Orville Dewey that he "did not want the labor of writing the discourse" but had been prevailed upon by members of the Historical Society. In Bryant's words, the event, held on April 4, Irving's birthday, turned out to be "a great affair," with an immense and attentive audience. He shared the evening at the Academy of Music with Edward Everett, who according to Bryant "delivered his remarks with more vehemence than usual." Bryant opened his own eulogy with a retrospective on Irving's birth at the very origins of the Republic, offering references as well to his departed friends Cole and Cooper. Irving's *Knickerbocker's History*, which Bryant had read with delight and laughter while at Williams College, and his *Life of Washington* were monuments to a glorious era and the iconic writer who embodied it. Bryant's remarks were elegiac: Irving's death recalled a brighter, purer age, populated by men of "steady rectitude, magnanimous self-denial, and cheerful self-sacrifice." Bryant declared, "It is as if some genial year had just closed and left us in frost and gloom; its flowery spring, its leafy summer, its plenteous autumn, flown, never to return."

Bryant's friends praised the poet's homage to Irving. Bigelow told Bryant that his discourse on Irving was "the model of *éloge*." Dana commented on the eulogy's "naturalness, simplicity, and beauty of expression, tender thoughtfulness with all due praise, yet nothing in excess." Even Seward, a political enemy, acknowledged the eulogy as "a monument of American literature." Bryant also received a letter praising the address from Cassius Marcellus Clay, an abolitionist editor from Kentucky. He thanked Clay for his kind remarks, but reminded the antislavery advocate of the new fate, so different from the "peaceful tenor" of Irving's life, that Providence had assigned him: "The great work of bringing a community prejudiced in favor of slavery to see their error, and to permit its evils to be freely discussed has been laid upon you and you have shown yourself fully equal to it."

Among the dozens of New York editors thronging Nassau Street's Newspaper Row, Bryant was the one who saw most clearly the need to end the spread of slavery by electing Lincoln. After the Illinois lawyer defeated Seward for the Republican presidential nomination at the party's convention in Chicago on May 16, Bryant threw the *Evening Post* behind Lincoln: "It is written on the tablet of destiny that Lincoln is to be the next President of the United States." Two days later, the editor waxed eloquently in "A Real Representative Man," composing a paean to the Republic and the ardent candidate who embodied the nation's virtues. Lincoln was "a personification of the distinctive genius of our country and its institutions. Whatever is peculiar in the history and development of America, whatever is foremost in its civilization, whatever is grand in its social and political structure, finds its best expression in the career of such men as Abraham Lincoln." The candidate was the epitome of the Western spirit, a self-made "child of our free institutions" who rose from poverty and obscurity to political fame. Bryant's prose, with its balanced biblical cadences, assumed an evangelical pitch as he lauded Lincoln as a champion in what was looming as "a monstrous political conflict."

Bryant wrote to Lincoln in June, offering frank advice from "an old campaigner who has been engaged in political controversies for more than a third of a century." He warned the Republican candidate against making pledges, stating opinions, or making "arrangements" with other politicians. Speaking for the candidate's many supporters, Bryant urged Lincoln to "make no speeches write no letters as a candidate, enter into no pledges, make no promises, nor even give any of those kind words which men are apt to interpret as promises." Lincoln replied on June 28:

"I appreciate the danger against which you would guard me; nor am I wanting in the *purpose* to avoid it. I thank you for the additional strength your words give me to maintain that purpose."

With the Democratic Party hopelessly split between its adherents in the North and in the South, and with a new Union Party with a nebulous platform adding to the chaos of the election year, Bryant was confident that Lincoln would achieve the presidency for the Republicans. As he predicted, Lincoln was elected the sixteenth president of the United States on November 6, 1860, winning less than 40 percent of the popular vote over three rival candidates, but amassing 180 electoral votes. Four days later, Bryant wrote to Lincoln warning the president-elect not to appoint Seward to his cabinet: "You have numerous friends in this quarter, and they include some of the most enlightened and disinterested men in the Republican party, who would be infinitely pleased if your choice of a Secretary of State should fall on Mr. Salmon P. Chase of Ohio." The editor was determined to surround Lincoln with former Free Soilers who would be unwilling to make concessions to the South.

Bryant miscalculated in thinking that the threat of secession by the states of the South was insane. In a leader, "Peaceable Secession an Absurdity," he charged that "if a State secedes it is in rebellion, and the seceders are traitors." The next day he proclaimed: "We look to Abraham Lincoln to restore American unity, and make it perpetual." Writing Robert Waterston, who was now residing in Boston, the editor exulted in the triumph of justice and liberty, predicting that "the people of South Carolina are making so much fuss about their defeat, but I have not the least apprehension that any thing serious will result from it." But even as he wrote, South Carolina's two senators had resigned, and a States Rights flag was flying over public buildings in Charleston.

Meanwhile the cabal controlled by Thurlow Weed was conspiring to place pro-South officers in Lincoln's cabinet with the goal of placating the South and avoiding disunion. Weed, a thin, dapper man with dyed hair, visited the president-elect on December 20 with the expressed purpose of keeping Chase, Gideon Welles, and Frank Blair out of the cabinet and advancing Whigs who were sympathetic to the South as members of Lincoln's administration. Learning of Weed's treachery, Bryant wrote immediately to Lincoln about the formation of the cabinet: "The rumor having got abroad that you have been visited by a well known politician of New York who has a good deal to do with the stock market and who took with him a plan of compromise manufactured in Wall Street, it has occurred to me that you might like to be assured of the manner in which those Republicans who have no connection with Wall Street regard a compromise of the slavery question." Any attempt to restore the Missouri Compromise, as Weed had proposed to the president, "would disgust and discourage" New York Republicans and "annihilate" the party nationally. As for South Carolina, which had approved an ordinance of secession on December 20, Bryant warned that the state "cannot be hired to return to the Union by any thing short of the removal of all restraints on the African slave trade." Cautioning Lincoln against appointing high-tariff politicians to the cabinet, Bryant closed by disavowing any interest in a position for himself.

Bryant and Frances spent a "rather solitary" Christmas together at Cedarmere, as he informed Reverend Waterston, "in sight of the tides wrought into white caps by the northeast wind dashing at the foot of our garden, with flocks of screaming seagulls sitting on them, or wheeling in the air." The wildness of nature reminded Bryant of the chaos of the times. He was convinced that slavery and the lucrative slave trade were fueling the Southern revolt. "The madness of the South," he declared, "astonishes me."

III

As the madness of the South accelerated in the months leading up to Lincoln's inauguration, with six states leaving the Union to establish the Confederacy, Bryant emerged as the standard-bearer for the Republic among New York's journalists. The *Evening Post*'s editor regretted that one of the paper's stalwarts would not be part of the crusade, for John Bigelow left the journal on January 16 in order to return to literary writing. In a move that surprised Bryant and everyone else, Bigelow sold his one-third share in the paper to Parke Godwin, who had been working at the city desk for $50 weekly, for $121,000. By agreement, the penniless Godwin would slowly reimburse Bigelow from the *Post*'s dividends.

To serve as new managing editor of the *Evening Post*, Bryant hired Charles Nordhoff, a former sailor and writer of sea tales whose brisk, aggressive manner, strong cigars, and equally pungent opinions would serve the senior partner well during the war years. Nordhoff, formerly an editor at *Harper's*, shared Bryant's disdain for the secessionists and advocated a vigorous prosecution of the war. Quick-tempered and bombastic but utterly principled, he must have reminded Bryant of William Leggett.

At the outset of 1861, Bryant was a minority voice among the city's powerful newspaper editors as he assailed the secessionists, branding the six original states that had formed the Confederacy a violent "species of Caesarian operation." By contrast, Greeley of the *Tribune*—"the Hon. Massa Greeley" as Bennett's *Herald* caricatured him—was inclined to let the states of the South depart peacefully if that was the will of their citizens. The *Herald*, along with the *Journal of Commerce*, the *Express*, the *Daily News*, and many smaller papers, was also willing to let the South leave in peace. Only Raymond of the *Times* seemed as militant as Bryant in condemning the secessionists, but Raymond would join Greeley in urging compromise shortly after Lincoln's inauguration.

Times had changed, and Bryant's hostility toward slavery had hardened. It was as if his moral compass had shifted and now centered on the preservation of the Union and the elimination of slavery. In late January, the editor dismissed the Crittenden Compromise, designed to restore the Missouri agreement, as a betrayal of the Constitution and of Republican Party principles. Slavery, Bryant declared, should not be allowed in any of the territories. This was not the time for concessions to "a blustering and cowardly traitor" like Senator Robert Toombs of Georgia or for mawkish complicity in such treasonable acts as the seizure of forts and arsenals. A week later, Bryant wrote in his leader that if the federal government resorted to force to restore the Union, it would not have started the war but merely recovered lands from a "foreign power." If the South invited conflict, Bryant warned, "eighty years of progress in all the arts of warfare have not been lost upon the North."

Trading on his influence with the president-elect and widely perceived as the head of the radical Republicans, the editor contrived to surround Lincoln with strong Union men. Charles Ray, the editor of the Chicago *Tribune* and a staunch Republican, informed Bryant on January 8 that Lincoln had "profound respect for your fidelity to the cause and for your disinterestedness, and will be greatly influenced by your advice." Bryant had made it clear to the new president that he opposed the appointment of Simon Cameron, a political boss from Pennsylvania who was willing to sell his vote to the highest bidder, to Treasury; he informed Lincoln of an "utter, ancient and deep seated distrust of his integrity—whether financial or political" that was shared by many of Lincoln's supporters in the East. Bryant was unaware that Lincoln had already made some decisions about his cabinet, including the treasury post for Cameron and the appointment of Seward as secretary of state. But Lincoln, aware of the need to placate the "Bryant faction," as he called it, ultimately shifted Cameron to War and gave Treasury to Chase, stating that the nomination of Chase "alone can reconcile Mr. Bryant and his class, to the appointment of Gov. S. to the State Dept." Bryant was a figure of authority and Lincoln could not ignore him.

In mid-February 1861, Lincoln passed through New York on his way to the inauguration in Washington, and Bryant saw the president, now sporting a full set of whiskers, at the Astor House. There is no record of their conversation, but it can be surmised that Bryant urged the president to stand firm against the South. At a reception at City Hall hosted by the mayor, Lincoln appeared on the building's balcony to address the crowd below. "There is nothing," he declared in language that appealed to Bryant, "that can ever bring me willingly to consent to the destruction of this Union, under which not only the great commercial city of New York, but the whole country has acquired its greatness."

Bryant applauded Lincoln's Inaugural Address. "Admirable as the inaugural address is in all its parts—convincing in argument, concise and pithy in manner and simple in style—the generous and conciliatory tone is the most admirable," he wrote. "Mr. Lincoln thoroughly refutes the theory of secession. He points out its follies and warns the disaffected districts against its consequences, but he does so in the kindly, pitying manner of a father who reasons with an erring child." Nevertheless, Bryant predicted war with the rebels: "the Unionists of our States will arise and deal them the destruction they deserve."

On Saturday, April 13, 1861, a strange day of sunshine and rain in the North, the South fired on Fort Sumter. Bryant, intent on giving "office beggars the slip" as he wrote Orville Dewey, had escaped from the "constant applications to help people to offices under the new administration" in order to visit old friends in Boston and Cambridge. Before his departure, he had complained to Gideon Welles that "men of democratic derivation have been excluded from office." Seeing the Danas, Deweys, Waterstons, and Willard Phillips, with whom he stayed in Cambridge, offered some relief from his campaign to influence Lincoln and even build courage and resolve in the president. Longfellow, happy to see his old friend and mentor, wrote to Henry Tuckerman: "Bryant has been here; very gentle and pleasant, with his benign aspect and soft blue eyes. He looks like a Prophet of Peace, amid the din of Civil War."

Bryant returned to New York City to news of proslavery riots that had broken out in Baltimore. He told Leonice Moulton that "if the administration acts with proper energy," martial law would be proclaimed. "Military rule is better than mob rule."

In May, Bryant made a two-week trip with Frances and Julia to visit his family in Illinois. John Bryant, more radical in his views than Cullen, had maintained a station on the Underground Railroad and was a close friend of the abolitionist Owen Lovejoy, brother of murdered newspaperman Elijah Lovejoy. Bryant was moved by John's advocacy of Emancipation; immediately on his return to New York he arranged for Owen Lovejoy to speak at Cooper Union on June 16. Introducing Lovejoy, who now represented Illinois in Congress, Bryant praised him as a man as fearless as his martyred brother and a man who "had never ceased since that day to protest against an institution upheld by suppressing the liberty of speech and by assassination." For years Bryant had been a cultural icon and now, influential with Lincoln, he would use his public authority to fight for democracy and the preservation of the Union.

15

DAYS OF SLAUGHTER

OH COUNTRY, marvel of the earth!
Oh realm to sudden greatness grown!
The age that gloried in thy birth,
Shall it behold thee overthrown?
—"Not Yet," 1861

I

Bryant's confidence that force would rapidly bring the South to its knees was shattered by the disaster at the First Battle of Bull Run in July 1861. Frederick Law Olmsted, who had taken a leave of absence as superintendent of Central Park to become secretary to the United States Sanitary Commission, told Bryant that "although it is not best to say it publicly, you should know, at least, that the retreat was generally of the worst character, and is already in its results most disastrous." Shortly after Bull Run, Bryant indicated that the rout was the "best thing that could have happened." The defeat would take the "conceit out of us" and "give the contest so serious a character that when we do settle it we shall insist on so crippling the slave interest that it will never lift its head again."

Aware that the war could be long and bitter, Bryant endorsed the radical wing of Lincoln's cabinet—Welles, Chase, and Blair—who favored a brisk prosecution of the conflict. These three men aligned themselves against the conservatives Seward, Bates, and Smith, who were advocating negotiation with the South. Bryant revealed his militancy in "Not Yet," written in the summer of 1861 and published in the August 17 issue of the *New York Ledger*:

OH COUNTRY, marvel of the earth!
  Oh realm to sudden greatness grown!
The age that gloried in thy birth,
  Shall it behold thee overthrown?
Shall traitors lay that greatness low?
No, land of Hope and Blessing, No!

Bryant criticized the "idle hands" that would tear the fabric of the "sister States"; such behavior undermined generations of Americans who had fought to create a powerful, unified nation stretching from the "hoarse Atlantic" to the "Ocean of the West." He reaffirmed the enduring strength of the Union:

For now, behold, the arm that gave
  The victory in our father's day,
Strong, as of old, to guard and save—
  That mighty arm which none can stay—
On clouds above and fields below,
Writes, in men's sight, the answer, No!

In late August, Bryant returned to the idea of emancipation when in a leader for the *Evening Post* he supported General John C. Frémont's declaration in Missouri that the slaves of Southern sympathizers in that state would be freed—"the most popular act of the war." Lincoln, however, countermanded the order. Bryant criticized the president's decision, explaining that Frémont had "done what the government ought to have done from the beginning."

Bryant was now committed to emancipation. By October, in "Playing with War," he labeled slavery "a prodigious wrong which ought to be abrogated." He warned that the masses "will tolerate no playing at war." In the event that "it becomes necessary to extinguish slavery in order to put down this most wicked and wanton rebellion, it will be swept from the board." He criticized the administration for its tepid response to insurrection and warned that the public demanded swift measures: "the more energetic, the more effective these measures, the more telling the blow, the more they will applaud."

Appropriating Lincoln's famous concluding remark in his Cooper Union speech that "right makes might," Bryant composed "Our Country's Call" for the November 2 issue of the *New York Ledger*:

Few, few were they whose swords of old
    Won the fair land in which we dwell;
But we are many, we who hold
    The grim resolve to guard it well.
Strike, for that broad and goodly land,
    Blow after blow, till men shall see
That Might and Right move hand in hand,
    And glorious must their triumph be!

He was concerned that Lincoln's administration apparently did not share his militancy.

By the end of the year, Bryant was having doubts about Lincoln's resolve. The editor worried about the president's penchant for inaction if not prevarication in the prosecution of the war. When the president's message to Congress in December was couched in language that lacked the clarity and logic Bryant had praised in Lincoln's Cooper Union and Inaugural addresses, the editor lamented the "evident eagerness to dispose of the slavery question without provoking any violent convulsion." Three decades earlier, Bryant had speculated on the practicality of the Colonization Society's efforts to ship black Americans back to Africa. Now, when Lincoln seemed to hint at the prospect in his message to Congress, Bryant found the idea to be impractical and a reflection of the president's "limited and perplexed" thinking on the subject.

To Bryant, the answer was simple: the South was in rebellion, and the federal government had the right to seize the property of the rebels—including slaves—and dispose of them as it saw fit. To John Bigelow, now serving as the American consul in Paris, he conveyed his "impatience with some difficulty at the tardy proceedings" against the Confederate states: "People wonder and wonder what is the reason for keeping such an immense army at Washington, an army now admirably disciplined and perfectly equipped, and ready for any expedition on which they may be sent—when it is clear that the seat of government might be defended with a quarter of the number."

A month earlier, Bryant had pondered the start of his sixty-seventh year in "The Third of November, 1861." Casting his inner life, as he typically did, against the rhythms of nature, Bryant exults in the streams of sunshine and "golden haze of the great autumn skies" that greet him on his birthday. But "manhood's summer" had passed for the poet, leaving him only with the desire for a bit of "pleasant sunshine left me." The wistful lyric ends in tension, with Bryant's premonition of a northern blast, howling like a wolf, warring against his desire for repose:

> Dreary are the years when the eye can look no longer
>   With delight on Nature, or hope on human kind;
> Oh, may those that whiten my temples, as they pass me,
>   Leave the heart unfrozen, and spare the cheerful mind!

In the autumn of his years, Bryant knew that there would be no repose: the blast of civil war was upon the Union.

II

As the new year began, Bryant and his family were in the city for the winter, living at Blancord's boardinghouse on Fourth Avenue. The weather was mild; the effect of the war on the city subtle. "There is the old bustle in the streets," Bryant wrote to Leonice Moulton, "there was the old hurrying to and fro on New Year's day. The war has seriously interfered with some old interests; it has promoted a few and created some new ones. There is little gaiety—few parties—and some check given to luxury." Still, he saw many friends at a Saturday evening gathering at the Century Club, including the Bancrofts—now "zealous abolitionists"—and Chase, who was staying at the Fifth Avenue Hotel and was not, according to Bryant, "in a very cheerful mood."

One problem that was vexing to both Chase as secretary of the treasury and Bryant was the decision of Congress to float $150 million in "greenbacks" or legal-tender paper currency. In several editorials, Bryant inveighed against the folly of greenbacks, advocating instead bond issues and tax increases to pay for the war effort. He confided to the Boston financier and railroad baron John Murray Forbes that the greenbacks measure was "financial folly" and that once again having to fight the battle for a sound currency filled him "with intense disgust—and is exceedingly discouraging." Chase supported the measure reluctantly, writing to Bryant on February 4: "Your feelings of repugnance to the legal-tender clause can hardly be greater than my own, but I am convinced that, as a temporary measure, it is indispensably necessary."

Bryant took some solace from Lincoln's decision in January 1862 to replace Secretary of War Cameron who, as the editor had predicted, had turned out to be incompetent and corrupt, with Edwin M. Stanton.

With rumors that the cabinet was hopelessly in disarray and that Lincoln was planning more changes, Bryant wrote to the president that he and other Republicans would lament any decision to replace Gideon Welles as secretary of the navy. Bryant worried about the clashing, often self-serving people surrounding Lincoln, frequently receiving confidential correspondence from friends in Washington and officers in the field. He especially distrusted George B. McClellan as general-in-chief of the Union armies, alluding obliquely to McClellan's inaction: "The success of our arms and the energies of our generals seem to increase as we get farther away from the capital; the men of the west do not stand on ceremony with the enemy. They regard rattlesnakes as rattlesnakes, and treat them accordingly."

Events soon proved Bryant's mistrust of McClellan correct. On February 6, the editor received a confidential letter from General James Wadsworth: "I repeat the conclusion intimated in my last letter," wrote Wadsworth, who would distinguish himself at the Battle of Gettysburg but would perish in the Wilderness campaign. "The commander in chief is almost inconceivably incompetent, or he has his own plans—widely different from those entertained by the people of the North—of putting down this rebellion."

Under pressure, Lincoln finally placed general command of the army under Stanton in the War Department. McClellan, relieved of overall command on March 11 and demoted to commander of the Army of the Potomac, conducted a fitful and ultimately disastrous advance on Richmond during the spring and early summer months. Despite vastly superior Union forces, the rebels threw back the Army of the Potomac, forcing McClellan to make a frantic retreat across the James River to save his army. On July 11, Bryant lambasted Generals Scott, McDowell, and McClellan, all of whom had advocated the capture of the South's capital. He thought it folly to attack the South's cities instead of defeating its armies in the field and called the plan to capture Richmond "our fixed idea, our enchantment, our pleasant illusion, our fatuity."

Bryant's steadfast opposition to disunion did little to erode the sympathy of many New Yorkers for the South. (Mayor Wood had even proposed that the city should also secede and form its own free port in order to sustain business with the Confederacy.) Still, he was heartened by the way in which the city became a dynamo for the Union war effort. Men by the thousands—many joining ethnic American detachments like the Irish Brigade and the Garibaldi Guard—rushed to sign up as volunteers. Even the city's notorious b'hoys and fire laddies formed their own regiments, fighting bravely but vainly from April through November 1862 as the rebels routed them at Shiloh and Second Bull Run and fought them to a standstill at Antietam in Maryland. Even the Union's qualified success at repulsing Southern forces at Antietam that September, which prompted Lincoln to issue a preliminary Emancipation Proclamation, proved disastrous for New York's volunteers. When Major General Ambrose Burnside ordered a suicidal assault on Confederate barricades, soldiers of the Fifty-First New York Volunteers charged across a narrow field and were decimated by rebel gunners.

Led by "Ninety-Two of the Most Respected Ladies" in New York, including Mrs. William Cullen Bryant, some four thousand women had organized the Women's Central Association of Relief for the Sick and Wounded of the Army to care for the maimed survivors who straggled back to the city. The war had already become, Walt Whitman wrote, a "butcher's shambles."

In his roles as president of the newly established Emancipation League in New York and one of the founders of the Committee on National Affairs and at the urging of some of New York's most distinguished citizens, Bryant traveled to Washington in early August in an attempt to rouse Lincoln. Before departing, he wrote: "A deep lethargy appears to have fallen upon the officers of our government, civil and military, from which they must be aroused, or it will resemble the sleep of death." It was the duty of journalists to warn the public of the dangers of inaction and to demand "of the government an energy and will of which it has yet shown no sign."

Accompanied on his trip to Washington by the Manhattan millionaire Charles King, Bryant suspected the "influence of Seward" at work, neutralizing the best efforts of radical Republicans to win over the president. "I saw Mr. Lincoln," he wrote to Horatio Powers, "and had a long conversation with him on the affairs of the country, in which I expressed myself plainly and without reserve, though courteously." Bryant informed Orville Dewey that Lincoln had admitted that McClellan was "wanting in some of the necessary qualities of a general officer." But in a September 15 editorial, Bryant wondered whether Lincoln, despite his "honest" and "determined" posture, suffered from a "want of decision and purpose" that was the result of "treachery" (and here Bryant probably had Seward in mind) lurking "in the highest quarters."

Bryant found one warrior on the western front willing to prosecute the war vigorously: Ulysses S. Grant, whose troops called him "the quiet man." After Grant captured Fort Donelson in Tennessee in April, Bryant praised Grant as a general who got things done. Following the battle at Corinth in early October, Bryant described Grant as the one officer "able not only to shake the tree, but to pick up the fruit." The editor was unworried about the rumors swirling around Grant's drinking problem. He assured John Forbes that he had a batch of testimonials in his desk drawer attesting to Grant's abstinence: "Whether he drinks or not, he is certainly a fighting general, and a successful fighter, which is a great thing in these days."

Bryant thought that Grant's aggressiveness was the perfect antidote to McClellan's indecisiveness, which had been apparent at Antietam Creek when McClellan failed to pursue retreating rebel forces. The mess at Antietam prompted Bryant to send yet another letter to Lincoln:

> We are distressed and alarmed at the inactivity of our armies in putting down the rebellion. I have been pained to hear lately from persons zealously loyal, the expression of a doubt as to whether the administration sincerely desires the speedy annihilation of the rebel forces. We who are better informed acquit the administration of the intention to prolong the war though we cannot relieve it of the responsibility. These inopportune pauses, this strange sluggishness in military operations seem to us little short of absolute madness. Besides their disastrous influence on the final event of the war they will have a most unhappy effect upon the elections here, as we fear they have had in other states.

Finally, on November 5, Lincoln bowed to the pressure exerted by Bryant and the radical Republicans and sacked McClellan, appointing Major General Burnside as commander of the Army of the Potomac.

Nevertheless, at the end of the year, Bryant's dark thoughts about the Union effort persisted. When plans for the battle at Fredericksburg in Virginia resulted in a disastrous loss for the Army of the Potomac, Bryant was appalled. Relating the events of December 12 and 13 at Fredericksburg to Dana, he confessed that he scarcely had the heart to write about the Union defeat. "The battle was a dreadful piece of butchery for which I fear General Halleck is responsible. They say that the officers of Burnside's corps were all against making the attempt to carry the enemy's intrenchments." Still, Bryant assured his friend, who was something of an

Anglophile, that their country was far superior to that of the decadent British, who were proving to be no great friends of the Union. He ended his letter on an optimistic note: "Let us be thankful that God is bringing so much good out of the terrible evil that has fallen on us."

III

On January 1, 1863, Abraham Lincoln enforced the Emancipation Proclamation he had announced the previous autumn, freeing all slaves in the states and territories still in rebellion against the Union. Thanking the Waterstons for a volume of Anna Waterston's verse that she had sent him, Bryant exulted in the president's action: "The new year which has opened so gloriously with the proclamation of liberty to the enslaved in the greater part of the United States where the law of bondage has been in force, will I hope close upon a republic entirely composed of free states." He trusted that the year would "see the Union reestablished on the basis of universal liberty."

Bryant suspected that conspiracies were afoot—all designed to undermine Lincoln, cripple the Union's war effort, and produce an armistice with the South—that would ruin the dream of universal liberty he had expressed in his letter to the Waterstons. Seward, he was convinced, was the "evil genius" behind these machinations, as Bryant intimated to William Pitt Fessenden, the United States senator from Maine: "A good many of us here believe that the views of the manner in which the slave-holders ought to be dealt with, entertained by Mr. Seward, are incompatible with a successful prosecution of the war. We think the salvation of the country depends on the immediate arming of the blacks for offensive as well as defensive purposes—and that the advisers of Mr. Lincoln ought to insist upon this being done. We do not expect any such advice to be given by Mr. Seward."

There were traitors, Bryant intimated, in New York City as well. He was perplexed—and then angered—when Samuel F. B. Morse and Samuel Tilden, one a former Nativist and the other a Peace Democrat and both opposed to the administration, invited him to a secret meeting at Delmonico's during the first week in February. Perhaps Morse, serving as president of the newly formed Society for the Diffusion of Political Knowledge, had decided to invite his old friend because of Bryant's acid editorials attacking the conduct of the war. Declining the invitation,

Bryant sent a reporter to the meeting instead—and uncovered what he imagined was a Copperhead cabal planning to undermine support for the war. Here, Bryant charged, was evidence of rich New York merchants and bankers led by August Belmont who were intent on colluding with the Copperhead editors of the *World*, *Express*, and *Journal of Commerce* to weaken the war effort. This conspiracy, Bryant charged in an editorial, was treasonous; it would hand the government over "to the malignant and slaveholding oligarchs."

Bryant's revulsion against Copperheads, compromisers, and conspirators prompted his renewed call for support of the Union and for a vigorous prosecution of the war. On February 14 he helped organize a Loyal Publications Association in opposition to the wealthy cabal that had met at Delmonico's. At Cooper Union on March 6, he presided at a rally denouncing a negotiated peace and advocating a strong war effort. Then, on the evening of March 20 at Cooper Union, an enthusiastic crowd elected Bryant and his friend Bancroft along with first citizens William Dodge, Francis Lieber, and A. T. Stewart to a council organizing the New York branch of the Union League.

With his aggressive pro-war stance, Bryant had been steering the *Evening Post* well ahead of the city's other newspapers in defense of the Union. Professor Charles Eliot Norton of Harvard conveyed his "hearty sympathy for the principles maintained by the *Evening Post*." In Philadelphia, the antislavery leader William Furness wrote to Bryant, telling him that the *Evening Post* "stands in my esteem as the head of the American press." Bryant's former partner John Bigelow wrote from Paris that the *Evening Post* was "the highest newspaper authority now in the country."

By April, Bryant, who was exceptionally well informed about the intricacies of the Union's war planning, was optimistic about the spring campaign. Replying to Bigelow, who had offered him the use of The Squirrels, Bigelow's house at Buttermilk Falls on the Hudson River just below West Point, for the summer months, Bryant detected a changed climate of opinion about the war. Quoting from *Richard III*, he commented, "The war goes on as slowly as the season. 'The winter of our discontent' is not yet 'made glorious summer.' Public opinion, however, on the subject of the war is rectifying itself very rapidly, and the people of the North are becoming more and more emancipationists. I look for the time, and it is not far off I believe, when to be called an anti-abolitionist will be resented as opprobrium."

But Bryant's entrenched cynicism about the ineptitude of Northern generals returned when news of the Union defeat at Chancellorsville filtered into the *Evening Post* in early May. Possessing twice as many troops as Robert E. Lee, General Joseph Hooker, now commanding the Army of the Potomac, had permitted himself to be outflanked by Stonewall Jackson (who was wounded fatally by his own troops) and driven back across the Rappahannock with more than twelve thousand men killed and wounded. On May 7, the *Evening Post* charged that Hooker's strategy had been insane and incomprehensible. Why hadn't Hooker deployed thirty-five thousand of his troops? Why hadn't he called on reserves from nearby Washington?

Still, Bryant prophesied on May 21 that Lee had suffered a Pyrrhic victory. Thinking that reserves would swell Lee's army to between 150,000 and 200,000 men (in fact he commanded about 70,000), the editor predicted with uncanny accuracy the train of events that would lead Lee to Gettysburg:

> As soon as it is ready Lee will move, we conjecture, not in the direction of Washington, but of the Shenandoah Valley, with a view to crossing the Potomac somewhere between Martinsburg and Cumberland. It will be easy for him . . . to defend his flanks . . . and to maintain also uninterrupted communications with Staunton and the Central Virginia railway. The valley itself is filled with rapidly ripening harvests, and once upon the river supplies may be got from Pennsylvania.

Bryant advised the fortification of towns in Pennsylvania and a confrontation with Lee. "How the war drags on!" he complained to Dana.

Bryant had high hopes that Lee's incursion into Pennsylvania would end—as it did—in disaster for the South. When Lee's advance troops crossed the Potomac on June 17, the *Evening Post* surmised gleefully that the rebels might extend themselves too far, be cut off, and be destroyed. Ten days later, after Confederate troops reached Carlisle, the *Post* exulted that "the great occasion has come." The Battle of Gettysburg, which began on July 1 and lasted three days under warm, fair skies, resulted in epic heroism and unspeakable carnage. Deadly artillery duels and hand-to-hand fighting produced more than twenty thousand casualties on each side. On the last day of the battle, Pickett's gallant but suicidal charge cost the South the battle. Lee retreated—just as Vicksburg in Mississippi was falling to General Grant. Bryant predicted that "the rebellion has received a staggering blow, from which it would scarcely seem possible for it to recover."

IV

As fateful as Gettysburg was for both the North and South, the battle was not as lurid for New Yorkers as were the draft riots that broke out in the city on Monday, July 13. From virtually the beginning of the war, Bryant had advocated conscription as the solution to the North's manpower needs; he was pleased when Lincoln signed the Draft Act on March 3. Bryant had led the "niggerhead press," as the *Post*, *Times*, and *Tribune* were labeled by their opponents, in advocating a draft, while attacking Copperhead newspapers like the *World* and *Express* and Fernando Wood's secessionist *Daily News* for their opposition to conscription. Governor Horatio Seymour, a Democrat, had heightened tensions when at a July 4 anti-conscription rally at the Academy of Music he warned, "the bloody and treasonable and revolutionary doctrine of public necessity can be proclaimed by a mob as well as by a government." Shortly after the *Herald*, which prided itself in being nonpartisan, stated ominously in its Monday morning edition that workers were organizing to protest conscription—a protest that had started peacefully enough on Saturday—the city erupted in violence.

During four days of insurrection and race riots, Bryant waged his own war to save the *Evening Post* and even his home at Cedarmere from destruction. Waves of workers, goaded to new heights of fury by "low Irish women" as George Templeton Strong called them, turned the city into a hellish landscape of blood, fire, and destruction. For four sweltering days, mobs attacked African Americans, well-dressed citizens, Fifth Avenue mansions, Broadway emporiums (Brooks Brothers was sacked on Tuesday), arsenals, draft stations, and identifiable Republican strongholds like Columbia College on Fifth Avenue at 49th Street. On the first day, rioters burned down the Colored Orphan Asylum on Fifth Avenue and 43rd, but not before the 237 children were shepherded to safety.

The rioters did not spare Newspaper Row across from City Hall Park and its three major pro-Union journals from their fury. Gangs stoned Greeley's *Tribune*, broke into the building, and set the editorial office on fire before being routed by police. Raymond of the *Times* mounted Gatling guns in the north windows and successfully thwarted the mob. Bryant barricaded the *Evening Post* building: Nordhoff hooked the paper's steam-driven press to hoses mounted in windows and prevented the mob from attacking. Learning of a threat to burn down his house in Roslyn, Bryant wrote to his caretaker George Cline: "Four revolvers and ammunition will be sent down this evening," with a request that the workmen on the property "aid in the defense of the house."

Only when federal troops, which Republican mayor George Opdyke had implored Secretary Stanton to send, began to arrive on Wednesday did the insurrection lose momentum. By Thursday, with the city filled with six thousand troops drawn largely from Meade's forces at Gettysburg and the rioters uprooted from their redoubts, the battle for New York was over. Nordhoff had calmly roamed the streets during the riots. On July 23, he wrote an eight-thousand-word history of the events for the *Evening Post* that was the most extensive contemporary account, estimating that between four hundred and five hundred people had lost their lives.

Bryant suspected once again that a well-organized conspiracy rather than a spontaneous outburst of resentment over conscription lay behind the Draft Riots. On the second day, Bryant wrote editorially that a "distinguished and sagacious Democrat" (probably Tilden) had visited his office to inform him that the riots "had a firmer basis and a more fixed object than we imagined." The rioters themselves were merely "a small band of cutthroats, pickpockets and robbers" engaged in a criminal spree while local police forces stood by idly. (Herman Melville, planning a return to New York, labeled the rioters "ship rats and rats of the wharves.") Bryant was convinced of the existence of "a regular conspiracy, a branch of the rebellion, and the work of those who hold communication with the rebels." "Out of this anarchy, there is very little doubt that these dreamers hoped to erect a revolutionary government."

Bryant's concern for the safety of his family and the *Evening Post* prevented him from accepting an invitation to Williams College, which on August 4 and 5 celebrated its fiftieth commencement. During the festivities, Bryant was restored to the class of 1813. He had been invited to deliver a poem for the occasion, but prevailed on Charles Sedgwick, Jr., to deliver his eighty-line blank verse tribute, "Fifty Years," at the end of ceremonies for alumni that Tuesday. Composing the lyric, Bryant was preoccupied with the war:

> For us, who fifty years ago went forth
> Upon the world's great theatre, may we

Yet see the day of triumph, which the hours
On steady wing waft hither from the depths
Of a serener future; may we yet,
Beneath the reign of a new peace, behold
The shaken pillars of our commonwealth
Stand readjusted in their ancient poise,
And the great crime of which our strife was born
Perish with its accursed progeny.

At the outset of the conflict, Bryant had written the blank verse tales "Sella" and "The Little People of the Snow" as fantasies of retreat from the shadows of war. Now he was a sober realist who looks forward in "Fifty Years" to conquering a "deadlier foe" than any ancient power. A "mighty and insolent" South "that scoffs at human brotherhood / And holds the lash o'er millions" simply had to be destroyed.

Bryant was convinced that Gettysburg and Vicksburg marked turning points against the mighty and insolent South, but he thought nevertheless that aggressive military action was required to achieve victory. Grant was getting things done: "If any one after this still believes that Grant is a drunkard, we advise him to persuade the Government to place none but drunkards in important commands."

Bryant spoke at a mass meeting at Cooper Union on October 2 to welcome a delegation of emancipationists from Missouri. He attacked the notion of gradual emancipation. "Gradual emancipation! Have we not suffered mischief enough from slavery without keeping it any longer? Has not enough blood been shed? My friends, if a child of yours were to fall into the fire would you pull him out gradually? If he were to swallow a dose of laudanum sufficient to cause speedy death, and a stomach pump were at hand, would you draw the poison off by degrees? If your house were on fire would you put it out gradually?"

On November 20, Bryant wrote a warm, puckish letter to his old friend Catharine Sedgwick, who was on the mend after a serious illness. For Bryant, her recovery was a metaphor for the war itself. "Your return to life of such a vivacity, cheerfulness and physical strength as I hear it is," he remarked, "makes me think of the return of Aeneas from the shades. . . . Now that you have accomplished the feat, I hope that you will stay with us a long time, to the delight of your friends, to see this cruel war ended and the new order of things fully established and proceeding gloriously. . . . The delays of the war, vexatious as they have been, will have brought a swifter and more complete extinction to slavery, and ought to be remembered among our occasions of gratitude in the great national Thanksgiving of next week."

In his annual message to Congress on December 8, Lincoln outlined a proclamation of amnesty and reconstruction that appealed to Bryant. The editor applauded Lincoln's leniency toward the rebels, who in fact had "put themselves beyond the pale of the law by their insanity." The president was offering the South peace on the most generous of terms if only the region would surrender and renounce "that monstrous idol of Slavery, which has been the source of all their sacrifices and sufferings and woes."

V

The publication of *Thirty Poems* by Appleton in January 1864 provided Bryant with a welcome distraction from his preoccupation with the war. Praise for the volume flowed from his friends. Catharine Sedgwick, impressed by "The Life That Is," wrote to him: "Mrs. Bryant may now hold her head above Beatrice and Laura." Lydia Maria Child informed Bryant that her favorite poem from the volume was "Robert of Lincoln," while Caroline Kirkland singled out "The Planting of the Apple-Tree" and "The Song of the Sower" as her favorites. Orville Dewey liked Bryant's translation of a passage from the *Odyssey*. Dana praised the "the perfect calm" of the entire collection. Longfellow, who had lost his wife two years earlier, found *Thirty Poems* "very consoling both in its music and in its meaning."

After reading *Thirty Poems*, Emerson wrote in his journal:

> Bryant has learned where to hang his titles, namely, by tying his mind to autumn woods, winter mornings, rain, brooks, mountains, evening winds, and woodlands. . . . He is American. Never despaired of the Republic. Dared name a jay and a gentian, crows also. His poetry is sincere. I think of the young poets that they have seen pictures of mountains, and sea-shores, but in his that he has seen mountains and has the staff in his hand.

Emerson, joined by Holmes and Lowell, invited Bryant to a celebration of the three-hundredth birthday of Shakespeare that Boston's Saturday

Club was planning for April. Bryant readily accepted the invitation but had to back out at the last minute because of pressing business at the *Evening Post*.

The last selection in *Thirty Poems* was "The Poet," a lyric in nine stanzas that Bryant had composed at Roslyn in 1863. Soon to be seventy, Bryant in "The Poet" repeats a theory of prosody that he had proposed in his lectures on poetry shortly after his arrival in New York City almost forty years earlier. The "witchery" of verse, Bryant declares, lies in the poet's ability to distill "impassioned thought"—to "Set forth the burning words in fluent strains." The blending of thought and emotion, tempered by the poet's "clear vision" and experience in the world, are the criteria for excellence:

> Of tempests wouldst thou sing,
>   Or tell of battles—make thyself a part
> Of the great tumult; cling
>   To the tossed wreck with terror in thy heart
> Scale, with the assaulting host, the rampart's heights,
> And strike and struggle in the thickest fight.

The lyric's martial imagery and passionate tone capture Bryant's preoccupation with the apocalyptic struggle still being waged to save the Republic.

Bryant was fiercely engaged in that struggle. He had planned to preside at a Cooper Union meeting on January 13 at which Frederick Douglass was scheduled to deliver an address, "The Mission of the War," but the death of his brother-in-law Egbert Fairchild forced him to miss the event. He was able to preside at a second anniversary meeting of the National Freedman's Relief Association at Cooper Union on the evening of February 26, at which Henry Ward Beecher and others spoke. In a brief address, Bryant looked forward to reconstruction and the welfare of the four million freed slaves that the Freedman's Association had to assist: "We must bind up his wounds; we must convey him to a place of shelter; we must see that he is healed; we must set him forward on his journey, and bid him God speed."

As early as February, Bryant surmised that if Lincoln could advance the mission of the war by the middle of the year, the president would be renominated "almost by acclamation." However, he withheld an early endorsement of Lincoln by the *Evening Post*, but did not go as far as the

Tribune's Greeley, who groused in an editorial that Grant, Chase, Frémont, or Butler would be a better choice than Lincoln at the Republican
National Convention in Baltimore on June 7. Bryant worried that the
war had settled into a gruesome stalemate; he had proposed in an April 2
editorial entitled "The Nomination for the Presidency" that the convention be postponed until a clearer resolution of the conflict emerged.

But he remained convinced that the war ultimately would be won.
Thanking Catharine Sedgwick on May 5 for a kind note in which she
praised "The Little People of the Snow," Bryant wrote: "You are watching, I dare say, as well as I, the progress of the war. It really seems to me
as if we could already see a space of clear sky back of the cloud and as if
the storm was nearly over blown. But what a shower of blood must first
fall—the clearing up shower as the farmers call it, I hope. The rebel army
must first be destroyed, and it will fight desperately. What a dreadful
penalty our country is paying for the sins of the last thirty or forty
years!" Catharine had informed him that she could no longer afford the
"luxury" of subscribing to the daily *Evening Post*, which for sixty-three
years had been her "daily bread." Bryant assured her that her subscription would continue at his expense.

Bryant had scarce time for poetry, but the verse that he did compose
continued to be influenced by the war. On May 9, Bryant sent a seven-
teen-stanza lyric, "The Return of the Birds," to editor James T. Fields for
publication in the *Atlantic Monthly*. Lines from the poem comprise a
meditation on songbirds fleeing northward to escape the carnage of battles raging in the South:

> Yet, haply, from the region where,
>   Waked by an earlier spring than here,
> The blossomed wild-plum scents the air,
>   Ye come in haste and fear.
>   . . . . .
> There mighty hosts have pitched the camp
>   In valleys that were yours till then,
> And Earth has shuddered to the tramp
>   Of half a million men!
>   . . . . .
> Stay, then, beneath our ruder sky;
>   Heed not the storm-clouds rising black,
> Nor yelling winds that with them fly;
>   Nor let them fright you back;—

Back to the stifling battle-cloud,
   To burning towns that blot the day,
And trains of mounting dust that shroud
   The armies on their way.

Bryant ends the poem with a hymn to the "conquering hosts" who ultimately will bring "Peace to the torn and bloody land, / And freedom to the slave!"

By spring, Bryant concluded that Lincoln's supporters controlled the convention and that Lincoln would be renominated. He praised Lincoln on the eve of the convention: "the plain people believed Lincoln honest, the rich people believed him safe, the soldiers believed him their friend, the religious people believed him God's choice, and even the scoundrels believed it profitable to use his cloak." In an editorial on June 9, Bryant ascribed Lincoln's renomination by acclamation to the president's "complete integrity" and "homely good sense and honesty of purpose." Lincoln might have surrounded himself with men of dubious talents and virtues, and his administration was assuredly not "heroic" in its war strategy, but the *Evening Post* admitted that the people recognized a good man. "They overlook his defects, they pardon his mistakes, they are prone to forgive even his occasional lapses into serious and dangerous abuses of power." Bryant saw to it that the *Evening Post*'s endorsement of Lincoln was firm if not robust.

The summer months, which brought news of horrendous Union casualties—some seventy thousand at the battles of the Wilderness, Spotsylvania, Cold Harbor, and Petersburg—seemed to confirm Bryant's doubts about Lincoln's abilities as commander-in-chief. "It is very remarkable," he wrote Frances, who was vacationing in the Adirondacks that August, "to what a degree Mr. Lincoln has lost ground since his nomination. A great many persons now say, that the advice of the Evening Post to postpone the sitting of the nominating convention at Baltimore until September, was wise and judicious." Alone at Cedarmere, enduring a hot, humid summer of drought, Bryant was in no mood to admit that Lincoln might have a better understanding of the conflict than he did.

Bryant's displeasure with Lincoln had been exacerbated when Secretary Welles removed Isaac Henderson as navy agent in New York and ordered his arrest on corruption charges on June 22. The scandal had been brewing since February, when a certain H. D. Stover was arrested for fraudulent dealings in the Brooklyn Navy Yard. Thurlow Weed quickly charged that Stover was allied with Henderson, declaring in vit-riolic articles in the Albany *Journal* that Bryant's partner had his "arms shoulder deep in the federal treasury." Bryant was more than happy to take on Weed in dueling editorials, suspecting (with some credence as it turned out) that his old adversary was engaged in a conspiracy against him. On June 25, he sent a tart letter to Lincoln protesting Henderson's "spotless" reputation and his innocence: "If you could suppose yourself removed from the office you hold, under circumstances of like indignity, by some branch of the government invested with the power, you would at once conceive what his feelings must be." Bryant closed his letter by reminding Lincoln that Henderson had hitherto been an ardent advocate of the president's reelection. "Of course no astonishment that he ever felt could equal his, at being so roughly treated by a government which in his mind had always been associated with the idea of fairness and equity."

Lincoln replied immediately—and in language that matched Bryant's cold tone. Henderson's support, Lincoln declared, was never solicited and was unneeded in any case. And as to Henderson's guilt or innocence, the president was apprised that his accuser had as "spotless" a reputation as the accused. "While the subject is up," Lincoln added, "may I ask whether the Evening Post has not assailed me for supposed too lenient dealing with persons charged with fraud & crime? And that in cases of which the Post could know but little of the facts? I shall certainly deal as leniently with Mr. Henderson as I have felt it my duty to deal with oth-ers, notwithstanding any newspaper assaults."

The Henderson case dragged on for almost a year, pitting Bryant against Lincoln and Welles and also against his associates Godwin and Nordhoff, who worried that the scandal whirling around Henderson's dealings was tainting the integrity of the *Evening Post*. In a letter to Lin-coln on June 30, Bryant acknowledged the president's "equity and love of justice," adding, "I greatly regret that any thing said of your public conduct in that journal should seem to you like an assault, or in any way the indication of hostility." But the *Evening Post*, he reminded Lincoln, retained the right of "respectful criticism" of any administration. When the Henderson trial finally opened on May 23, 1865, the jury quickly dismissed the case. Three days later Bryant exulted that the attacks on "an innocent and worthy man" and the "innumerable malignant allu-sions" to the *Evening Post* had ended.

Even as the Henderson imbroglio distracted him, Bryant was angered anew when in late August Lincoln replaced Hiram Barney, the collector of the port of New York, with Simon Draper, a Weed protégé. At the outset of Lincoln's administration, Bryant had urged the president to appoint Barney to what was arguably the most important patronage position in New York. Now Lincoln was surrounding himself with the "creatures" of Weed and Seward, as Bryant grumbled to John Murray Forbes. "I am so utterly disgusted with Lincoln's behavior," he told Forbes, "that I cannot muster respectful terms in which to write him."

Bryant's personal displeasure with Lincoln did not compromise his determination to support the president and the Republican Party in the November presidential election. When the Democrats nominated McClellan as their candidate on August 29 on a platform condemning "four years of failure" by the Lincoln administration and advocating an end to hostilities, Bryant was amused. He wrote to Frances that McClellan's pledge to move for an immediate end to hostilities whenever the South was willing to reenter the Union "makes people laugh." In an editorial on September 20, "A Certain and Uncertain Policy," he contrasted the platforms of the Peace Democrats, led by the "political jumping-jacks who have constituted themselves leaders of the opposition," and the stalwart Union Republicans under the leadership of Lincoln. "The policy of Mr. Lincoln is declared and known. He has now guided the ship of state for more than three years; in that time of tremendous difficulty he has perhaps made mistakes, but he has acted throughout conscientiously, honorably, and with an honest and patriotic desire to do right." To his nearby neighbor George Porter, a Presbyterian minister in Manhasset, he wrote on October 10: "It appears to me that the success of Lincoln and Johnson is a moral certainty."

Bryant was "so beggar ridden and politician ridden," as he confided to Julia, that he had to rely for lunch on bread and cheese stuffed in his pocket, but he did find time, while family members toured the Adirondacks and Finger Lakes, to assemble occasional hymns he had written over the years for private publication and to send a new poem to James T. Fields for the *Atlantic Monthly*. "Ask me for no more verses," he warned Fields. Quoting from Pope's *Horace*, he confessed, "A septuagenarian has past the time when it is becoming for him to occupy himself with, 'The rhymes and rattles of the man and boy.'" He added, "Nobody, in the years, after seventy, can produce any thing in poetry, save the thick and muddy last runnings of the cask from which all the clear and sprightly liquor has been already drawn." Bryant invited Fields to give the poem a title, and Fields suggested "The Autumn Walk" or "My Autumn Walk."

Like his earlier "The Return of the Birds," the new poem depicted nature disrupted by the slaughter of soldiers in Georgia and Virginia. Sixteen quatrains, composed in varying rhythms of three and four feet, trace the suffering of soldiers and civilians during the Civil War, set against the backdrop of altered but enduring nature:

> The golden-rod is leaning,
>   And the purple aster waves,
> In a breeze from the land of battles
>   A breath from the land of graves.
>   . . . . .
> Again I turn to the woodlands
>   And shudder as I see
> The mock-grape's blood-red banner
>   Hung out on the cedar-tree;
>
> And I think of days of slaughter,
>   And the night-sky red with flames,
> On the Chattahoochee's meadows,
>   And the wasted banks of the James.

Shifting to more militant cadences, anticipating a "fresh spring season," Bryant concludes with a hard-won assertion:

> The leaves are swept from the branches;
>   But the living buds are there,
> With folded flower and foliage,
>   To sprout in kinder air.

In his letter to Fields, Bryant had been coy. In "My Autumn Walk" he demonstrated that, nearing seventy, he could still employ a range of poetic devices—short lines, feminine endings, varying metrical rhythms, heavy stresses as in "The mock grape's blood-red banner"—to compose a deft meditation on the personal loses caused by the Civil War.

VI

As his seventieth birthday neared, Bryant received an invitation from the Century Club's president, George Bancroft, to a celebration in his honor.

"I hope," Bryant replied, "I shall not be accused of affectation when I say that I sincerely think I have no title to such a testimonial of their regard, and yet I will add that there is no set of men from whom I would accept with less hesitation than from the body over which you preside and with the members of which my relations have always been so delightful." With Farragut's success at Mobile Bay, Sherman's occupation of Atlanta, Sheridan's decisive rout of the Confederates in the Shenandoah Valley of Virginia, and Lincoln's anticipated reelection, Bryant was in an expansive mood as the date—November 5—of the "Bryant Festival" neared. To a letter from Lydia Sigourney, who shared with him a verse tribute hailing Bryant as the "master of our Western lyre!" that she had composed for the occasion, he replied, "I shall reckon it among the fortunate circumstances of a rather fortunate life, that my entrance on my seventy-first year was marked by so kind a testimonial of approbation from such a quarter."

On Saturday evening, November 5, almost five hundred members of the Century Club and their guests gathered to pay tribute to William Cullen Bryant. The club's hall was filled with flowers, and twenty-five new pictures by Bryant's many artist friends graced the walls. Serving as toastmaster, George Bancroft introduced his friend of forty years as America's foremost poet. "While the mountains and the ocean-side ring with the tramp of cavalry and the din of cannon," the historian told the guests, "we take a respite in the serene regions of ideal pursuits." Adopting an air of amused perplexity, Bryant responded by quoting Shakespeare's Lear and Samuel Johnson on the "barren topic" of "one's senility," saying that he found it baffling and paradoxical to be honored for merely having survived for seventy years. Bryant was adept at cultural performance.

But the remarkable gathering of Bryant's friends and admirers testified to the fortunate conjunction of old age and greatness that they beheld in the poet. One by one, the nation's leading poets, some present and others sending tributes, confirmed the seismic effect that Bryant had had on the nation's literature and public life. Longfellow wrote from Cambridge that Bryant, who had served as a mentor for the younger poet's early verse, "has led a noble life; and we are proud of him." Lowell, who had planned to attend but had to deal with the death in battle of a relative, sent an ode praising Bryant's role in manning the guns during the Union's "dark hour" and calling him "our bravest crown." As a younger, more impetuous man, Lowell had satirized Bryant in his *Fable for Critics*, but now he praised the poet-editor, his verse rising to a reverential climax:

But now he sang of faith to things unseen,
Of freedom's birthright given to us in trust;
And words of doughty cheer he spoke between,
That made all earthly fortunes seem as dust,
Matched with that duty, old as time and new,
       Of being brave and true.

To Whittier, Bryant's personal and public life was "his noblest strain." Julia Ward Howe, instantly famous when her "Battle Hymn of the Republic" was published in the *Atlantic* in 1862, had entered the hall on Bryant's arm and read a poem in eleven stanzas, "A Leaf from the Bryant Chaplet," in his honor. Richard Henry Dana, Jr., praised "Thanatopsis," reminding the audience of Bryant's true greatness: "Mr. Bryant has always been true to Nature and to Freedom. . . . Never did he pervert his sacred trust of divine poetry to the service of fashion, or trade, or party. True to nature, nature was true to him."

It was left to Emerson, representing Bryant's many New England friends who were unable to attend the celebration, to provide the most comprehensive assessment of America's first poet. Reformulating lines he had written in his journal after reading *Thirty Poems*, Emerson stressed Bryant's uniqueness:

I join with all my heart in your wish to honor this native, sincere, original, patriotic poet. . . . I found him always original—a true painter of the face of this country, and of the sentiment of his own people. . . . It is his proper praise that he first, and he only, made known to mankind our northern landscape—its summer splendor, its autumn russets, its winter lights and glooms. And he is original because he is sincere . . .

At the climax of the celebration, the Century's artists, represented by Daniel Huntington, presented Bryant with a portfolio of forty-six paintings and sketches, bound in morocco, and including work by Church, Durand, Kensett, Leutze, Hicks, and many other artists whom Bryant had known and championed from his earliest days in Manhattan. Never had so many leading American writers and artists gathered to pay tribute to one of their own.

Three days after the Bryant Festival, New Yorkers braved fog, rain, and long lines to vote on election day. With memory of the Draft Riots still raw, troops had been positioned on vessels in the Hudson and East rivers in the event of disturbances, but aside from a street fight in one ward, the day passed peacefully. By midnight, citizens who had been thronging the hotels and newspaper offices sensed that Lincoln would be reelected in a landslide. Lincoln's electoral vote was 212 against 21 for General McClellan, who carried only three states and, scarred by yet another lost battle, promptly departed for Italy.

Although New York City had voted for McClellan by 73,716 to 36,687, Lincoln won the state by a narrow margin, and Bryant rejoiced in the overall results of the election. Still, dangers remained, etched against the splendors of late November weather at Cedarmere. Bryant wrote to Dana: "This is a beautiful day—a soft south west wind, the grass still green about my house, and roses and two other of the very hardy flowers in bloom in my garden, beneath a golden sunshine. But what frightful crimes are committed in the world of mankind! That attempt to set the whole city of New York on fire!" On November 25 and 26, eight Confederate spies had infiltrated the city and attempted to set off a firestorm by torching thirteen leading hotels including the St. Nicholas, Fifth Avenue, Metropolitan, and Astor House, two theaters, Niblo's Garden, and Barnum's Museum. With fires erupting along Broadway, Gotham's citizens panicked; but the fires were quickly extinguished and the damage limited. The Confederacy, like the mixtures of camphene and phosphorus that the spies had used in their feeble effort to burn down New York City, was sputtering out.

VII

On New Year's Day, Bryant published "To the Soldiers of the Union Army" in the *Evening Post*. In words and cadences casting the Civil War as an epic battle, the editor valorized the ordinary and extraordinary men—Grant, Sheridan, Sherman, Thomas, Farragut—whose victories during the past year were slowly strangling the Confederacy. With high confidence, Bryant looked forward to the dawning of a new age. "Be strong," he implored the soldiers, "be hopeful! your crowning triumph cannot be far distant. When it arrives, our nation will have wiped out a dark stain, which we feared it might yet wear for the ages, and will stand in the sight of the world a noble commonwealth of freemen, bound together by ties which will last as long as the common sympathies of our race."

The next day, Bryant sent a petition to Edward Everett, whom he had known for twenty years, asking the former American minister to the

Court of St. James to support a law immediately abolishing slavery throughout the Union. In his reply, written just days before his death, Everett indicated that such a law was probably unconstitutional; he also warned that such congressional action would "only render more difficult the adoption of the constitutional amendment now pending." Bryant was apparently convinced by the arguments of the powerful Massachusetts statesman. Thereafter, he urged in his editorials the passage by the states of the Thirteenth Amendment abolishing slavery.

Throughout the winter and spring of 1865, Bryant was in an expansive mood, his spirits raised by Grant's relentless siege on Lee's diminished army around Petersburg and Richmond. Now that the Union seemed omnipotent, he rejected any attempts to compromise with the South. In early January, under the leader "Fool's Errands," Bryant ridiculed Francis Blair's trip to Richmond to seek an armistice with the rebels. "No, our best peacemakers yet are Grant, Sheridan, Thomas, Sherman, and Farragut, and the black-mouthed bulldogs by which they enforce their pretensions over more than half of what was once an 'impregnable' part of rebeldom." He urged the public to plan for reconstruction. At a meeting of the National Freedmen's Relief Association on January 25, he reminded those citizens who were not combatants that they too had a duty to help free the slaves and rebuild a free nation.

Bryant greeted the news of Lee's surrender to Grant at Appomattox Courthouse on April 9 in messianic terms. "GLORY TO THE LORD OF HOSTS" read the *Evening Post*'s leader:

> The great day, so long and anxiously awaited, for which we have struggled through four years of bloody war, which has so often . . . dawned only to go down in clouds of gloom; the day of the virtual overthrow of the rebellion, of the triumph of constitutional order and of universal liberty,—of the success of the nation against its parts, and of a humane and beneficent civilization over a relic of barbarism that had been blindly allowed to remain as a blot on its scutcheon—the day of PEACE has finally come. . . .

The city that had trounced Lincoln in November's election suddenly surged with waves of patriotic fervor. Stores closed, flags were unfurled, and Broadway became a sea of cheering and singing men and women. The city's leading citizens, gathering at the Union League Club to celebrate Lincoln's great victory, called on Bryant to express the gratitude of a nation. To have Bryant as a speaker was to convey legitimacy to the event.

But on the night of April 14, Lincoln was shot; he died the next morning. Once again the stores along Broadway closed, but this time they were shuttered in black. The journals along Newspaper Row also were bordered in black. Even the weather turned dark and rainy— "black, black, black" as Whitman wrote, "long broad black like great serpents." Bryant shared with his fellow poet and the nation a sense of biblical doom:

> How awful and solemn the blow which has fallen upon every true heart in the nation! Abraham Lincoln, the man of the people, whom the Providence of God had raised to be "the foremost man of all this world," in the flush of his success over the enemies of his country, while the peals of exultation for a great work accomplished were yet ringing in his ears, when his countrymen of all parties, and liberal minds abroad, had just begun to learn the measure of his goodness and greatness, is struck down by the hand of the assassin. All of him that could perish now lies in the cold embrace of Death.

Two months later, in a letter to Catharine Sedgwick, Bryant still was haunted by a vision of biblical destruction. "When I think of this great conflict and its great issues my mind reverts to the grand visions of the Apocalypse, in which the messengers of God come down to do his bidding among the nations and the earth is reaped and the spoils of its vineyards are gathered and the wine press is trodden and flows with blood, and the vials of God's judgments are poured out and the rivers are turned into blood, and finally the dragon is cast into the bottomless pit."

But now, in April, he sat down to compose an elegy, "The Death of Lincoln." As the president's funeral train wound its way from Washington to Baltimore, Harrisburg, and Philadelphia, Bryant prepared an elegy with an innovative rhyme scheme, stately cadences, and plain diction. On the evening of April 24, one day before Lincoln's cortege crossed the Hudson to Manhattan's Desbrosses Street dock, where his body was placed in a glass hearse drawn by six horses and taken to City Hall for viewing, thousands of mourners gathered at a ceremony for the president in Union Square. The Unitarian minister Samuel Osgood recited Bryant's elegy, its last line reminding many in the crowd of the conclusion of Lincoln's Cooper Union speech five years earlier:

Oh, slow to smite and swift to spare,
   Gentle and merciful and just!
Who, in the fear of God, didst bear
   The sword of power, a nation's trust!

In sorrow by thy bier we stand,
   Amid the awe that hushes all,
And speak the anguish of a land
   That shook with horror at thy fall.

Thy task is done; the bound are free:
   We bear thee to an honored grave,
Whose proudest monument shall be
   The broken fetters of the slave.

Pure was thy life; its bloody close
   Hath placed thee with the sons of light,
Among the noble host of those
   Who perished in the cause Right.

A few days later, Reverend Osgood told Bryant that that night he had seen his friend standing near Henry Kirke Brown's huge statue of George Washington on horseback that dominated Union Square. "You seemed to me standing there as the 19th Century itself," Osgood recalled, "thinking over the nation and the age in that presence."

16

LIKE ONE SHUT OUT
OF PARADISE

The morn hath not the glory that it wore,
   Nor doth the day so beautifully die,
Since I can call thee to my side no more,
   To gaze upon the sky.
                              —"A Memory" (1866)

I

Through the difficult years of the Civil War, Bryant—unlike the erratic Greeley and most other New York editors—had positioned the *Evening Post* squarely and consistently for the Union. He had introduced Lincoln to New York and the nation at Cooper Union, supported the president (even as he lamented Lincoln's penchant for procrastination), and bade the assassinated hero farewell with his elegy at Union Square. Now he planned to step back from the daily routine at the *Evening Post*, cultivate his "farm," as he called the property in Roslyn, reclaim and restore his boyhood home at Cummington, and begin to translate his beloved Homer. But Bryant's fame—and his fondness for civic events and fraternal gatherings—prevented him from leading a purely bookish life.

Soon after Lincoln's funeral train departed Manhattan, influential friends urged Bryant to write a biography of the president. After all, readers across the country had read his elegy for Lincoln; moreover, friends and associates remembered his orations after the deaths of Cole,

Cooper, and Irving. It was only fitting, declared several friends, that Bryant write the chronicle of the nation's fallen hero. George Bancroft suggested that Bryant, as always, would offer "delight and instruction" if he undertook the project. Oliver Wendell Holmes testified, "No man combines the qualities of for his biographer so completely as yourself and the finished task would be a noble crown to a noble literary life." John Greenleaf Whittier added, "It would give great satisfaction to all loyal men, to know that the work was in thy hands."

Bryant, however, declined to undertake the Lincoln biography. Replying to Holmes, he hinted at his reluctance: "There are various reasons . . . some of which are personal to myself, and others inherent in the subject, which discourage me from undertaking the task of writing Mr. Lincoln's life. It is not only his life, but the life of the nation for four of the most important, critical, and interesting years of its existence, that is to be written. Who that has taken part like myself in the controversies of the time can flatter himself that he shall execute the task worthily and impartially?"

Bryant's refusal to undertake a Lincoln biography derived from a conviction that he could never be as magnanimous toward the Confederacy as Lincoln had planned to be. He hewed to a middle way between "those who are for punishing almost everybody, and those who are for punishing nobody," asserting to Dana that the "men who took the lead in the rebellion" should be brought to justice. He was convinced that there should be limited retribution. But Jefferson Davis, attempting to elude capture by dressing as a woman, was a sneaking, ordinary criminal who needed to be brought to justice. However, in an editorial entitled "What Should Be Done with Jefferson Davis?" Bryant claimed that it was unwise to implicate the president of the Confederacy in the assassination of Lincoln. Justice had to be tempered by common sense and compassion for the defeated.

Still, treason *was* a crime, as Bryant wrote in an October editorial endorsing President Andrew Johnson's plans for Reconstruction, and the leaders of the rebellion had to be held accountable. As for Reconstruction, Bryant urged Negro suffrage at the time black Americans were prepared to exercise the right to vote; but he rejected Sumner's plan to immediately grant suffrage, fearing that it could precipitate violence in the South. When the Thirteenth Amendment to the Constitution outlawing slavery was ratified in December, Bryant exulted in a letter to Miss Sedgwick: "It is a great thing to have lived at a time when so magnificent an act of justice has been done—it is worth living for even were there no hereafter."

Since he was "little occupied with the Evening Post, passing the greater part of my time in the Country," as he informed the lawyer Reginald Parker, an old friend in England, Bryant had time to realize a more private dream. That May, he had repurchased the Cummington Homestead and two hundred acres that his brother Austin had sold when the family moved to Illinois in 1835. Visiting his old home and the haunts on the property that had inspired poems like "The Rivulet" and "Inscription for the Entrance to a Wood," Bryant made plans to expand the house so that it could accommodate family members during summer reunions and be made comfortable for Frances. Above all, Bryant hoped that the Homestead's high elevation and cool summer air would be beneficial to his wife's health.

But by the spring of 1866, Frances Bryant was in slow, painful decline; she died at Cedarmere on July 27 in her seventieth year. In a private account "intended for my own eyes, and the eyes of my children," Bryant detailed the last ten weeks of his wife's illness and her stoical decline. Early on, the family physician, Dr. Gray, had diagnosed Frances's condition as "an obstruction of the bile, with water on the heart," and said that he had never seen anyone recover from this malady. Frances placidly resigned herself to her fate, prepared to "pass the gates of death without fear." When she was strong enough, she liked to be placed in a chair near the corridor of her chamber where she could look out at the pond in front of the house. She reminded Cullen of their time in Naples when the view of the sky and mountain was so striking: "What a beautiful world," she murmured. In her last days of acute suffering, Frances's pain was alleviated by the administration of *cannabis medica*.

A day after her death, Frances Fairchild Bryant was buried in the family plot at the new Roslyn cemetery that had opened near the woodlands south of Cedarmere. The mourners "spoke well of her virtues, her love of doing good, her compassionate temper, her cheerfulness, her charities, the rectitude of her mind, and her sincerity." Cullen and Julia kissed Frances's brow before the coffin was closed and lowered into the ground. Recalling their first meeting in the autumn of 1815 and his immediate attraction to her, Bryant wrote, "I think the wedded life of few men has been happier than mine."

In his private memoir, Bryant acknowledged, "I never wrote a poem, that I did not repeat to her, and take her judgment upon it. I found its success with the public to be precisely in proportion to the impression it made upon her." The last poem that he read to her during her illness was "The Death of Slavery," to which she "added some kind words of commendation." Composed in May and published in the July issue of the *Atlantic Monthly*, the seven stanzas of "The Death of Slavery" were an extravagant rendition in verse of the nationalistic passion, religious fervor, and moral outrage that had characterized Bryant's editorials during the Civil War:

> O THOU great Wrong, that, through the slow-paced years
>   Didst hold thy millions fettered, and didst wield
>   The scourge that drove the laborer to the field,
> And turn a stony gaze on human tears,
>   Thy cruel reign is o'er;
>   Thy bondsmen crouch no more
> In terror at the menace of thine eye;
>   For He who marks the bounds of guilty power,
> Long-suffering, hath heard the captive's cry,
>   And touched his shackles at the appointed hour,
> And lo! they fall, and he whose limbs they galled
> Stands in his native manhood, disenthralled.

Frances had not liked all of his poems equally well, Bryant recalled, but she approved of "The Death of Slavery." Although she was dying, Frances Bryant could still appreciate a bravura performance by her husband.

Writing to Dana after his wife's death, Bryant confessed that he felt "like one shut out of Paradise and wandering in a strange world." To his brother Arthur he recalled Frances's "tender sympathies" and "her sense of right and justice." He distilled his grief in "October, 1866," a lyric composed in fourteen quatrains:

> Autumn is here; we cull his lingering flowers
>   And bring them to the spot where thou art laid;
> The late-born offspring of his balmier hours,
>   Spared by the frost, upon thy grave to fade.
>
> The sweet calm sunshine of October, now
>   Warms the low spot; upon its grassy mould
> The purple oak-leaf falls; the birchen bough
>   Drops its bright spoil like arrow-heads of gold.

. . . . .
I gaze in sadness; it delights me not
  To look on beauty which thou canst not see;
And, wert thou by my side, the dreariest spot
  Were, oh, how far more beautiful to me!

In a note thanking him for his letter of condolence and praising his *History of the United States*, Bryant informed George Bancroft, "I am just on the point of going to Europe." The sorrow that had befallen him required a change of scene.

II

On November 17, 1866, Bryant sailed for France on the steamer *Pereire*. Julia, who was overcome by the calamity of her mother's death, accompanied him, along with Laura Leupp, the daughter of his deceased friend and traveling companion Charles Leupp. After a "remarkably smooth and prosperous passage" that nevertheless left Bryant and his traveling companions "a little qualmish," as he admitted to Isaac Henderson, the party landed at Brest and traveled by train to Paris, checking in at the Hotel Wagram on the Rue de Rivoli on November 28.

Paris was dark, chilly, and wet: Bryant likened the experience to living in a barn. The city was a "melancholy place," reminding him of his time there with "some one now in the grave." Still, Fanny and her family were in Paris, along with his old friend Morse, who was fitfully trying to organize the International Exposition of 1867. And Bryant was happy to see John Bigelow, soon to retire as minister to Paris. Writing to the editor Evert Duyckinck, Bigelow remarked, "The *Evening Post* is now here in force."

Bigelow told Bryant of the recent incursion by American troops into the Mexican town of Matamoros, and the *Post*'s editor immediately wrote to Henderson with instructions for Charles Nordhoff to protest the affair. He deplored America's attempt "to exhibit ourselves to the eyes of the world as a military power" and added, "I fear that our Executive is bent, through Mr. Seward's advice, on getting up some new subject of discussion in which it hopes, by appealing to national vanity, to get the advantage of the opposition."

Anxious to leave Paris for the warmer, sunnier south of France, Bryant was unable to preside at a testimonial dinner for Bigelow given by 137 members of the American colony. The night before his departure on December 13, he dreamed "with great joy" of meeting his wife. Rapidly traveling south with his companions in tow, Bryant rejoiced five days later at seeing the sun and walking the dry streets of Amelie les Bains, in the eastern Pyrenees. The skies were serene, but the city's sulfur springs, which attracted hundreds of invalids, made the place "rather sad," he admitted in a letter to the *Evening Post*. He enjoyed the warmth, the foliage, the inviting landscape. "I climb the crags back of the house where I lodge," he wrote Catharine Sedgwick, "and the air is fragrant with lavender and rosemary, and other aromatic herbs."

The new year found Bryant and his companions in Spain, somewhat uncertain of their itinerary and suffering from colds. Barcelona, Valencia, Cordoba, and Seville were pleasant enough—the great mosque at Cordoba conveyed a "sense of sublimity"—but the midwinter mornings and evenings in Andalusia were "miserably chilly." Writing from Seville to his Roslyn neighbor Leonice Moulton, Bryant confessed, "I must own that I never traveled with so little curiosity to see what is peculiar or admirable in foreign countries." Sad memories of his wife and longing for Cedarmere distracted him, "constantly diverting my attention from what is before my eyes."

Seeking literary diversion, he continued to translate Homer in his spare moments. (That January, the *Atlantic Monthly* published the first half of the first book of the *Iliad* detailing the contention between Achilles and Agamemnon.) "It differs from all others in English," he wrote John Durand, who had accompanied the Bryant party as far as Paris, "in its greater simplicity." Earlier, Bryant had attempted to render Homer's hexameters, but now he experimented with a supple five-foot line:

> O GODDESS! Sing the wrath of Peleus' son,
> Achilles; sing the deadly wrath that brought
> Woes numberless upon the Greeks, and swept
> To Hades many a valiant soul, and gave
> Their limbs a prey to dogs and birds of air,—
> For so had Jove appointed,—from the time
> When the two chiefs, Atrides, king of men,
> And great Achilles, parted first as foes.

Bryant thought that his rendition was closer to the original than the translation by Cowper, a poet whom he otherwise admired, and than the recent translation by the British statesman Edward Stanley.

By early February, Bryant and the ladies were in Nice, where they checked into rooms that had just been vacated by General McClellan. The American consul, Asa Aldis, entertained them for a week before the Bryant entourage left for Florence, traveling for six days along the military road from Nice to La Spezia and stopping over at Pisa and Lucca.

Talking to sculptor Hiram Powers, Bryant learned of plans by Congress to levy a heavy duty on foreign works of art—legislation that would undoubtedly provoke retaliation by European nations. For decades a leading advocate of free trade, Bryant wrote an article for the *Post* deploring the move by Congress and attaching a letter of protest from Powers. From Florence, he wrote to his brother John, "I do not like the aspect of our politics in America. It is impossible to imagine public men behaving worse than the President and Seward are doing; the Republican party is so strong that it is lunging into grievous follies, and may yet wake up to find the other party strong enough to dispute its ascendancy."

Joining Fanny at the Godwin's quarters in Rome in early March, Bryant still seemed low in spirits; his mood darkened even more when, following an argument over rent with Fanny's landlady, he had to relocate to rooms at a hotel. "For my own part," he wrote Jerusha Dewey, "I have been so little interested in what I have seen during this visit to Europe that I have often wished that somebody were in my place whose curiosity had a sharper edge than mine, and that I were back at Roslyn." Nevertheless, he tried to convey a sunny disposition for the *Evening Post*'s readers, describing the "splendid capital" of Vienna for them, as well as the "Gothic invasion" of Rome by American tourists that had almost made it "a Yankee city." But a month later, writing to John Durand from Baden-Baden, he gave a more sober appraisal of this Gothic horde: "Almost every where on the continent the Americans swarm this year, and are not always the cream of our countrymen." Bryant's mood became bleaker still when he learned that his daughter Fanny's fourth son, six-year-old Walter, had died in early April.

"I have been wandering about Europe for the past five months," Bryant confided to Orville Dewey, "till I am quite tired, and wish myself back to Roslyn among my books in the old library." He worried about another great war in Europe—this time between France and Prussia over the two powers' designs over Luxembourg. On his arrival in Paris on May 1, as he poured over a large bundle of newspapers that awaited him, Bryant's bleak thoughts returned to American politics. He gave instructions to Isaac Henderson: "I wish you would say to Mr. Nordhoff that I hope he will keep in mind that what is now called the Republican party has no bond of cohesion except the question of the rights of the Negro in the late slave states and that just as soon as that question is settled and put aside, the cards will be shuffled again, a new deal made and there will be a change of partners." But he was pleased by the *Post*'s profits— $88,975 for the last five months, according to Henderson, who wrote, "This I know will please you as it will tend to make the winter of your life more agreeable."

Trusting Henderson and admiring Henderson's wife as well, Bryant asked his assistant to rent rooms or a house for him prior to his return to the United States. Instead, Henderson, with John Bigelow, Samuel Tilden, and Julia Sands concurring, took the liberty of buying a four-story brownstone residence for the editor at 24 West Sixteenth Street for the bargain price of thirty thousand dollars, including "2 large Mantle Mirrors worth about $1000." After forty years of wandering among rented rooms and boardinghouses in Manhattan, Bryant would finally have a place of his own there.

Crossing to England in early June, Bryant grumbled to John Durand that he and his traveling companions had "a rainy time in getting from Paris to London and were all of us made sick in crossing the Channel" in a wretched steamer. But seeing old friends—among them Edwin, Ferdinand, and Alfred Field and Christiana Gibson—in England and Scotland helped revive Bryant's spirits. Spending ten days at the Gibson family home in Crieff, he rode out into the countryside with Christiana and her sister Jesse; in his spare time, he dabbled in Homer. During the second week in July, he set out with Christiana for the Scottish Lakes and Wales, where Laura and Julia, who had stayed over in Edinburgh, joined them.

Despite the kindness of friends and his pleasant surroundings, Bryant was eager to depart for America. He confessed to Christiana Gibson, "I am counting, as I have done for some time past, the days that separate me from Roslyn, and shall soon begin to count the hours." His trip to Europe had been undertaken to assuage his and Julia's grief over Frances Bryant's death. Boarding the steamer *Persia* in Liverpool on August 23, Bryant, contending with a "not very favorable passage of eleven days across the Atlantic," was glad to get back to New York on September 5.

III

Soon after his return, Bryant set off for Cummington to check on the improvements he had requested at the old family homestead. Returning through the Berkshires, he spent four pleasant days at Orville Dewey's home in Sheffield, delighted to see that his friend had not "grown older for these last ten years. At my time of life," he informed Dewey's sister Jerusha, "it is a great comfort to meet any person in whom the mental and physical faculties do not seem to decline with advancing years." But he grieved over the loss of Catharine Sedgwick, who had died in July, consenting shortly afterward to compose a reminiscence of his longtime friend for a collection of items covering her life and letters. "I have never known a person of more generous sympathies," he would later confide to Orville Dewey, "or a stronger sense of justice or a more ready and cheerful activity in her benevolences."

Back at Cedarmere, Bryant immersed himself in the improvement of his property—a renovated icehouse with milk and fruit rooms, a new greenhouse, an enlarged dining room, and two expanded bedrooms— that he had dreamed about while overseas. Meanwhile, Julia, aided by Julia Sands, who had been invited to live with them as a housekeeper, attended to the furnishing of Bryant's new residence on West Sixteenth Street in Manhattan, which they planned to move into in December. Autumn at Cedarmere was beautiful: "the maples, at the end of our little lakelet, are glowing with the hues of autumns, and over all lies the sweetest sunshine. I look out upon the landscape from the bay-window while I write, but in a different mood from that in which I should have beheld it formerly."

Bryant's interest in the daily rituals of the *Evening Post* had diminished, and he rather enjoyed "the habit of seclusion." It was as if his double sense of self—the private and public man—had returned to its inner wellspring. Working on the grounds at Cedarmere, luxuriating in Longfellow's new translation of *The Divine Comedy*, and pursuing the translation of his beloved Homer took precedence over civic affairs. But that October, he was happy to preside at a farewell banquet given for the retiring Mexican ambassador, Matías Romero, at Delmonico's. Bryant toasted the outgoing envoy, who had admired the editor ever since the *Evening Post* defended Mexico against the French invasion and the installation of the puppet Maximilian.

However, Bryant declined an invitation to attend a banquet for Longfellow in Boston celebrating the poet's translation of *The Divine Comedy*. Instead he sent a tribute to be read at the Union Club dinner: "Mr. Longfellow has translated Dante as a great poet should be translated. After this version, no other will be attempted until the present form of the English language shall have become obsolete." Bryant's own translation of the *Iliad* was moving along fitfully: "I piddle a little with Homer, whose poem," he confessed to Dana, "does not seem to me the perfect work that critics have made it, notwithstanding its many undeniable beauties." He favored the Trojans over the Greeks, and he thought that the conduct of the gods was often detestable and disapproved of their meddling in human affairs. Nevertheless, working on Homer in the morning distracted him from the "flatness" of life.

With the return of Charles Dickens in December for a second speaking tour after an absence of twenty-five years, Bryant looked forward to renewing a literary friendship. Dickens apparently also wanted to see Bryant and, learning his address from John Bigelow, left his card at the editor's door. But when Bryant returned the visit, the novelist's imperious valet, who had been instructed to reject all visitors, refused to take his card to Dickens. The two men finally did manage to get together for dinner, but Bryant thought that Dickens's refusal to accept social invitations uncivil. In any case, he did not attend any of Dickens's performances. "I cannot muster up curiosity enough," he told Christiana Gibson, even though everyone was running after the celebrated novelist. He had heard from friends that Dickens's "voice is not good—neither strong nor musical—and while they admit his comic power as an actor, they call his reading of parts that are not comic monotonous—and sometimes, in pathetic parts, doleful."

The times in general seemed doleful to Bryant. On Christmas day, in a melancholy mood, the poet reflected: "the banquet of Life . . . has grown somewhat insipid of late." Old friends had died: Miss Sedgwick the previous July, and Fitz-Greene Halleck in November. His brother Cyrus had died in 1865, and early in 1866 his brother Austin had passed away. Now in December, he learned that his second sister, Charity Olds, had joined the procession. Still, at seventy-three he was among the living, astonished at times by his vitality and "firm and steady health." Moreover, the world would not let him rest or retreat into utter seclusion: from Paris, where he was now American minister, George Bancroft urged Bryant to succeed him as president of the Century Association. "The choice should fall on you alone."

Whether he liked it or not, Bryant—that "cute, wise old man," as Whitman later described him—had become communal property. Gotham's most famous septuagenarian was in constant demand at civic functions. On January 1, as Bancroft had predicted, he was elected president of the Century Association, a post he would hold the rest of his life. On January 22, at a dinner held at Delmonico's uptown restaurant on Broadway at Fourteenth Street, just east of Bryant's new townhouse, the poet offered the principal toast to his old friend and mentor in the arts, Jonathan Sturges, who was closing his "business career without a stain on his reputation." On January 30, he again found himself at Delmonico's, where one hundred members of the American Free-Trade League gathered to celebrate Bryant's five years as president of the organization. The league conveyed to Bryant, long an advocate of free trade, "the debt of gratitude which the American people owe to you for the enlarged and statesmanlike view you have ever advocated, and the courageous opposition you have ever made to spoliation, under the name and guise of protection."

Despite constant snowstorms and a cholera outbreak that winter, Bryant acknowledged that life in town was "quite gay—parties and dinners, masked balls and other amusements have been frequent." Sleighs cruised down "Ladies Mile" on Broadway below Madison Square, where emporiums—Lord and Taylor, R. H. Macy's, Tiffany's, and A. T. Stewart's "Cast Iron Palace" on Union Square—attracted throngs of customers. Bryant found changing social rituals amusing. He informed Jerusha Dewey that "the male part of fashionable society" had adopted the new fashion of exchanging visits in the afternoon after business— "for the male part of even fashionable society in our country cannot afford to dispense with business."

The business and editorial policies at the *Evening Post*, whose offices he now visited once or twice weekly, walking three miles from his house on Sixteenth Street to Park Row, were to Bryant's liking. He trusted Henderson's business acumen but disliked the constant squabbling between his partner and Parke Godwin. He was not unhappy when Godwin once again decided to divest himself of interest in the journal. Bryant and Henderson bought Godwin out for two hundred thousand dollars. Henderson, who purchased most of Godwin's share, now controlled half of the *Evening Post*.

With a new editorial writer, Charlton T. Lewis, at the helm, Bryant had gladly relinquished the composition of daily leaders for the *Evening Post*. The senior editor approved of Lewis, a former Methodist minister, professor of foreign languages, and deputy revenue commissioner for New York. He liked Lewis's progressive politics, scholarly background, and lucid style. Now and then Bryant contributed a leader, as he did on February 7, 1868, when he recommended General Ulysses S. Grant as the Republican candidate in November's presidential election. Grant was no great thinker, Bryant admitted, but he had a "frank and manly mode of stating his opinions." As for the impeachment proceedings against President Johnson, Bryant found that this "unhappy quarrel," as he termed it in an editorial on February 27, demanded "moderation, calmness, justice, and freedom from prejudice."

When spring came, Bryant returned to Cedarmere, venturing into the city and the offices of the *Evening Post* no more than two days weekly, normally on Tuesdays and Fridays. Finding Bryant at his editorial desk on one occasion, Thomas Nast, already savaging the Tweed Ring with his virulent cartoons in the *New York Times* and *Harper's Weekly*, sketched the famous editor. It was a good-natured drawing: Nast depicted the gnomish editor scribbling away with an enormous quill pen. "As to the caricature," Bryant confessed to a correspondent, "it is very clever, and if the subject were any other than myself, I have no doubt that I should like it."

Whether in the city, at Cedarmere, or at the Cummington Homestead, where he spent time during the summer and fall months, Bryant relished his mornings, which he devoted to translating the *Iliad*. Another literary project that filled his time throughout 1868 was the translation from Spanish of Carolina Coronado de Perry's prose romance, *Jarilla*, for the *New York Ledger*. The popular weekly's owner, Robert Bonner, had urged Bryant to undertake the project, offering him the astonishing sum of two thousand dollars (equivalent to forty thousand dollars today) for the effort. *Jarilla* would appear in the *Ledger* in seven installments between October 30 and December 11, 1869.

The results of the presidential election that fall were no surprise to Bryant: the *Evening Post* had declared for Grant, and on November 3, the Republican candidate triumphed over his Democratic rival, Horatio Seymour, by 214 electoral votes to 80. Prior to the election, Bryant had predicted that Grant would be the victor. "The sober people of this country are for him almost to a man, and this class includes many who have not hitherto belonged to the Republican party." Closer to home, Bryant deplored the way in which Tammany's boss, William Marcy Tweed, had rigged the New York State gubernatorial election, propelling Manhattan's mayor, John Thompson Hoffman, to Albany. He wrote to his brother John at the end of November: "We do not make much progress in the investigation of the frauds which gave the vote of New York to Hoffman as Governor, nor do I expect any very important results from what the Union League is doing. The public conscience is terribly debauched in regard to the frauds of voting."

The end of the year found Bryant, much as he had started the year, translating Homer and dining at Delmonico's. On December 29 at Delmonico's, he gave the main toast to his old friend Samuel F. B. Morse, who was being honored for his invention of the telegraph. The two men had gone their separate ways politically, but both had come to New York in 1825 to seek their fortunes, and each had prospered in his own realm. Representing the press, Bryant offered a graceful tribute to Morse, who had "annihilated both space and time in the transmission of intelligence. The breadth of the Atlantic, with all its waves, is as nothing." Bryant then spun a mystical conceit of his friend's telegraph wires snaking through the ocean's depths: "That slender wire thrills with the hopes and fears of nations; it vibrates to every emotion that can be awakened by any event affecting the welfare of the human race." He ended by saluting the man who had demonstrated the triumph of mind—and spirit—over matter.

Bryant had turned seventy-five; he was an old fish in the sea, and his sense of life's transience had become acute. Increasingly he worried that he would not live long enough to complete his translation of Homer. In early February, he informed his brother John that he had completed the twelfth book of the *Iliad*: "I would observe that Pope's translation is more paraphrastic than mine, and will probably have more than seven thousand original lines." Translating up to sixty lines of Homer daily—the equivalent of seventy or eighty lines of blank verse—Bryant felt that he was in a race against time.

Perhaps, as he pondered his mortality, he even lost a degree of closeness with nature. In "Among the Trees," published in *Putnam's Magazine* in January 1869, Bryant offers a melancholy vision of his fragile communion with the natural world. He apostrophizes the trees, an old convention with him, but admits that the environment is dumb:

> Have ye no sense of being? Does the air,
> The pure air, which I breathe with gladness, pass
> In gushes o'er your delicate lungs, your leaves,
> All unenjoyed? When on your winter's sleep
> The sun shines warm, have ye no dreams of spring?

Nature has its own rhythms and seasons divorced from the plight of humanity: "Our sorrows touch you not." Bryant can offer only a weak affirmation that some objects of Nature—like the old oak on his property at Cedarmere—outlive the "flitting generations of mankind." The

poet of nature sounds like a Stoic. George Bancroft sensed the uniqueness of the poem, finding the lyric to be "by far the best American short
poem or English or German" to have appeared in some time.

The memorial service for Fitz-Greene Halleck at the New-York
Historical Society on February 3 again reminded Bryant of his mortality
and his fear of a protracted, painful death. Asked by the society's members to deliver the oration for his old friend, who had died at the age of
seventy-seven, Bryant prayed for a similarly swift ending: "He was
spared the suffering which is the lot of many to whom, in their departure
from life, are appointed long days and nights of pain."

There were memories of Frances. His short lyric "May Evening,"
published that same month in *Appleton's Journal*, celebrates the "breath
of Spring-time" but turns in several stanzas to the death of his wife:

> Yet there is sadness in thy soft caress,
>   Wind of the blooming year!
> The gentle presence, that was wont to bless
>   Thy coming, is not here.

Bryant was feeling sorry for himself and the times. "All manner of
knaveries grow like Jonah's gourd," he wrote John Gourlie in June.
"Luxury grows apace; prices grow like weeds; rents grow; taxes grow. I
do not, however, hear that any man has grown wise and good, so suddenly and so greatly, as to astonish his friends. But we grow old fast
enough, both in town and country." Even the Green River, which he had
apostrophized in his younger years, must have forgotten him.

But this lachrymose mood was something of a pose, for Bryant was
still a man about town. "Bryant appears frequently at public dinners and
meetings," the scholar Evert Duyckinck informed William Gilmore
Simms. The poet "always makes the best speech of the evening . . . for he
works straight into the subject in hand and his mind once within
explores the dormant material in brilliant fancies."

Warm weather and time spent in New England helped to restore
Bryant's buoyancy. In late June, he visited Williamstown and spoke at the
commencement dinner for Williams College graduates. After attending an
alumni meeting, he contributed five hundred dollars to his alma mater.
The college's president, Mark Hopkins, was amazed at the generosity of
the gift: "Strange times we live in, when poets not only possess money,
and patronize literature, but make better speeches than anyone else."

Wandering the woods and fields near Cummington later that summer, often with his brother John, Bryant encountered local residents
who were surprised to see the famous poet. One day near Windsor Lake,
he purchased honey from a man named Hollis, who asked if he was not
Mr. Bryant—"that some people in his neighborhood would give as much
to see Cullen Bryant as to see a bear." In late August, he visited Newport
with Julia, staying with the organist and composer John Knowles Paine.
Appearing at a Sunday service at the Unitarian Church, Bryant's face
struck a reporter from the New York *Tribune* as belonging to an ethereal
realm: "Through the crowded tide of New York life, through the changing fashions of manners and politics, it has represented the one moral
aspect, the one democratic idea."

Passing his seventy-sixth birthday quietly at Cedarmere, intent on
completing his translation of the *Iliad* by the end of the year, the old
democrat still found time for civic affairs. "I have promised to take part
in a public demonstration in favor of founding a Museum of Art in New
York, at a meeting called on the 23rd of November." On that day, three
hundred cultural and civic leaders assembled at the Union League Club
to plan a Metropolitan Museum of Art. Elected president of the meeting, Bryant in his speech before the city's leaders took the opportunity
to allude to the scandals of the Tweed Ring and the corruption—"vice"
he called it—rampant in Manhattan. "Our city is the third great city of
the civilized world," he declared. "My friends, if a tenth part of what is
every year stolen from us . . . in the city where we live, under pretence
of the public service . . . were expended on a Museum of Art, we might
have . . . a collection formed of works left by the world's greatest artists,
which would be the pride of our country." Within two months, the
Metropolitan Museum of Art would be founded, and Bryant, who contributed one thousand dollars to the enterprise, was chosen as one of its
vice presidents.

IV

As a new decade began, New York City's population had soared to
almost one and a half million inhabitants—some living in ostentatious
luxury while tens of thousands huddled in tenement houses. Money had
flowed into the city from Civil War contracts, fueling business expansion and a real estate boom, including a newfangled phenomenon—the

apartment house. Elegant shops, restaurants, and theaters catered to the city's middle class and its emerging "Four Hundred." William B. Astor headed the *Evening Post*'s list of the ten wealthiest New Yorkers, his fortune estimated at $75 million.

Much of the wealth flowing from city government was tainted. William "Boss" Tweed, whose humble origins in the Seventh Ward made him a hero to immigrant and working-class families, headed Tammany Hall, located conveniently close to City Hall at the corner of Nassau and Frankfort streets. The city's Democratic bastion, Tammany dispensed largess to contractors, politicians, city workers, and the poor. "Big Bill" Tweed and his cronies—Mayor A. Oakey Hall, City Chamberlain Peter Sweeny, and Comptroller Richard Connolly—took a minimum of 15 percent for their services. Tweed, the grand sachem of Tammany, presided over a city submerged in unparalleled corruption.

That spring, the *Evening Post* would run a series of articles condemning (to no avail) a revised charter that surrendered the city to the Tweed Ring, but Bryant was more absorbed in literary projects than in political battles. Fields and Osgood released the first volume of Bryant's translation of the *Iliad*—twelve of twenty-four books—in February 1870. "I have endeavored," Bryant explained in the preface, "to preserve the simplicity of style which distinguishes the old Greek poet, who wrote for the popular ear." Friends praised the result. Dewey, merrily calling his friend "Master," liked the "smooth, easy, simple style. . . . It is charming—not only because it is Homer, but because it is Bryant." Another old friend, William Gilmore Simms, who reconciled with Bryant after their estrangement during the Civil War, approved of the "strong, manly English heroic blank verse." Professor Taylor Lewis of Union College immediately adopted the book for use in his class, telling Bryant that he took pains to point out to his students "its surpassing excellence."

English writers and reviewers also applauded the new translation. Edward Bulwer-Lytton was struck by Bryant's talent for letting Homer speak in his own words rather than those of the translator and especially appreciated—as did Bigelow—the "masculine and vigorous flow of his verse." The *British Quarterly* anointed Bryant as "*The* poet of America," while the *Saturday Review* declared that Bryant's version was far superior to Derby's: "We congratulate our American kinsfolk on having a poet among them who in his green old age has produced a translation of the *Iliad* worthy to live amongst the best experiments of the kind in our common language."

After he corrected proofs for the second half of the *Iliad* (published in June), Bryant embarked on a translation of the *Odyssey*. "I do not intend to hurry the task, nor even to translate with as much diligence as I translated the *Iliad*; so I may never finish it," he told his brother John. "But it will give me an occupation which will not be an irksome one, and will furnish me with a reason for declining other literary tasks, and a hundred engagements which I want some excuse besides old age for declining."

However, he did consent to one new task—the editorship of an anthology entitled *The Library of Poetry and Song*. J. B. Ford and Company invited him to write an introduction for the book, which compilers had already organized into thematic chapters: "Nature," "Religion," "Childhood and Youth," and so forth. But Bryant insisted on reviewing the entire anthology, discarding poets and poems he found to be weak and strengthening selections by those poets—including Dana and Very—he admired.

In "Poets and Poetry of the English Language," his "brief survey" as he called the introduction, Bryant echoed a theory of prosody that he had first enunciated forty-five years earlier in his Athenaeum lectures. "To me," he now wrote, "it seems that one of the most important requisites for a great poet is a luminous style. The elements of poetry lie in natural objects, in the vicissitudes of human life, in the emotions of the human heart, and in the relations of man to man. He who can present them in combinations and lights which at once affect the mind with a deep sense of their truth and beauty is the poet for his own age and the ages that succeed it."

The "vicissitudes of human life" touched Bryant once again when Gulian Verplanck died in New York City on March 18 at the age of eighty-four. Overcome by a sense of loss, Bryant told Orville Dewey that Verplanck "was one of our best public men—a politician without a politician's vices—sturdily independent, though sometimes wrong; much in public life, yet never stooping to any act or any compromise of any sort to gain the public favor." Once they had been "intimate friends" and literary collaborators; now the Historical Society insisted that Bryant compose a discourse on Verplanck's life and character. Bryant obliged, delivering his eulogy on May 17. In his oration, Bryant surveyed Verplanck's private and public life, stressing his "eloquent pleas for freedom, political equality, and toleration" and his numerous contributions to New York City, especially his years of service as head of the Board of Emigration Commissioners. Near the end of his eulogy, Bryant alluded to current conditions in Gotham and the machinations of the Tweed Ring: "Even the shameless corruption which has seized on the local government of this city did not dismay or discourage him. He maintained, in a manner which it was not easy to controvert, that the great cities of Europe are quite as grossly misgoverned, and that every overgrown community like ours must find it a difficult task to rid itself of the official leeches that seek to fatten on its blood."

With the Tweed Ring raiding city and state coffers, Bryant found himself being drawn back into editorial policies at the *Evening Post*. The flamboyant and unflappable William Marcy Tweed, weighing almost three hundred pounds and sporting a diamond stickpin worth fifteen thousand dollars, controlled all levers of political power and patronage in New York City and Albany. When Samuel Tilden told Bryant that Tweed, now a state senator, was devising a city charter revision that would effectively place the city's finances in his hands and the hands of his cronies, the senior editor instructed the *Evening Post* to launch a series of articles and editorials attacking the scheme.

Among the New York dailies, only Manton Marble's *Sun*, Dana's *World*, and the *Evening Post* had followed the career of Boss Tweed and his cronies with unrelenting disdain. The *Times*, which would finally expose the complex financial machinations of the Tweed Ring after receiving documents from the former sheriff, James O'Brien, was a latecomer to the crusade. And Greeley, whom Bryant disdained, waffled, opposing the charter one minute and supporting it the next, prompting the *Post* to accuse the *Tribune*'s editor of "a gross breach of trust." In April 1868, under its managing editor Nordhoff, the *Evening Post* had run an editorial, "Thieves Growing Desperate," attacking the Tweed Ring: "The vampires of the city treasury are well aware of the growing determination of the people to make away with them. They must choose between two alternatives. They must either aim at prolonging their privilege of plunder by moderating and disguising their use of it, or they must steal so enormously for the short time remaining as to compensate them for soon losing their chance."

And "steal enormously" they did, once the Tweed Charter passed the Albany legislature in April, enabling the Tweed Ring to dominate the city's new Board of Special Audit, which had the power to dispense millions without accountability. The *Evening Post* excoriated the new charter: "The true democratic doctrine of city government," it insisted, "is that power ought to be simple, responsibility undivided and direct." But nothing was simple or direct in the charter that Tweed, elected head of the New York State Senate, had crafted along with Sweeny. Under the guise of home rule, the Board of Special Audit, consisting of the mayor, comptroller, chamberlain, and presidents of the supervisors and aldermen, monopolized all financial powers in the city in an interlocking cabal of self-aggrandizement. With Tweed serving as Commissioner of Public Works and Sweeny as head of the Public Parks Board, the Ring promptly raised its fee for doing business with the city to 75 percent.

Apparently there was corruption at the *Evening Post* as well, although Bryant, immersed in Homer and intent on cutting back on his time at his newspaper (often escaping down rickety back stairs when uninvited visitors besieged his office), did not want to face it. He was annoyed when in February 1870 Parke Godwin accused Isaac Henderson of defrauding him and his father-in-law through "the systematic undervaluation of your property." Although Godwin had profited handsomely from the earlier sale of his shares in the paper, he had suspected Henderson of unsavory financial dealings for some time. Godwin warned Bryant that he regarded Henderson as "a most subtle, adroit, and thorough rascal . . . who in less than ten years will, in ways that you will hardly suspect, defraud you of the better part of your interest in the Evening Post." Unwilling to believe that Henderson would defraud him, Bryant informed his son-in-law that he was "perfectly willing to make amends" if Godwin felt he had been defrauded when he sold his shares in the *Evening Post*.

Bryant apparently was also unaware of the growing rancor between Henderson and Nordhoff as well as between Henderson and other employees of the *Evening Post*. Henderson owned fifty shares of the paper and owned the building outright. Running the paper on a day-to-day basis, he effectively controlled the *Evening Post*. He was training his son, Isaac Jr., to succeed him, and he hired his son-in-law, Watson Sperry, a Yale graduate, as a managing editor. Employees and others outside the journal referred to Henderson as "the wicked partner." Intent on maximizing the paper's profits, he kept employees' wages low and micromanaged operations—even requiring the building superintendent to send him daily reports on the amount of coal used. And he argued with Nordhoff over editorial policy.

The clash between Henderson and Nordhoff came to a head in early 1871, when the business manager insisted on moderating the *Evening Post's* assault on the Tweed Ring. Henderson worried that the *Post's* attacks on Tweed would cost it business—business that often flowed through Tammany. (All of New York's major newspapers received significant sums from Tammany for running "necessary legal advertisements of the city," with the *Evening Post* profiting by some five thousand dollars monthly.) Rather than submit to Henderson's meddling in editorial policy, Nordhoff, who had always disliked the publisher, resigned that spring. Bryant did not interfere, escaping the imbroglio by visiting his relatives in Illinois for the last time. As penance, he surrendered his Pullman berth to two ladies, taking their uncomfortable seats in the last car of the train and bouncing uncomfortably to his destination.

Bryant's health and stamina remained superb. When in town, he continued to walk to the *Evening Post* and back, a distance of almost six miles. He described his daily regimen to Joseph Richards, a former publisher of the *Nation* and now a principal owner of the *Herald of Health*:

> I rise early, at this time of the year about 5:30; in Summer, half an hour, or even an hour earlier. Immediately, with very little incumbrance of clothing, I begin a series of exercises, for the most part designed to expand the chest, and at the same time call into action all the muscles and articulations of the body. These are performed with dumb bells, the very lightest, covered with flannel; with a pole, a horizontal bar, and a light chair swung around my head. After a full hour, and sometimes more, passed in this manner, I bathe from head to foot.

His breakfast, he informed Richards, was simple: hominy, brown bread, oatmeal or buckwheat cakes, milk but no tea or coffee, occasionally a cup of chocolate, and always fruit. His main meal of the day consisted of a small amount of meat or fish but "mostly . . . vegetables." Water, and occasionally wine, were his favorite drinks. "I abominate all drugs and narcotics, and have always carefully avoided everything which spurs nature to exertions which it would not otherwise make."

More and more he relished the spring and early summer months at Roslyn and late summers at Cummington. He especially enjoyed entertaining friends at Cedarmere, including James and Annie Fields who came from Boston to stay with him, Samuel Tilden, and the Swedish soprano Christine Nillson. Earlier he had written to Fields telling him of his surprisingly rapid progress on the *Odyssey*: "In the case of the Odyssey I have finished the first volume two months sooner than I promised. I do not think the Odyssey the better part of Homer, except morally. The gods set a better example, and take more care to see that wrong and injustice are discouraged among mankind." But the story, he concluded, was better than that in the *Iliad*, whose plot was unsatisfactory—"and there is, besides, a monotony of carnage—you get a surfeit of slaughter."

Often using his "literary task of considerable magnitude" to escape public engagements, Bryant nevertheless agreed to deliver the principal address at the unveiling of a statue to Samuel F. B. Morse on the Mall in Central Park in June 1871—"a debt due to an old and valued friendship." But he enjoyed the temperate season—"the greenest meadows, the richest foliage on the trees and the most luxuriant gardens"—too much to venture into Gotham any more than he had to. On July 4, Samuel Tilden, scheming to oust the Tweed Ring, paid him a visit, as did the Dicksons from Philadelphia and the portrait artist George Hall. "This is a very quiet fourth of July in these parts," he informed Christiana Gibson, "people in their holiday dresses—men, women and children are silently passing in the streets; the temperature is most agreeable; the sun is shaded by floating clouds; quails—the American quail—are whistling in the fields calling out the familiar name 'Bob White.'"

Bryant's halcyon mood was shattered on July 12 when the deadly Orange Riot broke out in Gotham. The previous year, Irish Catholics had attacked the city's Orangemen—Irish Protestants—at their Elm Park picnic commemorating a battle that took place in 1690, killing fourteen and injuring scores of men, women, and children. This year, the Orangemen planned a Boyne Day parade through Manhattan. Mayor Hall and Superintendent of Police Kelso warned that they would have no protection during their march. The *Evening Post* renewed its opposition to the Tweed Ring, charging it "with a cynical contempt for law and order" and taking "the part of the mob." Governor Hoffman overruled Mayor Hall, providing an escort of police and militia, but violence broke out nevertheless, precipitated by a shot fired by an Irishman as the parade passed along Eighth Avenue near Twenty-Sixth Street. In the ensuing riot, the Eighty-Fourth Regiment fired on the mob, littering the street with dead and dying.

Dismissing any concern that Henderson might have over the loss of city advertising revenues, Bryant took up his quill pen to denounce the role of the Tweed Ring in the sordid affair:

> New York, like every great city, contains a certain number of idle, ignorant, and lawless people. But these classes are not dangerous to our peace, either by their numbers or by their organization. They are dangerous and injurious only because

they are the tools of Tweed, Sweeny, Oakey Hall, Connolly, and the Ring of corruptionists of whom these four persons are the leaders. Dispose the Tammany Ring and all danger from the "dangerous classes" will cease. . . .

The Tammany Ring purposely panders to the worst and most dangerous elements and passions of our population. It cares nothing for liberty, nothing for the rights of the citizen, nothing for public peace, for law and order; it cares only to fasten itself upon the city, and chooses to use, for that end, the most corrupt and demoralizing means, and the most lawless and dangerous part of our population. It is the Head of the Mob. It rules by, and through, and for the Mob; and unless it is struck down New York has not yet seen the worst part of its history.

Although he preferred to keep a comfortable distance from the *Evening Post*, the old man still could compose ringing sentences. By July 22, when the *Times* began publishing O'Brien's damning revelations, the Tweed Ring had begun to unravel.

Bryant was already in Cummington before the *Times* launched its exposé of the Tweed Ring's thievery. That summer, he expanded the Homestead by acquiring his grandfather Snell's property up the hillside from the main house; he now owned 465 acres. Accompanied by his surviving brothers, John and Arthur, he renewed the country rambles that they had enjoyed so much in their youth. Meanwhile, Julia would ride out in a carriage drawn by matched chestnut horses and driven by Jerry Mayhew, a black coachman from Roslyn who "delighted in fresh white gloves and big silver-plated buttons." Old friends came to visit, including Reverend Waterston from Boston, who gave an impromptu Sunday sermon while neighbors sat on boxes and sawhorses. The Bryants apparently were something of a sight for local residents.

Bryant continued to occupy his mornings with the *Odyssey*. Intimations of mortality hounded him; he had to be "frugal of my days," he wrote stoically to Orville Dewey, prompting Dewey to reply waggishly that he found his "venerable" friend amusing: "For it seems you grow old, and count the diminishing days, as a bankrupt counts his ducats." Willard Phillips, who was eighty-seven himself, also received one of Bryant's mordant letters: "at my age there are a great many holes in the bridge, and if I waste any part of my time which should be given to the translation, I may drop through one of the holes before my task is ended."

Bryant returned to Roslyn in late September to enjoy the lingering sunshine and summer flowers. The changing season reminded him of two "bad lines" in Goldsmith's "Deserted Village":

Where smiling Spring her earliest visit paid,
And parting Summer's lingering blooms delayed.

"Observe the cacophony," he informed Robert Waterston—"'ing ing ing ing' and observe what is worse, the tautology of the second line. 'Smiling,' too, in the first line is a trivial epithet, and has no business there." Skilled in prosody, Bryant was keeping his translation of the *Odyssey* as simple as possible, attempting to demonstrate that Homer's greatest strength was his ability to tell a good story. By the holiday season, his translation of the *Odyssey* was finished and the last books sent to Osgood and Company. He wrote in the preface, "I have found this a not unpleasing employment for a period of life which admonishes me that I can not many times more appear before the public in this or any other manner. . . . This gentler exercise of the intellectual faculties agrees better with that stage of life when the brain begins to be haunted by a presentiment that the time of its final repose is not far off."

V

Bryant was in his seventy-eighth year when, early in 1872, he once again felt the urge to travel. Too many supplicants—autograph hounds, would-be poets, office seekers, aspiring journalists, organizers of public events—were demanding his help and encroaching on his precious time. "They are like mosquitoes in your room at night," he complained to Dana; "they break your quiet whether they bite you or not." To escape the distractions and the bites, he told Dana, he was embarking on a trip to the Bahamas, Havana, Vera Cruz, and Mexico City.

On January 25, accompanied by Julia, her cousin Anna Fairchild, his brother John, and John Durand, Bryant left for Nassau aboard the *Morro Castle*. Fellow passengers included General George McClellan and Mrs. Henry Ward Beecher, who were traveling to Cuba as guests of A. W. Dimmick, the president of the Atlantic Steamship Line. Rough seas made for a difficult passage, and the Bryant party was relieved to disembark in Nassau on January 30.

Settling into a cottage attached to the Cleveland Hotel, Bryant and his entourage spent two weeks visiting schools, markets, plantations, and Granttown, "a district inhabited altogether by the negro population." Bryant was gratified by the "spread of education among the colored population," which, he felt, would "be certain to elevate their character." He luxuriated in the lushness of nature, the tropical warmth, and the "brilliant blue tint of the sea. . . . I could only compare its color to that of the globular vessels of glass in an apothecary's window, filled with a blue liquid and placed in front of a gaslight." Writing to the *Evening Post*, he predicted: "This place becomes more and more, with every year, the resort of invalids from the United States, who seek to escape the rigors of a northern winter. At some time not far distant this will become one of the most thronged watering-places in the world."

Bryant reached Havana on February 15, finding the city strikingly altered since his last visit in 1849. Havana now had decent hotels; the Bryant party stayed at the San Carlos Hotel, where "the rooms are airy and the table excellent." The city was a beehive of activity and political intrigue, with persistent speculation about the island's revolt against Spain. Bryant's fame had preceded him, and journalists and government officials feted him. At one dinner, Cuban and Spanish dignitaries asked Bryant to convey to Washington their desire for a reciprocal trade treaty with the United States—a request endorsed in an editorial by Parke Godwin, who had returned to the *Evening Post* as "an adjunct and advisory editor" during Bryant's absence.

Warned about dangers posed by bandits on the 120-mile stretch from Vera Cruz to Mexico City, Bryant left the women at the San Carlos Hotel, where they would be safe and comfortable, while he and the other men embarked for Vera Cruz aboard the British steamer *Corsica*, crossing the Gulf of Mexico in four days. Bryant's friend Matías Romero, now minister of finance for the Mexican government, had instructed officials in Vera Cruz to be on the lookout for the famous American; when the poet reached the city, he and his party were escorted to shore in a boat sent by the port captain. Vera Cruz turned out to be a cleaner and less dangerous city than Bryant had been led to expect, but yellow fever was raging, and the party left a day later by rail and then stagecoach for Mexico City, which they reached on March 1.

Bryant spent thirteen days in Mexico City and its environs, filing six long letters to the *Evening Post* with descriptions of the city's history, culture, and inhabitants. He was struck by the contrast between "the utter poverty" of the masses and the "great luxury" of the ruling class, whose hospitality he sampled at a private banquet in his honor. The Catholic clergy, he learned, was "fearfully corrupted" and "loose in their morals." Bryant visited Chapultepec, the Floating Gardens, and the American Cemetery. He was made an honorary member of the Philharmonic Society and of the Geographical and Statistical Society. His stay ended memorably when Matías Romero presented Bryant to President Benito Juárez; the two men had a long conversation about the Aztec race, the unsuccessful insurrection by Porfiro Díaz, and Mexico's need for American investment. After Bryant's departure on March 13, Major George W. Clarke, editor of the English language paper the *Two Republics*, wrote: "We believe that no foreigner ever was the subject, in this capital, of a warmer, a more sincere and eloquent reception."

Bryant and his companions returned to Havana to pick up Julia and Anna before embarking for New Orleans, a city he had never seen. He wandered the French Quarter and was the guest one evening of Louisiana governor Henry Clay Warmoth, then under heavy criticism for his attempts to improve relations between blacks and whites. Boarding a riverboat on April 8, Bryant headed up the Mississippi. At Cincinnati, the city's dignitaries, joined by Rutherford B. Hayes, the governor of Ohio, gave him a reception. "His looks and manners," Hayes wrote in his diary, "are very winning and lovable. His intellect is clear, his talk vigorous, interesting, pithy, and friendly. Modesty, kindness, and serenity possess him, or he possesses them." Hayes was amused by Bryant's imitations of Negro and Yankee dialects and by his many anecdotes, including one involving an old Irish servant in his Havana hotel, who had exclaimed, "Oh, sir, I welcome you back; you are like one of the old Saints."

The old saint had traveled widely in his lifetime, speaking in several voices and assuming various personas: shrewd social observer, celebrity tourist, cultural guide and authority, keen naturalist, aesthetic judge, alert social and political commentator. Through travel, Bryant had assumed many identities—but above all he remained a representative American democrat.

17

A CENTURY'S SPACE

Through calm and storm the years have led
Our nation on, from stage to stage—
A century's space—until we tread
The threshold of another age.
—"The Centennial Hymn," Roslyn, 1876

I

Returning to Manhattan, Bryant was immediately caught up in election year politics. The scandals of the Grant administration had fractured the Republican Party, with the liberals intent on preventing Grant's renomination. When a Liberal Republican Convention opposed to Grant met in Cincinnati on May 1 and two days later nominated Horace Greeley as its candidate for the presidency, Bryant was dismayed. He had endorsed the convention, hoping that a more likely candidate such as Charles Francis Adams or Lyman Trumbell would be nominated. Bryant told his brother John that he was "sorely disappointed" by the outcome.

There had been bad blood between Bryant and Greeley for years, dating back to 1831 when Leggett had summarily fired the unkempt journeyman printer who bobbed over his type in "a peculiar way." In 1849, Greeley had responded to a Bryant editorial by writing, "You lie, you old villain, you basely, wickedly lie!" In 1864, Bryant found himself at a breakfast that Greeley also attended; when the host asked him if he did not know his rival editor, Bryant replied, "No, I don't; he's a blackguard—he's a blackguard." There was something about the mercurial Greeley that offended Bryant.

As soon as he learned of Greeley's nomination, Bryant rushed into the *Evening Post* and insisted on writing the day's editorial. Appearing in a later edition on May 3 under the caption "Why Mr. Greeley Should Not Be Supported for the Presidency," Bryant enumerated the reasons as if he were presenting a legal brief. In his most vitriolic style, Bryant listed Greeley's failings: the man was devoid of courage, firmness, and consistency; coddled corrupt friends, including members of the Tweed Ring; lacked political principles; and was a "bigoted protectionist." Overall, Greeley betrayed a certain "grossness of manners"; such a leader could not manage the affairs of the nation "with common decorum."

Bryant made his disdain for Greeley equally clear in a letter to Lyman Trumbull, an original Free Soiler, founder of the Republican Party, and since 1854 the United States Senator from Illinois: "We who know Mr. Greeley, know that his administration, should he be elected, cannot be otherwise than shamefully corrupt. His associates are of the worst sort, and the worst abuses of the present administration are likely to be even caricatured under his. His election would be a severe blow to the cause of revenue reform. The cause of civil service reform would be hopeless with him for President. . . . the other wretches by whom Greeley is surrounded, will never give up the patronage by which they expect to hold the power." According to Bryant, Greeley lacked scruples and suffered from "an infirmity of judgment."

Greeley's nomination, Bryant observed wryly to employees at the *Evening Post*, made the Grant administration look not so bad after all. He still had some hope that an alternative to Grant could be found, but when a May 30 meeting of the Free Trade League at Steinway Hall that he presided over could not settle on a rival candidate, Bryant tepidly swung the *Evening Post* behind Grant. At the same time, Bryant quickly suppressed rumors that he would be a good presidential candidate, inserting a "card" in the *Evening Post* protesting the absurdity of the idea. Rumors that he would make a strong presidential nominee had circulated for years, but Bryant had always denied any interest in elected office. Still, John Bigelow observed in his journal that Bryant was "the only man in the United States who cannot be replaced, whose death would leave the country substantially poorer in genius, in character, in moral courage and purpose."

Greeley, unpredictable as always, campaigned vigorously for the presidency on the Liberal and Democratic tickets, but was trounced by Grant, who received 286 electoral votes to Greeley's 62 and won by a plurality of three-quarters of a million popular votes. Three weeks later, exhausted by the campaign and his defeat, hurt by Nast's drawings in *Harper's Weekly* depicting him conspiring with Boss Tweed, and devastated by his wife's death, Greeley suffered an emotional breakdown and died.

The *Evening Post* offered a generous obituary for the man it had attacked so vehemently. The obituary's balanced cadences were vintage Bryant, guilt-ridden perhaps over his harsh indictment of Greeley: "By good natural abilities, by industry, by temperance, by sympathy with what is noblest and best in human nature, and by earnest purpose, the ignorant, friendless, unknown printer's boy of a few years since became the powerful and famous journalist, whose words went forth to the ends of the earth, affecting the destinies of all mankind."

Distracted more than he had planned to be by presidential politics, Bryant had cut back on his public engagements and writing during the year. He did offer speeches at the unveiling of Shakespeare's statue in the Mall at Central Park in May and the dedication of Walter Scott's statue on November 4. With Evert Duyckinck, he undertook an edition of *The Complete Works of Shakespeare*, a project that would be published in three volumes after his death. And he agreed to write an introduction for a lavish two-volume pictorial book, *Picturesque America*. With the Homer translations behind him, he wrote little new poetry, publishing only two minor poems on Indian themes, "Tree Burial" and "A Legend of the Delawares," in the *Ledger*.

One project wholly absorbed Bryant: the construction of a library for the residents of Cummington. He purchased eleven acres of land for three hundred and fifty dollars, set aside eight thousand dollars for the construction of the building, and hired a local widow, Henrietta Nahmer, as a cataloguer. With the help of his friend George Palmer Putnam, Bryant then gathered 3,618 volumes, arranging to have the catalog printed on the *Evening Post*'s steam press. Bryant managed every detail, including the correction of errors (a misspelling of Garibaldi's name did not escape his editorial eye) in Mrs. Nahmer's catalog.

At seventy-eight, Bryant still sought new projects to fill his time; he told Dana that he felt "rather urgently the need both of bodily and mental exercise. Yet though while employed I am not much haunted with the consciousness of being old yet the fact is almost always present to my mind that the time of my remaining here is necessarily short, and that whatever I am to do must be done soon or it may not be done at all." He only had to think of Morse, who had first painted his portrait for twenty-five dollars in 1825; Kensett, "the amiable and generous artist"; and Putnam, "the liberal-minded and kindly bookseller," who had died during the year, to realize that Time's chariot was drawing near.

Bryant had so enjoyed his adventures in the Caribbean and Mexico that he decided to resume the life of a vagabond in February 1873, this time taking his daughters Fanny and Julia, Anna Fairchild, and John Durand to Florida. "We old men are like snakes," he confided to James T. Fields, "fond of the sun, and inclined to crawl to sunny places." The Bryant party visited Jacksonville, Saint Augustine, Palatka, Green Cove Springs, and Silver Spring. In letters to the *Evening Post*, the editor described life along the St. John River—"a broad, deep, placid stream, as black as a Claude Lorraine mirror." He stopped at Harriet Beecher Stowe's mansion, "Mandarin," and predicted that an invasion of ordinary citizens would soon follow Mrs. Stowe to warm winter climes. "At some future time here will be groves of the date palm, which has flourished at St. Augustine, and gardens with hedges of myrtle, and walks embowered with the arbutus, and the laurel of Europe, and every beautiful evergreen which grows under the skies of Italy, for the refreshment of those who come from the snow fields of our harsher clime."

Peering beneath the luminous Florida landscape, Bryant also detected a grimmer reality: the physical and material decline of the black population. When he had first visited Florida thirty years earlier, he recalled, the "negro race" in St. Augustine "had a sleek, well-fed look, and were for the most part neatly attired. In both respects it has seemed to me that there is a change for the worse." As Bryant made a leisurely return through the South in April, stopping at Savannah, Charleston, Wilmington, Norfolk, and Richmond, he was struck by the failure of Reconstruction to materially improve the region's newly freed slaves. Equally abject were the "Crackers" or poor whites—"a degraded race," he informed Christiana Gibson's sister Janet. Only the education of the poor black and white populations, he surmised, held the promise of substantially improving their lot. But he observed that replacing competent white public officials with corrupt black politicians did not bode well for Reconstruction.

After he returned to New York in mid-April, Bryant was little occupied with affairs at the *Evening Post* or literary projects. He eschewed new literary ventures, turning down among other projects William Dean Howells's request from the *Atlantic* for "a series of articles—the more autobiographical the better—on such phases of our literary, social and political past as have most interested you." Howells had read Bryant's recently collected *Orations and Addresses* "with very great pleasure."

But Bryant was content to devote his time to the evolving library at Cummington and a new library project at the College of New Jersey, subsequently Princeton University. He journeyed to Cummington in May and was charmed by the completed library and dwelling house. In late June, he traveled to Princeton at the invitation of President James McCosh to receive an honorary degree of Doctor of Laws and to give the principal address at the dedication of the new Chancellor Green Library. During his remarks on June 24, Bryant invited the guests to imagine that the South American white ant (or termite) had invaded other continents, devouring all of the world's books. Our understanding of the past and the contours of civilization would be obliterated, Bryant declared, and the human race would "drift hopelessly into barbarism."

How humanity had managed to evolve out of barbarism was a perpetual wonder to Bryant. Darwinism posited the evolution of the species; Bryant was skeptical but mildly intrigued by the theory. Offering some remarks on Darwin at a Williams College alumni dinner in late 1871, Bryant had speculated humorously that the current state of humanity might actually represent Darwinism in reverse. "Our race," Bryant mused, "may be frittered away into the meaner tribes of animals. . . . Then may our Tweeds become the progenitors of those skulking thieves of the western wilds, the prairie-wolves, or swim stagnant pools in the shape of horse-leeches; our astute lawyers may be represented by foxes; our great architects by colonies of beavers; our poets by clouds of mosquitoes, famished and musical." With politicians like Boss Tweed squeaking like bats and gibbering like apes and with Grant's administration transformed into a paradise for swinish scoundrels, Darwinism in reverse might be unfolding. The Crédit Mobilier and Whiskey Ring scandals, Indian land grabs and congressional salary grabs, all symptomatic of the "Era of Good Stealings," was clear evidence of a jungle world.

The Grant administration's foreign policy was equally distressing to Bryant. When his old friend Hamilton Fish, now secretary of state, asked Bryant for advice on the tense relationship with Cuba after a Cuban gunboat had intercepted a U.S. freighter shipping arms to rebels and executed eight American sailors, Bryant urged caution. "A war with Spain would be a real disaster," he warned, in large part because the country would inherit an "ignorant population of negroes, mulattos and *monteros* or white peasantry" that had been degraded by slavery and "centuries of the most grinding despotism." Here was Darwinism in reverse in its baldest outline. "We have trouble enough already with the freed men our own country." A war with Spain and the acquisition of Cuba, he concluded, "should be sedulously avoided."

In December, Bryant declined an invitation from the Massachusetts Historical Society to participate in a centenary celebration of the Boston Tea Party. But he did offer words to be read by Robert Waterston, who was hosting the event at his home. Apostrophizing "the mighty fortunes of nations," Bryant in his most hortatory style highlighted the progress of civilization in America and around the world, emphasizing the cyclical turns of history that he had first embraced in "The Ages." New ages begin, he declared, then decline, and are reborn. Wrongs are committed, are redressed, and recur. Ancient despotisms are overturned and new empires formed. "History," Bryant concluded, "will have much to do in recording the events of the century which ends with the sixteenth of this month."

II

On the afternoon of November 3, 1874, a delegation of prominent citizens headed by Jonathan Sturges arrived at Bryant's brownstone on West Sixteenth Street to pay tribute to the poet on his eightieth birthday. They presented Bryant with a printed declaration prepared by Dr. Samuel Osgood and signed by hundreds of friends and admirers around the country. His friends had decided that a commemorative vase would be designed by Tiffany's to reflect "the lessons of your literary and civic career in its relations with our country, whose nature, history, liberty, law, and conscience you have so illustrated." Sturges lauded his friend as a poet who had given America "the purest language of the English-speaking race," as a journalist who had "vindicated the duties as well as the rights of man," and as a citizen who had "stood up manfully for justice and humanity." In his modest reply, Bryant reviewed the progress of humanity in his lifetime, praised the end of slavery in the United States, and applauded the rise of emerging democratic movements worldwide. He looked forward to a day of "universal peace" when nations would send "their soldiery back to the fields and workshops."

Literary societies and newspapers across the country paid homage to a man who had entered into the ethos of American life. His brother John, who had appeared with Arthur at the celebration sponsored by the Chicago Literary Club, pointed to the "great shower of kind notices" that greeted the octogenarian. Bryant replied, "I am quite uncertain how to take the compliments 'showered' upon me on the occasion of my eightieth birthday, recalling what Charles Lamb somewhere says, 'I stink in the midst of respect.' But I account in part for what the newspapers say of me, almost with one consenting voice. 'I, too, am a journalist,' and a natural feeling leads them to commend one of their own number, who has been fortunate enough to stand pretty well in the opinion of his countrymen."

The year had started on a painful note when Bryant took a tumble on Broadway's icy winter streets, bruising his right shoulder. He described the episode to Christiana Gibson: "It always seems to me that there is a kind of disgrace in falling to the ground. Drunken people fall. As I got up, I thought to myself, 'Nobody, at least, is here who knows me.' At that very moment a gentleman, whom I did not know, asked: 'Are you hurt, Mr. Bryant?' 'Of course not,' I answered, and I marched off down town as if I had just come from my door."

Bryant's damaged shoulder, which would bother him for several months, did not dampen his revived capacity for civic life during the year. He gave a half dozen speeches on varied topics: Benjamin Franklin as a poet before the New York Typographical Society; "Freedom of Exchange" at the Cooper Union; toasts to the actress Charlotte Cushman at the Booth Theatre and to Peter Cooper at the Arcadian Club; and a talk on the genius of Shakespeare at the Saint George's Society. One Friday evening in late January, just before his fall on Broadway, he spoke at the request of the inspectors of the city's female evening schools to four hundred "scholars . . . a large proportion of them women grown— a great many of German and Irish birth, who are at work all the day and come at night to get the rudiments of an English education." Bryant was impressed by the women's "intelligent looks."

With the *Iliad* and *Odyssey* translations behind him, Bryant undertook a new literary project—a four-volume *Popular History of the United States*, which would occupy him during his remaining years. Sydney Howard Gay, a former Abolitionist editor and managing editor of the *Tribune* and now managing editor at the *Evening Post*, would be his coauthor (actually the lead writer) for the work. Numerous artists, including Albert Bierstadt, whom Bryant had helped when the German painter had first come to the United States, and Winslow Homer, would provide illustrations. Bryant acknowledged to his brother John: "The real hard work of writing the history itself is to be done by Mr. Gay, but is all to pass through my hands." As it turned out, Bryant only wrote the preface and carefully edited the manuscript of *A Popular History of the*

United States, which Scribner, Armstrong and Company would publish in successive volumes.

Bryant served as editorial guide and grammatical guru for his partner as they worked through the first two volumes of *A Popular History of the United States* that were published in his lifetime. He filled forty letters to Sydney Gay with the same advice on clarity and purity of language that had made him a stylistic arbiter at the *Evening Post*. His stylistic recommendations expanded the *Index Expurgatorious* he had distributed to his writers: avoid slang, substitute fresher language for a trite word or hackneyed expression, use specific words, pay attention to syntax, grammar, and mechanics. Reviewing page 50 in the galleys, he cautioned: "'the cattle supported themselves' a phrase not properly applied to animals. Men support themselves—cattle are fed or pastured." Bryant was meticulous and thorough—the arbiter, as he styled himself, of commas and semicolons. But he was careful to balance his rigorous correction of the galleys with overall praise for Gay's chapters. He wrote to Gay on November 11, 1875, "You have told the story of the Discoveries and Explorations of the Spanish Leaders who immediately succeed Columbus—so far as concerns our part of the continent—in a picturesque manner, and in such a way as to give it an air of novelty." As to his "verbal suggestions," Bryant assured his partner that he was free to ignore them, but Gay rarely did.

There was always some new enterprise—funding a reading room and assembly hall for the residents of Roslyn, hosting a meeting of the old Sketch Club, embarking on a nostalgic trip back to Plymouth, Massachusetts, where he had first practiced law—to occupy the octogenarian. In fact, there was never sufficient time to read everything at hand or to honor every invitation. In the spring of 1874, he started to reread *Don Quixote*. The book had amused him when he first read it as a boy; now, reading Cervantes' novel backward, the octogenarian laughed again, "filled with wonder at the fertility of his invention and the narrative skill." In early 1878 Bryant would agree to write a poem, "Cervantes," for a celebration by New York's Spanish residents honoring the anniversary of the writer's death. The lyric's opening quatrain captures the comic spirit of *Don Quixote* that so delighted Bryant as he reread Cervantes' picaresque narrative:

> As o'er the laughter-moving page
>   Thy readers, oh, Cervantes, bend,

What shouts of mirth, through age on age,
   From every clime of earth ascend!

Occasionally in the rush of life and laughter, Bryant forgot social obligations and civic commitments. He begged John Bigelow to remind him of a service he had agreed to perform for the amateur poet and literary hostess Anne Botta: "I must have got into that stage of life when today forgets yesterday." His public refused to forget Bryant, who now seemed indispensable to New York society and civic life—the very embodiment of American civilization.

He had been born in the first year of George Washington's second administration, and in his lifetime the nation had grown from fifteen to thirty-nine states. The nation's first president was very much on Bryant's mind. On Tuesday, February 22, 1876, he penned one of his few editorials that year, a leader entitled "Washington's Birthday—His Parting Counsels." Bryant began by recommending to the *Evening Post*'s readers Washington's "Farewell Speech," reprinted in that day's issue, and reminding them of the first president's refusal to consider a third term. The concerns raised by Washington in his farewell address—"the dissolution of our union of states," "obstructions to the execution of laws," party prejudice and party zeal, the danger of foreign entanglements— were as pertinent to modern times, he thought, as they were during the Republic's first years.

A year later, still thinking about Washington, Bryant composed "The Centennial Hymn," a conventional lyric churned out by America's titular poet laureate:

Through calm and storm the years have led
   Our nation on, from stage to stage—
A century's space—until we tread
   The threshold of another age.

We see where o'er our pathway swept
   A torrent-stream of blood and fire,
And thank the Guardian Power who kept
   Our sacred League of States entire.

Our chequered train of years, farewell!
   With all thy strifes and hopes and fears!

Yet with us let thy memories dwell,
   To warn and teach the coming years.

And thou, the new-beginning age,
   Warned by the past, and not in vain,
Write on a fairer, whiter page,
   The record of thy happier reign.

Bryant visited the grounds of the Centennial Celebration prior to its opening in May, but he declined an invitation to serve as the grand exhibition's president. His hymn and a second lyric, "The Flood of Years" (published in *Scribner's Monthly Magazine* in July), would have to serve as his contributions to the occasion.

The year 1876 was also an election year, and Bryant believed that the nation badly needed George Washington's expansive vision and spirit of self-sacrifice. The election presented Bryant with one of the most agonizing political decisions of his life. Samuel J. Tilden, who had been elected governor in 1874, was running for the presidency on the Democratic ticket. Bryant had known Tilden for a third of a century, and he especially admired the younger man's austerity and strong moral compass. They had drifted apart during the Civil War but had joined forces again when Tilden exposed the corruption of the Tweed and "Canal" rings, the latter a group of corrupt contractors and politicians who had earned fabulous sums of money from fraudulent repairs of the state's canal system.

Tilden for his part saw much of his own rigorous morality in Bryant, and early in his gubernatorial administration accorded the poet-editor what in Bigelow's words was "a compliment which had never before been paid in this country to a man of letters." On February 6, 1875, Bryant traveled to Albany at the new governor's invitation to spend time at the executive mansion and receive the accolades of both houses of the state legislature. Two days later, the chairman of the welcoming committee presented Bryant to the Senate as "the most distinguished citizen of our state—I might say of our country." After a standing ovation, Bryant was cheered again when in a wry reply he likened his own insignificance before this "imposing ceremony" to the funeral in ancient Greece of a child whose father had apologized to a large gathering of mourners "for the smallness of the infant that was brought out." A similar scene unfolded in the lower chamber and again Bryant responded with levity: "Old men, my friends, are rarities. . . . If pebbles were scarce they would not be picked up and thrown at dogs, but would be sought after and collected by mineralogists."

Governor Tilden was a shrewd politician who clearly hoped that his old friend would swing the *Evening Post* behind his candidacy for the presidency. Bryant had in fact been disgusted with the Republican Party for some time, writing as early as November 1873 in an editorial entitled "A Word for the Republican Party" that "the party is going down hill, and we should be very much obliged to any one who will tell us where it is likely to stop." But Bryant also had no attachment to the Democratic Party, whose platform on civil service and financial and revenue reform, he thought, was even worse than that of the Republicans. Throughout the early months of the campaign year and even after both party conventions, Bryant refused to pronounce his paper's endorsement of either Tilden or the Republican nominee, Rutherford B. Hayes. Tilden was a friend and a man of admirable qualities, but Bryant also like Hayes's record as a reform governor. He realized that Bigelow, who still wrote occasional editorials for the *Evening Post*, was Tilden's campaign manager and would become secretary of state if the Democrat won. Bigelow implored Bryant to head the Tilden electoral ticket, but Bryant, with "great pain," declined.

Bryant apparently had succumbed to the wishes of his business partner, Isaac Henderson. The "wicked partner," as he was generally perceived, was now de facto head of William C. Bryant and Company, controlling half the shares and the entire ten-story building that housed the *Evening Post*. Henderson clearly wielded power over the paper's editorial policy. When on June 29 the paper had offered warm but noncommittal praise of Tilden's nomination, Henderson immediately closeted himself with Bryant for a long discussion of the paper's position on the election. Then on July 5, the paper began a series of editorials denouncing the Democratic Party and attacking Tilden for his soft money policies. On July 10 the *Evening Post* endorsed Hayes.

Bigelow was dismayed. He wrote to a confidant: "I can hardly trust myself to talk about the *Post*. I hope to be spared the necessity of writing about it. But the *Evening Post* that you and I have known and honored, which educated us and through which we have educated others in political science, I fear no longer exists. . . . I only wish Mr. Bryant had his name stricken out of it." Bigelow and other friends wondered whether the old crusader and apostle of radical democracy had compromised his principles by submitting to Henderson's single-minded devotion to the bottom line.

Bryant in fact preferred the Republican Party platform to the soft-money policies of the Democrats. While believing that Tilden was the superior candidate, he was convinced that Hayes would make a surprisingly strong reform president. But he never divulged how he voted on November 7. Bigelow claimed that he knew on "perfectly competent authority" that Bryant had abstained. The "competent authority" was probably Julia Bryant, who had been distressed by the machinations at the *Evening Post* and wrote Tilden to explain her father's removal from the paper's policies.

A prediction that Bryant had made that summer—that the election would be "one of the greatest contests for the presidency"—turned out to be prescient. Tilden trounced Hayes in the popular vote for president and led in the electoral vote 184 to 165, one vote short of victory. But the outcome was uncertain in four contested states—Florida, South Carolina, Georgia, and Oregon. With the House controlled by Democrats and the Senate by Republicans, Congress created a special fifteen-member commission to resolve the crisis. "We have chosen a President of the United States," Bryant wrote to Christiana Gibson in late November, "and do not yet know who it is—We are to be gainers any how—we are to have a better administration than the present one whether it be Hayes or Tilden that is chosen. I have never before felt so lukewarm an interest as now in any previous contest for the Presidency."

In late February, the commission, on which the Republicans held a majority of one, voted strictly along party lines, and delivered the election to Rutherford B. Hayes. On March 5, 1877, Hayes took the oath of office, becoming the nineteenth president of the United States. Four days later, Bryant wrote to his brother John that he had been surprised by the outcome: "I confess that it seemed to me from the first that Tilden would win and I could hardly help expecting after the Electoral Commission was appointed that something would happen to throw the office into his hands."

Matched against the great cycles of history and nature, as he had framed his favorite theme in "The Flood of Years," the presidential election year had been a mere speck in the vast expanse of the cosmos:

A Mighty Hand, from an exhaustless Urn,
Pours forth the never-ending Flood of Years,
Among the nations. How the rushing waves
Bear all before them! On their foremost edge,

And there alone, is Life. The Present there
And there alone, is Life . . .

The flood sweeps on, the old Stoic believed, and the torrent bears everyone under.

Slowly, in the last full year of his life, the flood would sweep away
all illusions that Bryant had about Isaac Henderson. For decades he had
sustained a warm regard for Henderson and his wife despite admonitions
from Godwin, Bigelow, and his daughters. However, on March 16, 1877,
Bryant informed Henderson by letter that, at the urging of his daughters,
he was asking his attorney, Andrew H. Green, to determine "the precise
situation" of his affairs at the newspaper. Green, a law partner of Tilden
since 1871 and comptroller of the City of New York, was a man acclaimed for his integrity. His scrutiny of the *Evening Post*'s books along
with a later examination of the ledgers by Judge John J. Monell revealed
that Henderson had been defrauding his partner for thirty years. The
money rightfully belonging to Bryant that had been systematically mis-
appropriated by Henderson came to more than two hundred thousand
dollars.

The Henderson affair was a painful blow to Bryant, who had
trusted, defended, and increasingly deferred to his partner in editorial
matters. As a result of the disclosures, Henderson was forced to resign as
publisher. To meet his debts, Henderson pledged thirty shares of the
company to Bryant, who would remain editor, and twenty shares to
Parke Godwin, who reentered the *Evening Post*. Judge Monell, who
wrote the opinion for the Bryant family, declared that Henderson could
never again gain control of the paper. The judge also agreed to serve as
the company's president.

Disillusioned by the Henderson affair, Bryant found consolation in
his active social and literary life—and especially in his warm relationship
with his Roslyn neighbor, Leonice Moulton. He was pleased with a new
edition of *Poems* that Appleton's had released in 1876, and he kept a keen
editorial eye on the *Popular History*, with a second volume scheduled for
publication in the spring of 1878. He also edited a new edition of *A
Library of Poetry and Song*, an anthology that would remain popular
well into the twentieth century. In his introduction, Bryant had emphasized the "luminous style" characterizing the best poetry in English.
(Walt Whitman would accord Bryant the same quality of luminosity,
writing of the "marvelous purity of his work in verse . . . never a waste

word—the last superfluity struck off; a clear nameless beauty pervading and overarching all the work of his pen.")

His health remarkably robust, Bryant still walked from his house on West Sixteenth Street to the new offices of the *Evening Post*, bounding up nine flights of stairs instead of taking the fancy new elevator to his office, and then hiding out with the compositors on another floor to avoid uninvited visitors. He was still a clubman and an occasional traveler. Whitman recalled that Bryant "would go off of an evening from club to club—the Union League, the Goethe Club, what not—being everywhere deferred to—meetings often 'perceiving the great so-and-so present,' inviting him to the platform, and so forth and so forth."

One evening in 1876, Bryant attended a lecture by Mark Twain, unnerving the normally unflappable raconteur. Starting with "flying colors," Twain told Annie Fields, he soon spied Bryant sitting in the front row: "Nobody told me that William Cullen Bryant was there, but I had seen his picture and I knew that was the old man. I was sure he saw the failure I was making, and all the weak points in what I was saying, and I couldn't do anything more—that old man just spoiled my work."

Bryant had to turn down more speaking engagements than he accepted, especially if they involved trips out of town. But he assumed a leading role in erecting a statue to his old friend Halleck in Central Park, offering the principal oration at the ceremony in May 1877, while trying to talk over the pandemonium created by the presence of President Hayes. (The following year Hayes asked Bryant to send him the plans for the library in Cummington, a request that would result in the construction of the Hayes Library, the first presidential library in the United States.) Pleading old age, Bryant found it easy to extricate himself from out-of-town invitations—whether to speak at two new women's colleges, Vassar and Wellesley, address the commemoration of the Battle of Oriskany in upstate New York, join Williams College alumni at their annual meeting in Boston, or participate in a literary congress in Paris, France. However, he did travel to Lafayette College in Easton, Pennsylvania, for the June 1877 commencement, where he presented a collection of his books to the student who had written the best study of the year's designated author, who happened to be Bryant. While at Lafayette, Bryant dined with an old friend, Professor Joseph Alden, author of the textbook *Studies in Bryant*, and with General Benjamin Harrison, the future president of the United States whose son was graduating.

As was his custom, Bryant declined to write poetry for special occasions. One exception was a lyric he agreed to write for a new journal, the

International Review. The sonnet, "In Memory of John Lothrop Motley," reflected Bryant's respect for the historian who had died earlier in the year:

> Sleep, Motley, with the great of ancient days,
>   Who wrote for all the years that yet shall be.
> Sleep with Herodotus, whose name and praise
>   Have reached the isles of earth's remotest sea.
> Sleep, while, defiant of the slow decays
>   Of time, thy glorious writings speak of thee
> And in the answering heart of millions raise
>   The generous zeal of Right and Liberty.
> Sleep, till the days o'ertake us, when, at last,
>   The Silence that ere yet a human pen
> Had traced the slenderest record of the past
>   Hushed the primeval languages of men—
> Upon our English tongue its spell shall cast,
>   Thy memory shall perish only then.

Motley had been a champion of freedom and an able emissary abroad, serving as minister to Great Britain before Grant summarily recalled him in 1870, an action that the editor had condemned in the *Evening Post*.

Bryant had turned eighty-three when his sonnet to Motley appeared in the November-December issue of the *International Review*. In Boston, Whittier was turning seventy, and Bryant regretted that he could not compose a poem or attend a dinner for "a poet whose life is as beautiful as his verse." Thanking Christiana Gibson for her birthday wishes, Bryant acknowledged that he was grateful for a comfortable old age and generally sound physical and mental faculties—unlike Emerson, then seventy-four, who, "they say, begins to feel the decays of age not only in physical but mental activity." Emerson's mind was increasingly feeble. He thought that his friend Henry Thoreau, who had died in 1862, was still alive, and he could not recall the name of another friend, Bronson Alcott. Neither could he remember the name of his favorite childhood flower.

Bryant, his poetry a repository of discrete details drawn from nature, retained an amazing memory; he could recite every line of his verse. A favorite was "To the Fringed Gentian," written during his early New York days, in which the poet set the autumn flower's heavenly blue against the violets and columbines of springtime:

Thou waitest late and com'st alone,
When woods are bare and birds are flown,
And frosts and shortening days portend
The aged year is near his end.

Then doth thy sweet and quiet eye
Look through the fringes to the sky,
Blue—blue—as if that sky let fall
A flower from its cerulean wall.

I would that thus, when I shall see
The hour of death draw near to me,
Hope, blossoming within my heart,
May look to heaven as I depart.

Bryant had composed the poem in 1829, when his departure from the natural world must have seemed a distant and fanciful poetic conceit.

Answering a letter from a correspondent wanting to know the background of an even earlier poem, "Green River," the intricately rhymed lyric in tetrameter couplets that he had first published in 1821, he could recall: "The Green River, which gave its name to my poem, is a beautiful little stream of Berkshire County Massachusetts. It flows through Great Barrington, passing by the dwelling of Mr. Mackie, author of *Casas de España*, and entering the meadows of the Housatonic pours itself into that river."

With his mental and physical faculties remarkably robust, Bryant had no intention of departing the beauties of this world any time soon. Whether strolling the streets of New York City, traversing the 175 acres of his "half-country place" in Roslyn, or wandering the Berkshire hills, he seemed to have conquered Time. "I certainly have no objection," he told Christiana Gibson, "to see a few more birthdays yet."

III

"Gone! Gone!" Leonice Moulton wrote in her private diary on June 12, 1876. Bryant had died at 5:30 that morning, two weeks after he had fallen on the steps of James Grant Wilson's brownstone on East Seventy-Fourth Street. According to Dr. Gray, his longtime physician, in the days following his fall, Bryant wandered about the library in his home on

West Sixteenth Street and sat in his favorite chair but showed little sign of recognizing people, including Julia, who had returned from Atlantic City. (Bryant had thought that Atlantic City was a decidedly "absurd" name for the new seaside resort.) On the eighth day, Bryant suffered a brain hemorrhage and paralysis down his right side. He remained comatose during the days leading up to his death—the relatively easy passing that he had prayed for.

No one was more grieved by Bryant's death than Leonice Moulton, a widow who occupied a cottage on Bryant's property. Twenty years younger than Bryant and apparently quite attractive, she had known Bryant since 1843, when the poet-editor purchased the forty acres of land that Bryant named Cedarmere from her husband, Joseph Moulton, a historian and writer in law who had died in 1875. Over the years, a close friendship developed between Bryant and Mrs. Moulton. Bryant's many letters to Leonice are warm, witty, and avuncular; as for Leonice, whose letters to Bryant are unrecovered, she adored "The Poet," as she often called him in her diary. They enjoyed many pleasurable hours together. In a typical entry in her diary, Leonice records a two-mile walk they embarked on, in which Bryant picked wildflowers for her and confessed, "I am not much of a poet."

Especially after the death of Frances, Bryant wrote warm letters to his female friends, as his correspondence with Catharine Sedgwick, Christiana Gibson, Jerusha Dewey, and Leonice Moulton demonstrates. But his relationship with Leonice Moulton, who was a constant neighbor, was notably affectionate. In his letters—often addressed to "My dear Mrs. Moulton" (an unusual tone of familiarity for the typically formal correspondent), Bryant discussed their mutual health, literature and gardening, local gossip, current events, and the condition of the times. "I begin to be uneasy at not hearing anything from Roslyn," he worries in an August 24, 1876, letter to her. Later in the year, he wishes her merry Christmas but worries about her "indisposition." Then on March 19, 1877, he writes, "I hope the dinner agreed with you—in a physical and material sense I mean." In the same letter he cautions her about the perils of remarriage; the widow apparently was contending with a suitor. On March 2, 1878, he offers a mock-complaint: "Is there a penny post, do you think, in the world to come? Do people there write for autographs to those who have gained a little notoriety? Do women there write letters asking for money? Do boys persecute literary men with requests for a course of reading? Are there offices in that sphere which are coveted and to obtain which men are pestered to write letters of recommendation?"

On April 10, 1878, Bryant provided Leonice Moulton with an amusing description of one of his last public appearances—a "Commers" given by the German Americans of the city for the poet Bayard Taylor, who had just been appointed minister to Germany. "There were five hundred people at fifteen tables in an immense dining hall, besides the [Arian?] singers in the gallery who in the clouds of tobacco smoke which ascended from the beer drinkers below looked like the gods of Olympus, as they are sometimes seen in pictures." It was a raucous, beery affair, during which the celebrants "drank the health of the Nestor of American poets"—yet another term of tribute applied to Bryant in his later years.

For her part, Leonice Moulton was enamored of Bryant, as her fragmentary, unpublished diary confirms. Often she fills entries recording meetings with "the Poet" with hearts, cryptic notations, and provocative allusions. One entry eliciting three hearts was Bryant's visit shortly after he had turned eighty in November 1874: "An octogenarian! WB came from New York. Then went to the office and brought our mail. Fulfilled a promise! Such a walk!" Another entry warranting three hearts records a visit Leonice made to Cummington to see Bryant in September 1875: "Went with the Poet to the 'old study' in which he wrote Thanatopsis before I was born." Frequently she prevails on Bryant to recite his poetry—she mentions "The Yellow Violet," "Entrance to a Wood," "The Rivulet," "Life," "October"—during their walks together.

News of Bryant's sudden death, which she apparently received that same day, shattered Leonice Moulton. Only three weeks earlier, she had dined with the Poet. "Oh how well and cheerful he was at dinner." What "promise" had he once made to her? "Why this burning in my brain? No tears. Oh! Oh!"

Bryant had left instructions for a simple burial with no procession or public service. Julia, who along with his niece Anna Fairchild and granddaughter Minna Godwin, had been with Bryant when he died (Fanny and Parke Godwin were in France), intended to honor the wishes of her father. But John Bigelow told Julia that it was unworthy to bury "so large a personality as if he were merely a favorite horse or dog." Bryant's pastor, Henry Bellows, suggested to Julia that her father "was a public man and a private funeral would be inappropriate." Julia agreed to a compromise: there would be no procession through the streets of New York, only a public service at the family church.

Bryant's death on June 12 had been immediately reported in newspapers from New York to San Francisco. John Bigelow recalled that "the flags of the city . . . and of the shipping were raised at half-mast, his portrait was displayed in all the shop windows, and his writings were in special demand at every bookstore and library." Hours before the service on June 14 at All Soul's Unitarian Church, New Yorkers thronged the area around Fourth Avenue and Twentieth Street, struggling to catch a glimpse of the pallbearers and coffin. Police struggled to contain the crowd that pushed into the church, spilled into pews, clogged aisles, and overflowed the balcony. Almost lost in the melee were former governors Tilden and Morgan, dozens of artists and members of the press, and naturalist John Burroughs.

Also in attendance was Walt Whitman, who had just come up from West Philadelphia and felt "a strong desire to attend. I had known Mr. Bryant over thirty years ago and he had been markedly kind to me. . . . We were both walkers, and when I worked in Brooklyn he several times came over, middle afternoons, and we took rambles miles long, till dark, out toward Bedford or Flatbush, in company."

In his eulogy, Dr. Bellows captured the essence of William Cullen Bryant's life: "It is remarkable that with none of the arts of popularity a man so little dependent on others' appreciation, so self-subsistent and so retiring, who never sought or accepted office, who had little taste for cooperation, and no bustling zeal for ordinary philanthropy, should have drawn to himself the confidence, the honor of a great metropolis, and become, perhaps it is not too much to say, our first citizen."

Following the service, the Bryant family, close friends, and staff members from the *Evening Post* took a special train to Roslyn for Bryant's burial beside his wife in the local cemetery. Reverend Bellows led the mourners in prayer and recited a selection of Bryant's poems. Sunday school girls and boys—some of the same children whom Bryant invited every fall to pick pears from his orchard—threw flowers on the coffin before it was lowered into the grave.

It was a beautiful day, and the mourners must have sensed the aptness of the lines from "June" that Dr. Bellows had read at the conclusion of his eulogy at All Soul's Church. Bryant had written the lyric in 1825 in Great Barrington just before he departed, a self-described literary adventurer, for an uncertain future in Gotham. In the lyric, Bryant imagined his own death:

I gazed upon the glorious sky
  And the green mountains round,
And thought that when I came to lie
  At rest within the ground,

'Twere pleasant, that in flowery June,
When brooks send up a cheerful tune,
    And groves a joyous sound,
The sexton's hand, my grave to make,
The rich, green mountain-turf should break.

It was not Berkshire but Roslyn hills—"very cliffy" as another Long Islander, Walt Whitman, described the terrain—that now held America's first poet and citizen. Bryant had prayed for a "green" grave in "June," and half a century later Nature had rewarded him.

The editor and poet George W. Curtis, speaking at a memorial service held at the New-York Historical Society shortly after Bryant's death, echoed Cooper's sentiments from long ago—that Bryant had been the author of America. "Whoever saw Bryant," Curtis declared, "saw America." In the closing lines of "June," a young poet had longed for a modest degree of immortality—a "living voice." His impact on American literature and culture had been more than that. In the end, as Curtis observed, William Cullen Bryant—poet, publisher, and patriot, a representative democrat— "had become universally familiar, like a neighboring mountain or sea."

SOURCE NOTES

Wherever possible, I have relied on Bryant's poetry, editorials, and letters to construct the story of his life and influence on American culture in the nineteenth century. The Rare Books and Manuscripts Division of the New York Public Library is the largest repository for primary material. The six-volume edition of Bryant's letters, including valuable interstitial notes by Bryant and Voss, is another valuable source of documentation on Bryant's life and work. The biographies by Godwin and Brown also provide useful information.

ABBREVIATIONS

B   Parke Godwin. *A Biography of William Cullen Bryant*. 2 vols. New York: D. Appleton, 1883.

EP   Alan Nevins. *The Evening Post: A Century of Journalism*. New York: Boni and Liveright, 1922.

L   William Cullen Bryant II and Thomas G. Voss, eds. *The Letters of William Cullen Bryant*. 6 vols. New York: Fordham UP, 1977–1992.

NYP   *New York Post*, 1825–1878.

NYPL New York Public Library, Rare Books and Manuscripts Division.

PW   Parke Godwin, ed. *Prose Writings of William Cullen Bryant*. 2 vols. New York: D. Appleton, 1889.

WCB Charles H. Brown. *William Cullen Bryant*. New York: Charles Scribner's Sons, 1971.

Unless otherwise noted, excerpts from Bryant's poetry appear in Parke Godwin, ed., *The Poetical Works of William Cullen Bryant*. 2 vols. New York: D. Appleton, 1883.

CHAPTER 1: AMERICA'S FIRST POET

1   "In my ninth year": "An Autobiography of Mr. Bryant's Early Life," In *B*, I, 22. Hereafter referred to as *Autobiography*. Bryant composed this autobiographical fragment in 1874–1875.

1   "America's first poet": As early as 1821, an English critic, reviewing Bryant's first collection of seven poems, wrote that the young poet "stood at the head of the American Parnassus." Bryant's iconic image as America's first true poet and New York City and State's—indeed the nation's—first citizen grew during his lifetime. In the November 1831 issue of the *New England Magazine*, a reviewer declared that "by common consent" Bryant headed "the list of American poets." Poets as diverse as Poe, Whitman, and Emerson also elevated Bryant to the rank of first American poet; Cooper called him the "author of America." After his death, George William Curtis in *Harper's Monthly* wrote that Bryant had been "universally familiar, like a neighboring mountain or the sea," while Dr. Holland in *Scribner's Monthly* called Bryant "the principal citizen of the great republic."

2   Carlyle: See Thomas Carlyle's *On Heroes, Hero-Worship and the Heroic in History*, first given as a lecture series in 1839. Godwin states that Bryant read Carlyle "attentively . . . but his taste was offended by the too obvious gymnastics of Carlyle's style, and his cynical worship of force of the gunpowder kind" (*B*, I, 370).

2   Cooper: Quoted in *B*, I, 368.

2   The Bryant Building: *WCB*, 509.

2   "extremely poor stuff": Quoted in *B*, II, 402.

3   "the whole field": Ibid., 403.

3   The previous Sunday: Ibid., 402.

3   "If you knew": Ibid., 401.

4   "Image of the illustrious": Quoted in *B*, II, 403.

4   It was close to four o'clock: Bigelow, 298–300.

5   Cullen . . . was born: *Autobiography*, 2ff.

5   Cummington: *Autobiography*, 2–7; *B*, I, 38–44; *WCB*, 4–8.

6   Both sides: *B*, I, 47ff.

6   "then lived": *Autobiography*, 2.

8   "I was always": Ibid., 25.

8   "He was a passionate": Quoted in *B*, I, 203. According to Colonel Taylor, Bryant "was curious also about the antiquities of every place."

8   Ralph Waldo Emerson: Quoted in *WCB*, 468.

8   To read Bryant's strongest poems: John Hollander in his introduction to the Chelsea House edition of John Bigelow's *William Cullen Bryant* (New York, 1980) calls Bryant "our first true poet," highlighting these poems as Bryant's best: "Thanatopsis," "To a Waterfowl," "Inscription for the Entrance to a Wood," "Green River," "The Ages," "A Winter Piece," "Summer Wind," "Autumn Woods," "A Forest Hymn," "June," "To the Fringed Gentian," the sonnet to Cole, "A Scene on the Banks of the Hudson," "The Conjunction of Jupiter and Venus," "The Prairies," "Earth," "The Snow-Shower," and "A Rain-Dream" (xv).

9   A family acquaintance: Hatfield, 69.

9   According to Senator Henry Dawes: Quoted in Bigelow, 259.

9   "My health was rather delicate": *Autobiography*, 24.

9   He was frequently sick: Ibid., 5, 7, 24, 25, 31.

10   Tutored by his mother: Ibid., 4.

10   "I ought to be fond": Ibid., 5; *WCB*, 13.

10   Bryant's grandfather: Ibid., 8–11.

11   Peter Bryant: Ibid., 2–3; *B*, I, 52–57.

11   Bryant recalled: Ibid., 7, 12, 36.

11   "Reading, spelling": Ibid., 15–16.

12   "American versifiers": *B*, I, 59.

12   "I was thought": *Autobiography*, 4.

12   His first published: Ibid., 23.

12   *The Embargo*: Ibid., 28; *B*, I, 71–74; Bigelow, 15–17; *WCB*, 24–30; McLean (1989), 73–76.

13   Cullen had uncritically absorbed: *Autobiography*, 27; *WCB*, 70–71.

13   "It was decided": *Autobiography*, 28.

14   Reverend Snell: Ibid., 28–33.

14   He was now sixteen: Ibid., 34–36; *B*, I, 85–93.

14   A classmate: *B*, I, 89.

15   "He was lively": Ibid., 94–95.

15   "receive the gift": *Autobiography*, 26.

CHAPTER 2: PEDLAR OF LAW AND POETRY

17 Bryant informed: Bryant to John Avery, January 9, 1812, *L*, I, 23–24; March 27, 1812, *L*, I, 25.

18 "consisting of a blacksmith-shop": *B*, I, 105.

18 "Ward's store": Bryant to George Downes, September 19, 1814, *L*, I, 34.

18 In fact, Worthington: *L*, I, 35n2.

18 "the only entertainment": *B*, I, 105.

18 She found Bryant: *B*, I, 103.

18 In a letter: Bryant to Elisha Hubbard, August 30, 1814, *L*, I, 33.

18 "You have cost me": *B*, I, 119.

19 The town's women: Bryant to George Downes, September 19, 1814, *L*, I, 34.

19 To Hubbard: Bryant to Elisha Hubbard, August 30, 1814, *L*, I, 32–33.

19 "What are the views": Bryant to William Baylies, October 20, 1814, *L*, I, 44.

19 "It is like the polypus": Bryant to Peter Bryant, October 10, 1814, *L*, I, 39. In a lengthy draft that he decided to withhold from this letter to his father, Bryant gave several reasons justifying his decision to join the state militia.

20 "His Imbecility": Bryant to William Baylies, September 26, 1814, *L*, I, 36.

20 "almost ashamed": Bryant to Elisha Hubbard, October 12, 1814, *L*, I, 42.

20 He railed against: Bryant to William Baylies, October 19, 1814, *L*, I, 45.

20 "the people of New England": Bryant to William Baylies, December 27, 1814, *L*, I, 49.

20 For a full week: See *NYP*, February 27, 28, March 1, 1815.

20 "a pedlar of law": Bryant to Elisha Hubbard, October 12, 1814, *L*, I, 42. Bryant agonized over his impending career in law. In an October 12, 1814, letter to Baylies, he confessed that reading law books was dull business. To his friend George Downes, he complained that "the day when I shall set up my gingerbread board is to me a day of fearful expectation" (*L*, I, 56).

21 Bryant creates: See Arms, "William Cullen Bryant: A Quiet Station on Parnassus," 219–221; also McLean (1989), who comments, "the concluding stanza can be read, both literally and figuratively,

as a statement about man's moral relationship to nature *and* as a comment upon one's social obligations," 29–30.

21 *Lyrical Ballads*: *WCB*, 56, 144, 147; McLean, 12, 110.

21 innovative form: Hollander, xvii.

22 Matthew Arnold: Ibid.

22 Richard Wilbur, concurs: "A Word from Cummington," in Brodwin, 32.

22 Ivor Winters called: Richard Elman states, "With Winters you never really knew if he really believed 'Thanatopsis' was the only truly great poem of the first half of the nineteenth century, or if that was a way of telling his scholarly and critical friends in American studies et cetera that they wouldn't know their own toe if they were eating it" (Brodwin, 58). The author, who also took Winters's course in American poetry at Stanford University, found the critic to be serious on the subject of Bryant's excellence as a poet—even as he disparaged Poe, Emerson, Whitman, and other of Bryant's contemporaries.

22 Years afterward: Godwin, *Poetical Works*, I, 329–330.

24 Dr. Bryant discovered: *B*, I, 149–152.

24 He was admitted: *L*, I, 62.

24 "You ask whether": Bryant to William Baylies, May 27, 1817, *L*, I, 71.

24 Earlier . . . while studying: Bryant to Jacob Porter, *L*, I, 28.

25 Baylies admonished him: Baylies to Bryant, January 24, 1816, *NYPL*.

25 "I had never before seen": *B*, I, 145.

25 "This is a pretty little village": Bryant to William Baylies, January 25, 1817, *L*, I, 65.

25 "I knew thee fair": *B*, I, 114.

26 In an unpublished memoir: July 31, 1866, *NYPL*.

26 "It is so long": Bryant to Frances Fairchild, March 31, 1817, *L*, I, 68.

27 Bryant's new association: *B*, I, 150.

27 In October 1817: Bryant to Willard Phillips, *L*, I, 75. Bryant knew Phillips from their childhood in Cummington. In a letter to Richard Henry Dana in September 1873 following the death of Phillips, Bryant observed: "To me he was particularly kind—unconsciously so as it seemed; it was apparently a kindness which he could not help."

27 Phillips in turn: *B*, I, 153. Willard Phillips to Bryant, February 14, 1818, *NYPL*.

27   "most of the American poets": Bryant to Peter Bryant, February 20, 1818, *L*, I, 80.

27   "We make": "Early American Verse," in *PW*, I, 46ff. See also Bigelow, 45–49.

28   "Mr. Brown has fallen": *North American Review* 7 (July 1818), 211.

28   "I doubt not": Channing to Bryant, September 3, 1819, *L*, I, 87n2.

28   "On the Use of Trisyllabic Feet": This essay appeared in the September 1819 issue of the *North American Review*. Reprinted in *PW*, I, 57–67. Bryant's essay is a seminal document in American literary criticism—the first to argue for substitution and metrical variation in iambic verse. Bryant cites Shakespeare, Spenser, Milton, and Dryden among the older English poets employing trisyllabic feet; among the newer poets, he singles out Cowper (especially "The Task").

28   "On the Happy Temperament": *North American Review* (June 1819). See *L*, I, 90n2.

28   his father's condition: *B*, I, 161–162.

28   He wrote to his sister: *L*, I, 91n2.

28   Sarah wrote to Charity: Ibid.

29   Writing to his Aunt Charity: Bryant to Charity Bryant, March 21, 1820, *L*, I, 91.

29   "a man so upright": Ibid.

30   he had written: Bryant to Peter Bryant, June 20, 1818, *L*, I, 84.

30   He was elected: *B*, I, 159.

30   For the July 4, 1820, celebration: Ibid., 164–165. William Pitt Palmer, who attended the event, recalled Bryant in an 1858 note quoted by Godwin: "It was the first time I ever saw the poet. He spoke from the pulpit of the Old Church; his delivery was modest and graceful. I got a position in the gallery near the speaker, and have not yet forgotten how fine, large, and prominent his forehead appeared to me under the brown locks that curled around it. He was already looked upon as a person of unusual literary attainments—one of the first botanists of Berkshire, one of the best classical scholars in all Massachusetts, and a poet *facile princeps* on this side of the Atlantic."

30   In a letter: Bryant to Henry D. Sewall, November 1, 1820, *L*, I, 96.

31   On January 11: *WCB*, 94–95.

31   "I hasten to communicate": Bryant to Sarah S. Bryant, January 16, 1821, *L*, I, 97.

31   "a long letter": Bryant to Sarah S. Bryant, February 4, 1821, *L*, I, 98–101.
31   "young women": *B*, I, 170.
32   "he was in health": *L*, I, 101n3.
32   By unanimous vote: *B*, I, 170.
32   a delightful letter: Bryant to Frances Bryant, August 25, 1821, *L*, I, 107–110.
33   tea at Waltham House: Ibid.
33   At noon: *B*, I, 173–175.
34   One listener: *B*, I, 175; *L*, I, 109–110n6.
34   Dana saw *Poems*: *B*, I, 175–177.
34   "Green River": Bryant apparently had written this poem at Great Barrington in 1819.
36   he had started to question: *B*, I, 182–187.
36   Phillips had hailed Bryant: Ibid., 178.
36   Verplanck: Ibid.
36   in England: Ibid., 180.

CHAPTER 3: THE DELECTABLE CITY OF GOTHAM

37   His dislike: *B*, I, 201–202; Bigelow, 38–39; *WCB*, 120–122.
37   "pure republican equality": Quoted in Wilentz, *Chants Democratic*, 61.
38   Henry and Robert Sedgwick: Henry Sedgwick to Bryant, March 20, 1824, *NYPL*.
38   He had known: *WCB*, 92–93.
38   In a memoir: *B*, I, 184.
38   He composed: In old age, Catharine Sedgwick wrote to Bryant, recalling "the day when the young poet, one of the first objects of my hero-worship, offered me in my dear home the six hymns; and but boring you, I would have described the color and form of his cloak, and the fire and countenance of his expression, but—." Quoted in *B*, I, 163–164.
38   American novelists: *WCB*, 119–120.
39   "Mr. Cooper": Bryant to Frances F. Bryant, April 29, 1824, *L*, I, 154.
39   Years later: See "James Fenimore Cooper," in *PW*, 299–331.
39   Despite bad spring weather: Bryant to Frances F. Bryant, April 29, 1824, *L*, I, 154.

39   "Every muscle": *WCB*, 112.

40   "fixed . . . beggarly profession": Bryant to Charles Sedgwick, December 24, 1824, Ibid., 146.

40   Dana encouraged his: *B*, 196.

40   "My residence": Bryant to Richard Dana, May 25, 1825, *L*, I, 184.

40   His law practice: *B*, I, 124–125. See also Bryant to Charles Sedgwick, November 24: "The law is a hag, I know, wearing the wrinkled visage of antiquity, toward which you can feel no complacency."

40   Bryant's state of mind: *WCB*, 113–114.

40   "Next to": Bryant to Sarah S. Bryant, September 8, 1817, *L*, I, 73.

40   inviting her to visit him: Bryant to Sarah S. Bryant, May 5, 1821, Ibid., 104–105.

41   Edgar Allan Poe: *WCB*, 114.

41   one of twenty-three poems: Between 1824 and 1825, Bryant wrote several strong poems while under contract with the *United States Literary Gazette*, among them "The Rivulet," "March," "Summer Wind," "Mutation," "Monument Mountain," "Autumn Woods," "November," "The Greek Partisan," and "A Forest Hymn."

41   If you can confer on me": Parsons to Bryant, December 19, 1823, *L*, I, 149n2. Bryant supplied Parsons with a "cargo of verse" on one occasion (156).

42   Wordsworth's "Tintern Abbey": McLean writes of Bryant: "He must have been aware, of course, of Wordsworth's successful use of reminiscence in 'Tintern Abbey' and other poems, and thus he cannot be considered, even in his early blank verse, as an innovator" (1989, 126). Gulian Verplanck, in his review of *Poems* (1821) for the New York *American* on October 4, 1821, was the first to detect a Wordsworthian strain in Bryant's poetry.

42   Bryant made a second trip: *WCB*, 123.

42   "To a Discontented Friend": Bryant to Elisha Hubbard, December 1, 1814, *L*, I, 46–47.

43   "I have got here": Bryant to Frances F. Bryant, February 18, 1825, Ibid., 173.

43   City Hotel: Burroughs and Wallace, 340.

43   "My friends here": Bryant to Frances F. Bryant, February 21, 1825, *L*, I, 174.

44   He told Frances: Bryant to Frances F. Bryant, March 23, 1825, Ibid., 176.

44   "At all events": Bryant to Frances F. Bryant, February 21, 1825, Ibid., 174.

44   With the support: *WCB*, 124–128.

44   "literary adventurer": *B*, I, 206.

45   the president . . . asserted: See Burns, 249–254.

45   "this beggarly profession": Bryant to Charles Sedgwick, December 21, 1824, *L*, I, 166.

46   "hobbledehoy metropolis": *B*, I, 206–208; *WCB*, 138. For a useful history of New York City during Bryant's early years there, see Burroughs and Wallace, 428–508.

46   "There was a crowd": Bryant to Frances F. Bryant, March 23, 1825, *L*, I, 176.

47   "We took lodgings": *WCB*, 139–140.

47   "at some distance": Bryant to Frances F. Bryant, May 24, June 3, 12, 20, 1825; *L*, I, 179–180, 186–187; 190–191; 192–193.

47   "I went yesterday": Ibid., 179.

48   "On the whole": Ibid., 187.

48   "the heat": Ibid., 192.

48   "Within the city": *B*, I, 207.

48   "To the Curious": *EP*, 63ff.

48   "I envy you": Bryant to Frances F. Bryant, *L*, I, June 12, 1825, 190.

49   "The space covered": Bigelow, 323–324.

49   Commissioners' Plan: Voorsanger and Howat, 7–10.

50   Bryant had learned something: *B*, I, 184–185.

51   "the fashionable lounge": Voorsanger and Howat, 32.

51   "This week": Bryant to Frances F. Bryant, June 3, 1825, *L*, I, 187.

51   Five Points: Burroughs and Wallace, 475–479.

52   "The business": Bryant to Richard H. Dana, May 25, 1825, *L*, I, 184.

52   In a rare moment: *WCB*, 136–137. See also Foshay and Novak, passim.

53   Berkshires neighbors: *B*, I, 202–204.

54   "I yesterday received": Bryant to George Bancroft, June 28, 1825, *L*, I, 193–194.

55   "The weather": Bryant to Frances F. Bryant, September 19, 1825, Ibid., 199.

55   Bread and Cheese Club: *WCB*, 136; Burroughs and Wallace, 469–470.

55 Bryant ran into Cooper: Wilson, 45.
56 Bryant's Lunch companions: *L*, I, 181–182. See also Callow, passim, for a detailed history of Bread and Cheese and its successor, the Sketch Club.
57 Paulding: Brooks, 193–195.
57 With friendships cemented: *WCB*, 137, 144; Voorsanger and Howat, 56–57, 60–92 passim.
57 Erie Canal: Burroughs and Wallace, 42–21, 429–431.

CHAPTER 4: APPRENTICE EDITOR

59 "If I keep to it": *WCB*, 141.
59 discourses: See "Lectures on Poetry," *PW*, I, 3–44.
60 William Coleman: On Coleman see *EP*, 14–34, 39–76, 101–105, 112–120, 133–134.
61 "The establishment": Bryant to Frances F. Bryant, August 2, 1826, *L*, I, 209.
61 Hamilton: *EP*, 9–34.
62 turbulent 1820s: For a concise analysis of the 1824 election, see Wilentz (2005), 240–253.
62 Coleman had endorsed: *EP*, 124.
63 "The Conjunction of Jupiter and Venus": See also McLean (1989), 80–81, 89.
64 "We now have": *NYP*, January 4, 1827.
64 "The watch": Ibid., January 11, 1827.
65 *Index Expurgatorius*: *EP*, 348. Bigelow writes: "Though he neither sought nor expected fame from his prose, he was careful to print nothing that could in any way compromise his reputation as a poet. As a consequence, in all his contributions to his paper, I doubt if as many erroneous or defective forms of expression can be found as in the first ten numbers of the 'Spectator'" (73).
65 "I drudge": Bryant to Richard H. Dana, June 1, 1827, *L*, I, 241.
66 "neglect of the public welfare": *NYP*, February 3, 1827.
66 "full make": in Bigelow, "Reminiscences of the Evening Post," 312–313.
67 One of his favorite books: *Autobiography*, 24–25, 32–33.
67 address to the Greek Meeting: *NYPL*.
68 poetry . . . on the Greek question: See also McLean (1989), 68, 79.
68 free trade: Spann (1972), 42–44.

69   "The members of Congress": *NYP*, February 12, 1827.

70   Bryant reminded: *EP*, 130.

70   Van Buren: Ibid.

70   "I am a small proprietor": Bryant to Richard H. Dana, February 16, 1828, *L*, I, 262.

70   Meeting at: *B*, I, 236–241.

70   "A Scene on the Banks of the Hudson" appeared originally in the *United States Review*, to which Bryant also contributed "October," "The Damsel of Peru," "The African Chief," "The Gladness of Nature," "The Greek Partisan," "The Two Graves," and "The Conjunction of Jupiter and Venus." Bryant confessed to one of his brothers that these poems were composed when he was greatly overworked; he wanted to omit them from his edition of 1832, but friends prevailed on him to include them (*B*, I, 233).

72   "Reminiscences of New York": *B*, I, 240–241; *WCB*, 165.

73   the Salazars: *WCB*, 140.

73   Ferdinand Field, *B*, I, 366.

74   *Hope Leslie*: *NYP*, June 19, 1827.

74   New York Theatre: *EP*, 111–120,

74   Edwin Forrest: *WCB*, 228–229, 353–354.

75   da Ponte: *WCB*, 135, 139, 167, 230.

75   "There are three classes": Bryant to Richard H. Dana, March 10, 1827, *L*, I, 232.

CHAPTER 5: JACKSON DEMOCRAT

77   "never having": Letter to the Editor, July 10, 1827; see *L*, I, 247.

78   "not remarkable": *NYP*, August 10, 1827.

78   Bryant also offered: *L*, I, 264n1.

79   Writing to Bryant, Verplanck: Ibid.

79   Fanny Wright: *WCB*, 176–177, 180, 220; Wilentz (2005), 313, 314, 352–353. See also Celia Morris Eckhardt, *Fanny Wright: Rebel in America* (Cambridge: Harvard UP, 1984).

80   "Suppose the singular spectacle": *NYP*, January 26, 1829.

81   "passed for Halleck's": Bryant to Guilian C. Verplanck, January 27, 1829, *L*, I, 273. Bigelow relates that Halleck denied authorship of the "Ode to Miss Frances Wright": "There is but one man in New York who could have written it, and that is Bryant" (*L*, I, 239n).

81   "she possessed herself": Kaplan, 57.
82   "acuteness in controversy": Quoted in *WCB*, 173–174.
83   In his series: See Lectures One and Two, *PW*, I, 3–24.
83   "large and comprehensive views": *NYP*, November 3, 1836.
83   Leggett had been court-martialed: *WCB*, 174–175.
83   "I like Leggett": Bryant to Frances F. Bryant, August 5, 1829, *L*, I, 280.
84   "In person": *New-York Mirror*, January 29, 1828; quoted in *WCB*, 167.
84   Sketch Club: For a comprehensive treatment of Bryant and the Sketch Club, see Callow, passim.
86   "Sonnet—To Cole": The poem appeared originally in the *Talisman* for 1829. Bryant delivered a eulogy for his friend, published as *A Funeral Oration, Occasioned by the Death of Thomas Cole* (New York, 1848). For a useful treatment of the Bryant, Cole, and Durand friendships, see Foshay and Novak.
87   "expose the robbery": Bryant to Gulian C. Verplanck, December 24, 1829, *L*, I, 283.
87   "The President's message": Bryant to Gulian C. Verplanck, December 15, 1829, *L*, I, 282.
88   "the vocation": *B*, I, 253.
88   Jackson's plan: For a comprehensive treatment of Jackson's policies, see Remini; for Bryant's views on Native Americans, see Ostrowski.
89   "Congress should set aside": *NYP*, January 4, 1830.
89   "universally commended": *NYP*, April 30, 1830.
90   "You see": Bryant to Richard H. Dana, September 15, 1821, *L*, I, 111.
90   "The nature": *NYP*, January 9, 1830.
91   "To General Jackson": *NYP*, May 28; February 26, 1831.

CHAPTER 6: YANKEE BRAWLS

93   "While I was shaving": *WCB*, 185–187; *L*, I, 303.
93   Bryant's fight with Stone: *EP*: 154–162; Hale, 21–23.
94   "vilest verbal attacks": Ibid.
94   in a lighthearted editorial: *WCB*, 185–187.
95   "On arriving opposite": *NYP*, April 21, 1831.
95   "Another year": *NYP*, January 2, 1830.

96   "The great city": Bryant to Richard H. Dana, April 17, 1830, *L*, I, 292.

96   "This patronage": *NYP*, January 9, 1830.

97   "a class of highly respectable citizens": *NYP*, January 25; March 6, 1830.

97   Bolívar: *NYP*, June 24, 1830.

97   "A dancing scene": *NYP*, May 1, 1830.

97   "Those passages": *NYP*, June 14, 1830.

97   "The metaphysics of Coleridge": *NYP*, February 12, 1831.

98   "The Buckwheat Cake": *NYP*, December 16, 1830.

99   Workingmen's Party: Spann (1972), 49–50; Burroughs and Wallace, 521–526; Wilentz (2005), 354–358.

99   "bee in a tar barrel": *NYP*, March 25, 1831.

100   "Call a rose": *NYP*, February 3, 1831.

100   "the candidate": *NYP*, July 26, September 2, 1831.

100   the rebellion of Nat Turner: *NYP*, August 27, September 20, 1831.

101   Not feeling well: Bryant to Frances F. Bryant, August 21, 1831, *L*, I, 307.

102   "a landed proprietor": Bryant to John Howard Bryant, November 21, 1831, *L*, I, 308–309.

102   His reputation: *L*, I, 304.

102   *Poems* appeared: *B*, I, 264–280; *WCB*, 190–196.

102   Emerson: *B*, I, 355.

103   Whittier: Quoted in *WCB*, 191.

103   Clay: *NYP*, January 14, 1832; Spann (1972), 51–53.

104   Bryant and Irving: *B*, I, 264–276; *L*, I, 311, 327.

104   "by land": Bryant to Frances F. Bryant, January 22, 1832, *L*, I, 313–314.

105   "lamentable tragedy": *NYP*, January 17, 30, 1832.

106   "a shabby place": Bryant to Frances F. Bryant, January 22, 23, 29, 1832; to John Howard Bryant, February 19, 1832, *L*, I, 313–320.

106   "the great center": *NYP*, March 14, 16; April 18, 24, 26, 28, 1832.

107   "to shake off the bile": Bryant to Richard H. Dana, April 9, 1832, *L*, I, 325.

107   "The season": *NYP*, April 18, 1832.

108   "Yesterday they got Mr. Burton": Bryant to Frances F. Bryant, June 28, 1832, *L*, I, 353. For extensive coverage of this trip, see Bryant's additional letters to his wife (329–355).

108   "Shall I confess": Ibid., June 12, 1828, *L*, I, 343.

109   "The appearance": Ibid., May 31, 1832, *L*, I, 334.

109   Amos Eaton: *B*, I, 165, 203; McDowell (1935), xxxiv; *L*, I, 105, n.2.

109   "I carry my plunder": Bryant to Frances F. Bryant, June 12, 1832, *L*, I, 343–344.

110   "These prairies": Bryant to Richard H. Dana, October 8, 1832, *L*, I, 360.

110   "What I have thought": *PW*, II, 22. Somewhat altered, Bryant's correspondence on his trip to the West appears here under the title "Illinois Fifty Years Ago" (3–22).

110   "The Prairies" first appeared in *Knickerbocker Magazine* in 1833. See Miller (227–232), Dahl (178–190), and McLean (1989, 23–26) for background and criticism.

111   "well-filled stagecoaches": quoted in *WCB*, 208.

111   "the cholera": Bryant to the Editor, October 30, 1832, *L*, I, 262. For background on the 1832 cholera epidemic, see Burroughs and Wallace, 589–594.

111   "witnessing": Bryant to Richard H. Dana, October 8, 1832, *L*, I, 359.

112   "The absence": *NYP*, July 23, 1832.

112   "It is to be hoped": *NYP*, August 10, 1832.

112   "mighty pecuniary institution": *NYP*, August 12, 1932.

112   Bank War: Spann (1972), 57–62; Wilentz (2005), 392–401.

113   Tocqueville: See *Democracy in America*, II, 408. Reviewing the first United States edition of the book on June 2, 1838, the *Evening Post* writes, "De Tocqueville appears to have had a clearer insight into the nature and peculiarities of our institutions, and their effect upon society, than any other foreigner who has written of this country."

114   *Tales of the Glauber Spa*: *B*, I, 286–287; *WCB*, 209–210.

114   "mountains and clouds": *WCB*, 212.

114   "a mere *party hack*": *WCB*, 211–212.

115   "a small party of enthusiasts": *NYP*, April 25, 1833.

116   "We have strong doubts": *NYP*, August 7, 1833.

117   The turbulence: *NYP*, April 12, May 31, June 5, 12, 13, July 26–31, August 15, 1833; *WCB*, 213–224.

117   "Did you not see": Bryant to Gulian Verplanck, [ca] January 1834, *L*, I, 391.

118   "the domineering spirit": *NYP*, February 11, 1834.

118   "the rich against the poor": *WCB*, 221.

118   "I am sick": Bryant to Richard H. Dana, April 22, 1834, *L*, I, 401.

CHAPTER 7: MY NATIVE COUNTRY

119   "literary enterprise": Bryant to Richard H. Dana, April 22, 1834, *L*, I, 402.

120   "suffered unmercifully": Frances Bryant, *Diary*, *NYPL*; see *L*, I, 413n2.

120   "Sea smooth and fair": Bryant, *Diary*, *NYPL*. Both Bryant and his wife kept diaries during their stay in Europe.

121   "the traces": Bryant to John Rand, July 20, 1834, *L*, I, 414.

121   Provençal poets: "Nostradamus's Provencal Poets," *PW*, I, 68–92.

121   "make love": Bryant to Thatcher T. Payne, August 9, 1834, *L*, I, 417.

122   "Monotonous plains": To the *Evening Post*, September 27, 1834; published in *Evening Post* for November 24, 1834. Six of seven letters that Bryant wrote for the *Post* were reprinted in revised form in *Letters of a Traveler*.

122   "I found": Ibid.

122   "I think": Ibid.

123   "as indolent": Bryant to William Ware, October 11, 1834, *L*, I, 422.

123   "Cole's fine little landscape": Ibid.

124   "I am tempted": Bryant to Julia Sands, October 12, 1834, *L*, I, 427–428.

125   "We had our apartments": Frances Bryant to Eliza Robbins, December 10, 1834, *L*, I, 134n2.

125   "the very seat": To the *Evening Post*, December 11, 1834. Published in the *Evening Post* for January 27, 1835, *L*, I, 430.

125   "I have my lodgings": Bryant to Austin Bryant, February 24, 1835, *L*, I, 436.

125   Before his departure: Ibid., 409, 429n1.

126   "My *labours*": Bryant to Horatio Greenough, February 27, 1835, *L*, I, 440.

127   Poe: *WCB*, 244.

128   "I cannot help": Bryant to Austin Bryant, February 24, 1835, *L*, I, 437.

129   "It is a magnificent": Bryant to William Leggett, April 15, 1835, *L*, I, 445.

129   "I have strolled": Bryant to William Leggett, June 12, 1835, *L*, I, 447.

129   "populous": Bryant to Julia Sands, September 7, 1835, *L*, I, 464.
129   "In Sardinia": Bryant to William Leggett, June 12, 1835, *L*, I, 447.
129   "a city which": Bryant to William Leggett, August 6, 1835, *L*, I, 451.
130   "I was glad": Bryant to William Ware, September 14, 1835, *L*, I, 465.
130   "climbed and crossed": Bryant to William Leggett, August 6, 1835, *L*, I, 451.
130   "glad to repose": Bryant to Susan Renner, September 7, 1835, *L*, I, 457.
130   Bryant and Longfellow: *WCB*, 143–144, 230–231; *L*, I, 478–479n2.
131   At first: *B*, I, 172–173; *WCB*, 231–232.
131   "the greater part": Bryant to Frances F. Bryant, April 1, 1836, *L*, I, 483–484.
132   Bryant's friends: *B*, I, 312–313; *L*, I, 486nn1,2; letter to Frances Bryant, April 14, 1836, *L*, II, 10.

CHAPTER 8: LEGGETT'S LEGACY

133   Leggett had alienated: *B*, I, 332–333; *WCB*, 232–237; Spann (1972), 157–158.
134   Loco Focos: Wilentz (2005), 421–423; Burrows and Wallace, 609, 610, 613.
135   "But when Congress": *NYP*, April 5, 1836.
135   "I found New York": Bryant to Frances F. Bryant, April 14, 1836, *L*, II, 10–11.
135   "You cannot think": Bryant to Frances F. Bryant, May 23, 1836, *L*, II, 24.
136   "Can you oblige": Bryant to Robert W. Weir, May 17, 1836, *L*, II, 20.
136   "Mr. Bryant's poetical reputation": Quoted in *WCB*, 244–245.
136   He read: Bryant to Frances F. Bryant, July 20, 1836, *L*, II, 44–45.
137   "monstrous doctrine": *NYP*, May 26, 31; July 7, 1836.
138   "Can any one": *NYP*, July 2, 1836.
138   "They were condemned": *NYP*, June 13, 1836.
138   ridiculed the Albany *Argus*, *NYP*, August 10, 1836.
139   It would be better: *NYP*, May 24, 1836.
139   In June: *NYP*, June 3, 1836.
139   "We are resolved": *NYP*, August 8, 1836.

139   the Whigs: Burroughs and Wallace, 573–575, 608–609, 614–615.
140   "Who stirred up": *NYP*, November 30, 1836.
140   "incapacity": *NYP*, August 27, 1836.
141   "When will the bubble burst?": *NYP*, April 7, 1836.
141   "financial storm": *NYP*, October 24, 1836.
141   Bryant and Simms: *Letters of William Gilmore Simms*, I, 109–113.
142   "The readers": *NYP*, November 3, 1836.
142   Bryant, Irving, and Leggett: *B*, I, 342–344; Bigelow (1909–13), 138, 182; *WCB*, 245.
143   "He was of middle age": *B*, I, 334.
144   Panic of 1837, riots: *NYP*, February 14, 16, 1837; *B*, I, 347–348; *WCB*, 248–249; Burroughs and Wallace, 611–614.
145   "the affairs": Bryant to Richard H. Dana, February 27, 1827, *L*, II, 64.
145   Bryant and Aaron Clark: *NYP*, June 17, 26, 1837.
145   "The states' rights party": *NYP*, June 29, 1837.
146   Calhoun: *NYP*, September 20, 1837.
146   Texas project: *NYP*, August 4, 1837.
146   "noisy and agitated": Bryant to William Ware, May 29, 1837, *L*, II, 71.
146   "atrocious violence": *NYP*, November 18, 1837.
147   "liberty of the press": Bryant to an unidentified correspondent, December 16, 1837, *L*, II, 95; Wiltse, 167–170.
147   "Over all the world": *NYP*, December 30, 1837.
147   deeply in debt: Bryant to John Rand, August 13, 1838, *L*, II, 100. "Do you not think that fewer ill natured speeches are made about you than about the editor of a principal democratic newspaper in the first city of America?"
147   "You cannot": Frances Bryant to Mrs. Ware: *B*, I, 357.
147   "To keep myself": Bryant to Richard H. Dana, June 28, 1838, *L*, II, 97.
148   "I had taken": Dana to Bryant, *B*, I, 364.
148   "I saw Bryant": Emerson to Margaret Fuller, May 4, 1838, II, 128–130.
148   Bryant's friends: *NYP*, April 13, 25, 1838; *WCB*, 253–255; *L*, II, 9n4, 5.
149   Beggars: *NYP*, May 11, July 18, 1838.
149   "blank verse": *NYP*, July 10, 1838.
149   Whittier and Simms: *NYP*, December 14, 22, 1838.
150   memory of a dead dog: *NYP*, July 31, 1838.

150   "to write more": Bryant to William Ware, September 19, 1838, *L*, II, 105.

150   "The sky": Bryant to Cyrus Bryant, January 8, 1839, *L*, II, 112.

150   New York press: *EP*, 154–163.

151   Catlin and Cooper: *NYP*, January 11, February 19, 1839.

151   "monstrous corruption": *NYP*, March 1839.

151   city election: *NYP*, April 12, 1839.

152   uncollected ode: *NYP*, May 1, 1839.

153   Leggett: *WCB*, 252–253; *L*, II, 108, 117–118.

153   "I write in behalf": Bryant to Martin Van Buren, April 27, 1839, *L*, II, 116.

153   Leggett's death: *L*, II, 118n2.

CHAPTER 9: POLITICS AND POETRY

157   *Amistad* affair: *NYP*, September 4, 5, 11, November 15, 1839; January 9, 10, 15, 1840; Wilentz (2005), 473–479, 521–522.

161   Audubon: *NYP*, September 30, October 21, 1839.

162   "Pauperism and mendacity": *NYP*, February 14, 1840.

162   "It is a class": *NYP*, January 9, 1840.

163   Bryant on Harrison: *NYP*, December 14, 1839, February 27, March 13, May 6, September 3, November 9, 10, 1840.

164   When Harrison died: *NYP*, April 5, 1841; *WCB*, 267.

164   "Departed this life": *NYP*, August 7, 1841.

165   "There is a valley": Thomas Cole to Bryant, June 15, 1840, quoted in *L*, II, 134n4.

165   "over scenes": Bryant, *A Funeral Oration*, 14.

166   "a grand mountain ridge": Quoted in Foshay and Novak, 26–27. For the connections between Cole, Bryant, and Durand, see Foshay and Novak; also Callow, 62–69.

166   "It is situated": Bryant to Richard H. Dana, September 12, 1840, *L*, II, 135.

167   another trip: Bryant to Frances F. Bryant, August 6, 1840, *L*, II, 133.

167   When Dana: *B*, I, 376. Godwin writes: "thus the four most famous poets that our literature had yet produced were brought together, and their conversations, we may well suppose, if they could have been reported, would have added a lively chapter to the best chronicles of table-talk."

167 "I like the book" Bryant to Richard H. Dana, June 24, 1839, *L*, II, 119.
168 *Selections from the American Poets*: *WCB*, 263–264.
168 trip to Illinois: *B*, I, 386–387; *WCB*, 268–269; *L*, II, 146–154.
170 John Hughes: Burroughs and Wallace, 629–633.
171 Dickens: *B*, I, 394–398; *EP*, 209–214; *WCB*, 273–274.
173 "I am thinking": Bryant to John Bryant, November 23, 1841, *L*, II, 166.
173 *The Fountain*: *WCB*, 280–282; McLean, 82–85, 125–127; *L*, II, 194–195n1.
175 "You gave": Bryant to Richard H. Dana, June 1, 1842, *L*, II, 176.
175 A month after: *WCB*, 277–279.
176 "to leave": *NYP*, August 12, 1839.
176 Cedarmere: *B*, I, 406, 408–409.
177 travels in the South: *NYP*, March 14, April 12, May 4, May 23, 30, 1843; reprinted in *Letters of a Traveler*, I.
178 "I remember": Bryant to William Gilmore Simms, February 9, 1844, *L*, II, 257.

CHAPTER 10: AMONG THE FIRST IN THE WORLD

179 "I place": Quoted in Spann (1972), 119.
180 Cooper and New York press: Ibid.
180 "every body allows": Bryant to Richard H. Dana, January 16, 1844, *L*, II, 255.
180 Polk: *WCB*, 240.
181 "Would that I": Bryant to Ferdinand Field, September 1844, *L*, II, 281.
181 Bryant told: Bryant to Frances F. Bryant, April 23, 24, 27, 1845, *L*, II, 302–305.
182 "To leave": Bryant to Frances F. Bryant, May 26, 1845, *L*, II, 307.
182 letters to the *Evening Post*: Bryant's letters appeared on June 20; July 5, 7, 22; August 1, 19, 20; September 11, 13, 16; and November 5. Save for the October 21 letter, they were reprinted in *Letters of a Traveler*, I, 144–240.
182 American writers in Europe: See Stowe, Mulvey.
183 "non-existence of literature": see Martineau, *Society in America*, 206, 314–315.

183   "We have been all looking": *Foreign Quarterly Review*, January 1844, 414–415.

184   "your sultry summers": *NYP*, July 22, 1845.

184   "a deficiency": *NYP*, May 10, 1833.

184   "saw nothing in it": To the *Evening Post*, June 18, 1845, *L*, II, 327. Bryant was far more impressed by an illustration he found in a print shop of the *Greek Slave*, a new statue by the American sculptor Hiram Powers that would cause an international sensation: "The statue represents a Greek girl exposed naked for sale in the slave-market. Her hands are fettered, the drapery of her nation lies at her feet, and she is shrinking from the public gaze. I looked at it with surprise and delight."

185   "to get a peep": Bryant to Frances F. Bryant, July 2, 1845, *L*, II, 333.

185   propose a toast: Ibid., 339*n17*.

185   Wordsworth: *B*, II, 8–9; *WCB*, 308–309.

186   Wordsworth "in the garden": Bryant to Frances F. Bryant, July 8, 1845, *L*, II, 343.

186   "among those we liked best": *L*, II, 348n16.

186   "full of life": Bryant to Frances F. Bryant, Ibid.

187   "If I had five minutes": Ibid.

187   "The streets": Bryant to Frances F. Bryant, August 5, 1845, *L*, II, 381.

188   "zig zagging": To the *Evening Post*, September 12, 1845, *L*, II, 396.

189   "decidedly bad": Bryant to Frances F. Bryant, October 5, 1845, *L*, II, 411.

189   "I certainly did intend": Bryant to Charles Elbert Anderson, October 1, 1845, *L*, II, 406. See Ibid., n3.

189   "dragging heavily": Bryant to Frances F. Bryant, October 5, 1845, *L*, II, 408.

189   "My heart yearned": Bryant to Richard H. Dana, December 4, 1845, *L*, II, 416.

190   "Amidst a thousand": Bryant to Frances F. Bryant, November 27, 1845, *L*, II, 414.

190   Texas and Oregon question: *EP*, 175–179; *WCB*, 314, 316; Spann, 161–164.

191   "Oh Mother of a Mighty Race": published in *Graham's Magazine*, July, 1847. Other lyrics commissioned by *Graham's*, including "The Stream of Life," "The Unknown Way," and "The Land

of Dreams," intimate at Bryant's forebodings over the problems facing the nation.

192 "an English cheap edition": Bryant to Richard H. Dana, January 13, 1846, *L*, II, 423.

192 Dana apparently read: *B*, II, 14–15.

192 "Such nonsense": Bryant to Richard H. Dana, April 6, 1846, *L*, II, 428.

192 "Let me say": *B*, II, 15–16.

192 seemed "more beautiful": Bryant to Henry W. Longfellow, January 31, 1846, *L*, II, 427.

193 "In return": Longfellow to Bryant, February 5, 1846, NYPL.

193 "I think very well": Bryant to Richard H. Dana, September 26, 1846, *L*, II, 473.

194 Central to the editor's creed: *L*, II, 420.

194 "It is an honor": Quoted in *L*, II, 471–472n9.

194 "a prodigious army": *NYP*, May 13, 1846.

194 "such demonstrations": *EP*, 179.

195 Whitman: Quoted in Kaplan, 130.

195 Illinois: *B*, II, 18–19; *WCB*, 322–325; *NYP*, August 1, 11, 13, 15, 24, 25, 27, 1846; *Letters of a Traveler*, 241–302.

196 Poe: *WCB*, 320–322; Bryant to Frances F. Bryant, September 14, 1846, *L*, II, 469.

196 "when they talked": *B*, II, 22n.

198 "The three things": Bigelow (1909–13), 291–292.

CHAPTER 11: KINDRED SPIRITS

199 Wilmot Proviso: See Wilentz, *Rise of American Democracy*, 596–601, 605–610, 623–628, 630–632.

200 "Slavery in California": *NYP*, January 25, 1847.

200 "We thank Mr. Calhoun": Quoted in *WCB*, 331.

200 "A man who": *NYP*, March 30, 1847.

201 Godwin: Spann (1972), 149–151; *WCB*, 329; *L*, II, 497n2.

201 Bigelow: *WCB*, 329.

201 "blameless and useful": Bryant to Charity Bryant, May 18, 1847, *L*, II, 495.

202 "Your praise": Bryant to an Unidentified Correspondent, November 27, 1847, *L*, II, 510.

202   "No man pledged": Bryant to John Bryant, February 7, 1848, *L*, II, 516.

202   Democratic Convention: Nevins (1947), II, 192, 195, 201.

202   "spurious": *NYP*, June 1, 1848.

203   conventions: *WCB*, 342–343; Spann (1972), 166–171; *L*, II, 514.

204   "Ever since meeting": Bigelow, *Retrospections*, I, 91.

204   "rooted up": *NYP*, April 24, 1848.

204   "Our leveling": Bryant to Ferdinand E. Field, May 31, 1848, *L*, II, 527.

205   various editorials: see *NYP*, September 30, 1830, November 21, December 18, 1839.

205   "Seating himself": Quoted in *L*, II, 528n3.

205   death of Cole: "A Funeral Oration"; *B*, II, 34–35.

205   "the most genial": Quoted in *L*, II, 534n2.

205   social life: *WCB*, 274–278.

206   Homoeopathic Society: Bryant had been a subscriber to homoeo-pathic medicine since the mid-1830s. When doctors practicing the Hahnemann method founded the Homoeopathic Society of New York Physicians on December 23, 1841, they elected Bryant as the organization's first president. See William Cullen Bryant, *Popular Considerations of Homoeopathia. Delivered Before the New York Homoeopathic Society, December 23, 1841.*

206   typical evening: Bryant to Frances F. Bryant, September 5, 1848, *L*, II, 529.

206   friends in the art world: Foshay and Novak, 31–32; Pinto (1981), 4–10; *L*, II, 515.

207   *Kindred Spirits*: Foshay and Novak, 11–12; *L*, II, 515, also Bryant to Asher Brown Durand, February 26, 1849, *L*, 541–542.

207   Lowell: *WCB*, 336–337n.

208   travels in South and Cuba: *B*, II, 45–47; *WCB*, 343–347; *L*, III, 5.

208   "insulting taunts": *WCB*, 344n.

208   two brides: To the *Evening Post*, March 29, 1849, *L*, III, 13. Bryant's correspondence covering the trip to the South and Cuba was reprinted in *Letters of a Traveller*, I, 336–401.

209   "I have since learned": To the *Evening Post*, March 31, 1849, *L*, III, 20.

209   "I feel a temptation": To the *Evening Post*, April 10, 1849, *L*, III, 27–28.

209   "The truth is": To the *Evening Post*, April 22, 1849, *L*, III, 46.

210 Astor Opera House disturbances: Burroughs and Wallace, 761–766; *L*, II, 537–538n2.

211 trip to Europe: *B*, II, 47–51; *WCB*, 346–348.

211 "overgrown city": Bryant to Frances F. Bryant, July 6, 1849, *L*, III, 57.

211 "You look hearty": Quoted in *WCB*, 347.

211 "Upon the whole": To the *Evening Post*, July 7, 1849, *L*, III, 61. "The annual exhibition of the Royal Academy is now open. Its general character is mediocrity, unrelieved by any works of extraordinary merit." Bryant's letters covering his European excursion were reprinted in *Letters of a Traveler*, 402–442.

211 "daisies nodding": To the *Evening Post*, July 19, 1849, *L*, III, 68.

212 Scott's home: *L*, III, 8.

212 "Whoever should visit": To the *Evening Post*, September 13, 1849, *L*, III, 95.

212 "The words, liberty": Bryant to Frances F. Bryant, August 13, 1849, *L*, III, 85.

212 "I could almost": To the *Evening Post*, September 13, 1849, *L*, III, 97.

212 "The political condition": Bryant to Fanny Bryant Godwin, September 11, 1849, *L*, III, 93–94. "particularly about the nose."

213 "the disconsolateness": Bryant to Leonice M. S. Moulton, November 14, 1849, L, III, 112. Bryant liked Mrs. Moulton, whose husband had sold him the Roslyn property. In a letter written to her in Edinburgh (July 27, 1849), he compared her beauty favorably to that of the English women.

213 "in a rather friendly manner": Bryant to Richard H. Dana, November 15, 1849, *L*, III, 114. The correspondence was published by Putnam as *Letters of a Traveler; or, Notes of Things Seen in Europe and America*, in 1850.

213 *Post* was prospering: *WCB*, 348–349.

213 "stock of good health": Bryant to Richard H. Dana, November 15, 1849, *L*, III, 114.

CHAPTER 12: OLD TEMPLES AND TOMBS

215 "fast assuming": "New York," *Sartain's Union Magazine of Literature and Art* (August 1851), 149.

215   *Post*'s offices: *EP*, 236–237.

216   Only the *Evening Post*: Ibid., 244.

216   Bryant and his Free Soil friends: Quoted in Kaplan, 162.

216   Whitman: *NYP*, March 2, 1850.

216   "young artist race": Quoted in Kaplan, 165.

216   "the cause": *EP*, 246.

217   Bigelow: Ibid., 231.

217   "most popular": Quoted in *L*, III, 117.

217   Maria Clemm: Ibid. Bryant quite possibly had been acquainted with Poe as early as 1837 when both families lived next to each other on Carmine Street.

217   "dear old poet": *Yesterdays with Authors* (Boston, 1893), 52–53.

217   "Monument Mountain": Bryant wrote the poem in Great Barrington; it was published in the October 1, 1824, issue of the *United States Literary Gazette*. McLean (1989) observes that the poem "treats nature, sexuality, and passion in a mature yet sensitive way" (36).

218   National Academy: Foshay and Novak, 31; *L*, III, 124n1.

219   inviting his Williams classmate: Bryant to Orville Dewey, April 8, 1850, *L*, III, 123–124.

219   "I hope": Bryant to Richard H. Dana, July 4, 1850, *L*, III, 131.

219   "fairly parboiled": Bryant to Frances F. Bryant, July 30, 1850, *L*, III, 132.

220   *Rural Hours*: Bryant to Leonice Moulton, August 7, 1850, *L*, III, 135.

220   "the greatest": Cooper, *Letters and Journals*, VI, 237.

221   homoeopathic remedies: See Bryant to John T. S. Smith, July 27, 1851, *L*, III, 157–158.

221   "He has grown thin": Bryant to Richard H. Dana, April 8, 1851, *L*, III, 150.

221   "not only": Bryant to Rufus W. Griswold, September 19, 1851, *L*, III, 165.

221   "deplorably": Bryant to Richard H. Dana, March 15, 1852, *L*, III, 166.

221   Cooper oration: Bryant's "Discourse on the Life and Genius of Cooper" appeared in *NYP* for February 27. It was reprinted in *Memorial of James Fenimore Cooper* (New York: Putnam, 1852), 39–73.

222   "made himself": Quoted in *L*, III, 117–119.

222 "A New Public Park": *NYP*, July 3, 1844. For Bryant's seminal role in the founding of Central Park, see *EP*, 201.

222 "fills the mind": Bigelow, 341. "Reminiscences," which Bigelow added in an appendix to the biography of Bryant, is the most accessible source for this work.

223 "cheered and strengthened": Quoted in *WCB*, 357.

223 "one of the most disgusting": *NYP*, January 26, 1851.

223 Fugitive Slave Act: Wilentz (2005), 645–655; *WCB*, 355.

224 "The Free-Soil Party": Bryant to John Howard Bryant, ca. August, 1852, *L*, III, 185.

224 "a man who": *NYP*, June 7, 1852.

224 Webster: *NYP*, September 24, 1852; *New York Times*, November 4, 1852; Bryant to the Editor of the *New-York Daily Times*, November 4, 1852, *L*, III, 191–192; Nevins, *Ordeal*, II, 180–182; *L*, III, 192n2.

225 Near East: *B*, II, 65–76; *WCB*, 361–367, L, III, 195–198. Bryant collected the correspondence covering his trip in *Letters from the East* (New York: G. P. Putnam and Son, 1869).

225 Egyptian Museum: Kaplan, 170.

225 *Arctic*: *WCB*, 361; *L*, III, 195.

225 "a blue-stocking lady": Quoted in *WCB*, 361.

225 "the monument": Bryant to Messrs. William Cullen Bryant & Co., November 25, 1852, *L*, III, 200.

225 "Such numbers": To the *Evening Post*, November 29, 1852, *L*, III, 201.

225 "There is not": reprinted in *NYP*, January 28, 1853.

226 "present order": To the *Evening Post*, December 7, 1852, *L*, III, 206.

226 "birds of every feather": Ibid., 205.

226 "proportion": Ibid., January 12, 1853, 221.

226 "good-natured Mussulmans": Ibid., 223.

227 "still almost as soft": Ibid., January 29, 1853, 229.

227 "From the summit": Ibid., 232.

227 "the once great city": Ibid., 235.

227 "The weather": Bryant to Frances F. Bryant, January 29, 1853, *L*, III, 227.

228 Bryant caravan: To the *Evening Post*, January 30, 1853, *L*, III, 241–245.

228 Bryant took to the desert: Ibid., February 22, 1853, 245–269 passim.

229　"came in sight": Ibid., 270.

229　"The Russian negotiators": Ibid., 279.

229　"broadbrimmed": Bryant to Frances F. Bryant, May 9, 1853, *L*, III, 293.

230　"I went down": Bryant to Richard H. Dana, July 5, 1853, *L*, III, 315.

CHAPTER 13: TUMULTS OF THE NOISY WORLD

231　"grinding at the mill": Bryant to Richard H. Dana, July 5, 1853, *L*, III, 315.

231　"party hack": *NYP*, July 14, 1853.

231　Crystal Palace Exhibition: Burroughs and Wallace, 669–672; Voorsanger and Howat, 40–42.

232　"I like more space": Bryant to Eliza Robbins, July 19, 1853, *L*, III, 318.

232　"a convenient agent": Quoted in *WCB*, 172–173; *L*, III, 309.

233　"It is mortifying": *NYP*, February 27, 1854.

233　"The President": *NYP*, March 5, 1854.

234　"If it should become": *NYP*, May 29, 1854.

234　Bryant despised: *WCB*, 378–380; *L*, III, 309–310.

234　Saratoga convention: *WCB*, 377.

235　"popular dissatisfaction": Quoted in *WCB*, 379.

235　"Every liberal sentiment": Quoted in *EP*, 250.

235　"ceased to serve": Quoted in *WCB*, 380–381.

235　Sumner: *EP*, 252–253.

236　"Allow me to add": Bryant to Charles Sumner, April 24, 1851, *L*, III, 151.

236　"Violence reigns": Quoted in *EP*, 253.

237　"deafening cheers": Quoted in *WCB*, 384.

237　"Buchaneers": *EP*, 211–212.

238　"one mighty stream": *NYP*, February 25, 1856.

238　"We have at least": *NYP*, November 6, 1856.

238　"dry, spare, hard visage": "Street Yarn," *Life Illustrated*, August 16, 1856.

238　"surfeited with politics": Bryant to John Howard Bryant, February 15, 1856, *L*, III, 379.

238　Sketch Club: *L*, III, 311–312.

239   "A Rain-Dream": Bryant wrote this poem at Cedarmere in 1854; it was published in the first issue of the *Crayon* (January, 1855), a new art journal started by the painter and art critic William James Stillman, who apparently gave the lyric its title.

239   Caroline Kirkland: Quoted in *B*, II, 58–61.

240   wife's health: *WCB*, 388–389.

240   Europe trip: *B*, II, 94–119; *WCB*, 390–403.

240   "looking exceeding well": Bryant to Julia Sands, June 17, 1857, *L*, III, 417.

241   Dred Scott decision: *EP*, 253–255; *WCB*, 389–390.

241   "Land of Bondage": Quoted in *EP*, 254.

241   "a Protestant": To the *Evening Post*, July 14, 1857, *L*, III, 420. Bryant collected correspondence covering this European trip in *Letters of a Traveler*, II.

241   "Shallows of the lake": Bryant to Orville Dewey, August 27, 1857, *L*, III, 425.

242   "My wife": Bryant to Christiana Gibson, September 3, 1857, *L*, III, 427–428.

242   "Spain is a backward country": Bryant to Charles M. Leupp, October 26, 1857, *L*, III, 464. Bryant was more critical of Spain in his personal correspondence than in the letters he filed for the *Evening Post*.

243   "and laid him": To the *Evening Post*, November 1, 1857, *L*, III, 468.

243   "one of the greatest poets": Quoted in *L*, III, 495n6.

243   "a Museum of pictures": Bryant to Caroline M. S. Kirkland, November 5, 1857, *L*, III, 477.

243   "I wanted to enjoy": To the *Evening Post*, November 15, 1857, *L*, III, 485.

244   "elegant wrapper": Quoted in *L*, III, 410.

244   "the pretty poetess": Ibid.

244   "Mother pronounced": Ibid.

244   In mid-November: See letters to the *Evening Post*, November 28, 29, December 2, 17, 1857, *L*, III, 496–527.

245   "rising from": To the *Evening Post*, December 17, 1857, *L*, III, 537.

245   The Bryant party: *B*, II, 103–109; *L*, IV, 5–6.

247   "in that twilight boundary": Quoted in *L*, IV, 6.

247   "the gentle methods": Bryant to John Howard Bryant, May 18, 1858, *L*, IV, 30.

247   During his two-week stay: To the *Evening Post*, May 21, 1858, *L*, IV, 31–35.

247   Hawthorne: *B*, II, 112–114; Bigelow (1909–13), 194; *WCB*, 400–402; Wineapple, 203.

248   "a weary look": Quoted in *L*, IV, 42n1.

248   "that disagreeable": Ibid., 54nn1, 2.

248   Two weeks later: *B*, II, 115; *WCB*, 401–402; *L*, IV, 71–72n3.

249   "aversion": Bryant to John Bigelow, July 9, 1858, *L*, IV, 64.

249   On July 20: *L*, IV, 9–10.

CHAPTER 14: LINCOLN

251   "The South is our best customer": Quoted in Burroughs and Wallace, 862.

252   "No man": *NYP*, October 18, 1858.

252   The conventional wisdom: See Bryant to John Bigelow, December 14, 1859, *L*, IV, 129–130.

252   "The Republican party": *NYP*, October 22, 1859.

252   "prosperous": Bryant to John Bigelow, April 11, 1859, *L*, IV, 104.

253   "We are all": Bryant to Cyrus Bryant, February 17, 1859, *L*, IV, 98.

253   "The Century": Bryant to John G. Chapman, November 8, 1858, *L*, IV, 91.

253   Artists insisted: *L*, IV, 79–80.

253   "in which thousands": Bryant to Christiana Gibson, April 19, 1859, *L*, IV, 107–108.

254   Leupp "was one": *NYP*, October 6, 1859.

254   "on excellent terms": Bryant to L. M. Gardner, December 12, 1859, *L*, IV, 128.

254   "The New and the Old": this poem along with "The Cloud on the Way," "Waiting by the Gate," "The Constellations," and "The Tides" appear in *Thirty Poems* (1864). Bryant wrote these five lyrics while residing at Cedarmere.

255   John Brown: Nevins, *Ordeal*, II, 472–475; Wilentz (2005), 748–753.

255   "crazy attempt": *NYP*, October 19, 1859.

255   "to the gallows": *EP*, 256–258; *WCB*, 407–408; Wilentz (2005), 751; Wineapple, 333.

256   February 1860: *EP*, 259–261; *WCB*, 409–411; *L*, IV, 133–134, 143n3.

256   "I can but think": Quoted in *L*, IV, 143n3.

257   The three men: *WCB*, 410.

258   "infinitely elastic": *NYP*, February 28, 1860.

258   "It is worth": Quoted in *EP*, 260–261.

258   "did not want the labor": Bryant to Orville Dewey, April 30, 1860, *L*, IV, 152.

258   "a great affair": Bryant to John Bigelow, April 13, 1860, *L*, IV, 148.

258   Irving: See "Washington Irving," in *PW*, I, 332–368.

259   Bryant's friends: Quoted in *L*, IV, 146n1; *B*, II, 136.

259   "The great work": Bryant to Cassius Marcellus Clay, May 4, 1860, *L*, IV, 152.

259   "It is written": *EP*, May 19, 1860.

259   "an old campaigner": Bryant to Abraham Lincoln, June 16, 1860, *L*, IV, 159.

260   "You have numerous friends": Bryant to Abraham Lincoln, November 10, 1860, *L*, IV, 184.

260   "if a State": *NYP*, November 12, 1860.

260   "the people": Bryant to Robert Waterston, November 6, 1860, *L*, IV, 185.

260   Thurlow Weed: Nevins, *Emergence of Lincoln*, II, 393–396.

260   "The rumor": Bryant to Abraham Lincoln, December 25, 1860, *L*, IV, 187.

261   "rather solitary": Bryant to Robert Waterston, December 26, 1860, *L*, IV, 189–190.

261   Bigelow left: *L*, IV, 194.

262   At the outset: *EP*, 226–227, 266–280 passim.

262   "blustering and cowardly": *NYP*, January 26, 1861.

262   "foreign power": *NYP*, February 2, 1861.

262   "profound respect": Quoted in *L*, IV, 192.

262   "utter, ancient": Bryant to Abraham Lincoln, January 3, 1861, *L*, IV, 197.

263   "alone can reconcile": Quoted in *L*, IV, 199n3.

263   "Admirable as": Quoted in *EP*, 278–279.

263   "office beggars": Bryant to Orville Dewey, March 13, 1861, *L*, IV, 211.

263   "men of democratic": Bryant to Gideon Welles, March 24, 1861, *L*, IV, 212.

263 "Bryant has been here": IV, 235–236.

263 "if the administration": Bryant to Leonice M. S. Moulton, April 24, 1861, L, IV, 216.

263 Illinois: *WCB*, 433–434.

264 "had never ceased": Quoted in *B*, II, 161. Lovejoy replied on June 18: "I thank you for your kindness in presiding at the meeting at Cooper Institute, and for the speech you made at the opening. I felt pleased and flattered that you should do so. It is also highly gratifying, on public grounds, that you should give the influence of your name and fame to the cause of emancipation."

CHAPTER 15: DAYS OF SLAUGHTER

265 Bull Run: *EP*, 285; *WCB*, 435–436; *L*, IV, 194–195.

265 "although it is not best": Quoted in *EP*, 285.

266 "done what the government": *NYP*, September 2, 1861.

266 "Playing with War": *NYP*, October 11, 1861.

267 "evident eagerness": *NYP*, December 4, 1861.

267 "impatience": Bryant to John Bigelow, December 23, 1861, *L*, IV, 237.

268 "There is the old bustle": Bryant to Leonice M. S. Moulton, January 2, 1862, *L*, IV, 247.

268 "zealous abolitionists": Bryant to Frances F. Bryant, January 12, 1862, *L*, IV, 248.

268 "financial folly": Bryant to John M. Forbes, January 25, 1862. See also *NYP*, January 15, 16, 1862.

268 "Your feelings": Quoted in *B*, II, 165.

269 "The success": *NYP*, January 11, 1862.

269 "I repeat": Quoted in *L*, IV, 243–244.

269 "our fixed idea": *NYP*, July 11, 1862.

269 men by the thousands: Burroughs and Wallace, 868–872, 879–882.

270 "A deep lethargy": *NYP*, August 1, 1862.

270 "influence of Seward": Bryant to Horatio N. Powers, September 15, 1862, *L*, IV, 270.

270 "wanting in some": Bryant to Orville Dewey, August 17, 1862, *L*, IV, 268.

271 "able not only": *NYP*, October 8, 1862.

271 "Whether he drinks": Bryant to John Murray Forbes, October 16, 1862, *L*, IV, 276.

271 "We are distressed": Bryant to Abraham Lincoln, October 22, 1862, *L*, IV, 278–279.

271 "The battle": Bryant to Richard H. Dana, December 18, 1862, *L*, IV, 290.

272 "The new year": Bryant to Robert and Anna Waterston, January 9, 1863, *L*, IV, 296.

272 "A good many": Bryant to William Pitt Fessenden, January 12, 1863, *L*, IV, 297–298.

272 secret meeting: *EP*, 304; *WCB*, 448–449.

273 Bryant's revulsion: *WCB*, 449.

273 aggressive pro-war: *L*, IV, 244.

273 "The war": Bryant to John Bigelow, April 9, 1863, *L*, IV, 304.

274 "As soon as": *NYP*, May 21, 1863.

274 "How the war": Bryant to Richard H. Dana, May 14, 1863, *L*, IV, 308.

274 "the rebellion": *NYP*, July 6, 1863.

275 draft riots: *EP*, 367–370; Nevins, *War*, II, 462–466; *WCB*, 251–253; Burroughs and Wallace, 887–899.

276 "Four revolvers": Bryant to George B. Cline, July 18, 1863, *L*, IV, 320.

276 "a regular conspiracy": *NYP*, July 16, 1863.

276 Williams College: *B*, II, 370; *L*, IV, 322.

277 "If any one": Quoted in *L*, IV, 246.

277 Cooper Union: Bryant wrote the account of the meeting that appeared in the *Post* the following day, October 3, 1863.

277 "Your return": Bryant to Catharine Sedgwick, private collection.

278 "put themselves": *NYP*, December 11, 1863.

278 *Thirty Poems*: *B*, II, 206–210; *WCB*, 455–457.

279 Frederick Douglass: See *NYP*, January 13, 1864; also Bryant to Oliver Johnson, January 11, 1864, *L*, IV, 343.

279 "We must bind up": Quoted in *WCB*, 439.

279 "almost by acclamation": Quoted in *L*, IV, 339.

280 "You are watching": Bryant to Catharine Sedgwick, May 4, 1864, private collection.

280 "The Return of the Birds": published in the *Atlantic Monthly*, 81 (July 1864).

281 "the plain people": *NYP*, June 3, 1864.

281 "It is very remarkable": Bryant to Frances F. Bryant, August 12, 1864, *L*, IV, 388.

281 Secretary Welles removed: *EP*, 427–428; *WCB*, 459–463.

283   "I am so utterly disgusted": Quoted in *L*, IV, 340–341.

283   "makes people laugh": Bryant to Frances F. Bryant, September 9, 1864, *L*, IV, 404.

283   "so beggar ridden": Bryant to Julia S. Bryant, September 16, 1864, *L*, IV, 409.

283   "Ask me": Bryant to James T. Fields, October 13, 1864, *L*, IV, 411–412.

285   "I hope": Bryant to George Bancroft, October 17, 1864, *L*, IV, 415.

285   "I shall reckon": Bryant to Lydia H. H. Sigourney, October 20, 1864, *L*, IV, 417.

285   On Saturday evening: *B*, II, 213–220; *WCB*, 467–469. See also *Bryant Festival*.

287   "This is a beautiful": Bryant to Richard H. Dana, November 30, 1864, *L*, IV, 425.

287   Confederate spies: Nevins, *War for the Union*, II, 138; *NYP*, November 26, 28, 29.

287   "To the Soldiers": *NYP*, January 1, 1865.

287   petition: Everett: *B*, II, 224.

288   Fool's Errands": *NYP*, January 10, 1865.

288   "Glory to the Lord of Hosts": Quoted in *EP*, 314–315.

289   "How awful": *NYP*, April 15, 1865.

289   "When I think": Bryant to Catharine Sedgwick, June 26, 1865, *L*, V, 31.

290   "The Death of Lincoln": Bryant published the poem in the April 20, 1865, edition of the *Evening Post*.

291   "You seemed to me": Samuel Osgood to Bryant, February 20, 1866, *NYPL*.

CHAPTER 16: LIKE ONE SHUT OUT OF PARADISE

291   influential friends: Quoted in *B*, II, 230–231; *WCB*, 472–473.

292   "There are various reasons": Bryant to Oliver Wendell Holmes, May 1, 1865, *L*, V, 21–22.

292   "those who are for punishing": Bryant to Richard H. Dana, May 4, 1865, *L*, V, 24.

292   "What Should Be Done": *NYP*, July 12, 1865.

292   Still, treason: *NYP*, October 23, 1865.

292   "It is a great thing": Bryant to Catharine Sedgwick, December 29, 1865, *L*, V, 64.

293 "little occupied": Bryant to Reginald Parker, December 7, 1865, *L*, V, 59.

293 death of Frances Bryant: Bryant's "private account" is in his papers at *NYPL*.

294 "like one": Bryant to Richard H. Dana, September 1, 1866, *L*, V, 116.

294 "tender sympathies": Bryant to Arthur Bryant, July 28, 1866, *L*, V, 111.

295 "I am just": Bryant to George Bancroft, November 12, 1866, *L*, V, 123.

295 "remarkably smooth": Bryant to Isaac Henderson, December 1, 1866, *L*, V, 125.

295 "melancholy place": Bryant to Christiana Gibson, December 18, 1866, *L*, V, 128.

295 "The *Evening Post*": Quoted in *L*, V, 67.

296 "with great joy": Ibid., 68.

296 "rather sad": To the *Evening Post*, December 24, 1866, *L*, V, 136.

296 "I climb": Bryant to Catharine Sedgwick, December 20, 1866, *L*, V, 132.

296 "sense of sublimity": To the *Evening Post*, January 22, 1867, *L*, V, 156.

296 "miserably chilly": To the *Evening Post*, January 12, 1867, *L*, V, 151.

296 "I must own": Bryant to Leonice M. S. Moulton, January 22, 1867, *L*, V, 157.

296 "It differs": Bryant to John Durand, February 22, 1867, *L*, V, 169.

297 By early February: Ibid.

297 Hiram Powers: To the *Evening* Post, February 27, 1867, *L*, V, 171.

297 "I do not like": Bryant to John Howard Bryant, February 27, 1867, *L*, V, 174.

297 "For my own part": Bryant to Jerusha Dewey, March 25, 1867, *L*, V, 177.

297 "splendid capital": To the *Evening Post*, April 12, 1867, *L*, V, 180–181.

297 "Almost every where": Bryant to John Durand, April 27, 1867, *L*, V, 188.

297 "I have been wandering": Bryant to Orville Dewey, April 29, 1867, *L*, V, 188.

297 "I wish": Bryant to Isaac Henderson, May 4, 1867, *L*, V, 191.

298 "This I know": Quoted in *L*, V, 192n3.

298 took the liberty: Ibid., n2.

298 "a rainy time": Bryant to John Durand, June 10, 1867, *L*, V, 198.

298 crossing to England: *WCB*, 480; *L*, V, 142–143.

298 "I am counting": Bryant to Christiana Gibson, August 20, 1867, *L*, V, 214.

298 "not very favorable": Bryant to Jerusha Dewey, October 14, 1867, *L*, V, 219.

299 "grown older": Bryant to Jerusha Dewey, October 14, 1867, *L*, V, 218.

299 "I have never": Bryant to Orville Dewey, October 1869, *L*, V, 340. See also *Life and Letters of Catharine M. Sedgwick*, 438–436.

299 "the maples": Bryant to Jerusha Dewey, October 14, 1867, *L*, V, 219.

299 "habit of seclusion": Bryant to James T. Fields, October 31, 1867, *L*, V, 222.

299 banquet: *NYP*, October 3, 1867.

299 "Mr. Longfellow": Bryant to James T. Fields, October 31, 1867, *L*, V, 222.

300 "I piddle": Bryant to Richard H. Dana, November 30, 1867, *L*, V, 226.

300 "I cannot muster": Bryant to Christiana Gibson, December 25, 1867, *L*, V, 236. See also Bigelow, *Retrospections*, IV, 129.

300 "the banquet of Life": Bryant to Christiana Gibson, Ibid.

300 "The choice": Quoted in *L*, V, 144.

300 communal property: *L*, V, 241–242.

301 "the debt": Quoted in *L*, V, 246n1.

301 "quite gay": Bryant to John Howard Bryant, January 24, 1868, *L*, V, 248.

301 "the male part": Bryant to Jerusha Dewey, March 4, 1868, *L*, V, 255.

301 business and editorial policies: *WCB*, 481; *L*, V, 242.

301 Charlton T. Lewis: *EP*, 397, 422–23.

302 "As to the caricature": Bryant to Julia Hatfield, August 1868, *L*, V, 285.

302 *Jarilla*: *L*, V, 264–265.

302 "The sober people": Bryant to Christiana Gibson, September 5, 1868, *L*, V, 287.

302 "We do not": Bryant to John Howard Bryant, November 30, 1868, *L*, V, 294.

303 "annihilated": See *Orations and Addresses*, 325–330.

303 "I would observe": Bryant to John Howard Bryant, February 10, 1869, *L*, V, 306.

304 "by far": Quoted in *L*, V, 301.

304 "He was spared": See *Orations and Addresses*, 157–194.

304 "All manner": Bryant to John Gourlie, June 19, 1869, *L*, V, 325.

304 "Strange times": Quoted in *B*, II, 280.

305 "Through the crowded": Quoted in *L*, V, 331n3.

305 "I have promised": Bryant to F. Seeger, November 16, 1869, *L*, V, 345.

305 "Our city": See *Orations and Addresses*, 333–341.

306 William "Boss" Tweed: Burroughs and Wallace, 937–932, 1008–1012.

306 Friends praised: *B*, II, 284–289; *L*, V, 352.

307 "I do not intend": Bryant to John Howard Bryant, July 1, 1870, *L*, V, 382–383.

307 *Library of Poetry and Song*: *B*, II, 294–296.

307 "one of our best": Bryant to Orville Dewey, March 24, 1870, *L*, V, 363.

307 Verplanck eulogy: See *Orations and Addresses*, 197–258.

308 Tweed Ring: *EP*, 376–388.

309 Henderson affair: *EP*, 426–441; *WCB*, 492–494.

310 "I rise early": Bryant to Joseph H. Richards, March 30, 1871, *L*, V, 413.

310 entertaining friends: *L*, V, 402.

310 "In the case": Bryant to James T. Fields, April 25, 1871, *L*, V, 419.

311 "a debt due": Bryant to George Hannah, April 22, 1871, *L*, V, 418.

311 "the greenest meadows": Bryant to Christiana Gibson, July 4, 1871, *L*, V, 425.

311 Orange Riot: *EP*, 385–386; Burroughs and Wallace, 1003–1008.

311 "cynical contempt": Quoted in *EP*, 386.

311 "New York": Ibid., 387.

312 Cummington: *L*, V, 402; see also Bryant to Christiana Gibson, September 4, 1871, *L*, V, 432.

312 "frugal of my days": Bryant to Orville Dewey, September 11, 1871, *L*, V, 436.

312 "at my age": Bryant to Willard Phillips, July 29, 1871, *L*, V, 429.

313 "Observe the cacophony": Bryant to Robert C. Waterston, September 23, 1871, *L*, V, 439.

313 "like mosquitoes": Bryant to Richard H. Dana, January 18, 1862, *L*, VI, 12.

314   "a district inhabited": To the *Evening Post*, February 5, 1872, *L*, VI, 18. Bryant wrote six long letters to the *Post* describing this trip. See also *B*, II, 318–323.

314   "brilliant blue tint": Ibid., 17.

314   "This place": Ibid., 20.

314   Havana: See Bryant to Isaac Henderson, February 17, 1872, *L*, VI, 21–22.

314   Mexico: To the *Evening Post*, March 5, 8, 10, 11, *L*, VI, 23–52, passim.

315   "We believe": Quoted in *L*, VI, 7.

CHAPTER 17: A CENTURY'S SPACE

317   "sorely disappointed": Bryant to John Howard Bryant, May 8, 1872, *L*, VI, 63.

317   Greeley: *EP*, 395–396; *L*, VI, 64n3.

317   "We who know": Bryant to Lyman Trumbull, May 8, 1872, *L*, VI, 63.

318   Bryant's "card": *EP*, July 8, 1872.

319   "By good natural abilities": *EP*, November 20, 1872.

319   speeches and projects: *B*, II, 346; *WCB*, 501.

319   Cummington library: *L*, VI, 8.

319   "rather urgently": Bryant to Richard H. Dana, September 1, 1872, *L*, VI, 81. In the same letter, he resumed his criticism of Greeley's "remarkable unfitness for the office" of the presidency.

319   "amiable": Bryant to Christiana Gibson, January 6, 1873, *L*, VI, 96.

320   "We old men": Bryant to James T. Fields, January 30, 1873, *L*, VI, 102.

320   "broad, deep": To the *Evening Post*, February 9, 1873, *L*, VI, 106.

320   "negro race": Ibid., March 23, 1873, *L*, VI, 109.

320   "a degraded race": Bryant to Janet Gibson, April 13, 1873, *L*, VI, 121.

320   Howells: See Bryant to William Dean Howells, August 22, 1873, *L*, VI, 134–135.

321   "drift hopelessly": See *PW*, II, 324–328.

321   "Our race": *PW*, II, 292–293.

321 "A war": Bryant to Hamilton Fish, November 19, 1873, *L*, VI, 144.

322 "mighty fortunes": Bryant to Robert C. Waterston, December 12, 1873, *L*, VI, 146–147.

322 eightieth birthday: *B*, II, 347–350.

322 Chicago Literary Club: Ibid., 350–351.

323 "It always seems": Bryant to Christiana Gibson, July 22, 1874, *L*, VI, 175.

323 speeches: *L*, VI, 149.

323 "scholars": Bryant to Jerusha Dewey, January 26, 1874, *L*, VI, 153.

323 "The real hard work": Bryant to John Howard Bryant, May 11, 1874, *L*, VI, 167.

324 "the cattle": Bryant to Sydney H. Gay, July 29, 1873, *L*, VI, 231–232.

324 "filled with wonder": Bryant to Orville Dewey, May 29, 1874, *L*, VI, 170.

325 "I must have got": Bryant to John Bigelow, November 25, 1874, *L*, VI, 194.

326 Centennial Celebration: *WCB*, 516; *L*, VI, 269–270. The poet placed the "Bryant Vase," which Tiffany had been commissioned to design after the firm won a national competition, on display at the Philadelphia celebration. The vase also was featured at the Paris Exhibition of 1878. Bryant donated the commemorative vase to the newly established Metropolitan Museum of Art as a permanent loan.

326 Tilden: *B*, II, 374–380; *WCB*, 510–515.

326 "a compliment": Bigelow, 238.

326 tribute from state legislature: Ibid., 238–242.

327 Election of 1876: *EP*, 400–405; *WCB*, 510–513.

327 "the party": *NYP*, November 17, 1873.

327 "great pain": Bryant to John Bigelow, August 28, 1876, *L*, VI, 315.

327 Henderson: *EP*, 403–405, 411, 420.

327 "I can hardly trust": Quoted in *EP*, 404.

328 "perfectly competent authority": Bigelow (1909–13), 251.

328 "one of the greatest": Bryant to John H. Gourlie, August 17, 1876, *L*, VI, 314.

328 "We have chosen": Bryant to Christiana Gibson, November 25, 1876, *L*, VI, 332.

328   "I confess": Bryant to John Howard Bryant, March 9, 1877, *L*, VI, 346.

329   all illusions: *EP*, 420–434, passim.

329   "marvelous purity": Quoted in *L*, VI, 338. In "My Tribute to Four Poets," Whitman ranked Bryant ahead of Emerson, Longfellow, and Whittier: "Bryant pulsing the first interior verse—throbs of a mighty world—bard of the river and wood, ever conveying a taste of open air, with scents as from hayfields, grapes, and birch borders—always lurkingly fond of threnodies—beginning and ending his long career with chants of death, with here and there through all, poems, or passages of poems, touching the highest universal truths, enthusiasms, duties—morals as grim and eternal, if not as stormy and fateful, as anything in Aeschylus." See *Specimen Days*: 109.

330   "would go off": Quoted in *L*, VI, 270.

330   "flying colors": Quoted in *L*, VI, 255n3.

330   Halleck: *L*, VI, 338.

330   Lafayette College: Ibid.

331   "In Memory of John Lothrop Motley": See Bryant to the Editors of the *International Review*, September 26, 1877, *L*, VI, 385–386.

331   "a poet": See Bryant to Edward Abbott, November 17, 1877, *L*, VI, 392–393.

331   Emerson "they say": Bryant to Christiana Gibson, December 10, 1877, *L*, VI, 410–411.

331   "To the Fringed Gentian": Harold Bloom, an admirer of Bryant's verse, writes of this lyric: "Bryant takes the gentian as the natural hope of heaven, which he is eager to share." He also notes the influence of Bryant's poem on Emily Dickinson, whose early verse includes "The Gentian Waves Her Fringes" and "Distrustful of the Gentian." See *The Ringer in the Tower*: 304, 309.

332   "Green River": Bryant to James Sutton, November 5, 1877, *L*, VI, 391.

332   "I certainly": Bryant to Christiana Gibson, Ibid.

332   "Gone! Gone!": Leonice Marston Sampson Moulton, *Diary*: June 12, 1878, *NYPL*.

332   According to Dr. Gray: *WCB*, 520.

333   "I am not": Moulton *Diary*, April 20, 1860.

334   prevails on the poet: Ibid., September 4, 5, 1875.

334   "Oh, how well": Ibid., June 16, 1878.

334   "Why this burning": Ibid., June 14, 1878.

334   Bryant had left instructions: *L*, VI, 417. Bryant's will, reprinted in the appendix in Bigelow (1909–13), excluded Parke Godwin from any part of his estate.

334   Bryant's funeral: Ibid. 417–419.

335   "a strong desire": *Specimen Days*, 76–77.

336   "Whoever saw": Quoted in *L*, VI, 418.

BIBLIOGRAPHY

PRIMARY SOURCES

"An Autobiography of Mr. Bryant's Early Life," in Parke Godwin, *A Biography of William Cullen Bryant, with Extracts from His Private Correspondence*. 2 vols. New York: D. Appleton, 1883: 1–37.

The Complete Works of Shakespeare edited by Wm. Cullen Bryant assisted by Evert A. Duyckinck. New York: 1888.

A Discourse on the Life, Character and Genius of Washington Irving, Delivered before the New-York Historical Society, at the Academy of Music in New York on the 3d of April, 1860. New York: Putnam, 1860.

A Discourse on the Life, Character and Writings of Gulian Crommelin Verplanck, Delivered before the New-York Historical Society, on the 3rd of February, 1869. New York: 1869.

The Embargo, or Sketches of the Times: A Satire, by a Youth of Thirteen. Boston: printed for the purchasers, 1808. Second edition, corrected and enlarged as *The Embargo; or, Sketches of the Times. A Satire. Together with The Spanish Revolution and Other Poems*. Printed for the author by E. G. House, 1809. A Facsimile Reproduction with an Introduction by Thomas O. Mabbott. Gainesville: U of Florida P: Scholars' Facsimiles and Reprints, 1955.

The Fountain and Other Poems. New York and London: Wiley and Putnam, 1842.

A Funeral Oration, Occasioned by the Death of Thomas Cole, Delivered before the National Academy of Design, New-York, May 4, 1848. New York: D. Appleton, 1848.

Hymns. 1864: n.p.

The Iliad of Homer. Translated into English Blank Verse. 2 vols. Boston: Fields, Osgood, 1870.

Letters from the East. New York: G. Putnam and Son, 1869.

Letters of a Traveler; or, Notes of Things Seen in Europe and America. New York: G. P. Putnam, 1850.

Letters of a Traveler. Second Series. New York: D. Appleton, 1859.

The Letters of William Cullen Bryant. 6 vols. Edited by William Cullen Bryant II and Thomas G. Voss. New York: Fordham UP, 1975–1992.

A Library of Poetry and Song, Being Choice Selections from the Best Poets, with an Introduction by William Cullen Bryant. New York: J. B. Ford, 1870.

The Odyssey of Homer. 2 vols. Boston: James R. Osgood, 1871–1872.

An Oration, Delivered at Stockbridge, July 4, 1820. Stockbridge, MA: Charles Webster, 1821.

Orations and Addresses by William Cullen Bryant. New York: Putnam's, 1873.

Picturesque America. New York: D. Appleton, 1872–1874.

Poems. Cambridge: Hilliard and Metcalf, 1821.

Poems by William Cullen Bryant: An American. Edited by Washington Irving. London: J. Andrews, 1832.

Poems. New York: E. Bliss, 1832; London: J. Andrews, 1832.

Poems. Boston: Russell, Odiorne & Metcalf, 1834.

Poems. New York: Harper & Brothers, 1836.

Poems. Fifth Edition. New York: Harper & Brothers, 1839.

Poems. 2 vols. New York: D. Appleton, 1854.

Poems. New York: D. Appleton, 1871.

Poems by William Cullen Bryant. New York: D. Appleton, 1876.

The Poetical Works of William Cullen Bryant. Edited by Parke Godwin. 2 vols. New York: D. Appleton, 1883.

Popular Considerations of Homoeopathia. New York: W. Radde, 1841.

A Popular History of the United States by William Cullen Bryant and Sidney Howard Gay. 4 vols. New York: Scribner, Armstrong, 1876–1881.

The Prose Writings of William Cullen Bryant. Edited by Parke Godwin. 2 vols. New York: D. Appleton, 1884.

Reminiscences of the Evening Post: Extracted from the Evening Post of November 15, 1851, with Additions and Corrections by the Writer. New York: Wm. C. Bryant & Co., Printers, 1851. Reprinted in Bigelow, *Bryant*, pp. 312–342.

The Talisman. 3 vols. Edited, with contributions by Bryant, Robert Sands, and Gulian Verplanck, as Frances Herbert. New York: Elam Bliss, 1827, 1828, 1829.

Thirty Poems. New York: D. Appleton, 1864.

The White Footed Deer and Other Poems. New York: I. S. Platt, 1844.

SECONDARY SOURCES

Alden, Joseph. *Studies in Bryant.* New York: D. Appleton, 1882.

Alder, J. H. "A Milton Bryant Parallel." *New England Quarterly* 24 (1951): 377–380.

Allen, Gay Wilson. "William Cullen Bryant." *American Prosody.* New York: American Book, 1935.

Amoruso, Vito. "La poesie de Bryant." *Studi Americani* 9 (1963): 39–67.

Arms, George. "William Cullen Bryant: A Respectable Station on Parnassus." *University of Kansas City Review* 15 (1949): 215–223.

Bancroft, George. *The Bryant Festival at the Century.* New York: D. Appleton, 1865.

Baxter, David J. "Timothy Flint and Bryant's 'The Prairies.'" *American Notes and Queries* 16 (1977): 52–54.

———. "William Cullen Bryant: Illinois Landholder." *Western Illinois Regional Studies* I (Spring 1978): 1–14.

Bender, Thomas. *New York Intellect.* New York: Alfred A. Knopf, 1987.

Bennett, Diane Tarleton. *William Cullen Bryant in Roslyn.* Roslyn, NY: Bryant Library, 1978.

Berbrick, John D. *Three Voices from Paumanok: The Influence of Long Island on James Fenimore Cooper, William Cullen Bryant, and Walt Whitman.* Port Washington, NY: Ira J. Friedman, 1969.

Bigelow, John. *Retrospections of an Active Life.* 5 vols. New York: Baker and Taylor, 1909–1913.

———. *William Cullen Bryant.* American Men of Letters Series. Boston: Houghton Mifflin, 1890.

Birdsall R. D. "William Cullen Bryant and Catharine Sedgwick: Their Debt to Berkshire." *New England Quarterly* 28 (1955): 349–371.

Bloom, Harold. *The Ringer in the Tower: Studies in the Romantic Tradition.* U of Chicago P: 1971.

Bonham, George V. "A Poet's Mother: Sarah Snell Bryant in Illinois." *Journal of the Illinois State Historical Society* (June 1940).

Booher, Edwin R. "The Garden Myth in 'The Prairies.'" *Western Illinois Regional Studies* 1 I (1977): 15–26.

Bradley, William Aspewall. *William Cullen Bryant.* English Men of Letters Series. New York: Macmillan, 1905.

Branch, Michael P. "William Cullen Bryant: The Nature Poet as Environmentalist." *ATQ* 12 (1998): 179–198.

Braudy, Leo. *The Frenzy of Renown: Fame and Its History.* NY: Oxford UP, 1986.

Brickhouse, Anna. "'A Story of the Island of Cuba': William Cullen Bryant and the Hispanophone Americas. *Nineteenth-Century Literature* 56 (2001): 1–22.

Brodwin, Stanley, and Michael D'Innocenzo, eds. *William Cullen Bryant and His America.* New York: AMS Press, 1983.

Brown, Charles H. *William Cullen Bryant.* New York: Scribner's, 1971.

Brooks, Van Wyck. *The World of Washington Irving.* New York: Dutton, 1944.

Bryant Centennial, Cummington. August the Sixteenth. 1894. Springfield, MA: Clark W. Bryan, 1894.

The Bryant Centennial: A Book about a Day. Galesburg, IL: Knox College, 1894.

Bryant Festival at The Century, November 5, 1864. New York: Appleton, 1865.

Bryant, William Cullen II. "Bryant: The Middle Years: A Study in Cultural Fellowship." Unpublished Ph.D. diss., Columbia University, 1954.

———. "The Genesis of 'Thanatopsis'." *New England Quarterly* 21 (1948): 163–184.

———. "Poetry and Painting: A Love Affair of Long Ago." *American Quarterly* 22 (1970): 859–882.

———. "'The Waterfowl' in Retrospect." *New England Quarterly* 30 (1957): 181–189.

———, ed. *Power for Sanity: Selected Editorials of William Cullen Bryant, 1829–1961.* New York: Fordham UP, 1994.

———, and Thomas G. Voss, eds. *The Letters of William Cullen Bryant.* I: 1809–1836, II: 1836–1849, III: 1849–1857, IV: 1858–1864, V: 1865–1871, VI: 1872–1878. New York: Fordham UP, 1975–1992.

Budick, Miller E. "'Visible' Images and the 'Still Voice': Transcendental Vision in Bryant's 'Thanatopsis'." *Emerson Society Quarterly* 22 (1976): 71–77.

———. "The Disappearing Image in William Cullen Bryant's 'To a Waterfowl'." *Concerning Poetry* (Western Washington State College) 2, 2 (1977): 13–16.

Burns, James MacGregor. *The Vineyard of Liberty*. New York: Alfred A. Knopf, 1982.

Burroughs, Edwin G., and Mike Wallace. *Gotham: A History of New York City to 1898*. New York: Oxford UP, 1999.

Callow, James T. *Kindred Spirits: Knickerbocker Writers and American Artists, 1807–1855*. Chapel Hill, NC: U of North Carolina P, 1967.

Cameron, Kenneth Walter. "An Early English Review of Bryant's Poems." *Emerson Society Quarterly* 13 (1958): 91.

Casale, Ottavio M. "Bryant's Proposed Address to the Emperor of Brazil." *Emerson Society Quarterly* 63 (1971): 10–12.

Christensen, Norman Ferdinand. "The Imagery of William Cullen Bryant." *Dissertation Abstracts* 21 (1960): 195.

Cody, Sherwin. *Four American Poets: William Cullen Bryant, Henry Wadsworth Longfellow, John Greenleaf Whittier, Oliver Wendell Holmes: A Book for Young Americans*. 1899. Reprinted, Folcroft, PA: Folcroft Library Editions, 1977.

Coleman, Earle E. "The Exhibition of the Palace: A Bibliographical Essay." *Bulletin of the New York Public Library* 64 (1960): 450–477.

Crapo, Paul. "Bryant on Slavery, Copyright, and Capital Punishment." *Emerson Society Quarterly* 47 (1967): 139–140.

Crino, Anna Maria. *Echi, temi e motivi nellapoesia di William Cullen Bryant*. Verona: Linotipia Ghidini e Fiorini, 1963.

Curtis, George William. *The Life of William Cullen Bryant*. New York: Scribner's, 1879.

Dahl, Curtis. "Mound Builders, Mormons, and William Cullen Bryant." *New England Quarterly* 34 (1961): 178–190.

Dendinger, Lloyd N. "William Cullen Bryant." *Critical Survey of Poetry*, vol. 1. Englewood Cliffs, NJ: Salem, 1982.

Douglas, Ann. *The Feminization of American Culture*. New York: Doubleday Anchor, 1988.

Drew, Helen L., ed. "Unpublished Letters of William Cullen Bryant." *New England Quarterly* 10 (1937): 346–355.

Duffey, Bernard. *Poetry in America: Expression and Its Values in the Times of Bryant, Whitman, and Pound*. Durham: Duke UP, 1978.

Eaten, Ernest R. "The Early Life of William Cullen Bryant." *Phi Alpha Gamma* (December 1933).

———. "William Cullen Bryant, Homeopathist, 1794–1878." *Phi Alpha Gamma* (February 1934).

Eby, Cecil D., Jr. "Bryant's 'The Prairies': Notes on Date and Text." *Papers of the Bibliographical Society of America* 56 (1962): 356–357.

Epstein, Daniel Mark. *Lincoln and Whitman: Parallel Lives in Civil War Washington*. New York: Ballantine, 2004.

Floan, Howard R. "The New York *Evening Post* and the Antebellum South." *American Quarterly* 8 (1956): 243–253.

Foerster, Norman. "Nature in Bryant's Poetry." *South Atlantic Quarterly* 4, 17 (1918): 10–17.

Foshay, Ella M., and Barbara Novak. *Intimate Friends: Thomas Cole, Asher B. Durand, William Cullen Bryant*. New York: New-York Historical Society, 2000.

Foster, Henry Halsey. *Catharine Maria Sedgwick*. Boston: Twayne, 1974.

Free, William J. "William Cullen Bryant on Nationalism, Imitation, and Originality in Poetry." *Studies in Philology* 66 (1960): 672–687.

Friedland, Louis S. "Bryant's Schooling in the Liberties of Oratory." *American Notes and Queries* 7 (1947): 27.

Gelpi, Albert. *The Tenth Muse: The Psyche of the American Poet*. Cambridge: Harvard UP, 1975.

Glicksberg, Charles I. "Bryant: The Poet of Humor." *Americana* 29 (1935): 364–337.

———. "Bryant and *The United States Review*." *New England Quarterly* 7 (1934): 687–701.

———. "Cooper and Bryant: A Literary Friendship," *The Colophon* (1934).

———. "From the 'Pathetic' to the 'Classical': Bryant's Schooling in the Liberties of Oratory." *American Notes and Queries* 6 (1947): 179–182.

———, ed. "Letters by William Cullen Bryant," *Americana* 33 (1939): 23–41.

———, ed. "Letters of William Cullen Bryant from Florida." *Florida Historical Society Quarterly* 13 (1934): 255–274.

———. "New Contributions in Prose by William Cullen Bryant." *Arcana* 30 (1936): 573–592.

———. "William Cullen Bryant: Champion of Simple English." *New England Quarterly* 26 (1949): 299–303.

———. "William Cullen Bryant and Communism." *Modern Monthly* 7 (1934): 353–359.

———. "William Cullen Bryant: A Reinterpretation." *Revue Anglo-Americaine* (1934): 495–503.

———. "William Cullen Bryant and Fanny Wright." *American Literature* 6 (1935): 427–432.

———. "William Cullen Bryant and Nineteenth Century Science." *New England Quarterly* 23 (1950): 91–96.

Goddard, Conrad Godwin. *The Early History of Roslyn Harbor, Long Island*. Printed by the Author [1972].

Godwin, Parke. *A Biography of William Cullen Bryant, with Extracts from His Private Correspondence*. (Published as Volumes I and II of *The Life and Writings of William Cullen Bryant*.) 2 vols. New York: D. Appleton, 1883.

———. *Commemorative Addresses*. New York: Harper, 1895.

Gonzalez, Manuel P. "Two Great Pioneers of Inter-American Cultural Relations." *Hispania* 42 (1959): 175–185.

Griffin, Max L. "Bryant and the South." *Tulane Studies in English* I (1949): 53–80.

Griswold, Rufus Wilmot. *The Poets and Poetry of America*. Philadelphia: Parry and McMillan, 1842.

Gross, Seymour L. "An Uncollected Bryant Poem." *Notes and Queries* 4 (1957): 358–359.

Grubbs, Henry A. "Mallarmé and Bryant." *Modern Language Notes* 62 (1947): 410–412.

Guilds, John C. "Bryant in the South: A New Letter to Simms." *Georgia History Quarterly* 37 (1952): 142–146.

Hale, William Harlan. *Horace Greeley: Voice of the People*. New York: Harper and Brothers, 1950.

Harrington, Evans. "Sensuousness in the Poetry of William Cullen Bryant." *University of Mississippi Studies in English* 7 (1966): 25–42.

Harris, Neil. *The Artist in American Society: The Formative Years, 1790–1860*, 2d ed. Chicago: U of Chicago P, 1982.

Hatfield, Julia. *The Bryant Homestead Book*. New York: 1870.

Hone, Philip. *The Diary of Philip Hone*. 1828–1851. Edited by Allan Nevins. 2 vols. New York: Dodd, Mead, 1927.

Hornberger, Theodore, ed. *William Cullen Bryant and Isaac Henderson: New Evidence on a Strange Partnership*. Austin, TX, 1950.

Hoyt, William D., Jr., ed. "Some Unpublished Bryant Correspondence." *New York History* 21 (1940): 63–70, 193–204.

Hudson, William P. "Archibald Alison and William Cullen Bryant." *American Literature* 12 (1940): 59–68.

Huntress, Keith, and Fred W. Lorch, eds. "Bryant and Illinois: Four Letters of the Poet's Family," *New England Quarterly* 16 (1943): 634–647.

In Memory of William Cullen Bryant. New York: Evening Post Presses, 1878.

Jelliffe, Rebecca Rio. "The Poetry of William Cullen Bryant: Theory and Practice." Unpublished Ph.D. diss. University of California at Berkeley, 1964.

Johnson, Curtiss S. *Politics and a Belly-Full: The Journalistic Career of William Cullen Bryant: Civil War Editor of the New York Evening Post.* New York: Vantage, 1962.

Jones, Howard M. *Belief and Disbelief in American Literature.* Chicago: U of Chicago P, 1967.

Kaplan, Justin. *Walt Whitman: A Life.* New York: Simon and Schuster, 1980.

Krapf, Norbert, ed. *Under Open Sky: Poets on William Cullen Bryant.* New York: Fordham UP, 1986.

Lazzerini, Edward J. "Bryant as a Writer of Friendly Letters." *Emerson Society Quarterly* 48 (1967): 125–131.

Lease, Benjamin. "William Cullen Bryant: An Unpublished Letter." *Notes and Queries* 197 (1953): 396–397.

Leonard, W. E. "Bryant." *Cambridge History of American Literature, Vol. 1.* New York: G. P. Putnam's Sons, 1917.

Link, Eric Carl. "American Nationalism and the Defense of Poetry." *Southern Quarterly* 41 (Winter 2003): 48–59.

Long, H. P. "The Alden Lineage of William Cullen Bryant." *New England History and General Register* 102 (1948): 82–86.

Longfellow, Henry Wadsworth. *The Letters of Henry Wadsworth Longfellow.* 4 vols. Ed. Andrew Hilen. Cambridge: Harvard UP, 1966–1972.

Mabbott, Thomas O. "Bryant's 'Thanatopsis'." *Explicator* 11 (1952): 15.

Marshall, P. David. *Celebrity and Power: Fame in Contemporary Culture.* Minneapolis: U Minnesota P, 1997.

Matthews, J. Chesley. "Bryant and Dante: A Word More." *Italica* 35 (1958): 176.

McDowell, Tremaine. "The Ancestry of William Cullen Bryant." *Americana* 22 (1928): 408–420.

———. "Bryant and *The North American Review.*" *American Literature* 1 (1929–1930): 14–26.

———. "Bryant's Practice in Composition and Revision." *Publications of the Modern Language Association* 52 (1937): 474–502.

———. "Cullen Bryant at Williams College." *New England Quarterly* 1 (1928): 443–466.

———. "The Juvenile Verse of William Cullen Bryant." *Studies in Philology* 26 (1929): 96–108.

———. *William Cullen Bryant.* American Writers Series. New York: American Book, 1935.

———. "William Cullen Bryant and Yale." *New England Quarterly* 3 (1930): 706–716.

———. "The Youth of Bryant: An Account of the Life and Poetry of William Cullen Bryant from 1794 to 1821." Unpublished Ph.D. diss., Yale University, 1928.

McLean, Albert F., Jr. "Bryant's 'Thanatopsis': A Sermon in Stone." *American Literature* 31 (1960): 474–479.

———. *William Cullen Bryant.* New York: Twayne, 1964, 1978, rev. ed. 1989.

McMartin, Gaines Noble. "A Perspective on Unity in the Poems of Bryant, Longfellow, Emerson, and Whitman: The Use of Analogy and Example in Metaphor." *Dissertation Abstracts International* 36 (1976): 4494A.

Meyer, Kinereth. "Landscape and Counter-Landscape in the Poetry of William Cullen Bryant." *Nineteenth-Century Literature* 48, 2 (1993): 194–211.

Miller, Ralph N. "Nationalism in Bryant's 'The Prairies'." *American Literature* 21 (1949): 227–232.

Monteiro, George. "The Patriarchal Mr. Bryant: Some New Letters." *Notes and Queries* 22 (1975): 440–441.

Morrill, Peter B. "Unpublished Letters of William Cullen Bryant." *Emerson Society Quarterly* 27 (1962): 47–48.

Morris, Timothy. "Bryant and the American Poetic Tradition." *ATQ* 8 (1994): 53–70.

Mulvey, Christopher. *Anglo-American Landscapes.* London and New York: Cambridge UP, 1983.

Murray, Donald M. "Dr. Peter Bryant: Preceptor in Poetry to William Cullen Bryant." *New England Quarterly* 33 (1960): 513–522.

Nevins, Allen. *The Emergence of Lincoln.* 2 vols. New York: Scribner's, 1952.

———. *The Evening Post. A Century of Journalism.* New York: Boni and Liveright, 1922.

———. *Ordeal of the Union.* 2 vols. New York: Scribner's: 1947.

———. *The War for the Union.* 4 vols. New York: Scribner's, 1959–1971.

Olson, Steve. "William Cullen Bryant's View of Prairie America's Conflicting Values." *North Dakota Quarterly* 53, 4 (1985): 35–43.

Onis, José de. "The Alleged Acquaintance of William Cullen Bryant and José-Maria Hérédia." *Hispanic Review* 25 (1957): 217–220.

———. William Cullen Bryant y José Maria Hérédia, vieja y nueva polemica." *Cuandernos Americanos* 17, ii (1958): 154–161.

Ornato, Joseph G. "Bryant and the *United States Literary Gazette.*" *Emerson Society Quarterly* 48 (1961): 135–139.

Ostrowski, Carl. "'I Stand Upon Their Ashes in Thy Beam': The Indians and Bryant's Literary Removals." *ATQ* 9 (1995): 299–312.

Parrington, Vernon L. *Main Currents in American Thought.* New York: Harcourt Brace, 1927, 1930.

———. "William Cullen Bryant, Puritan Liberal." *The Romantic Revolution in America.* New York: Harcourt, Brace and Co., 1927.

Pattee, F. L. "The Centenary of Bryant's Poetry." *Sidelights on American Literature.* New York: The Century Co., 1922.

Pearce, Roy Harvey. *The Continuity of American Poetry.* Princeton, NJ: Princeton UP, 1961.

Peck, Richard E. "Two Lost Bryant Poems: Evidence of Thomson's Influence." *American Literature* 39 (1967): 88–94.

Peckham, Harry Houston. *Gotham Yankee: A Biography of William Cullen Bryant.* New York: Vantage Press, 1950.

Petrino, Elizabeth A. "Late Bloomer: The Gentian as Sign or Symbol in the Work of Dickinson and Her Contemporaries." *Emily Dickinson Journal* 14, 1 (2005): 104–125.

Phair, Judith Turner. *A Bibliography of William Cullen Bryant and His Critics: 1808–1972.* Troy, NY: Whitston, 1975.

Phelps, C. Deidre. "The Edition as Art Form: Social and Authorial Readings of William Cullen Bryant's Poems." *Text* 6 (1994): 249–285.

Pinto, Holly Jean. *William Cullen Bryant and the Hudson River School of Painting.* Roslyn, NY: Nassau County Museum of Art, 1981.

———. *William Cullen Bryant, The Weirs, and American Impressionism.* Roslyn, NY: Nassau County Museum of Art, 1983.

Poger, Sidney. "William Cullen Bryant: Emblem Poet." *Emerson Society Quarterly* 43 (1966): 103–106.

Rebmann, David R. "Unpublished Letters of William Cullen Bryant." *Emerson Society Quarterly* 48 (1967): 131–135.

Reeve, Clayton C. "Kindred Spirits: William Cullen Bryant, Thomas Cole, and Asher Durand." *Tennessee Philological Bulletin* 32 (1995): 6–17.

Remini, Robert V. *Andrew Jackson and His Indian Wars.* New York: Viking, 2001.

Ringe, Donald A. "Bryant Criticism of the Fine Arts." *College Art Journal* 17 (1957): 43–54.

———. "Bryant and Whitman: A Study in Artistic Affinities." *Boston University Studies in English* 2 (1956): 85–94.

———. "Bryant's Use of the American Past." *Papers of the Michigan Academy of Science, Arts, and Letters* 41 (1956): 323–331.

———. "Kindred Spirits: Bryant and Cole." *American Quarterly* 6 (1954): 233–244.

———. "Painting as Poem in the Hudson River Aesthetic," *American Quarterly* 12 (1960): 71–83.

———. *The Pictorial Mode: Space and Time in the Art of Bryant, Irving and Cooper.* Lexington: UP of Kentucky, 1971.

———. *Poetry and the Cosmos: William Cullen Bryant.* Harvard UP, 1953.

———. "Two Items of Midwest Folklore Noted by William Cullen Bryant." *Midwest Folklore* 6 (1956): 141–146.

———. "William Cullen Bryant and the Science of Geology." *American Literature* 26 (1955): 507–514.

———. "William Cullen Bryant's Account of Michigan in 1846." *Michigan History Mind* 40 (1956): 317–327.

Rocks, James E. "William Cullen Bryant." *Fifteen American Authors: Bibliographical Essays on Research and Criticism.* Robert A. Res and Earl N. Hurbert, eds. Madison UP, 1971: 37–62.

Rusk, Ralph L., ed. *The Letters of Ralph Waldo Emerson.* 6 vols. New York: Columbia UP, 1939.

Sanford, Charles L. "The Concept of the Sublime in the Works of Thomas Cole and William Cullen Bryant." *American Literature* 37 (1957): 434–448.

Scheich, William J. "Bryant's River Imagery." *College Language Association Journal* 20 (1976): 205–209.

Schlesinger, Arthur M., Jr. *The Age of Jackson.* Boston and Toronto: Little, Brown, 1945.

Sedgwick, Catharine. *The Life and Letters of Catharine M. Sedgwick.* Ed. Mary E. Dewey. New York: Harper, 1871.

Smith, Gerald J. "Bryant's 'Thanatopsis': A Possible Source." *American Notes and Queries* 13 (1975): 149–151.

Snow, Vernon F. "'Where Rolls the Oregon'." *Western Humanities Review* 10 (1956): 289–292.

Spann, Edward K. "Bryant and Verplanck, The Yankee and the Yorker, 1821–1870." *New York History* 49 (1968): 11–28.

———. *Ideals and Politics: New York Intellectuals and Liberal Democracy 1820–1880*. Albany: State U of New York P, 1972.

Spivey, Herman E. "Bryant Cautions and Counsels Lincoln." *Tennessee Studies in Literature* 6 (1961): 1–13

———. "Manuscript Resources of the Study of William Cullen Bryant." *Papers of the Bibliographical Society of America* 44: 254–268.

———. "William Cullen Bryant Changes His Mind: An Unpublished Letter About Thomas Jefferson." *New England Quarterly* 22 (1949): 528–529.

Stimson, Frederick S., and Robert J. Biniger. "Studies of Bryant as Hispanophile." *American Literature* 31 (1959): 189–191.

Stowe, William W. *Going Abroad: European Travel in Nineteenth-Century American Culture*. Princeton, NJ: Princeton UP, 1974.

Tocqueville, Alexis de. *Democracy in America*. 2 vols. Translated, edited, and with an introduction by Harvey S. Mansfield and Delba Winthrop. Chicago: U of Chicago P, 2000.

Trimpi, Helen P. "Three of Melville's Confidence Men: William Cullen Bryant, Theodore Parker, and Horace Greeley." *Texas Studies in Literature and Language* 21 (1979): 368–395.

Tucker, Edward L. "Two Letters from William Cullen Bryant to Emily C. Hardy." *ANQ* 17, 1 (Winter 2004): 40–43.

Van Doren, Carl. "The Growth of 'Thanatopsis.'" *Nation* 101 (1915): 432–433.

Vespa, Jack. "The Unsurveyed Interior: William Cullen Bryant and the Prairie State." *ATQ* 11 (1997): 285–308.

Voorsanger, Catherine Hoover, and John K. Howat. *Art and the Empire City: New York, 1825–1861*. New York: The Metropolitan Museum of Art; New Haven: Yale UP, 2000.

Voss, Thomas G. *William Cullen Bryant, an Annotated Checklist of the Exhibit Held in the Mullen Library of the Catholic University of America, October 30–November 10, 1967*. Washington, DC: Catholic U of America P, 1967.

———. "William Cullen Bryant's New York *Evening Post* and the South: 1847–1856." *Dissertation Abstracts* 28 (1967): 698A-699A.

Weinstein, Bernard. "Bryant, Annexation, and the Mexican War." *Emerson Society Quarterly* 63 (1971): 19–24.

Weisbuch, Robert. *Atlantic Double-Cross: American Literature and British Influence in the Age of Emerson*. Chicago: U of Chicago P, 1986.

Whitman, Walt. *Specimen Days* (1882, 1892). Boston: David Godine, 1974.

Wilentz, Sean. *Chants Democratic: New York City and the Rise of the American Working Class, 1788–1850*. New York: Oxford UP, 1984.

———. *The Rise of American Democracy*. New York: Norton, 2005.

Williams, Stanley T. "William Cullen Bryant: Illinois Landowner." *Western Illinois Regional Studies* 1 (1977): 1–14.

———. "William Cullen Bryant." *The Spanish Background of American Literature*. vol. 2. New Haven: Yale UP, 1955: 122–151.

Wilson, James G. *Bryant and His Friends: Some Reminiscences of Knickerbocker Writers*. New York: Ford, Howard and Hulbert, 1886.

Wiltse, Charles M. *The New Nation, 1800–1845*. New York: Hill and Wang, 1961.

Wineapple, Brenda. *Nathaniel Hawthorne: A Life*. New York: Knopf, 2003.

Woodward, Robert H. "Bryant and Elizabeth Oakes Smith: An Unpublished Bryant Letter." *Colby Library Quarterly* 5 (1959): 69–74.

———. "Bryant and the Oriskany Centennial." *Emerson Society Quarterly* 63 (1971): 19–24.

———. "'The Wings of Morning' in 'Thanatopsis'." *Emerson Society Quarterly* 58 (1970): 153.

Yates, Norris. "Four Plantation Songs Noted by William Cullen Bryant." *Southern Folklore Quarterly* 15 (1951): 251–25.

INDEX

K

CO-2
L-2015